Discovery Guide to

Eastern Turkey

and the Black Sea Coast

by Diana Darke

Other *Discovery Guides* cover Aegean and Mediterranean Turkey, Egypt, Cairo, Jordan and the Holy Land, West Africa, Zimbabwe, Vietnam, Rajasthan, etc.

Please send for our complete list:
Discovery Guides
Michael Haag Limited
PO Box 369
London NW3 4DP
England

The author wishes to thank John and Mary Swift for their help with the section on birdwatching, and Sidney Nowill for his help with the section on mountains.

Discovery Guide to Eastern Turkey and the Black Sea Coast, second edition

Cover photograph by Andrew Powell; cover design by Colin Elgie

Photo credits: Diana Darke and the Turkish Tourist Office, London

Text © 1990 by Diana Darke

Typeset in 9/10pt Times and printed in Great Britain by litho at the Bath Press, Lower Bristol Road, Bath BA2 3BL

Published by Michael Haag Limited, PO Box 369, London NW3 4DP, England

ISBN 0 902743 74 0

CONTENTS

*Practical Information sections follow each chapter, and there is an index at the
rear.*

4

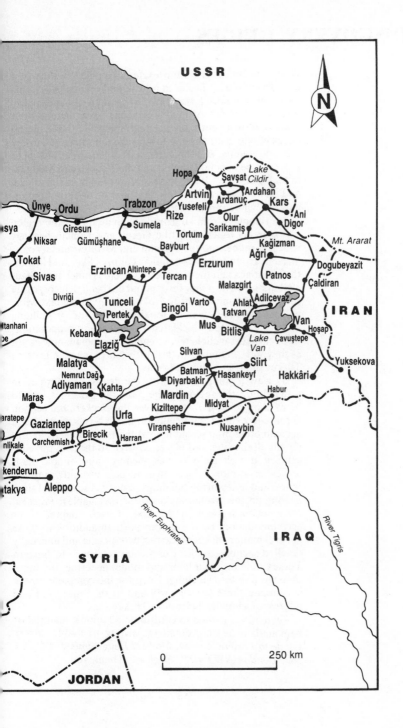

DISCOVERY GUIDES

Discovery Guides cover the less familiar places of the world or look at familiar places in a fresh and original way. This *Discovery Guide to Eastern Turkey* covers a vast and largely unknown expanse of land which has never before been treated in such depth, having been relegated to the last 50 pages of books attempting to squeeze the whole of Turkey into one volume. But this guide starts where others begin to peter out, ie beyond Istanbul and the Aegean and Mediterranean coastlines. It encompasses everything from Ankara and Konya eastwards, a few sites that lie west of Ankara, and the whole of the Black Sea coast.

Far removed from all European civilisations, the region was scarcely touched by the Greek and Roman heritage which so influenced the Aegean and Mediterranean coastlines. Surrounded by unfamiliar cultures like the Hittites, the Urartians and the Armenians, there is much that needs explanation. The policy throughout has been to incorporate such background and historical insights into the text while you are actually standing looking at the site or building in question, often elucidated by entertaining quotations from earlier travellers whose comments remain now as apt as they were in their own day: little has changed in Eastern Turkey in the last hundred years.

By way of compensation for the dearth of information provided on the region in the past, the guide sets out to be as comprehensive as possible: the *Background* section is full and explicit, especially on the subjects of food and accommodation; a scaled map at the head of each chapter details all the sites and places covered so that the traveller can see at a glance what lies ahead of him; simple plans are given of most larger towns to help instantly pinpoint hotels and noteworthy buildings (a distinct scarcity of signposting on the ground makes these invaluable); *Practical Information* sections at the end of each chapter cover accommodation, food and transport. In addition to these general matters the book carries two specific and unusually detailed sections, both of particular relevance to Eastern Turkey: one on mountains and mountaineering, the other on birds and birdwatching. Even for the complete novice it is hoped these sections will add to the enjoyment and interest of a holiday in Eastern Turkey.

Readers are invited to contribute additional material or help update existing detail by writing to the *Discovery Guide to Eastern Turkey, Michael Haag Limited, PO Box 369, London NW3 4DP, England*. Thank you.

BACKGROUND

Dispelling the myths

Turkey as a whole has long suffered from an image problem in the eyes of the West, an image that began at the time of the Crusades, was continued throughout the Ottoman period and perpetuated in such films as *Midnight Express*. The West was in no doubt: Turkey was a dark barbaric place of guaranteed stomach upsets, where the slightest misdemeanour would lead to instant and indefinite imprisonment. Turkey's Aegean and Mediterranean regions are at last beginning to shed this image, as increasing numbers of foreign visitors discover for themselves the difference between the image and the reality.

Eastern Turkey however remains for most people an unknown, a complete blank, and many are convinced that much of it is totally out of bounds to travellers. Twenty-five years ago this was largely true, with whole tracts designated military zones and with travel for sheer interest or pleasure's sake virtually impossible to arrange.

Now you can travel freely anywhere you are likely to want to go. Where certain sites lie very close to the borders with Russia, Iran, Iraq or Syria, permits are required to visit them. Ani, the Armenian ghost town on the Russian border, is the case that will affect most people, but obtaining a permit is a routine process undertaken at the local tourist office at Kars. Beyond these border regions the only other part of Turkey where travel is in any way restricted is in the Hakkâri, the extreme southeast. Even here, the main roads are open, and it is only if you decided to head up into the hills and villages that you would probably be stopped and questioned.

The east of Turkey does however remain a very different part of the country to the western and southern coastal regions. Whole stretches are vast tracts of bleak wilderness, the climate is subject to harsh extremes of heat and cold, and facilities for food and accommodation are generally meagre. Despite all this, the country has a power in its sheer scale and roughness that is almost demonic. Most surreal of all is the vast and eerie Lake Van, its thin piercing blueness ringed with snow-covered peaks as high as anything Europe can offer.

The flat central plateau

Large areas of the east and some areas of central Anatolia have been covered in sheets of lava which are often of such recent occurrence that soil has not yet been formed — consequently there are wide expanses which are sterile and uninhabited. The Van region, once heavily wooded, is now denuded after centuries of man chopping down trees for fuel in the long hard winters and for building material. Though the average altitude of the central plateau is 1500 metres you are not aware of being so high as the land itself is often flat with distant mountains rimming the horizon. Much of the scenery is therefore far from inspiring and long drives between towns can be very tedious with little to break the monotony: hence the later birdwatching section.

Van and volcanoes

Lake Van creates a special landscape of its own which despite the starkness of its shores has a memorable quality. A few magnificent extinct volcano cones, Mount Erciyes, Suphan Dağı and above all Ararat, snow-capped all the year round, lend majesty to the bleakest of horizons, and in the Hakkâri the river and gorge scenery is often spectacular in an alpine way.

The lush Black Sea coast

The most attractive and surprising landscapes of Eastern Turkey are, however, to be found in the Georgian valleys and the Pontic mountains between Erzurum and the Black Sea. The lush greenness here, in such contrast to the bleakness of the plateau, lends a variety of colour and texture to the landscapes which is often sorely missed elsewhere.

Where to Go for Information

Before any trip to Turkey it is well worth visiting the Turkish Tourist Office in your own country. If it is not practicable to visit, then you can phone and they will answer questions and gladly send you free of charge all the leaflets and maps you ask for. Particularly useful is their mini-booklet called *Turkey: Travel Guide* which, apart from listing all the state-registered hotels, also provides summarised practical information with many useful addresses.

In Britain, the Turkish Tourist Office is at Egyptian House, 170 Piccadilly, London W1; Tel: 071-734 8681.

In the USA the address is 821 United Nations Plaza, New York, NY 10017; Tel: (212) 687-2194.

There are also Turkish Tourist Offices in Paris, Brussels, Amsterdam, Copenhagen, Vienna, Frankfurt, Munich, Zürich, Rome, Madrid, Stockholm, Tokyo, Kuwait and Jeddah.

In almost every town of any size in Turkey you will find a Tourist Information Office run by the Ministry of Culture and Tourism. These are generally stocked with maps, town plans and summarised leaflets for the regions given free of charge, and their staff will also help you with any special local information you require.

Getting to Turkey

By air

İstanbul, Ankara, İzmir, Adana, Antalya and Dalaman are all international airports. Antalya and Dalaman are largely used in the summer months by charter flights. Turkish Airlines (Türk Hava Yolları-THY) links all the major

Turkish airports with the major European cities, the Middle East and North Africa. Flying time from London to İzmir is around $3\frac{1}{2}$ hours. From the USA connecting flights via Europe are plentiful.

If your local travel agent looks rather blank when you ask about travel to Turkey, visit or phone the Turkish Tourist Office and ask for their list of travel agents and tour operators specialising in Turkey. Some of these specialise in flights only, some in fly-drive, but the list will be comprehensive and detailed, so by making a few phone calls you can easily get some comparative quotes for fares.

By sea   If you are driving from Europe in your own car, you can spare yourself some driving and arrive suitably rested by taking one of three car ferries:

From Venice
The luxury Orient Express ferry, operated by British Ferries Limited (20 Upper Ground, London SE1 9PF; Tel: 071-928 6000), runs its popular new service weekly from April through October, leaving Venice at 6pm, arriving in İstanbul on Tuesdays at 9am and in Kusadası on Wednesdays at 10.30am. Prices are from £175 one way per passenger (£315 return) (including cabin, meals and port taxes), and cars are from £100 one way (£180 return). Eight decks, six types of cabin, excellent food, four bars, two pools, a sauna and gymnasium. If you take your car across the Channel on a Sealink ferry or hovercraft, British Ferries will reduce your Channel fare by 50 percent. For the carless person who wants to do things in style, you can travel to Venice and back on the refurbished Venice–Simplon Orient Express train. Luxurious, but expensive.

From Ancona
Turkish Maritime Lines (TML) runs a service from June to September leaving Ancona in the morning on Saturdays, arriving in İzmir in the morning on Tuesdays. Fares are similar to the Venice ferry. In Britain, contact the TML agents: Walford Lines Limited, Ibec House, 42–47 Minories, London EC3N 1AE; Tel: 071-480 5621.

From Brindisi or Piraeus
Libra Maritime, a Greek company, runs car ferries three days a week in summer connecting Brindisi, Patras, Piraeus and İzmir in 40 hours, leaving Piraeus on Mondays, Wednesdays, and Fridays at 8pm, and leaving İzmir on Tuesdays, Thursdays and Sundays at 2pm.
Libra in Piraeus: Plateia Loudovicou 4; Tel: (1) 411 7864.
Libra in Brindisi: 54 Corso Garibaldi; Tel: 21 935 28 004.

From the Greek islands there are ferries from Lesbos, Chios, Samos, Kos and Rhodes running to the Turkish mainland, though not much advertised. The only formality is handing in your passport 24 hours before the trip, which is then returned to you when you board. The service from Rhodes to Marmaris is daily in summer, as is the service from Samos to Kuşadası. Boats from Lesbos to Ayvalık, Chios to Çeşme, and Kos to Bodrum are not daily, but at least two or three times a week in summer. See the *Practical Information* section at the back of the relevant chapter for further details.

Turkish Maritime Lines ferries also run regularly from Turkish Cyprus to the Turkish mainland: from Taşucu near Silifke to Kyrenia three times a week, and from Mersin to Famagusta also three times a week (see the *Practical Information* section of the relevant chapter).

By train Trans-European trains to Turkey, once they reach Yugoslavia, are crowded, uncomfortable, dirty, often late, and generally not to be recommended.

By bus There are several companies offering coach runs from major French, Italian and German cities. They take two to three days each way and are very cramped. For most people the slightly lower cost does not compensate for the extra time lost in getting there.

Passports and Visas

Normally, no visa is required for any national of Western Europe, the US, Canada, Australia, New Zealand or Japan; a valid passport permits a stay of up to three months. However, for the time being, British travellers do require a visa. Package tour visitors can obtain one on arrival (about £5); independent travellers must obtain a visa in advance from the Turkish Consulate in London (about £20). All British travellers would do well to phone the consulate first (071-589 0360), as the situation could change. British Visitors Passports (available from the Post Office) are valid for travellers arriving from Britain by air, or by land or sea via Italy and Greece.

Vaccinations

No vaccinations are required, but for those who want to be totally safe, the following precautions are recommended: typhoid (injection effective for 3 years); cholera (injection effective for 6 months); polio (sugar lump effective for 5 years); tetanus (injection effective for 5 years); and malaria (paludrine tablets from the chemist to be taken daily and continued for 3 weeks after your return). These precautions are not generally considered necessary for travel in the Aegean and Mediterranean areas, but would be advisable in Eastern Turkey. Despite Turkish claims otherwise, there are isolated cases of malaria.

The Turks

From their origins in the steppes of Asia the Turks arrived in Asia Minor in the 10th C having adopted the religion of the Arabs enroute, and for the last six centuries they have lived half in and half out of Europe. Today they are neither Asian nor Middle Eastern nor European, having traces of all three yet being distinct from them. Although Islam is the religion of 95 percent of the population, the country uses the Christian weekend of Saturday and Sunday, and there are also elements of Shamanism, Taoism, Zoroastrianism and fragments of the Chinese and Byzantine cultures.

A personality of extremes

David Hotham, who spent eight years in Ankara as *The Times* correspondent, sums it up: 'The Turk is unusually full of contradictions. Not only has he East and West in him, Europe and Asia, but an intense pride combined with an acute inferiority complex, a deep xenophobia with an overwhelming hospitality to strangers, a profound need for flattery with an absolute disregard for what anybody thinks about him. Few people, capable of such holocausts, are at the same time so genuinely kind, helpful, magnanimous and sincere as the Turks. It is as if his nature compensated its capacity for one extreme by a propensity towards the other'.

The importance of honour

The Turks' attitude to money is usually one of disdain; it is beneath their dignity to appear preoccupied with it. Correspondingly, trust is very important to a Turk for whom the most contemptible of all crimes is theft, which, except in the big cities, is almost unknown. In prison a thief is the lowest form of life and is spat upon by the other prisoners. A murderer on the other hand is the elite of the prison. Murder is often a question of honour and is therefore respected. A Turk who returned home to find his wife in bed with another man promptly went out to fetch an axe from the shed, hacked the couple to pieces and then calmly gave himself up to the police, his honour avenged. Crimes of this sort are never, it is important to mention, committed under the influence of drink. Public drunkenness is almost unknown among the Turks.

The Turks on the whole do not make good businessmen. Until the 1920s it was the Greeks and the Armenians who busied themselves with the country's commerce. Unused to trade, the Turks are still not very adept at selling themselves or their goods. But they do have great national pride. Atatürk's dictum 'Ne mutlu Türküm diyene' (How happy is he who can say he is a Turk) still lives in their hearts.

After centuries of ruling an empire pride dies hard. This pride can often be carried to excess, however, with the Turks taking credit for everything in sight. Anamur castle for example is believed by many Turks to be Turkish, whereas it was built by the Armenians. The Turks have a weakness for equating what they want to believe with the truth.

The Terrible Turk

Though generally placid and even-natured, the Turk when pushed too far lashes out, and has a tendency to live up to his epithet 'terrible'. The Turks themselves admit it and a Turkish diplomat once confided to Western friends, 'Mind you, if I was an Armenian or a Greek, I'd be terrified too'. As Aubrey Herbert put it, 'The Turk was unbusinesslike, placid, and lazy or long-suffering. But when he turned in his rage he poured out death in a bucket, and guilty and innocent suffered from his blind anger'. This capacity for violent action showed itself in the massacres of the Kurds and the Armenians, and most recently in 1974 in Cyprus where, having been goaded and maltreated by the Greek Cypriots for years, the EOKA-B guerilla attacks in support of Enosis were the final straw. The Greeks totally underestimated the Turkish response. Many educated Greek Cypriots admit that they were wrong to push the Turks so far and that they brought the calamity on themselves. The Turkish soldier has always been extremely tough, though in battle his leaders have often let him down. C B Norman, special correspondent of *The Times* in 1877 during the war with Russia, wrote: 'Of the bravery of the Turkish troops it is impossible to speak too highly; of the utter incompetence of their leaders it is equally impossible to speak in terms of sufficient disparagement'.

Physically, though the vast majority of Turks have thick dark hair, eye colour varies and a noticeable number have green or less often blue eyes. Some young children are blond and blue-eyed, especially the girls, but they seem to lose this fairness when they get older. In the Georgian areas north of Erzurum you will still notice a sprinkling of ginger-haired freckly Turks. With the racial mix of Asian, Kurd, Caucasian, Arab and European, there is also enormous variation in features and build, but as a generalisation the Turks are a hirsute nation with paler skins than the Arabs. Some have a noticeable propensity to a flatness of the back of the head. The men are often very attractive in a masculine and hirsute way with strong features, while the women, tending to share the strong heavy features of the men, are not by and large very good-looking. In the eastern provinces, the women are frequently so heavily concealed that quite frankly there could be anything beneath the layers of unflattering sackcloth that go past.

Virility is prized by the Turks almost more than any other quality and Turkey is still an essentially male society. A

Women in a man's world man's most important relationships are with other men, and even in the cities it is surprising how rarely you see a man walking with a woman. When couples meet it is usually the men who embrace and kiss and fall into conversation, while the women stand lamely aside. Women have, however, made enormous strides since Atatürk's reforms. Turkish women long ago entered the professions and there are Turkish women in parliament and the universities, and working as writers and journalists. In the arts there are excellent actresses, ballet dancers, opera singers and musicians. In banks you will be struck by the number of senior women working behind the counter and in the Turkish civil service there are many women in prominent positions. Turkish women got the vote before British women. Despite all this, there is far less equality between the sexes than might be suggested by these high profile Westernised ladies, especially in the eastern provinces: there, old attitudes die hard, and in cinemas and schools there is still usually separate seating for women. As Hotham says, 'You can change a law but not a mentality'.

In hotels and restaurants in the eastern provinces all the staff and waiters are men, whereas in the Aegean and Mediterranean parts there are almost more women than men to be seen behind the reception desks. On the rare occasions when you do see women in Eastern Turkey, you are inclined to feel that the remarks of Frederick Burnaby, the Englishman who travelled these parts in the 1870s, still hold some truth. 'The faces of the ladies were not prepossessing, and sadly wanted expression — a defect which I subsequently observed in almost every Turkish woman whose countenance I had the opportunity of seeing. We need not be surprised at this. I have been informed by the Turks themselves that very few women, not one per 1000, can read or write. They amuse themselves with gossip and eating. Their mental faculties become absorbed. They live for the moment, and pine after the coarser and more sensual pleasures'.

As the Turkish proverb says 'The thicker the veil, the less worth lifting'.

The views of men in Eastern Turkey today probably do not differ much from those expressed by a Turk whom Burnaby exhorted to educate women as they were educated in Europe. 'It would be difficult to do so', said the Turk coldly. 'Their women uncover their faces; I have heard that some of them declare that they are the equals of their husbands. What ridiculous creatures they must be', he continued, 'not at once to accept that inferior position which Allah in His wisdom has awarded to them!' Again, on the practice of receiving money from future sons-in-law, as opposed to giving their daughters dowries; 'Our daughters are maid-servants; when they marry we lose their services. It is quite right that the husband should compensate us for our loss. Europeans educate their girls very well, but the latter are utterly useless as cooks or sweepers. When they marry, the fathers lose nothing, but, on the contrary, gain, as they no longer have to pay for their daughters' maintenance and clothes. It is quite proper that you should give a husband something when he saddles himself with such a useless incumbrance, and you have no right to find fault with us for our system'.

Today still, even at sophisticated parties in the cities, the women tend to huddle together in one part of the room leaving the men to talk seriously among themselves, and you will never see a woman sitting in the coffee shops.

Dense oceans of maleness
These are packed with men, 'dense oceans of maleness'. As a Western woman you can drink in the coffee houses and tea houses and eat at the local restaurants. You will be stared at and whispered about, but you should simply ignore it and behave normally and respectfully. Dress is important in the eastern provinces, and you should always make sure you are not too scantily clad. Tight shorts and low-cut T-shirts are not at all appropriate and will cause offence. If you are decently dressed and behave sensibly and discreetly you will cause no offence but will simply be regarded with great curiosity by men and women alike.

The pressure to educate
Young Turks are very keen to be educated and the pressures on them to succeed at university and vocational schools are enormous. Unemployment is beginning to be a serious problem even in the professions. The only fields which guarantee work are medicine and engineering, so the top students compete for places to study these subjects. A doctor can earn good money in Turkey in private practice in the cities, though only after a period of enforced practical training in the eastern provinces. The less able students study subjects like history, French and English, and as a result the English students often speak English less well than the medical or science students. Children from the state schools who want to fight their way to the coveted medicine and engineering places have a real struggle on their hands, especially if they come from the east where the standard of teaching is lower, particularly in the villages. Those with wealthier backgrounds whose parents can send them to the private schools of Ankara and İstanbul have a definite advantage. Among schoolchildren it is not uncommon to hear of suicides when they can no longer stand the pressure of the intense competition.

Potential Europeans
Turks today, especially the younger ones, are increasingly regarding themselves as European. Associate members of the EEC since 1964, they are now intensifying their efforts to gain full membership. They are desperately

anxious for acceptance by the West, anxious to cast off their barbaric image. David Hotham, posing the question at the beginning of his book *The Turks* (John Murray), 'Is the Turk a European?', ends by concluding that the Turk is a potential European, poised to move towards Europe. But if Europe does not prove welcoming, who knows what reaction that will provoke?

Turkish Proverbs

The Turks are so rich in proverbs that many have been used as illustrations of particular characteristics throughout the text of this book: many others, however, which could find no suitable insertion without great contrivance, are too fine to be omitted. With no pretence at relevance therefore, the following selection is given for the reader's edification, though one might add by way of justification that the study of a people's proverbs is one of the most interesting and entertaining ways to gain insight into their mentality and mores.

Stretch your feet only as your blanket allows.

Sweeter than honey is anger.

God created serpents, rabbits and Armenians!

Every bachelor is a sovereign.

The man who weeps for all soon loses his eyes.

Destiny caresses the few and molests the many.

Beware of dwarfs, for God has seen fit to strike them on the head.

The first time even a duck dives in tail first.

The man who has scalded his lips on milk will blow on his ice-cream.

Trust in God but tie your camel.

Grieve for the living, not for the dead.

Like a child, the heart hopes for what it desires.

If you accept the wolf's invitation, take a dog.

Should my beard catch fire, others will use it to light their pipes.

When a man hears his own lie at the end of the market he believes it.

Nine out of ten men are women.

When the times don't suit you, make sure you suit the times.

For the birds that cannot soar, God has provided low branches.

They may be brothers but their pockets are not sisters.

Sweet words lure the snake from his hole.

Never tell the truth unless you already have one foot in the stirrup.

Even from a crooked chimney, the smoke rises straight.

And finally, a proverb that rings particularly true in Eastern Turkey:

When the flood recedes the mud remains.

Religion
Over 95 percent of Turks are Moslems, but as Turkey since Atatürk's reforms in the 1920s has been a secular state, non-Moslem religions are tolerated. The main division in Islam between Sunnis and Shi'as can be traced back to the years immediately following Mohammed's death. The Shi'as believed that Mohammed's son-in-law Ali and his descendants were the rightful successors to the caliphate, while the Sunnis believed it should pass to the person chosen by the Ulema or Islamic clergy. The vast majority of Turks are Sunnis (the orthodox and majority sect within Islam), though a minority are Shi'as (as are almost all Iranians), called also Alevis, or partisans of Ali. The Sufi and dervish orders with their mystical elements formed another sizeable minority which were very popular in Turkey until Atatürk officially disbanded them in the 1920s.

Religious conservatism in Eastern Turkey

In the eastern provinces religious adherence is more noticeable than in other parts of Turkey, and so in mosques and generally your dress should be more discreet. It is fine to show bare arms and legs in the streets but not in a way that exposes too much or is too figure-hugging. In mosques, bare arms and legs are not permitted for men or women, and women should also cover their hair with a scarf.

Ramadan, the month of fasting, is far more strictly observed in the east than it is in the Aegean and Mediterranean areas where you would not even notice it; in the east most restaurants will be closed, and only a very few in the biggest hotels will serve alcohol. For this reason it is worth avoiding the east during Ramadan if you are travelling independently as it will seriously affect your ability to get food. Fasting also badly affects the mood of the people, who become very grumpy and bad-tempered and do everything half-heartedly. If you complain, shoulders are shrugged helplessly and the word Ramadan is uttered as an excuse for everything that malfunctions or is not available. It also means that at sundown the restaurants are packed to bursting point with men waiting for the Ramadan cannon to signify the end of fasting each evening. After eating a mountainous plateful they lean back, burp, and then smoke continuously to make up for the abstinence of the day.

Economy
Turkey is a predominantly agricultural economy, with 57 percent of its population living in the countryside. Main crops are wheat, cotton, tobacco and fruit. The main export

earner is cotton, and with abundant sheep Turkey is Europe's main wool producer. Among the widespread economic reforms introduced by Prime Minister Turgut Özal since he took office in 1983, two priorities have been privatisation of state-owned concerns and an ambitious programme of capital infrastructure construction. Both of these will serve to develop the growing tourist industry which Turkey is now keen to encourage.

Turkey has oil resources in the southeast but not sufficient to meet its needs. It therefore buys crude oil from Saudi Arabia, Iraq, Iran, Algeria and the Soviet Union. It already has a pipeline direct to Iraq and there are plans to build an Iranian pipeline.

With its large quantities of sheep and goats, Turkey exports in bulk to Syria and Libya, especially before the two major Islamic festivals. It is hoped that the ambitious Southeast Anatolia Project consisting of a series of dams on the Upper Euphrates will by the 1990s produce enough water to transform the wasteland around Urfa and Harran into fertile agricultural land for growing cereals; it is also hoped that the project will make Turkey self-sufficient in electricity, thereby releasing it from dependence on the Russian grid. The Atatürk Dam, the main dam of the project, will be the fourth largest dam in the world. The life of the peasants and semi-nomads in the region will be transformed.

Security
The Jandarma or gendarmerie is a branch of the armed forces which polices the rural areas where there are no civilian police. Military presence in the east is more marked by far than in other parts of the country, especially in the four southeastern provinces (out of a total of 67 in the country as a whole) which still retain martial law. These are Diyarbakır, Hakkâri, Mardin and Siirt, all provinces in which troops have been attacked by Kurdish rebels. The situation is reviewed three times a year and, if considered necessary, martial law is extended for another four months. No foreigners have ever been involved in such incidents.

Low crime rate   Crime rates are very low. The widespread petty theft in Italy, for example, hardly exists in Turkey. As long as you behave sensibly, dress decently and do not take any photos near military zones, you will have nothing but courtesy from the Jandarma and the other arms of the police. Horror stories of people being clapped in prison only apply if you are carrying drugs or have infringed the law. Make sure your passport and car documents are in order. There are no road blocks on the main roads, except one on the Hakkâri road in the extreme southeast, and on the minor dirt tracks the only road blocks are where the road passes very close to the Iranian or Russian borders.

The only other way you can fall foul of the law is to attempt to export any antiquities from the country. Buried treasure is an obsession in Eastern Turkey and illicitly dug up Urartian bronzes and Byzantine coins are always checked to see if they are gold. Beware that the legislation on antiquities introduced in 1967 carries severe penalties if you are found with any in your possession.

Human rights

Human rights issues continue to trouble Turkey, and organisations like Amnesty International are always investigating cases. Of the 850 prisoners who have died in Turkish prisons since 1980, the Minister of Justice says that 813 died from natural causes, 13 from fighting among the inmates, 33 were suicides and two died from maltreatment by prison officers. Turkey does seem to be making efforts to improve the situation and a martial law court in Erzurum in 1986 jailed six policemen for 64 months for torturing a man to death in police custody.

The Language

Turkish derives from a Turco-Tartar language group called Altaic, a distinction it shares with Mongol, Tunguz and possibly Korean. The migrations of the Turkic peoples from the central steppelands and their consequent intermingling with other peoples of non-Turkic speech over the course of history has created a linguistic structure of great complexity which has not yet been sufficiently researched for the final word to be said on the matter. In the 19th C it was widely believed that Finnish and Hungarian were related because they share with Turkish certain features such as vowel harmony and no grammatical gender, but this view is no longer widely supported.

Nomad origins

A language of nomadic tribesmen from Central Asia, it had a wealth of vocabulary for describing livestock and weather conditions. But this vocabulary was inadequate for coping with the complexities of civilised urban life the Turks discovered in the countries they conquered. So they borrowed the bulk of their abstract and intellectual vocabulary from Arabic (about 40 percent of the language, similar to the position of French in medieval English), and borrowed from Persian most words to do with crafts, trades and their associated objects. With the Turks' conversion to Islam and their adoption of the Arabic alphabet, their language became increasingly artificial. The Arabic alphabet was never suited to Turkish, being based on three root consonants with vowels generally left out, whereas vowels and vowel harmony are crucial to Turkish grammar.

Atatürk's reforms

When Atatürk came to power in the early 1920s he set about removing foreign influences in the language, and tried to find Turkish substitutes for Arabic and Persian words. He also abandoned the Arabic alphabet and adopted the Latin alphabet in use today. Along with many other of Atatürk's reforms, the effect was to shift Turkey away from the East and towards Europe. But this led to some problems in communication between generations, where even today there are grandparents who grew up with Arabic and Persian words while their grandchildren at school are taught a new vocabulary. The language reform also had the effect of greatly simplifying the over-elaborate use of language so favoured under the Ottomans. For example, the modern Turkish civil servant will now write: 'I have been thinking about your suggestion'. His Ottoman predecessor would have written: 'Your slave has been engaged in the exercise of cogitation in respect of the proposals vouchsafed by your exalted person'.

The amount of English and German spoken east of Ankara is, not surprisingly, far less than in İstanbul and the Aegean and Mediterranean regions. Most hotel and restaurant staff do speak limited English, however, so you will always be able to get by without a knowledge of Turkish. For visitors who do speak some Turkish, it is worth mentioning that the kind of Turkish spoken in the east of the country is very different to what you will be used to in İstanbul and the west. The difference is not in dialect but in pronunciation, and the Turkish sounds which are quite soft and pleasant on the ear in the western parts become very harsh and gutteral.

The ultimate negative

One of the most infuriating characteristics of the Turk, as any traveller to Turkey soon discovers, is the way he says no. The famous Turkish negative *yok*, accompanied by an upward movement of the head with eyes half closed, is the negative to end all negatives as it also manages to convey complete indifference on the part of the person using it. When the hotel is full, or there is no orange juice, no fish, no fruit, no vegetables, this upward nod of the head and weary closing of the eyes says 'No, there isn't any (and who cares anyway)'. Freya Stark described it as 'that eloquent gesture which is the Turkish equivalent of a blank wall'.

Coping with Turkish

Pronunciation

Vowels and consonants are pronounced as in English, except for: ö = oe (Göereme); u = as in French *tu*; ı = the dotless ı which is peculiar to Turkish and is pronounced as the initial 'a' in 'away' (Topkapı = Topkapeu); c = j (cami, meaning mosque = jami); ç = ch (Foça = Focha); ş = sh (Kuşadası = kushadaseu); ğ is unpronounced, but lengthens the preceding vowel (dağ, meaning mountain

= daa); h is always pronounced; e on the end of a word is always pronounced, so Pamukkale has four syllables. Stress falls evenly over the syllables in Turkish rather than being concentrated on one syllable as tends to be the case in English.

Greetings

For simple greetings in Turkey, you need only know two things: when you arrive somewhere you will be greeted by *Hoş geldeniz* (welcome), to which you reply *Hoş bulduk* (happy to be here); when you leave, those staying behind will say to you *Güle güle* (go with a smile), to which you, as the person leaving, reply *Allaha ısmarladık* (we have committed ourselves to God) — a bit of a mouthful, but worth practising as it will go down very well.

Food and drink

Other words and phrases (all given in their true Turkish spelling) you may find useful are:

breakfast	*kahvaltı*
eggs	*yumurta*
tea	*çay*
more tea	*daha çay*
coffee	*kahve*
milk	*süt*
sugar	*şeker*
bread	*ekmek*
butter	*tereyağ*
jam	*reçel*
cheese	*peynir*
soup	*çorba*
salad	*salata*
tomato	*domates*
fish	*balık*
chicken	*tavuk, piliç*
fried	*kızatma*
grilled	*grill*
roast	*rost*
chips	*patates*
fruit	*meyva*
ice cream	*dondurma*
cake	*pasta*
packed lunch	*piknik*
salt	*tuz*
pepper	*biber*
water	*su*
mineral water	*maden suyu*
hot water	*sıcak su*
fruit juice	*meyva suyu*
beer	*bira*
wine	*şarap*
red wine	*kırmızı şarap*
white wine	*beyaz şarap*
dry	*sek*
sweet	*tatlı*
the bill	*hesab*

Practical situations		
	hello	*merhaba*
	yes	*evet*
	no	*hayır*
	please	*lütfen*
	thank you	*teşekkür ederim*
	very beautiful	*cçk güzel*
	how much?	*ne kadar?*
	cheap	*ucuz*
	expensive	*pahalı*
	money	*para*
	shop	*dükkan*
	open	*açık*
	shut, closed	*kapalı*
	bank	*banka*
	post office	*postane*
	chemist	*eczane*
	hospital	*hastahane*
	police	*polis*
	ticket office	*gişe*
	toilet	*tuvalet*
	towel	*havlu*
	soap	*sabun*
	gents	*baylar*
	ladies	*bayanlar*

Travel		
	shared taxi	*dolmuş*
	private car	*özel oto/araba*
	good road	*iyi yol*
	bad road	*bozuk yol*
	road closed	*yol kapalı*
	is this road possible for my car?	*bu yol arabamla gitmeye musait mıdır?*
	no entry	*girilmez*
	attention	*dikkat*
	stop	*dur*
	right	*sağ*
	left	*sol*
	straight on	*doğru*
	far	*uzak*
	near	*yakın*
	petrol	*benzin*
	where?	*nerede?*
	bus	*otobus*
	ship/ferry	*vapur/feribot*
	small boat	*sandal/kayık (ie caïque)*
	motor boat	*motörbot*
	to let/hire	*kıralık*
	room	*òda*
	forbidden	*yasak*
	forbidden zone	*yasak bölge*
	municipality	*belediye*
	governor (of a province) in larger towns	*vali*
	province	*vilayet*

head man or mayor in small towns	*kaymakam*
director, manager	*müdür*
primary school	*ilkokul*

Road signs

Here are some words you will not use, but will see so often on signs at the side of the road that not knowing what they mean will drive you insane:

Karayolları (+ numbers): Highways Department, ie that number department is responsible for looking after the roads at this point.

Orman: forest or wood.

Dinar-il Sınırı: province boundary of Dinar.

On town signs you will see *rakım*, altitude, and *nufus*, population. Written on public bins you will see *cöp bana at*, Throw the rubbish into me. Carved into hillsides or written in slogans above the entrance to military camps you will see *Ne mutlu Türküm diyene*, How happy is he who can say he is a Turk, and *Her şey watan için*, Everything for the homeland.

Accommodation

Because of the high rate of inflation it would be ridiculous to offer any hotel or other prices expressed as Turkish lira in this book. Instead, where prices are mentioned at all, they are given in pounds sterling and US dollars. Sometimes the Turks will themselves express room rates (or car hire rates, etc) in dollars.

Hotel rating system and prices

The range of accommodation in Turkey is enormous, from luxury complexes down to small family-run pensions. In the Ministry of Culture and Tourism's own listings the grading of accommodation is somewhat random, and far from comprehensive as well. Many good hotels and pensions choose not to be registered. The distinction between hotels and motels is blurred as many establishments calling themselves motels are in fact perfectly normal hotels, not chalet- or bungalow-style accommodation. In view of the general confusion in the official system, this guide dispenses with Turkish classifications in favour of its own star-rating system reflecting the level of comfort and standard of facilities offered. The following prices are the average cost of a double room with breakfast included.

5-star is a luxury hotel with full facilities: £55 to £65 or $83 to $98.

4-star is a very good hotel with above-average facilities: £45 to £55 or $68 to $83.

3-star is a good tourist hotel with a moderate level of comfort, almost always with private bathroom: £25 to £45 or $38 to $68.

2-star is a simpler hotel with a moderate level of comfort, usually with private bathroom: £15 to £25 or $23 to $38.

1-star is a modest hotel or pension with simple facilities, often with no private bathroom, but clean: £10 to £15 or $15 to $23.

The rock-bottom hotels cost £5 to £10 or $7.50 to $15.

Any establishments registered with the Ministry of Culture and Tourism automatically add a 10 percent tax to the bill. Price fluctuations in the 2- and 3-star category are considerable, often for no discernible reason. Some are surprisingly cheap for the facilities offered, others surprisingly expensive.

The good . . . The standard of hotels in Eastern Turkey leaves a lot to be desired. At the top end there are now a few good hotels in the cities, like the Büyük in Diyarbakır, the Akdamar in Van and the Harran in Urfa, all built in the last five years or so. These are the ones the coach tours use and if you can get in they are fine, with functioning private bathrooms, good restaurants and bars attached. If, however, as is increasingly becoming the case, they are full with pre-booked tours (not only British but German, Dutch, French, Italian and even American), you face a colossal drop in standard down to the local hotels that have always existed before the tourists — there is nothing between. There are no pensions, as there are in the Aegean and Mediterranean areas, of the clean and simple variety, but rather they are of the simple and squalid variety. It is worth getting your hotel to book ahead for you each night: the tours rarely fill every room, so there are usually a few left on a first come first served basis. If you do not arrive at the hotel by 7pm and you have not made a reservation, the chances are that any spare rooms will have been taken.

The bad . . . The bad hotels that remain if the good ones are full are such as to warrant a cockroach rating rather than a star rating system; they often have fleas in the bedding and very rarely offer breakfast or any meals. Hot water is a distinct rarity in these hotels and usually gets charged extra anyway, as it involves lighting the heater specially. In practice, the communal bathrooms are so unsavoury that you generally feel disinclined to use them, feeling you would be cleaner to stay as you are and wait till you can get into one of the better hotels. Take an anti-cockroach aerosol with you or buy one there.

It may, if you are forced to stay in any of these fleapits, be of some small comfort to know that matters used to be even worse. Freya Stark writing in 1959 complained bitterly: 'The Turks, with the most splendid, varied and interesting country in the world, are naturally anxious to obtain tourists, and their difficulties in this respect are caused chiefly by the quite phenomenal badness of their hotels. Leaving İstanbul and Ankara out of count, where better conditions naturally exist, I have not found more than one among about 40 small provincial inns able to compare with even a fourth-rate pub in England. Now it is no act of friendship to disguise this fact, when it is preventing people you like from getting what they wish for, especially since it would be a simple matter to remedy and since the Turks are perfectly able to organise a good hotel. It is not the building but the running of the inns that is so bad. When they are started — new and clean and rather expensive, with the latest available devices — the owner sets out his chair in the shade of his doorstep, places his magenta stockinged feet comfortably out of his shoes on to an opposite chair, reads his paper, and expects his clients to carry on with all remaining details. Some crone upstairs with one tooth in her head is walking around with a handful of rushes that stroke the dust along an unwashed floor; the beds are made with sheets or quilts that may or may not be changed when the guests depart in the morning; and in a year or two every one of the modern devices is wrecked. There is an improvement, though a slow one: single rooms or rooms with running water are making their way, and it seems to me that the percentage of clean sheets is a good deal higher: but the central problem remains in the person of the innkeeper himself. To tell him that his profession is an art, that it requires several years of industry and patience to learn, would surprise him. And no real progress will be made until the Turkish Government, which is admirably ready to send young men abroad to learn this and that, includes a proper training of hotel-keepers in its programme'.

... and the
unspeakable
Frederick Burnaby, a traveller in these parts of Turkey in the 19th C, frequently had to put up with extreme squalor when he stayed in the private houses of various hosts before the days of any kind of hotel. He ranked them in descending order of squalor from Turks, to Armenians, to Kurds, to Nestorians at the very bottom.

'The Armenians in their habits of body are filthy to the last degree. Their houses and clothes are infested with vermin. The Turks, on the contrary, are much cleaner, and are most particular about the use of the bath. An Englishman would not be pleased if his house became filled with what it is here not necessary to mention.'

Another Armenian he stayed with 'had no ideas beyond that of manufacturing cows' dung. His conversation was entirely engrossed with it. It was also an important topic with the rest of his family, who were all longing for the frost to go, so as to commence making the article in question on a large scale'.

Fleas often stopped him sleeping and his English man-servant complained to their host: 'There are many fleas; my Effendi cannot sleep'.

'It is true', replied the Armenian, 'but there are by no means so many here as in a Kurd village a few miles distant. The Kurds have been obliged to abandon their houses in consequence of these insects. They have had to live in tents for several months past'.

A Turkish major staying in a Kurdish house had moved out of the room before Burnaby's arrival, the insects proving too much for him. The Kurdish host said disparagingly: 'These Turks have thin skins; only think of their being frightened by a few fleas. You Ingliz are much braver people'.

'My Effendi is very particular about these matters', remarked his servant, 'if he is bitten, there will be no baksheesh.'

When there was a choice about where to stay the night between Kurdish or Nestorian villages, Burnaby says: 'The inhabitants of these hamlets possess the reputation of being dirtier than the Kurds, so the traveller who is wise will invariably elect to pass the night with the mountaineers'.

Cleaner than all these however, Burnaby found the Persians, and when he commented to his Turkish escort that the Persian roads and houses were much better and cleaner than those in Turkey, the captain replied sorrowfully: 'That is true: the little dogs can do some things well, but they are sly and deceitful'.

Last but not least All classified hotels have normal Western-style bathrooms with conventional sit-down toilets. Most have an additional feature that requires some explanation, namely a puzzling small metal pipe that protrudes from just under the rim of the bowl. The position of this pipe is perfectly set so that when seated you can operate the tap (usually set in the wall to the right of the cistern) and a jet of water will hit you in exactly the right place to wash all impurities from the rear. You can then use the paper to dry off — a most satisfying and hygienic operation.

In the unclassified fleapit hotels, however, the lavatory is usually of the squat-over-a-hole variety, where you inevitably miss the hole and are then forced to confront your daily achievement from close quarters as you try to flush it away with the jug of water provided — a most messy and unhygienic operation. Take your own paper.

Camping

There are few campsites in this area of Turkey: Cappadocia and Adıyaman are about the only areas where camping sites of a sort exist. Rough camping is legal except where notices state otherwise, but it is not generally advisable. If you do decide to camp rough it is best to do so near a local Jandarma, after first asking permission.

Food and Drink

Basse cuisine

While Turkish cuisine has been called, even by French gourmets, one of the finest in the world, such praise does not unfortunately apply in Eastern Turkey, and the food available here is far more limited than in the rest of the country. Hors d'oevres or *meze*, usually the highpoint of Turkish cuisine, are conspicuous here by their almost total absence except in the extreme southeast around Antakya and Mardin: in most parts soup is the only thing on offer as the prelude to the main course. When you pass food markets an impressive array of fruit and vegetables is generally on display but for some reason it never finds its way into appetizing dishes in restaurants.

Limited menu

The fare you will generally come across is so limited that the following is virtually an exhaustive list:

Hot yogurt soup with rice and mint, usually quite good

Tomato soup, a Heinz look-alike, very bland

Potato or lentil soup, variable and should be inspected before deciding

Luke warm or cold green beans cooked in tomato sauce and grease

Baked beans

Chips or pilav rice

Salads with tomatoes, cucumber, onion and green chillies

Stuffed green peppers with rice and pine nuts, usually cold, and though rather greasy, not at all bad when they are available (These are also suitable to buy from restaurants as picnic lunch fare, as long as you have water or cloths to wash off the grease afterwards.)

Chicken cooked in grease

Meat (mutton) stew with aubergine and okra

Meat kebab, lamb or mutton

Rice pudding

Creme caramel

Baklava

Fresh fruit in season; strawberries (May), oranges, apples (late summer), guavas and green *erik* (a small sharp kind of plum), peaches, cherries (May and June)

Nuts to nibble

With the possible exception of the Melita restaurant in Malatya, the only really good meal you are likely to get in Eastern Turkey is in someone's home, proof that all the ingredients are there but that in restaurants it lacks the people willing to take the time and trouble to produce it properly. In homes you can be offered delicious and delicately prepared rice wrapped in vine leaves (invariably prepared by women), which you will never see in a restaurant.

In the central Anatolian areas and along the Black Sea coast the food is noticeably better than in the east proper, and there is more variety and imagination shown in the preparation. The eastern areas are also the worst for bringing you your food in a totally random order. If you are brought your main course at the same as your soup the best course of action is simply to send it back and then get it brought again later so that it stays at least half-way warm. Since almost all the food is pre-prepared in large open aluminium tureens in the kitchen it is luke warm in the first place. The best way to choose your meal is to go into the kitchen and look for yourself, even in the big hotels, then point out your choice to the waiter. In the restaurants used as meal stops by the buses, service is so quick that you have to hold onto your plate to prevent it being snatched away. Food is clearly not something to be savoured in Eastern Turkey and there is little or no concern to present it well. It is definitely a case of eating to live rather than living to eat. The consolation however is price, and these restaurants do generally offer very good value, and because of the constant turnover the food is usually quite fresh. In the towns it is the restaurants attached to the best hotels which most often offer the best food in the most salubrious surroundings, in contrast to the Aegean and Mediterranean regions, where you are likely to enjoy a far better meal in a restaurant than in a hotel.

Surviving breakfast   The standard Turkish breakfast of black olives and white cheese washed down with strong sugared black tea, however, applies in the east as it does in the rest of the country, though the bread, butter and jam varies considerably from town to town. Coffee of the Nescafé variety is extremely expensive, more so than in the south and west, so take your own if you want it. In some hotels, like the Akdamar in Van, they will run to freshly squeezed orange juice if you ask for it, and eggs cooked as you want them. Service in the bigger hotels can sometimes be rather slow at breakfast, so it is a good policy to send the fastest person down first to give in the order. A few hotels, again like the Akdamar, will bring you breakfast in the room.

If you are unfortunate enough to find the better hotels full and are compelled to stay in a fleapit hotel, breakfast is not offered at all, and you must head off in search of the nearest pastahane where you can have sweet cakes, the standard olives and cheese, sometimes with honey, and often washed down with hot milk. Tea frequently has to be fetched from a nearby tea house by an errand boy. In the Van area the breakfast cheese may be the local otlupeynir (herb cheese), a succulent Kurdish delicacy.

Quenching your thirst   Like the food, all drink in Turkey, alcoholic or not, is very cheap. Exact prices are given in the budgeting section.

Water is usually drinkable but often does not taste very nice as it is likely to be heavily chlorinated. Bottled mineral water is readily obtainable, cheap and usually drunk in preference. Water from a spring (çeşme) along the side of the road is drinkable and tastes good; though it may come out of a tap its origin will be from a freshwater spring. If in doubt, ask: *içilir* means drinkable, *içilmez* means not drinkable.

Ayran is the non-alcoholic national drink, a chilled unsweetened yogurt liquid, thirst-quenching and slightly sour.

Rakı (an aniseed spirit similar to ouzo) is the national alcoholic drink, usually mixed with ice and water. It goes well with Turkish food.

As befits the place where it is thought the grape was first cultivated, Turkey today has the fourth largest area in the world under viticulture, and is the sixth largest wine producer in the world. Very little of this is exported. The red tends to be better than the white. On the red side the best is Buzbağ, a full-bodied red, closest to a Burgundy; the other good reds to ask for are Villa Doluca (pronounced Doluja), Yakut, Dikmen and Trakya. The premium whites are Çankaya, Villa Doluca again, and in the next rung, Kavak, Kavaklıdere and white Trakya.

While alcohol — spirits, wine and beer — is available in all the better hotels in the cities, around 60 percent of the local restaurants never serve it at all, and during Ramadan this percentage may go as high as 90 percent. If you want a drink with your food, therefore, it is best to ask before ordering so that you are not disappointed once it is too late. Of the non-alcoholic drinks available ayran and water are the commonest, but Coke and fizzy orange are usually available as well.

Tipping
Tipping is something which Turks do not generally expect as the automatic right that it has become in the West. It is regarded rather as a gesture of appreciation for good service (as tipping originally was), and since service in Turkey is usually excellent, most Turks do in practice leave tips. In restaurants ten percent is usual, though in smaller basic restaurants, especially in rural areas, tips closer to five percent are fine. In some hotels and restaurants, notably those registered with the Ministry of Culture and Tourism, ten percent is added to your bill willy-nilly, in which case there is no need to add anything more unless you wish to express particular gratitude. Taxis are the exception worth knowing about: Turks never tip taxi drivers.

Money and Currency
The unit of currency is the Turkish lira. Coins are rare, and notes come as 5, 10, 20, 50, 100, 500, 1000, 5000 and 10,000 lira.

Inflation   The inflation rate in Turkey is high, between 60 and 75 percent, but the exchange rate moves to balance this so that in practice the cost of holidaying in Turkey for foreign visitors has remained fairly static over the last five years.

The bigger hotels (3-star and upwards), international car hire agencies like Hertz and Avis, and the more expensive shops in cities will usually accept American Express, Diners **Credit cards**   Club, Visa, Access and Eurocard, though unless you are always staying in the top class hotels, it is best not to rely on them but rather to take them as a fall-back. They are not in general use in the more rural areas.

The exchange rate is better inside Turkey than outside, so it best only to change a small amount in advance of your arrival. The hotels in Eastern Turkey are not so geared up to changing money at the reception desk as they are in the Aegean and Mediterranean areas (where this will be done for you, without commission, by any 3- to 5-star hotel and many 2-star ones as well). You may therefore have to go to a bank, but be warned that not all banks **Changing money**   change all travellers cheques. For Eurocheques it may be, for example, that the local Etibank will not accept them and they will send you to the İşbank instead. It is worth showing the hotel reception your travellers cheques first and they can then advise you of the nearest bank that will change them for you. When you do find the right bank you must allow 15 to 20 minutes for the highly elaborate process to be completed. The rate at the bank is usually slightly better than at the hotels, but not remarkably so. Most people would probably consider it worthwhile to lose one percent or so commission in order to avoid the hassle of the queuing process in the bank. There is so much other hassle in Eastern Turkey that when it can be avoided, you generally do.

Budgeting and Prices

The cost of actually getting to Turkey will be by far the greatest element in your holiday budget. Car hire is the only other major expense. Once these two expenses are settled, the cost of holidaying in Turkey is very low indeed, far lower than most Mediterranean countries.

A reasonable daily budget for two people, including accommodation in a 2-star hotel, meals, drinks, entry fees and 300 km-worth of petrol is £30 to £35 or $45 to $53. In the good hotel restaurants a meal for two with wine generally costs between £5 and £7.50 or $7.50 and $11.

Average prices in hotels for drinks are: rakı (1 glass, the equivalent of a quadruple measure) 30p or 45c; beer (a bottle) 30p or 45c; a bottle of wine £1 to £2 or $1.50 to $3; Coke and soft fizzy drinks 20p or 30c; a cup of tea

10p or 15c; Turkish coffee 25p or 40c; Nescafé with milk 45p or 70c.

Electricity
220 volts all over Turkey, from continental 2-pin plugs.

How to Use Public Telephones
No coins are accepted: you have to buy little brass coloured 'jetons' from the post office. First you pick up the receiver, then insert the jeton in the slot on the top of the box. Next you dial the number, it rings at the other end, and you can speak as soon as it is answered. If it is engaged or there is no reply, you press the silver button near the top of the box to get your jeton back.

Weights and Measures
Turkey officially employs the metric system.

Temperature			Linear Measure	
Fahrenheit	=	Celsius	0.39 inches	1 centimetre
122		50	1 inch	2.54 centimetres
113		45	1 foot (12 in)	0.30 metres
110		43.3	1 yard (3 ft)	0.91 metres
107.6		42	39.37 inches	1 metre
104		40	0.62 miles	1 kilometre
102.2		39	1 mile (5280 ft)	1.61 kilometres
100		37.8	3 miles	4.8 kilometres
98.6		37	10 miles	16 kilometres
96.8		36	60 miles	98.6 kilometres
95		35	100 miles	160.9 kilometres
93.2		34		
91.4		33		
90		32	**Square Measure**	
87.8		31	1 sq foot	0.09 sq metres
86		30	1 sq yard	0.84 sq metres
84.2		29	1.20 sq yards	1 sq metre
80		26.7		
75		23.9		
70		21		
65		18.3		
60		15.6	**Weight**	
55		12.8	0.04 ounces	1 gram
50		10	1 ounce	28.35 grams
45		7.2	1 pound	453.59 grams
40		4	2.20 pounds	1 kilogram
32		0	1 ton (2000 lb)	907.18 kilograms
23		−5		
14		−10		
0		−17.8		

Fahrenheit into Celsius: subtract 32 from Fahrenheit temperature, then multiply by 5, then divide by 9.
Celsius into Fahrenheit: multiply Celsius by 9, then divide by 5, then add 32.

Liquid Measure

0.22 imperial gallons	1 litre
0.26 US gallons	1 litre
1 US gallons	3.79 litres
1 imperial gallon	4.55 litres

Opening Hours

Turkey shares with Europe the Saturday and Sunday weekend.

Banks: 8.30 am to noon, 1.30 pm to 5 pm

Shops: 9am to 1 pm, 2 pm to 7pm

Museums: All close Mondays but are open on all other days. The exception is the Topkapı Palace Museum which closes on Tuesdays.

Time

GMT +2 all the year round (ie noon GMT in London is 2pm in Turkey). As Britain may change either or both its winter and summer times to match the rest of the EEC, check what the time difference will be in practice.

Calendar of Festivals and Public Holidays

Turkey follows the Gregorian calendar like Europe, and it has weekends of Saturday and Sunday in the same way. However, being a predominantly Moslem country it celebrates the major Islamic festivals. The dates for these festivals are not fixed in our Gregorian calendar but are timed according to the lunar system which is 11 days shorter per year than our solar one. For example the approximate dates of the month of Ramadan in 1990 are 27 March to 24 April and it falls about 11 days earlier in each successive year.

Lunar calendar

There are two major Islamic holidays, the approximate equivalents if you like of our Christmas and Easter. The first is the Feast of the Sacrifice (Turkish *Kurban Bayramı*) which commemorates Abraham's willingness to sacrifice his son Isaac. Each family buys an animal for sacrifice according to his means (usually a sheep, or a very rich person might buy a camel) and then it is cooked and much of the meat is given to the poor. It is a national four-day holiday, occurring in 1990 from about 2 to 4 July, and in 1991 from about 23 to 25 June. Most banks close for a full week and everyone is on holiday.

The second celebrates the end of the month of fasting in Ramadan and is called in Turkish *Şeker Bayramı*. It is a three-day national holiday when much visiting of friends and family and feasting takes place to make up for the deprivation of the previous month.

During both of these major festivals, especially when they fall in the summer, Turks pour out in a mass exodus from the cities, packing the resort towns all along the coasts to bursting. This is the only time you will experience difficulties in finding accommodation, and for this reason, if you are on a touring holiday, it can be wiser to plan to be inland for the duration of one of these festivals. The inland lakes like Eğridir remain surprisingly uncrowded during the festivals, so they can be an ideal spot to stay if you are keen to continue swimming.

1 January: a public holiday for New Year's Day.

23 April: a public holiday for National Sovereignty Day.

3 to 5 June: Aksaray Ihlara Folk Festival.

5 to 10 July: Akşehir Nasreddin Hoca Festival in honour of the famous wit, consisting of plays of his anecdotes and folk dancing.

1 to 25 August: Samsun Fair and Folk Dance Festival.

20 to 25 September: Çorum Hittite Festival held in Boğazkale, Alaca and Sungurlu, an open-air festival with displays, music and folklore shows among the ruins.

21 to 25 September: Cappadocia Festival, grape harvest celebration and folkloric festival.

15 September to 5 October: Mersin Fashion and Textile Show, with music and folklore.

29 October: Republic Day, to commemorate the proclamation of the republic by Atatürk in 1923.

9 to 17 December: Mevlana Festival at Konya. Hotels are packed for this, the only occasion in the year when the Whirling Dervishes can be seen performing.

Climate

Extremes of temperature are the order of the day in Eastern Turkey, not just between winter and summer, but also between night and day. The most extreme example of this is Kars, in the northeast, where the highest temperature recorded has been +35°C and the lowest −37°C.

The *Practical Information* section at the back of each chapter carries full details of the year-round climate in the major towns of that region, but generally speaking the best time to visit the east is between May and September, with June probably the best month of all for most places. The tourist season now, as a result of sheer demand, runs from as early as 1 April till as late as 31 October. July and August are extremely hot during the day, though the temperature still drops sharply at night. Some parts can be especially attractive in the winter months, notably Cappadocia and Lake Van.

Clothing

The emphasis is definitely on casual and strong clothes for Eastern Turkey. The dining rooms in the best hotels are not formal and most people are dressed for comfort rather than style. Trousers or skirts and short sleeves are fine for most occasions, but shorts are generally to be avoided except on the northern and southern coast resorts. Low-cut

Casual but covered

or tight-fitting T-shirts are not a good idea either. Loose clothes will be far more comfortable for walking around in the heat of the day anyway. A thick pullover or jacket is essential for the evenings when the temperature drops sharply, and a thin waterproof plastic garment is advisable in the Black Sea areas where sudden rainstorms are common. Strong shoes are a must for the towns as well as the sites; sandals are hardly ever suitable as there is too much dust, mud and dirt around. Women should be especially careful to cover bare arms and heads for entering mosques. Bikinis are fine in the few hotels that have pools and on the Black Sea and Mediterranean coasts. Toplessness is not the practice, and nudity is illegal.

Health

Stomach upsets are difficult to avoid in Eastern Turkey so you should be careful and go prepared with suitable pills, the stronger the better. Lomotil and antibiotics can in fact be bought over the counter in chemist shops (*ezcane*) all over Turkey, so if you know which type to ask for you can just buy your antibiotics then and there as necessary. In central Anatolia and Cappadocia standards of hygiene are higher so you are unlikely to pick anything up until you hit the east proper, ie Adıyaman and eastwards.

In summer months the dust in Eastern Turkey is excessive. Even for those not normally sensitive to such things, this can cause much discomfort with streaming irritated eyes, aggravated catarrh in the nose and sore throats. It is therefore a sensible precaution to take an eye bath lotion and throat lozenges or gargling fluid.

Useful Items to Take

Toilet paper, and more toilet paper!

Soap is not always provided at hotels, though towels are. Bring your own suntan potions, toothpaste and medicines, as you may not find the brands you want in Turkey. Bring an initial supply of toilet paper, and keep yourself stocked with it as you travel — amazing how useful it can be and how often it is not there. It is cheaper to bring film with you, and if you want coffee, bring your own jarful, as it can be difficult to find in Turkey and is always expensive. Also bring a tyre pressure gauge so that you can check the pressures after a day's crunching into potholes; a powerful flashlight for exploring caves, tunnels or the toilet when the light does not work; eye bath for sore dusty eyes and sore throat medicine; a travel plug adapter as the 2-pin shaver sockets are likely to be a different gauge to British and other 2-pin sockets; and a sheet sleeping bag to insulate you from the dirtiest sheets of fleapit hotels in case you are forced to stay in them. Hotels rarely provide bath or basin plugs: bring your own universal size.

Shopping for Souvenirs

Cappadocia the best

This is not as straightforward in the east as it is in other parts of the country. In Cappadocia there are many souvenir shops selling colourful woollen socks and gloves, embroidered headscarves, jewellery with semi-precious stones, carved wooden boxes, alabaster and pottery, and this is certainly the best place to do your shopping if it is on your itinerary. The woollen socks are good as slipper socks or inside rubber boots. In the east proper, however, souvenir shops are few and far between and tend to be kitschy when they do exist. The Kurdish areas like Siirt, Diyarbakır and Hakkâri are the best places to buy Turkish kilims or saddlebags.

In Erzurum you can buy the local black jet made into artefacts like worry beads and necklaces. Eros underpants, sold all over Eastern Turkey, make a suitably crass present.

Bargaining

Bargaining is normal if the price is not marked, and as a rough guideline you should offer a third of the price asked and then haggle towards the middle. To bargain successfully an air of complete indifference to the object being haggled over is essential. Once you make the fatal error of showing, either through your facial expression or the tone of your voice, that you like something and want it, you are doomed to the losing end of the transaction. In some of the towns where the locals have grown used to influxes of coach tours, young boys lie in wait near the shops for enthusiastic but bewildered tourists, offering their services as guides. 'I am student, I go with you to practice my English, no money.' When you demure politely, they insist, 'You need me, to keep the others away.' Once you have given in, their real purpose soon becomes clear: their uncle just happens to have a carpet shop nearby, or they surreptitiously produce a priceless fragment of something to sell you, convinced that the more illicit their manner, the more convinced you will be of its genuineness and its immense value.

Turkish Carpets

Most Turkish carpets are of the 'kilim' variety, kilim being a Turkish word meaning 'flat woven'. This is quite an accurate description as they are characterised by their almost total lack of pile and their rug-like size. Kilims were traditionally made by women for use in their own homes and not for sale. The patterns and colours were therefore never dictated by commercial motives but reflected the identity of the weaver's family and tribe. The wool used is normally sheep's wool, but cotton and goat hair are sometimes used as well. Silver thread and even gold lurex thread is also sometimes incorporated in the kilims of the Hakkâri and Malatya areas of Eastern Turkey, as it is thought to be a lucky charm for the user of the kilim in protecting him against the devil or the evil eye.

Kilims were used not only as floor coverings in the home but also as wall hangings, door curtains, tent dividers and prayer rugs, as well as being made into large bags for cushions or saddlebags or smaller bags for salt, bread, grain or clothes.

Natural and chemical dyes

Traditionally, natural dyes were used for colours from roots, bark, berries, vegetables and minerals. In the second half of the 19th C aniline chemical dyes became available and their use has gradually replaced most of the old vegetable dyes. Pink and orange are colours which could never be produced from natural dyes so the presence of these colours and any other colours with a harsher brightness to them is always an indication that the weaver used chemical dyes and that the carpet is relatively recent. The quality of chemical dyes has now improved considerably and can sometimes be quite convincing. Obtaining natural dyes often involved a lengthy and laborious process and also had the problem that no two colour mixes ever came up quite the same: this difference in colour 'mid-weave', so to speak, is another indication of the use of vegetable colours in a kilim. Today's weavers are often all in favour of the new chemical dyes for the sake of convenience. They have also been freed from the constraints of the availability of plants in their particular region, a factor which traditionally dominated the choice of colours, such as the Turcoman red, the blue of southeast Turkey and the blue and red of the Balıkşehir region in northwest Turkey.

The designs and patterns on a kilim also gave clues to its region, though you would have to be quite an expert before you could identify these differences. Some designs however are common to all rugs, the best known pattern being the prayer rug with its solid arch-shaped block of colour representing the mihrab or prayer niche which faces Mecca in a mosque wall. Such rugs were used exclusively for prayer and the range of symbols frequently to be seen on them are the hands of prayer, the mosque lamp, the Tree of Life, the water jug, the jewel of Mohammed or the Star of Abraham.

How to tell new from old

As older kilims are becoming rarer and fetch more money, dealers have not been slow to develop techniques for fading newly woven rugs. Fading in sunlight is the commonest method and can often produce quite effective and pleasing results with mellower colours. Parting the surface, to look at the very bottom of the weave, you can compare the colouring with the top surface to check this. Comparing the colours on the top with those on the underside also gives an indication. More harmful, however, is the practice of washing a kilim in bleach to produce the effect more quickly, as this reduces the life of the weaving. A quick sniff usually reveals this. As smaller kilims sell more quickly than larger ones, some dealers will cut up the larger ones into pieces and sell them as original. Watch out for the newer ends added to make them complete or an unnatural break in the pattern. If colours have been touched up to hide repairs or fading, the felt-tip colouring or shoe polish used may be disclosed by rubbing a wetted cloth or handkerchief over the surface; these may even come off on your hand as you run it across the weave. Another common aging trick is dirt, along with deliberate scorch marks. Always look at both sides of a carpet to compare the colours and look at the closeness of its weave. The closer the weave and the smaller the knots the better the quality and durability of the carpet.

Agreeing a price necessitates the usual bargaining: aiming for around a third off the price first asked is usually the norm. If you want to pay by credit card you may do less well as the dealer will be losing 6 to 8 percent to the credit card company.

Kilims are best used on top of another carpet or on an overlay to help them wear well. They should not really be used under a dining table or in a corridor where they would get heavy wear. Sharp pointed furniture legs or pointed heels can also damage them. For cleaning, a cylinder vacuum cleaner is gentler than an upright one especially on the fringes. By hanging a kilim on the wall you can prolong its life indefinitely and it will certainly outlive you if hung correctly with the fringes top and bottom. For cleaning you can use the hose pipe to simulate the river water which is the traditional method or, far easier, use a good carpet cleaning powder and then just vacuum it and the dirt off. One age-old method is treading the carpet into the snow and then shaking it out vigorously before it gets wet, but this is obviously an annual event at best. Dry cleaning is not recommended. A simple outdoors shake-out of the dust is still the best method for more routine cleaning.

Kindness to kilims

Museums and Sites
Museums are generally shut on Mondays (with the exception of the Topkapı Palace in İstanbul which closes on Tuesdays). The usual opening hours are 8.30am to 12.30pm and 1.30 to 5.30pm. There is usually a small charge for entry. All sites too carry a small entry fee, unless they are still under excavation. They are usually open throughout daylight hours. On Saturdays and Sundays the entry fee is halved as an encouragement to local people to visit in their spare time.

An important point to note when visiting sites in Eastern Turkey is that they are generally small in size, like Nemrut Dağ, the Cappadocian churches and the Doğubeyazıt palace, and this means that if you coincide with a coach tour the site will be swamped and your enjoyment inevitably diminished. In the Aegean and Mediterranean areas sites like Ephesus and Pergamum are so extensive that thousands can pour over them in a day and the sites will still not appear unpleasantly crowded. A hundred people visiting Nemrut Dağ on the other hand can seem quite oppressive. You should make it your business therefore, as an independent traveller, to try never to coincide with a coach tour, or if you do to wait until they have left before beginning your own tour. The key to this is to cultivate somewhat unorthodox timing.

Avoiding the coach tours...

A second point about the sites in Eastern Turkey is that almost all of them are in cities or close to habitation of some sort, so you will not find deserted sites like Arycanda and Patara of the Lycian shores. Thirdly, you should be prepared as an evident Westerner to be pestered by children and youths asking for money (*para*) and pens (*kalem*). The mentality of these children is quite different to those in the southern and western parts of the country, and while they are not hostile, they lack the charm and innocence of their southern and western counterparts. If the adults catch them pestering you, they will shout at them and tick them off, but the moment their backs are turned the children return. This change in behaviour begins as soon as you leave the coast at Adana and Antalya and stays with you till the Georgian valleys in the final approach to the Black Sea coast. It is also less marked in central Anatolian areas from Ankara to Elazığ and also in the Arab-influenced areas like Diyarbakır and Mardin. It is at its worst in the Van region and north to Erzurum. You will doubtless find the best way to deal with this to suit your temperament. A stick is an effective deterrent; ignoring it does not alas work at all; but the best way if you have the patience is firmly and politely to discourage them.

...and avoiding the children

Mountains

Eastern Turkey offers a tremendous range of climbing for the mountaineer: from near-tropical landscapes in the Pontic mountains just inland from the Black Sea to arctic peaks with permanent snow-covering like Mt Ararat and the Hakkâri range in the extreme southeast. Mountains form an important part of the landscapes of Eastern Turkey. Much of the plateau, though itself already high at 2000 metres, is very flat and the surrounding countryside is therefore dominated for miles around by any major peaks. This is especially true of the volcanoes which tend to rise up in splendid isolation, their majesty undiluted by a cluster of lesser peaks.

Volcanic peaks

There are five volcanoes in Eastern Turkey, all of which can be climbed. They are more for the mountain wayfarer than for the real alpinist, though Ararat requires proper equipment and altitude acclimatisation.

Mt Ararat, 5137 metres. Turkey's highest mountain and the only one that requires a permit from the authorities to climb it due to its proximity to the Russian border. Sometimes compared to Mt Kilimanjaro, it is one of the world's most imposing mountains. The standard ascent takes three days from the base camp of Doğubeyazıt, then one or two days for the descent, but presents no real technical difficulty apart from a few glaciers near the top. The high winds near the summit can be very unpleasant and even dangerous. The easier approach is up the east face from the base of Iğdir. July and August are the best months to get snow-free terrain but June has the clearest weather.

Suphan Dağ, 4058 metres. From Adilcevaz this is a fairly straightforward climb with fine views over Lake Van.

Erciyes Dağ, 3916 metres. Near Kayseri this is the volcano that spewed forth the lava that created the Cappadocian landscapes. There is a *kayak evi* or mountain hut with 100 beds at the top. Leaving Kayseri by the airport road you drive to the village of Hisarlık (14 km) and then continue to the kayak evi. There is good scenery enroute even if you do not climb.

Hasan Dağ, 3268 metres. South of Aksaray near the Ihlara Gorge, a straightforward climb but without spectacular scenery.

Nemrut Dağ, 2935 metres. A walk of several hours from Tatvan and offering the bonus of being able to go down into the lush vegetation of the crater with its lake and hot and cold springs. Though the outer cone is bleak and denuded of greenery the views over Lake Van compensate.

Hakkâri range

This range in Turkey's southeast corner south of Lake Van has Turkey's second highest peaks after Ararat, and used to be the most exciting climbing Turkey had to offer the experienced mountaineer. Many well-travelled climbers still consider these mountains, especially the two main peaks of Çilo and Sat, to be among the world's most curious and fascinating, in no small part because of their sheer remoteness. Today and for the forseeable future they are alas forbidden to climbers because of the Kurdish guerila activity which has seen a resurgence in recent years.

Ala Dağ

Since the loss of the Hakkâri area to climbers the Ala Dağ range southeast of Niğde offers the best substitute and has the great advantage of easy access. It is possible to drive in one long day from İstanbul to Niğde and from there up to Çamardı, a small town at 1500 metres reachable on tarmac road in a saloon car. Guides and mules can be arranged in Çamardı with no difficulty and no permits are required. About ten days would be needed in total from İstanbul to make a worthwhile trip.

Kaçkar range

The best climbing in Turkey after the Hakkâri and Ala Dağ is to be found in the Kaçkar range. Also known as the Little Caucasus this is the range inland from the Black Sea between Rize and Pazar. The approach is from the coast through Çemlihemsin and past the hot mineral springs at Ayder Kaplıcaları. From this northern approach through the lush rain forest the peaks of the Kaçkar (highest 3932 metres) offer good rock climbing (mainly granite) and ice and snow climbing, comparable to good second-class alpine peaks of 2500 to 3200 metres. Because of the high level of rainfall, glaciers are frequent and the rain, drizzle and mist does not stop until 3000 metres. A total of three weeks should be allowed from İstanbul. For non-mountaineers the approaches through the tea plantations and lush semi-tropical vegetation make interesting walking. The wetness and frequent rainfall are a nuisance but the compensations are the rich and colourful flora, with yellow azaleas, rhododendrons and pontic lilies, especially in June. All the peaks can also be approached from the south on dry routes which are mountain walks rather than climbs, but which offer bleaker landscapes as most of the vegetation and rainfall is on the northern side.

Munzur range

Located between Erzincan and Tunceli this is one of the least explored ranges in Turkey. The peaks rise to between 3000 and 3400 metres. In difficulty they are not in the same league as the Hakkâri or Ala Dağ but are well-suited to those who are between mountaineer and mountain wayfarer. The range offers fine scenery with many rivers and springs and is genuinely remote. Starting points are either Çağlıyan from Erzincan or Ovacık from Tunceli.

Arrangements and equipment

With the exception of Ararat, no permits are required for climbing. The best procedure is to organise yourself and supplies, drive to the base town and call on the local Wali or, if it is a smaller town, the kaymakam, and ask for help in providing guides and if necessary mules. For this reason a knowledge of Turkish is a distinct advantage in making yourself understood, though someone can usually be found to interpret.

Normal mountaineering equipment is required including ice axes, pitons, crampons and ropes. Sun block creams for the face and windproof clothing are needed for peaks higher than 3000 metres. Your own food supplies should be taken with you. The suitable supplies to be found locally are limited to tinned sardines, tea, salt, sugar, bread and margerine. The local chocolate is flimsy and lacking in energy and nutrition value.

The beauty of climbing in these remote mountains is summed up well by Sidney Nowill, the experienced English climber of these parts, as that sensation of living 'for a time completely free of every worldly link, self-reliant and untrammelled by any human agency or service, something which is healthful and cleansing to achieve, if only once in a lifetime'.

Wildlife

Along the roadsides the large hairy Bactrian camels are still to be seen in the southern Mediterranean areas, giving way in the central Anatolian regions to the distinctive black water buffalo with their long beards and fierce horns. Both are used as beasts of burden. Sheep and goats in many shapes and forms abound and there is also plentiful cattle. Chickens, geese and ducks are often all over the roads in the villages of the interior.

Further afield in the remoter and more mountainous areas, the game which the Turks shoot includes badgers, bears, boars, deer, ibexes, jackels and gazelles on the Turkish–Syrian border areas and wild cats and even leopards in the forests. There are also many wolves and wild dogs in the mountains.

Common game birds are wild duck, wild geese, quail, partridge and pheasant.

Birds and Birdwatching

Travel in Eastern Turkey means long distances, sometimes through a spectacular and dramatic landscape, at other times through scenery that is less immediately interesting. But there is one feature of the landscape that can always keep you on your toes and which gives every stop an extra dimension and an interest beyond the immediate archaeological, architectural or scenic. That is the birdlife.

An extra dimension

Carrying a pair of binoculars and a field guide will enhance the holiday even for the inexperienced birdwatcher, or indeed, for anyone who has never watched or systematically observed birds before. The only available volume which covers the whole of Turkey is *The Birds of Britain and Europe with North Africa and the Middle East* by Heinzel, Fitter and Parslow (Collins), and this is the best book to have along for reference. Bird identification can at times be a frustrating and disappointing experience if you are not an expert, though it is always challenging and continues to exercise the mind long after the bird has disappeared from view.

Turkey offers a wide range of birdlife in what is a comparatively small area. What is it that makes the country so worthwhile for the birdwatcher?

Just as its geographical position between the land masses of Asia, Africa and Europe laid it open to the movement of peoples and armies from the north, east and south, so too Turkey has elements of the birdlife of all three continents. This diversity is increased by the very wide range of climatic conditions which occur within the compact area of Turkey. There is the semi-desert of the Syrian border and the Mediterranean coastland with its hinterland of scrub-covered mountains. Then there is the bare central Anatolian plateau ringed and divided by naked mountain ranges, but holding within it natural and artificial lakes, many of them saline. Finally there is the almost temperate, humid Black Sea coast with its own forested mountains. So semi-desert, bare mountain, forested mountain, steppe and wetlands all add to the diversity of birdlife and make this an exciting country for the Northern European birdwatcher. If you are here in the spring or autumn there is the added attraction that two of the major north–south migration routes cross this land mass. To the east, their flight pattern follows the western flanks of the Caucasus and over the passes of the eastern Karadeniz (Black Sea) mountains. These migrations are on a huge scale; nearly 400,000 birds of prey were recorded passing the northeast coast between mid-August and mid-October 1976.

What can an inexperienced birdwatcher see on a touring holiday in Eastern Turkey? May is the best time, and on a typical three-week tour you can be assured of spotting, if not always identifying with certainty, well over 100 species. Nearly 50 of these are not to be seen in Britain. There are of course in addition, the inevitable 'big brown birds' of prey and numerous 'little brown birds', which are aggravatingly difficult to identify because of distance, lack of experience or inability to distinguish birdsong. It is worth stressing that all the birds mentioned here are to be seen while travelling from one town to another and along the routes you would be following to visit the various sites anyway. Birdwatching can therefore be easily incorporated to add interest to the long drives without necessitating any detour.

Storks and herons Sticking to the itineraries described in this book, the first group of birds to look out for are white storks in meadows by the Kızılırmak river east of Ankara, with grey herons fishing in the river shallows. Stork nests are common on buildings, minarets and telegraph poles. It is along this road from Ankara to the Hittite heartlands that you first notice the crested larks which are, in much of this part of Turkey, the bird which is always running off the tarmac

Remarkable diversity (marginal note beside second paragraph)

and flying up under the wheels of vehicles. They seem less common in the eastern parts of the Anatolian plateau.

The Hittite sites are rich with birds: red-backed shrikes and the black-eared wheatears in the open spaces of Boğaz-kale, the rocks of Yazılıkaya echoing to the sharp cries of families of rock buntings. After Alacahüyük in the failing light a small artificial lake among the hills enroute to Amasya reveals more grey herons and night herons, little egrets, a family of ruddy shelducks and white-winged black terns sweeping across the water.

Ibises, cranes and hoopoes Birds of the central Anatolian plateau are many and varied: redshanks, little ringed plovers, rose-coloured starlings and glossy ibises are to be seen by flooded fields besides the Sivas to Divriği road. Brightly coloured bee-eaters are the birds of the roadside telegraph wires, swooping down to feed, then back up to look out for the next morsel. The bright blue, brown and black rollers can be found nesting in the ruined caravanserais at Pazar and near Bitlis. At other times cranes, golden orioles, lesser grey shrike, black-headed buntings and hoopoes are to be seen as well as more familiar birds such as jays, starlings, blackbirds and many magpies.

Overhead, vultures and birds of prey are common if not always readily identifiable. The easily distinguished black **Vultures and eagles** and white Egyptian vultures circle overhead singly or in groups, but griffon vultures are also to be seen. On the open roads are buzzards and long legged buzzards. Black kites, seen near Sivas, are often devouring their prey perched on telegraph poles within a few yards of the road. There are also hobbies, kestrels, golden eagles and booted eagles. Just south of the Great Salt Lake (Tuz Gölü) between Ankara and Cappadocia you may spot Montagu's harriers, twisting and turning above a dried-out marsh, with a greylag goose in the distant marshland.

Around Gaziantep and Carchemish near the Syrian border Saker falcons, short-toed larks, black-headed buntings, Upcher's warblers, barred warblers, Montagu's harriers and white-breasted kingfishers can be spotted. On the banks of the Euphrates which flows through Birecik, pied kingfishers can be seen in abundance.

Lake Van, always the highpoint of any visit to Eastern Turkey, is also the ornithological highpoint. On the north-eastern shore beyond Adilcevaz and on the eastern shores where the Bendamahi river flows into the lake there is marshland where, driving past, a smudge of white by the water can be transformed by binoculars to a large flock **Pelicans and flamingos** of some hundred white pelicans. A short walk from the road across the fields closer to the lake can often reveal a flock of a few dozen greater flamingos. Among the reeds there are often black-winged stilts flying overhead trailing their fantastically long red legs, calling as they circle. In the shallow water others step like awkward robots, while their long black beaks poke the mud. The reeds conceal both the reed warbler and the greater reed warbler. Also to be seen in spots like this are little-ringed plovers, common sandpipers, redshanks, lapwings, black-headed buntings and corn buntings. On the water are black-necked grebes, great-crested grebes, potchards, ruddy shelducks and shelducks as well as herring gulls and the oddly-shaped white-headed duck.

On Akdamar Island and at Hoşap Castle there are alpine swifts and kestrels, while on the rocky Van Kalesi citadel itself there are hoopoes calling, kestrels, bee-eaters and rollers, together with black redstarts and rock nutlatches with their young. On the mountainous road from Van to Hakkâri, Lammergeier's vultures can often be seen circling overhead.

On the bare plains near Erzurum the roads are sometimes lined with poplars containing extensive rookeries, although the other members of the crow family to be seen are hooded crows, jackdaws and ravens.

The northern mountains and the Black Sea coast are disappointing in comparison to the rest of the country. Cloud-shrouded woods near Borabay Gölü reveal only pied and grey wagtails, dippers and coal tits as well as lots of infuriatingly unidentifiable little brown birds flitting about among the trees. The coast itself is not especially rich in birdlife, with mallards, coots and only herring gulls and lesser black-backed gulls. Cormorants can be seen in the water or on the offshore rocks.

In addition to the birds of the countryside there are the birds of the town: apart from the ubiquitous feral pigeons and house sparrows there are the lesser kestrels wheeling round the minarets of the city mosque, but over all is the abiding memory as dusk falls, above the street noises and the cry of the muezzin, of the squeals of the flocks of hundreds of wheeling swifts.

For the serious ornithologist prepared to make specific detours from his itineraries, visits to well-known birdwatching spots can be made where some 250 species can be seen. Such sites include Kulu Gölü about 100 km south of Ankara and the Sultan Marshes (Aya Gölü) south of Kayseri where immense numbers and varieties of birds can be seen by the enthusiast. There are also several bird sanctuaries to visit. At the Pines National Park 5 km from Yozgat near the Hittite sites of Boğazkale and Yazılıkaya, 13 king eagles reside, said to be over 400 years old. They are only found in the Caucasus mountains and have a wingspan of 3.5 to 4 metres. The nests are on the southwest side of the peak and the best chance of a sighting is to be concealed

Bird sanctuaries

near the nests at dawn or sunset. The wild Yozgat tulip is also to be found in the national park. At the Manyas Bird Sanctuary 17 km from Bandırma on the Sea of Marmara, Lake Manyas is surrounded by a wood of willow trees. Many migratory birds are to be found here nesting each year, arriving in February with the young appearing in April and May. Towards autumn they migrate to India and Africa where they spend the winter months. The common species to be seen here are grey herons, small white herons, cormorants and pelicans. The rarer species include crimson heron, waterfowl, wild duck, falcon, titmouse birds, nightingale and blue crow. 179 varieties have been seen in the sanctuary. Finally, at Birecik near the Syrian border between Gaziantep and Urfa, you can visit the reserve of the bald ibis, a large and extraordinary bird on the verge of extinction and currently the subject of a World Wildlife Fund rescue operation.

For those with a serious interest in the birds of Turkey contact with or better still membership of the Ornithological Society of the Middle East, c/o The Lodge, Sandy, Bedfordshire SG19 2DL, England, is recommended.

Travel within Turkey by Public Services

By air On arrival at İstanbul International Airport a very sophisticated and ultra-modern terminal building is there to greet you. All facilities are to hand, with restaurants, bars, shops, banks and a post office. The only rather surprising omission is a left-luggage section to leave your bags if you have a long wait for your connection and want to make a trip into İstanbul for a brief tour. The journey from the airport into the town centre takes only 40 minutes, so if your wait is anything over 3 hours it leaves you time to get a bus or a taxi into the centre and have a stroll round Haghia Sophia or the Blue Mosque or even the Topkapı Palace. Left-luggage facilities do exist however in the otherwise appallingly equipped Domestic Terminal, 1 km away, and a courtesy bus shuttles between the two terminals every few minutes.

If you are making an onward internal flight from Istanbul, which will usually be the case if you are intending to tour the eastern part of Turkey, you must go out of the International Terminal and wait for the courtesy bus to the Domestic Terminal. Be sure to collect your luggage first, as even if your ticket shows an onward flight your baggage will not be forwarded automatically or loaded onto the internal flight for you. You must collect it yourself and then check it in again at the Domestic Terminal. This procedure is far from obvious as there are no signs telling you what to do or pointing to the Domestic Terminal from inside the International one, so you could be forgiven for assuming your onward flight was from the same terminal. As always it is advisable not to have too much luggage as you have to hump it on and off the bus yourself. The check-in desks at the Domestic Terminal only open an hour before take-off, so do not hurry over there if you have a longish wait for your connection. Facilities at the Domestic Terminal are very limited indeed, with just one shabby 'restaurant' offering variations on a toasted sandwich. The toilets are extremely smelly and mainly of the squat-over-a-hole-in-the-ground variety. All in all it is a depressing place to have to spend any time and you are far better advised to wait and eat at the International Terminal, just coming across to the Domestic Terminal an hour before your flight to check in.

Tickets for internal flights are between 15 and 20 percent cheaper when bought in Turkey than abroad, so you may feel you want to wait and buy them at the Domestic Terminal. Because internal air travel in Turkey is quite good value, however, the flights are well-used and can frequently fill up. For destinations like Ankara, where there are six or seven flights a day from İstanbul, even if one flight is full your chances of getting on the next one are good. But if your destination only has one or two flights a day, like Adana or Trabzon, it may be preferable for peace of mind's sake to buy the ticket in advance. There is no bank at the Domestic Terminal so if you need to change money remember to do it at the International Terminal.

The contrast between the plush sophisticated International Terminal and the shabby little Domestic Terminal is so marked that you cannot help feeling that the one is the face Turkey puts on for the outside world, while the other is the real face without the make-up. As if to rectify the situation, a dreadful propaganda film runs on the TV screen in the spartan departure lounge with an American voice-over lauding the country's and Atatürk's achievements.

All domestic flights are operated by Turkish Airlines (Türk Hava Yolları: THY), the national carrier. It does not have the best of reputations for safety and service, and certainly the food is more what you would expect from a rock-bottom charter than a scheduled airline. No alcohol is served.

The pilots on the internal domestic flights are often like bus drivers. They taxi along the runway at great speed to the take-off point while the cabin crew struggle to keep their balance in demonstrating the emergency procedures. On landing they are inclined to slam the brakes on the second the wheels touch the ground, so that they take an earlier slipway turn-off as a short cut to the docking bay.

By rail İstanbul is linked by an express train to Ankara (c8 hours) and İzmir ($12\frac{1}{2}$ hours), and links between these cities are good, though scarcely faster than the bus. Other links, however, tend to be slow and services not that frequent. The Van Gölü Ekspresi from İstanbul (Haydarpaşa) to Lake Van at Tatvan, 1900 km away, takes nearly two days. The following towns east of Ankara are all connected to a rail service of some sort: Samsun, Amasya, Sivas, Divriği, Erzincan, Elazığ, Malatya, Kayseri, Konya, Niğde, Adana, Mersin, Maraş, Gaziantep, Diyarbakır, Tatvan, Van, Kars and Erzurum. The only railway on the Black Sea is at Samsun.

By sea The only ferry along the Black Sea coast now is run by Turkish Maritime Lines (TML) (London agents: Walford Lines Limited, Ibec House, 42–47 Minories, London EC3N 1AE; Tel: 071-480 5621). It is a weekly service from Istanbul, calling at Samsun and Trabzon only. See the Black Sea *Practical Information* section for full details and timings.

By bus Buses are a highly practical way of travelling around Turkey. There are several independent companies, varying slightly in frequency and comfort. The competition between them means that the system is efficient and cheap. Services are punctual, and on board there are pleasantnesses such as bottled drinking water and copious sprinklings of cologne provided free by the bus-boy. Stops of half an hour or so are made for breakfast, lunch and dinner, often at restaurants attached to petrol stations where the meals are basic but adequate. Buses run between almost every town in the country, leaving from the *otogar* (bus station) in the larger places or from the central square in the small places. Efficiency and practicality apart, the buses also provide an amusing and interesting way to travel and to meet people, and for a girl on her own are the safest way to get about the country.

Seats are reserved, so to ensure the best position on the bus you should buy your ticket a day or two in advance at the otogar office. There is also the possibility that by leaving your purchase to the last moment you will not get a seat at all. The middle seats are generally considered the best, as the ride can be bumpy towards the front or rear.

The more rural areas may not be so well served, and travel by bus is not recommended except to those with plenty of time to spare owing to the less frequent connections. Even in areas where the service is good, there is still the problem of how to reach the sites from the bus stop, as many sites lie a few kilometres off the main road. Walking or getting a taxi are then the only options, and so extra time and perhaps extra money must be allowed for the journey.

By taxi and dolmuş

Taxis in cities are recognisable by their chequered black and yellow bands. Although meters are usually fitted, they rarely work, so it is wise to agree on the fare first.

The dolmuş is a shared taxi which follows specific routes within larger towns and cities and is recognisable by its yellow band. The fares are fixed by the relevant municipality and each passenger pays according to the distance travelled and can get off at any of the specified stops. Much cheaper than a taxi, it is often good to get a dolmuş from the airport to the bus station or to the centre of town for example. As well as linking city centres with the suburbs, there are also some inter-city dolmuş, but these are more expensive than the bus, and often less comfortable.

Driving a Car Around Turkey

Travel by car is by far the best way of exploring Turkey. Without one you will be able to see less, or you will need more time (adapting your plans to bus schedules, etc) to see more. It is not advisable to take your own car unless it is especially hardy and you do not mind it taking a battering on the poor road surfaces.

In central Anatolia and along the northern and southern coasts of Eastern Turkey the road surfaces are fine. From around Urfa eastwards and northwards to the Black Sea, however, although all main roads have tarmac surfaces, they are often extremely potholed as a result of both extremes of temperature and general lack of maintenance.

Potholes

In fact the key on the tourist map provided by the authorities would do well to have an extra category called 'road under deterioration' to warn people of this. In a hire car you will usually end up by abandoning any pretence of avoiding the potholes and just grit your teeth as you fly over them at speed. If you try and avoid them you will have to reduce your driving speed considerably and your travelling times between stops will be seriously affected.

The roads in central Anatolia and Eastern Turkey are usually very empty. The number of private cars on the road is still quite small in relation to the number of buses and trucks, due to the high price of cars in the country. The only area where you do get heavy traffic is on the E5 main transit highway from Ankara south through Aksaray and Pozantı to Tarsus, along the coast to Adana, Gaziantep, Urfa and Nusaybin, where the transit route enters the eastern corner of Syria or transits to Mosul in Iraq.

Stray animals

The only road hazard for the most part is therefore livestock, the large quantities of sheep and cows which frequently stray all over the road and stay there insistently, to the total indifference of the shepherds. Their dogs, some with spiked anti-wolf collars, are often quite ferocious and will chase your car as if it is a runaway outsize sheep, snarling at the wheels. One other thing you will learn to ignore on the roadside is the insistent waving down by people standing in the middle of nowhere. The frantic waggling hand motion suggests that there has been an awful accident or that you are being warned about something dreadful round the next corner, when in fact all the fellow wants is a lift.

Lunatics   Driving at night is not recommended as the road markings are usually poor and other vehicles, especially trucks, can often have faulty lights or no lights at all.

Traffic drives on the right. In towns the speed limit is 50 km per hour, outside towns 90 km per hour. Important road signs include:

DUR: stop

DIKKAT: attention (warning you, eg, of road works)

ŞEHIR MERKESI: town centre

Archaeological and historical sites are indicated by yellow signs.

Car hire   For car hire in the east, Avis has by far the best network, as it is the only agency to have offices in Samsun and Trabzon, as well as in Ankara and Adana. This makes planning a circuit easier as you can leave the car in Trabzon, say, having picked it up in Adana or Ankara, at no extra cost. Otherwise, Europcar has offices in Adana, Ankara and Mersin, and Hertz has an office in Ankara, but this may restrict your flexibility and there is an extra charge for leaving the car at a different office to where you picked it up. Some fly-drive arrangements are cheaper than buying the flight and hiring the car separately, and it is worth shopping around. Obtain a list of tour operators from the Turkish Tourist Office and compare prices, which vary from operator to operator, destination to destination, and with the time of year. Of the two usual models for hire, the Renault 12 and the Murat (Fiat) 131, the Fiat is the stronger, and is therefore the one you should express a preference for when driving in the east. All these hire cars use the standard Benzin type of petrol, not the Super. The only cars requiring Super are cars like Mercedes which are not manufactured locally.

Maps and licences   A good map is essential: that produced by the Turkish Tourist Office is better than nothing, but it is not the best. Kümmerley and Frey produce the best one for Eastern Turkey.

Drivers must have a licence from their own country, and it is advisable to have an International Driving Licence as well because of the photograph. These licences are obtainable from your national automobile association.

Forbidden Zones

There is still a widespread belief that much of Eastern Turkey is out of bounds and heavily militarised. While this was true until 1960 it is no longer the case, and with very few exceptions all areas of the country can now be travelled with ease and with no necessity for permits.

To avoid all possible ambiguity these exceptions are spelt out below:

Ani: a permit is necessary because it is located in the no-man's land between the Russian and Turkish borders, but obtaining the permit is a straightforward process from the Kars Tourist Office requiring no planning in advance and taking a maximum of 30 minutes.

Digor: used to require a permit obtainable from Kars but from 1986 this is no longer necessary. There are a few Armenian churches to visit in the area, and proximity to the Russian border is again the reason for any circumspection.

Toprakkale and Yedi Kilise: require a permit from the Wali in Van (which can be arranged via the Van Tourist Office) because they are both within military zones.

Small villages and mountains in the Hakkâri range: the main road from Van to Hakkâri town is always open, even at night, and though there are road blocks, as a tourist you are waved through after a cursory search and document inspection. The side roads up into the valleys and villages are to be avoided however. Mountaineering in this area of the Sat and Çilo peaks has been forbidden since 1985 because of Kurdish guerilla activity in the hills.

Siirt: like Hakkâri, the main roads are open in the area but it would be advisable to keep off the smaller roads into the villages because of the risk of guerilla activity.

Carchemish: requires a permit because of its proximity to the Syrian border.

Itineraries

The best direction of travel is from Adana to Van to the Black Sea. The following two-, three- and four-week itineraries show what can be done at a reasonable pace of travel. Those wanting to incorporate a period of rest and recuperation by the sea would be best advised to spend several days at one of the beach hotels near Silifke, before returning from Adana or Ankara.

two weeks	two weeks	two weeks
Adana	Ankara (two days)	Ankara
Adıyaman (two days)	Boğazkale	Boğazkale
Urfa	Amasya	Amasya
Diyarbakır	Sivas	Ünye
	Elazığ	Trabzon (two days)

Tatvan	Diyarbakır	Artvin
Van (two days)	Urfa	Erzurum
Doğubeyazıt	Adıyaman	Doğubeyazıt
Kars	Antakya	Van (two days)
Erzurum	Adana	Diyarbakır
Trabzon	Göreme	Adana
Samsun	Ürgüp	Fly to İstanbul
Boat/fly to İstanbul	Ankara	

three weeks	*three weeks*	*four weeks*
Ankara	Adana	Ankara
Boğazkale	Adıyaman	Boğazkale
Amasya	Urfa	Amasya
Ünye	Diyarbakır	Sivas
Trabzon (two days)	Mardin	Elazığ
Erzurum	Tatvan (two days)	Malatya
Kars	Van	Kayseri
Doğubeyazıt	Hakkâri	Ürgüp
Van (two days)	Van	Ortahisar
Diyarbakır	Doğubeyazıt	Adana
Adıyaman	Kars	Adıyaman
Antakya	Sarıkamış	Urfa
Silifke (three days)	Erzurum	Diyarbakır
Konya (two days)	Hopa	Mardin
Ankara	Trabzon (two days)	Tatvan (two days)
	Samsun	Van
	Boat to İstanbul	Hakkâri
		Van
		Doğubeyazıt
		Kars
		Sarıkamış
		Erzurum
		Hopa
		Trabzon (two days)
		Samsun
		Boat/fly to İstanbul

ANKARA AND ENVIRONS

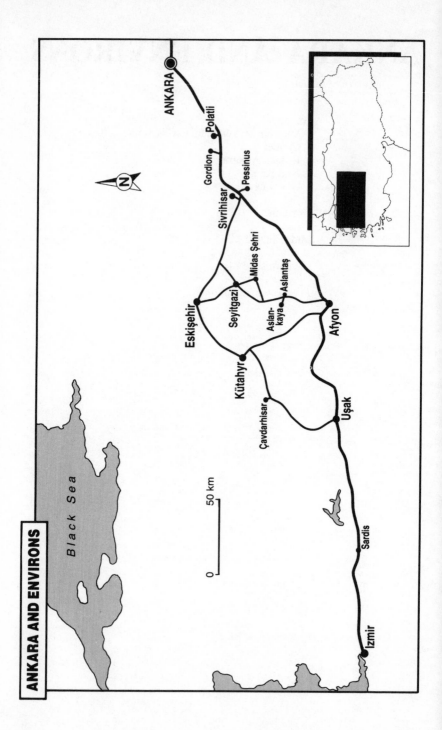

ANKARA AND ENVIRONS

Black Sea

50 km

ANKARA
Polatli
Gordion
Pessinus
Sivrihisar
Midas Şehri
Aslantaş
Seyitgazi
Aslan-kaya
Eskişehir
Afyon
Kütahya
Çavdarhisar
Uşak
Sardis
İzmir

ANKARA

Arrival in **Ankara** is a curious experience. As modern Turkey's capital it has many new roles to play and it is the conflict of these roles that makes the city so intriguing today.

First Impressions

The first glimpse for many coming from the west will be on the drive in from the international airport 28 km to the north. The road leads through green undulating hills and then suddenly drops down into a basin with colourful houses clinging to the steep rocky sides. As the view unfolds you realise that the entire city is in fact built on a series of small steep hills within the basin, the wide main roads running in straight lines along the open valleys, and the narrow sidestreets winding off uphill in zigzags. In spring there is a constant strongish wind with kite-flying a popular pastime. The houses on the steep slopes are highly distinctive, painted in blues, greens, mauves and yellows with red tiled roofs. The whole effect is unlike anything European or Mediterranean, yet also unlike anything Middle Eastern or Arab. Huddled together covering every inch of available ground, house of cards fashion, the impression is that if one collapsed it would bring down the entire hillside. These are the houses built by the rural immigrants in their ever hopeful search for work and a better standard of living. In 1919 when Atatürk moved his headquarters here at the beginning of the War of Independence the town had only 30,000 inhabitants. The recent rural influx has however been almost wholly responsible for the surge in Ankara's population from a mere 500,000 in 1960 to 2,257,000 in 1985. Yet despite this astonishing quadrupling of the population in the last 25 years, the *gecekondu* as the Turks call them (literally night lodgings), far from taking on the dreary aspect of shanty towns, have remarkably quickly acquired a permanence and become real neighbourhoods with their own schools and utilities. In many parts where they are particularly well established, you could be forgiven for mistaking them for colourful if eccentric garden suburbs.

The contrast between these gay crowded hillsides and the wide open boulevards of the new city centre adds to the oddness of Ankara and points towards the split identity of the city which is more marked than that of any other in Turkey. While the main boulevard is lined with luxury high-rise hotels, European-style restaurants and cafés,

Rapid, eccentric growth

Dilemma of roles

53

impressive new embassies, ministries, government buildings and the fine Hacetepe University, in the old streets
around the citadel and the Ulus Meydanı (The People's
Square) you are back in a simple Anatolian town with traditionally dressed peasants going about their lives as they
have always done. This split symbolises in a very real way
the curious dilemma of Turkey as a whole, trying on the
one hand to project itself as a semi-European state with
a face acceptable to doubting Western observers, and clinging on the other to traditional customs and values nurtured
and unchanged for centuries. In the Aegean and Mediterranean areas of Turkey, this dilemma has now been largely
resolved with change and development welcomed by most
because of its attendant improvement in living and educational standards. East of Ankara the story is different. The
sophisticated cosmopolitan Turk becomes harder to find,
and the rougher side of the Turkish character comes to
the fore.

Ancient and Modern

Ankara stands on the boundary of this divide, one foot
in the 20th C, the other firmly implanted in the lifestyle

Astride the divide of centuries ago. Chosen by Atatürk officially in 1923 as
Turkey's new capital, Ankara is far from being a new city.
Its origins go back to the 2nd millenium BC when it was
a Hittite settlement called Ankuwash on the Royal Road
from Hattuşaş to Sardis. A great Phrygian necropolis was
found here in 1925 to the south of the railway station.
The Phrygians called their settlement here 'Ankyra' and
the prefix '*ank*' is known to mean 'gorge' or 'ravine' in
early Indo-European languages, an obvious reference to
the town's setting. The name Ankyra appears in historical
records for the first time in the Persian period (546–334 BC)
where it is mentioned as a stopping place on the Royal
Road.

   It is fitting given Ankara's background that the two major
sights the city has to offer the visitor today should reflect
its ancient and its modern ties, the Museum of Anatolian
Civilisations and the Cyclopean Anıt Kabir, Atatürk's
Mausoleum. One day should be sufficient to visit Ankara's
attractions; in fact in an energetic half-day you can visit
the museum (two hours), take a brief stroll round the citadel (45 minutes) and visit Anıt Kabir (one hour), then have
lunch and leave Ankara behind for the Hittite heartlands,
feeling fairly happy that you have not missed much. The
most important thing to linger over is undoubtedly the
museum, so if you are really pushed for time, this is the
essential. The visit to Anıt Kabir is the next most important

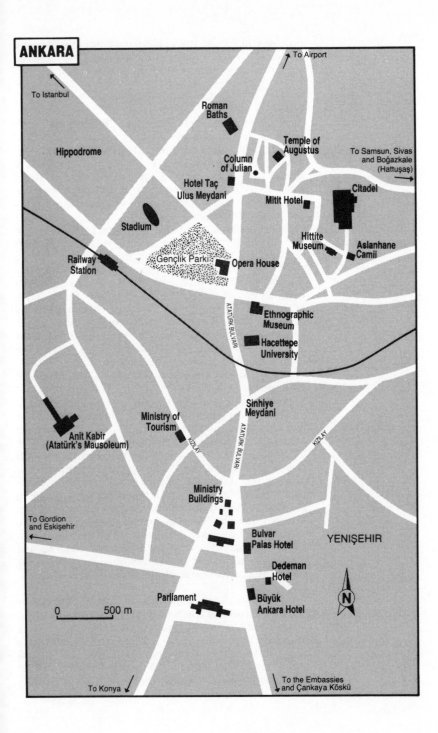

ANKARA

To Airport

To Istanbul

Roman Baths

Temple of Augustus

Hippodrome

Column of Julian

To Samsun, Sivas and Boğazkale (Hattuşaş)

Citadel

Hotel Taç Ulus Meydani

Mitit Hotel

Stadium

Hittite Museum

Aslanhane Camii

Railway Station

Gençlik Parki

Opera House

ATATÜRK BULVARI

Ethnographic Museum

Hacettepe University

Anit Kabir (Atatürk's Mausoleum)

Ministry of Tourism

Sinhiye Meydani

KIZILAY

ATATÜRK BULVARI

KIZILAY

Ministry Buildings

To Gordion and Eskişehir

Bulvar Palas Hotel

YENIŞEHIR

Dedeman Hotel

Parliament

0   500 m

Büyük Ankara Hotel

N

To Konya

To the Embassies and Çankaya Köskü

because it helps give you an understanding of the immense awe in which this one man is still held and of the powerful sense of Turkish identity which the monument represents.

Visiting the Museum of Anatolian Civilisations

No signs

For a capital city Ankara has an extraordinary dearth of signposts and reference to the city plan is essential. Distances are small and so if you choose to stay in the modern part of town in one of the more expensive hotels, it will still only take ten minutes to drive into the old part to visit the citadel and museum. Taxis are efficient and cheap with working meters.

From the Ulus Meydanı, the main square of the old town, recognisable by the inevitable equestrian statue of Atatürk in blackened bronze, you follow the road uphill till you reach a set of traffic lights on the brow. The one-way system can play havoc with map-reading in the old town and from here, instead of forking diagonally right in the direction of the museum, you continue straight ahead towards the citadel in front of you, the road dropping down to the very foot before winding up to reach the front of the museum, recognisable at most times of the year by the large numbers of coaches parked outside.

It is to visit the **Museum of Anatolian Civilisations** that most people will make the trip to Ankara and it has achieved wide renown for the most spectacular and comprehensive display in the world of Hittite and Urartian

World famous exhibition

finds. Small but carefully and clearly laid out, the museum lives up to its reputation. The building is a renovated 15th C Ottoman bedestan (covered market) which lends itself very well for conversion into a museum because you can progress round the four galleries on all sides of the courtyard moving logically through time from the neolithic to the Roman eras. In the centre, the big hall, the first part to be renovated in 1950, contains monumental Hittite stone carvings from sites like Carchemish. The idea to begin such a collection was, like everything in Ankara, Atatürk's, and it was originally called the 'Hittite Museum' to draw the world's attention to the newly discovered culture of Anatolia's forbears.

It is set in well-kept and colourful gardens with various statues and rock-cut reliefs on display among the trees and shrubs, and benches where it is pleasant to sit and relax in the sun afterwards. Opening hours are 8.30am to noon and 1.30 to 5.30pm in summer and 8.30am to 12.30pm and 1 to 5pm in winter. It is closed Mondays like all museums in Turkey. Inside there is also an attractively laid out drinks and coffee area.

Stone Age Exhibits

On entering the museum and buying your ticket you turn right past the bookshop and postcard displays to come to the neolithic (late Stone Age) displays.

The first exhibit is a reconstruction of a cave sanctuary at Çatalhüyük, 8000 years old, which has the earliest murals ever discovered on a plaster coating of cave walls and showing paintings of bulls' heads, humans and leopards. These are the original reliefs, removed from the walls with great care, though they are heavily restored.

Ancient cave sanctuary

The Çatalhüyük excavations in 1958 by James Mellaart revealed what is thought to be the oldest known city in the world and indicate a remarkably advanced Anatolian culture with sophisticated tools, jewellery and sculpture. The houses were quite large with one or two sitting rooms and one or two large storage areas. Among the permanent furnishings were benches, ovens and fireplaces, and entry was by a ladder from a flat roof. Rubbish was covered with clay and stamped into the ground. Burials were also made under the floor. While this is of course a godsend to the prehistorian, it does not suggest very salubrious living conditions. Murals were found on many of the walls of the houses, showing scenes of dancing and hunting, musicians and acrobats, all thought to be taking part in various religious rituals.

The exhibits here demonstrate that neolithic Anatolian man in the 7th millenium BC developed earlier and more artistically than his neighbours. He was the first to apply his knowledge of plant and animal domestication, and so leave behind his hunting and gathering lifestyle and his caves as well, to live in settled villages instead. Older even than these paintings on man-made walls are the cave paintings found recently in the Van area, unable to be displayed here, but which have been dated to 15,000 years ago. The paintings, in red or dark brown, show the images of dancing human figures, deer, mountain goats and scenes of hunting and trapping now extinct animals. Also represented are gods and goddesses standing on deer and other animals, goddesses with exaggereated genitals and motifs of the sun, all of which were important symbols passed down to the Hurrian and Hittite cultures.

Among the most intriguing exhibits in this section are what could pass for a neolithic cocktail stick and an exquisite cup-shaped obsidian mirror, highly polished, perhaps the oldest mirror in the world. The earliest known seals, symbols of private property, are also to be seen here.

Fat is beautiful

In the next display cases are the earliest known examples of the Anatolian earth mother, grotesquely fat by modern standards with colossal arms, legs, breasts and belly. Female corpulence was much admired in Turkey until relatively recently. An Ottoman saying runs: 'She is so beautiful she has to go through the door sideways'. In one of the displays the earth mother is sitting calmly resting her hands on two lions either side of her: this is one of the earliest representations of her in her dual role as fertility goddess and mistress of the animal kingdom. It is a conception that can be traced through the Phrygian Cybele, the Greek Artemis, the Roman Diana and ultimately the Christian Virgin Mary.

The Copper and Bronze Ages

The next period you come to is the Chalcolithic (Copper Age). Hacılar is the main site excavated of this period and shows the first evidence of an enclosing city wall. The pottery is richer; it is shiny and painted; the geometric shapes used on it are similar to patterns seen in modern kilims.

An entrance to the vast central hall is marked by the colossal sideways-striding Hittite relief of the war god, **Smiling war god** muscle-calved and smiling very slightly. Wearing the typical Hittite short kilt and conical hat (signifying that he is a god), he stood originally outside the King's Gate at Hattuşaş. To preserve the chronology of your tour, however, you should not enter this hall of Hittite sculpture yet, but enter it later from the second gallery where the other Hittite finds are displayed.

Instead, next are the exhibits of the third millenium BC, the Early Bronze Age, with a wealth of objects in copper, lead, tin, gold, silver, bronze, electrum (a mixture of gold and silver) and even iron, a metal many times more valuable than gold at that time. They reveal a high degree of metallurgical competence and an opulent lifestyle, with golden goblets, crowns and jewellery. There are some gold necklaces that are so finely worked in delicate filigree that you have to marvel at the precision tools they must have used, probably made from hard vitrous obsidian, found locally.

Spectacular finds Most of these exhibits are finds from the royal tombs **from royal tombs** of Alacahüyük and are the most spectacular exhibits in the museum. Thirteen of these tombs were excavated between 1935 and 1939. The women were found accompanied by their jewellery and toilet articles, the men by their personal ornaments and weapons. In each grave the body was surrounded by elaborately wrought bronze 'sun discs'. These distinctive discs with their criss-cross patterns evidently had some mystical property which scholars still argue about. They are generally agreed to be cosmological symbols of some sort, possibly representing the sun and its rays, sometimes with antlered stags in the centre. They are called 'standards' for want of a better word, as they appear to have been designed to be mounted at the head

A cornucopia of flesh: the Anatolian earth mother

of a pole and used as a processional staff in rituals. These symbols continue to fascinate modern Turks and one was chosen as the emblem for the Ministry of Culture and Tourism. The abundance of bronze bulls, stags and cows all points to the fact that central and eastern Anatolia were far more heavily forested than now. The prominence given to the stag suggests the mentality of a mountain people, and the deers and bulls which also figure frequently are un-Mesopotamian in style and subject. The culture of this indigenous Anatolian people, the Hatti, influenced that of their later conquerors, the Hittites.

Artefacts from the Assyrian Colonies

Having completed the first side of the courtyard you now turn left to enter the second side running across the back of the bedestan cum museum, with a wealth of objects on display from the Assyrian colonies (1950–1750 BC). Assyrian merchants from northern Mesopotamia arrived in Anatolia attracted by the prosperity of the Hittite empire. They established large trading colonies and introduced their long-developed cuneiform writing system. The main site for these discoveries was at Karum, the trading centre at Kültepe, near modern Kayseri. This writing looks dishearteningly difficult to decipher with endless repetitive symbols differing only slightly from each other. Maybe the Hittites too found it difficult, for they later changed to adopt a hieroglyphic script which was deciphered by a Czech linguist, Hrozny, in 1912.

Futuristic pottery
The pottery of Kültepe was very advanced and shows for the first time the painting in geometric shapes, often stripes and zigzags, which is now called Cappadocian ware as it is thought to have been a development indigenous to that region. Some of the tall vases and jugs have shapes that are to our eye modern, not to say futuristic. Among these elegant vases and jars there are also large numbers of drinking vessels or rhytons (libation vases) in the shapes of animals and humans. Many of the animals are lions and large cats and have a comic and again almost modern appearance. What the liquid was that they drank out of these vessels is not certain, but with Anatolia being the home of both the cultivated grape and barley, perhaps the Hittites asked their servants for 'a lion of wine' or a 'stag of beer'. As well as the drinking vessels there are many cylindrical seals and lead figurines of deities.

Exhibits of the Old Hittite Kingdom

Monumental sculpture
You come next, towards the far end of the second gallery, to the Old Hittite Kingdom exhibits (c1700–1450 BC). Many of the vases show reliefs of the sideways-on people similar to contemporaneous Egyptian and Minoan art. The Hittites

were not, unlike the Hatti, indigenous, but came in a great wave from southern Russia and central Asia, making their appearance in Anatolia at the end of the Early Bronze Age. Under the Hittite dynasty the ceramic industry declined and the first stone upright reliefs appeared. Turning back to retrace your steps to the middle of the second gallery, you enter the central hall which houses an astonishing display of monumental Hittite sculpture covering a span of eight centuries, from Hattuşaş (Boğazkale) and Alacahüyük to the Neo-Hittite sites at Carchemish and Aslantepe. Of particular note is the Chimaera from Carchemish, dated to the 8th C BC. This mythical creature had its home on Mt Olympos in Lycian Turkey and was passed to Greece through Homer's *Iliad* and Corinthian vase painting at the beginning of the 7th C BC. By the 6th C BC it was also found in Etruscan art.

From Phrygians and Urartians to Greeks and Romans

You now arrive in the third side of the courtyard, turning left into the Phrygian exhibits, the Phrygians being the people who ruled central Anatolia after the collapse of the Hittite empire (8th C BC). Most of these exhibits were found in the royal tombs at Gordion and are of special interest because of the extent to which they foreshadow the later artistic and cultural developments in classical Greece.

Forgotten craftsmen   The next section displays the Urartian objects, the Urartians being contemporary with the Phrygians but ruling in Eastern Turkey over an empire that stretched from Lake Urmia near Tabriz in northwestern Iran to Sivas and Trabzon in the north and to Aleppo in the south. Their characteristic sites were steep rock citadels on long thin spurs and their ruined fortresses can still be seen on mountain tops throughout the Van region. They were a people, like their predecessors the Hittites, largely forgotten until rediscovered by archaeologists this century. Urartian metal and ivory objects were highly prized and were exported to Phrygia, Greece and Italy. There are gold, silver and bronze objects and cauldrons with human and animal attachments. One of these, a huge bronze cauldron on a three-legged stand with cloven-hoof feet and bulls' head handles, is the earliest known prototype of a style which found its way to Etruria and was passed from there to classical Greece. Especially lovely are the intricately worked wide gold belts and a superb ivory seated lion, reminiscent of the Chinese lion. If your itinerary takes you near Elazığ, you must make a point of stopping off at the new museum at the Euphrates University, Elazığ, where a much larger and even more impressive set of Urartian exhibits is now on display.

The world's first coin   The final part of the courtyard completing the three sides contains exhibits of the classical Greek and Roman periods. The most impressive exhibit here is an excellent coin collection, gold and silver, with all the city states in Anatolia represented, showing the heads of various kings and emperors. Here you can see the world's first ever coin, made from a mixture of gold and silver. It is from Sardis in Lydia and dates from 615 BC.

Walking Around Medieval Ankara

From the museum you can go on a short ten-minute walk up the road to the right towards the old **citadel** of Ankara to get a glimpse of the contrast between Turkey old and new. The powerful walls still stand tall and on climbing up the steps through one of the gates you step back into medieval times. Cars can only penetrate to the outer edges, and the crumbling houses line the narrow winding streets with barefoot children playing in the dirt and dust, cut off and oblivious to the pace of change in the modern city below.

Gauls in Turkey   The earliest citadel foundations discovered belong to the Gauls, a wild and warlike race invited into Asia in 279 BC from southern Europe as mercenaries by the king of Bithynia (on the southern shores of the Sea of Marmara). They made a nuisance of themselves all down the Aegean coast till the powerful king of Pergamum, Attalus, drove them inland. The Gauls settled in the Ankara region and even today there are a number of red-haired freckled Turks to be found here.

The main part of the **defence walls** standing today are Byzantine with much subsequent Turkish construction. The geographical location of Ankara is on one of the great natural east-west highways of Asia Minor. Invading armies have marched to and fro throughout its history. After the Phrygians, Persians, Alexander and the Gauls, came the Romans, Arabs, Turks, Crusaders and Mongols. The walls of the citadel and the houses within it reflect this variety with a hotchpotch of stones from different eras, with fragments of ancient columns and capitals in modern use as doorsteps, window sills, garden seats and lintels.

Angora wool   From the 11th C Ankara was in the hands of the Seljuks and it was presumably Turcoman tribesmen who brought the long-haired goats from central Asia to Angora (as Ankara was known until Atatürk's time), the fine wool from these Angora goats the foundation of the town's prosperity.

Byzantium saved by the Mongols   Ankara, though it has seen many armies march by, has been the setting for only one major battle: in 1402 the army of the Ottoman Sultan Beyazıt was devastated by the Mongol hordes under the ferocious Tamerlane. The

Ottoman Turks had been penetrating the shrinking borders of the Byzantine Empire, and until this battle it seemed certain that Constantinople would fall to Beyazıt. Instead Byzantium was reprieved for 50 years yet. The final assault came in 1453, when Beyazıt's great-grandson, Mehmet II, overwhelmed Constantinople's walls. There was also a more recent battle, in a valley near Ankara, where the climactic scenes of *The Charge of the Light Brigade* were filmed. The landscape was suitable and the Turkish government made available free of charge 600 cavalry and 3000 infantry for the 12 weeks of shooting in the hope of obtaining good publicity.

Ankara replaces İstanbul as capital

By the end of the First World War, which ended so disastrously for Turkey and brought about the disintegration of the Ottoman Empire, Ankara was no more than a small country town lost in the steppes. It became the centre of national resistance during the Greek War of 1920 and Mustafa Kemal Atatürk, leader of the revolution and generalissimo of the Turkish army, made it the new capital on 1 October 1923. It is to its geographical position that Ankara owes this honour. The shift to central Anatolia was a deliberate break with the Ottoman past and an assertion that Turkey was not İstanbul as many Westerners believed but Anatolia. One of the favourite Nationalist epithets for İstanbul is *kozmopolit*, a word with disparaging overtones unlike the the the English 'cosmopolitan'. A recent Turkish dictionary defines it as: '[a person] having no national and local colour but assuming the outward form that suits his purpose'. Atatürk himself did not once set foot in the old imperial capital from 1919 to 1927. For all the encouragement given to Ankara to supplant İstanbul as Turkey's first city, it has not and is unlikely ever to do so. On holidays and at any other excuse armies of civil servants rush lemming-like from their smart modern flats in Ankara to the charm of their decaying homes in overcrowded İstanbul.

Atatürk's patronage apart, Ankara has never been favoured by Turkey's rulers. It was too far from the major Seljuk cultural centres and the Ottomans largely ignored it. The only mosque to consider visiting is the **Aslanhane Camii**, a 13th C Seljuk mosque with a blue tiled mihrab and lovely carved woodwork on the ceiling and the 24 wooden columns that support it. A stone lion in the court gives its name *aslan*, lion. It is below the citadel, to the northeast of the Museum of Anatolian Civilisations.

Ankara's Roman Monuments

The Province of Galatia was annexed to the Roman Empire by Augustus in 25 BC, and the three remaining Roman monuments in the city can be visited on foot in an hour. Returning down the hill from the citadel towards the Ulus

Meydanı, you can pay a brief visit to the **Temple of Augustus**, the most prominent of the few Roman monuments remaining in Ankara, by turning off to the right about 100 metres before the square. Follow this road as it winds slightly for about 400 metres and you will then see on your left in an open square next to a mosque the high wall of the temple. It began life as a temple to Cybele, the Anatolian fertility goddess and was then a Phrygian temple to the phallic god Men before it became the Temple of Augustus and Rome. During his lifetime Augustus encouraged the deification of Rome and would only permit his own worship after his death, since his advisers assured him the people in the eastern provinces of Syria and Asia Minor expected it. At the beginning of the 6th C the temple was converted to a church, and following the Turkish conquest the church was converted to a madrasa (theological college) attached to the adjacent mosque. When Lord Warkwork, an English MP, stayed in Ankara in the 1890s he found the Turkish governor of Ankara 'an intelligent and liberal-minded soldier, cleaning and repairing the Temple of Augustus'. The setting, as so often in Eastern Turkey, does much to detract from the attractiveness of the temple, and it can only be viewed from outside its tall green railings, usually kept locked. The adjacent **Haci Beyram mosque** is dedicated to Ankara's favourite saint, the founder of the Beyrami order of dervishes, and his türbe (tomb) immediately in front of the mosque is a popular place of pilgrimage.

Rome and Augustus deified

On your way to the Roman Baths you pass the **Column of Julian**. This stands in the centre of the Hükümet Meydanı now, having been moved from its original site between the İş Bankası (Work Bank) and the Ministry of Finance. It is thought to have been erected in AD 362 in honour of the Emperor Julian, but is known locally as Belkis Minaret or the Queen of Sheba's minaret for no reason anyone can establish. It usûally has a large storks' nest on top. You can now walk from here out along the main road to see the **Roman Baths**, some 500 metres from Ulus Meydanı. These were discovered by chance in 1926 by architects making soundings for the construction of the nearby Ministry of Defence. The remains are not particularly impressive, but ten rooms can still be made out with central heating piping, fragments of marble paving and statues.

The Heart of the Nation
The visitor with little time on his hands would be better off, having visited the Museum of Anatolian Civilisations, to make a trip to Anıt Kabir, Atatürk's Mausoleum. From Ulus Meydanı you follow the Atatürk Bulvarı back towards Yenişehir (The New City) to reach its main square, called

Kızılay (Red Crescent, the Turkish Red Cross equivalent which used to have its headquarters here.) After Atatürk decided to make Ankara the new capital, town planners were enlisted from central Europe to create the new city. The district around the Ulus Meydanı was the first to be built. Here is the **palace of the National Assembly** and the **Merkez Bankası** which prints the country's banknotes. Devotees of modern Turkish history can visit the **National Assembly Museum**, a grey building just off the square where Atatürk founded his first parliament and where the 'Turkish nation', a new country, even a new concept, had its beginning. The early history of the assembly and the republic is documented here in detail.

Atatürk was especially keen on trees and greenery and the planners did try and preserve some green open spaces in the city, notably the **Gençlik Parkı** (Youth Park). 'The planting of one tree', he exhorted, 'is worth the prayers of a whole year'. Previously a swamp, the park now has a large man-made boating lake and fountains, cafés and gazinos, and a little opera house.

It was also at Ataturk's instigation that the **Ethnographic Museum** was built in 1925 off Atatürk Bulvarı near the university, displaying a wide range of Turkish crafts from Seljuk times onwards. It has the usual colourful dervish and wedding costumes, musical instruments, household items, weapons, carpets, kilims, copperware, some tiles and wood carving. Atatürk's body also lay in state here on his death in 1938 till Anıt kabir was completed in 1953.

Atatürk's Mausoleum

The main interest in visiting **Anıt Kabir** is to see, in tangible form, the personality cult built around this remarkable man who died half a century ago, a man whose picture still hangs in every private house and public place and building.

An atmosphere of reverence The sheer scale of the monument is the real shock. The sacred area occupies an entire hill over one kilometre square in the centre of Ankara, analogous, say, to the whole of Hampstead Hill in London being a mausoleum precinct for Queen Victoria. There are two entrances at the foot of the hill which are guarded by neatly uniformed and armed soldiers. The monument is open daily from 9am to 5pm in summer and from 9am to 4pm in winter. In summer a sound and light show is held here four evenings a week at 9pm.

The entrance road leads up through beautifully kept gardens to a parking area at the top. Guards in smart black and white uniforms stand at 10-metre intervals round the edge. From here a colossal avenue 300 metres long flanked by lions of Hittite inspiration leads off in a dead straight line across the top of the hill to a vast open courtyard, and on the highest point, up a massive flight of steps, stands the monumental limestone mausoleum itself. The inspiration here is closer to the classical Greek temple. Inside the room is empty and stark, the walls and floor covered in marble and in the centre the colossal stone of the sarcophagus itself, weighing 40,000 kilos. An atmosphere of reverence pervades and Turkish families walk around whispering. Nowhere outside are there any benches and no one is allowed to sit on the steps or walls or to walk on the grass. The guards keep a sharp lookout for such irreverence and are not slow to tick you off should you transgress.

In the buildings surrounding the courtyard below the mausoleum are various pieces of Atatürk memorabilia, the most interesting of which is Atatürk's huge black car of 1932–34, looking as if it has been lifted straight out of an Al Capone movie. Among these buildings at the far end, opposite Atatürk's own, is the **mausoleum of Ismet Inönü** (1884–1973), Atatürk's first prime minister and his successor as president.

If you are still starved for Atatürk memorabilia and are in Ankara on a Sunday afternoon, you can visit the **Çankaya Atatürk Muzesi**, the house where he lived during the War of Independence.

The Rise of Modern Turkey
This is perhaps a suitable place to talk about the history of Atatürk and how modern Turkey came into being, as some understanding of this becomes essential as you travel eastwards. Mustafa Kemal, later surnamed Atatürk (Father of the Turks), was born in Salonika, now Greece, then an Ottoman city, in 1880. He entered the army at the age of 12 and graduated from the War College in İstanbul in 1905. After serving with distinction in the Balkan Wars in 1911 and 1912, he led the Turkish forces in 1915 to defend the Gallipoli peninsula and was largely responsible for repelling the British and forcing their subsequent evacuation. He also distinguished himself on the Russian front and in Palestine, emerging as the only real Turkish hero of the debacle of the First World War.

Carving up the Sick Man of Europe The victorious Allies drew up their arrangements for the dissolution of the Ottoman Empire, 'the sick man of Europe', in the form of the Treaty of Sèvres in August 1920. The provisions of the treaty were very harsh, far harsher than those imposed on Germany. It has been described by historians as 'the signing of the death warrant of the Ottoman Empire'. The Arab provinces were to be placed under British and French mandates to prepare them for eventual independence. Anatolia's eastern provinces were to be divided between an autonomous Kurdistan and an independent Armenia. Greece was to have İzmir and

Atatürk's mausoleum

its hinterland and Thrace, regions with a heavily Greek population going back to ancient times. Italy would get the southern half of western and central Anatolia, while France took the southeast. The straits were to be neutralised and administered by a permanent Allied Commission in Constantinople and Constantinople itself would remain in Turkish hands as long as the rights of the minorities were upheld.

The War of Independence

The treaty was never implemented however, for while the Allies were imposing their terms on the Sultan and his government in İstanbul, a new Turkish state was rising in the interior of Anatolia based on the total rejection of the treaty. Though the British and French were successful in establishing their mandates over the Arab lands, and the Italians were able to secure at least the Dodecanese for themselves, Kurdish and Armenian hopes were suppressed, and the Greek army, after landing at İzmir in May 1919 and pushing deep into the interior, was routed by forces under the command of Atatürk. The Turkish nationalist movement, which had started among a small class of intellectuals, mushroomed during these struggles into a countrywide uprising bent on creating an Anatolian-based state for the Turks alone. The campaign against Greek forces, from 1919 to 1922, became known as the War of Independence. Atatürk's efforts were crowned by the Treaty of Versailles in 1923, which recognised Turkish sovereignty over approximately its present-day borders.

During the remaining 15 years of his life Atatürk carried through a series of far reaching reforms which were intended to westernise Turkey and integrate it into the modern world. His regime was effectively a dictatorship, and a single party, the Republican People's Party, enforced government policy. Atatürk terminated the caliphate, exiled the Sultan and in a series of edicts the Ministry of **Freedom from** Religious Affairs was abolished, religious orders dis-**religion . . .** banded, religious property sequestrated and religious instruction forbidden. The Arabic alphabet was abolished and Atatürk gave the academics six months to devise a new Latin alphabet for Turkish. The fez, which he called a 'Greek headdress' was forbidden. In 1928 Islam itself was disestablished and the constitution amended to make Turkey a secular state. Atatürk was not opposed to religion itself. His aim was to free the Turks from the clutches of the fanatics. Everyone could be a devout Moslem in his private life but was not to mix religion with politics.

. . . and from the Continuing his theme of moving towards the West he **veil** did much to improve the position of women, wanting them to be recognised as equals. One of his speeches ran: 'In the course of my trip I have seen that our women comrades — not in the villages but particularly in the towns and cities — are careful to muffle up their faces and their eyes. I should think this habit must cause them great discomfort, especially now, in the hot weather. Men, this is to some extent the result of our selfishness . . . Let them show their faces to the world and let them have the chance to see the world for themselves. There's nothing to be afraid of in that'. The majority of educated women had in fact discarded the veil years before, many during the First World War when they entered the civil service. His speeches, helped by increased interest in Western fashions, did accelerate the disappearance of the veil from the large country towns, but in the rural areas most women continued to be shut off from the equality Atatürk invited them to enjoy, and today still in many parts of central and eastern Anatolia, you will see women draw their shawls over their faces when you pass, or cringe towards the walls, just as Atatürk saw them 50 years ago. You can change the laws but not a mentality. Atatürk died in the Dolmabahçe Palace in İstanbul on 10 November 1938.

The political parties today, ironically, usually ignore Atatürk's exhortation to keep religion and politics apart, and at every election still pander to religious traditionalism to get out the rural vote.

Environs of Ankara

Various recreational areas have developed around Ankara for the use of residents who want to get out of the city, rather than for tourists, but just in case you find yourself in Ankara with a lot of time on your hands, it is probably worth mentioning them.

The closest, originally a few kilometres west of Ankara, but now almost swallowed up in the outskirts, is the Atatürk Forest Farm (Atatürk Orman Çiftiğli), which Atatürk set up towards the end of his life as a model farm to introduce new agricultural methods to Turkey. While being an experimental farm, it is also a recreation area with restaurants and a pool in the shape of the Black Sea.

Other recreation areas include the Bayındır Dam for good swimming, 17 km out of town on the Samsun road; Gölbaşı beach, 24 km southwest of Ankara on Lake Moğan; and for skiing and climbing, there is Elmadağ, 18 km to the south of Ankara.

EXCURSIONS WEST OF ANKARA

If you are based in Ankara for a while or have a couple of days to travel overland from Ankara to İzmir, there are a series of unusual and interesting places you can visit on the way to help break the journey. This route leads into what was known by the ancient Greeks as Phrygia, not a particularly scenic region, its occasional fertile river valleys surrounded by endless stretches of bare hills. Along this route are the relics of Phrygian civilisation, including Gordion, the first Phrygian capital, Midas Şehri with the tomb of King Midas, and finally, much further west, the Temple of Zeus at Aezani (Çavdarhisar), the most perfectly preserved temple in Turkey.

Along the way to İzmir and İstanbul

It is a route difficult to incorporate into any itinerary and as a result the sites are spared the attentions of the coach tours. If you happen to be passing this way they are certainly worth a visit, though none of them would warrant a major detour. From Ankara you could visit Gordion and Midas Şehri and stay at Eskişehir or Kütahya. On the second day you could drive via Çavdarhisar and Sardis to reach İzmir that evening. Gordion, some 100 km west of Ankara, can also be a short detour off the road to İstanbul.

The Kingdom of Phrygia

Setting off southwest from Ankara towards Polatlı and some 16 km beyond this town, a yellow sign points off to the right 12 km to Yassı Hüyük and **Gordion**, once the Phrygian capital. Its remains stand out on a great mound to the right of the road, colossal, nearly half a kilometre long and 350 metres wide. Enough remains here for specialists to have drawn up a ground plan of the palace but nothing particularly impressive remains for a non-archaeologist. The palace square was bordered by large buildings called megarons (large front vestibules opening out onto a larger inner room with a round hearth near the centre).

Earliest mosaic

One megaron was paved entirely with pebble mosaics, the oldest mosaic floor discovered (8th C BC), with geometric patterns of dark red, white and deep blue. As the largest megaron on the site, it is thought to have been the **palace of the Phrygian kings**. These megarons are also known to have had gabled roofs, a feature first seen in Urartian buildings much further to the east, and passed from there via Gordion westwards to Greece and the rest of Europe. The most prominent structure on the site today is the great gateway, originally flanked by two huge towers.

The Phrygians are thought to have been a Thracian people, speaking a language akin to Greek, who crossed the Hellespont to invade Anatolia, becoming, according to Homer, neighbours of the Trojans.

Royal burial mounds
From the mound you have a good view of the various tumuli or burial mounds of the Phrygian kings. The largest, over 250 metres in diameter and 53 metres high, is known as the **Great Tumulus**. The only tumulus in Turkey larger than this is that of a Lydian king at Bintepe near Sardis. Which king was buried here is not known though it is thought to date to the late 8th C BC. The man was small, only 1.57 metres and nearly 60 years old. Excavation of these mounds was especially difficult as the Phrygians left no passages into them. Having built wooden burial chambers, loose stones were then piled on top to make ever higher mounds. They usually placed the burial chamber off-centre to try to foil later grave robbers. The interior grave chamber in the Great Tumulus can be visited today thanks to the complex labours of Professor Rodney Young who began excavating here in 1950 with his American team. Of its contents — dozens of pots and well-made furniture (no gold, belying the legendary wealth of the Phrygian kings) — that which has not been removed to Ankara is still on display in the site museum.

Alexander Hellenises Asia

The Gordion knot
Historically Gordion lives on for most people as the place where Alexander cut the Gordion knot. This was the knot which the Phrygian king (of peasant extraction) tied to fix the yoke to the pole of his ox-cart. A prophecy said that whoever could undo the knot would be master of Asia. What the knot was meant to represent remains in dispute, some saying it was the symbol of the importance of the peasant to the kingdom, others that it was the importance of Gordion as the key to the ancient road network. Alexander had heard the legend of the knot and felt obliged to fulfill the prophecy on his way through, since conquering Asia and driving out the Persians was precisely what he had in mind. He simply sliced it through with his sword.

The Persian Medes had first entered Anatolia in 585 BC under Cyrus II and made the Halys, today's Kızılırmak, the boundary between their kingdom of Media and Lydia. When later that century the Persians captured Sardis, the Lydian capital, they established their satrapies or governorships all over Anatolia. Apart from some Ionian revolts, Anatolia was to remain largely in Persian hands until the advent of Alexander.

Alexander's cultural corridor
When in the spring of 334 BC this 21-year-old Macedonian crossed the Hellespont into Asia Minor at the head of 35,000 soldiers, it was to herald the dawn of an era that

was to last a thousand years, terminating with the rise of Islam. As age-old enemies the Greeks and the Persians had battled for decades over the cities of Asia Minor and it was Alexander's resolve now to drive the Persians out once and for all. In so doing, he created a corridor for cultural action and reaction which was to leave an immeasurable legacy to both East and West.

Alexander proceeded through western and southern Anatolia, the cities falling to him along the way so quickly that by 333 BC he stood poised at Issus in the easternmost corner of the Mediterranean, where he and his men routed a Persian army three times their number. Great as his military exploits were, greater still were the cultural consequences. A corridor was opened through which Greek and Near Eastern ideas could confront one other, harmonise and fuse — Hellenisation.

The city of Gordion dwindled after the Phrygian kingdom fell in c700 BC and by Roman times was reduced to a mere village.

Some 50 km further on a turn-off to the left leads 13 km to **Pessinus** (Ballıhisar), once the religious centre of Phrygia. Archaeologists have made finds here but almost nothing remains to be seen of the site today beyond the **fragments of a temple to Cybele**, the Anatolian fertility goddess from whom the Greek Artemis later derived. In Phrygia Cybele was worshipped as a bee, which explains the Turkish name for the site, Ballıhisar, Honey Castle.

Cybele the bee

The City of King Midas
From Sivrihisar you now follow the route west towards Eskişehir before forking left at Hamidiye for 27 km to Seyitgazi. From here signs mark the way southeast 25 km on dusty roads to the village of Çukurca and then on to **Midas Şehri** (or Yazılıkaya).

Of the sites west of Ankara this is the most impressive but is very rarely visited due to its remote position. Although the name Midas Şehri (Midas' City) implies that a whole town is left here, there is in fact just one monument, a colossal gabled rock-cut building with an ornamented façade. It was thought by the first 19th C travellers to write about it to be the tomb of King Midas because the word 'Midai' was found inscribed on it. The modern village of Yazılıkaya huddles below.

The golden touch

Midas was the king of Phrygia during its most prosperous times in the 8th C BC, and his kingdom had so much gold from the nearby river as to create the legend of his 'golden touch'.

As the most spectacular tomb-like structure in the neighbourhood it was a natural conclusion that this should be

Midas' tomb. Now it is known that the monument was not a tomb but a **temple linked with the cult of Cybele**; a statue of the goddess, flanked by her attendant lions, once stood in the doorway. The vast building, 17 metres high, cut into the rock of the steep hill behind the village is in good preservation and is very impressive. Nearby in the hills are several further rock-cut tombs or monuments, niches, altars and a monumental rock stairway leading up onto the acropolis.

More remote and difficult to find are two further Phrygian monuments similar in style to Midas Şehri, at **Aslantaş** and **Aslankaya**. Both are façades cut from the rock with two lions guarding the entrance to a niche with a statue of Cybele. That at Aslankaya is the more impressive. Both these sites are more easily reached from Afyon, though the maze of dusty dirt tracks are often unsignposted and the dearth of landmarks makes it difficult to distinguish them.

Fertility and Barrenness

From Afyon or Kütahya you can make a further excursion to **Aezani**, the site of one of the largest and best preserved temples in Turkey, near the village of Çavdarhisar. Because of its remote and difficult position it is rarely visited. It would be possible in a day to stay at Eskişehir or Kütahya, then drive via Çavdarhisar to Uşak and continue via Sardis to İzmir for the night.

Spectacular remains of a small ancient town

The magnificent **Temple of Zeus or Jupiter**, built in the Ionian style in the 2nd C AD and virtually intact, stands alone on the barren plateau, dwarfing Çavdarhisar village. Inside you are surprised to discover a **subterranean sanctuary** dedicated to the worship of the Phrygian Cybele, the earth and mother fertility goddess and predecessor of Artemis. In front of the temple is a vast **agora**, while beyond it are a **stadium** and **theatre**, reasonably well-preserved. On the stone blocks of the walls of the temple are animal figures which were executed by the old Turkish nomadic and semi-nomadic clans. The stylised goats, bisons, hunting scenes and magical symbols resemble the drawings and emblems found in the Cunni cave near Erzurum and the even earlier rock paintings of the Hakkâri region of 6000 to 10,000 years ago, showing how these ancient signs were passed down the ages by the clans.

The Anatolian plateau was not always as barren as it is here: centuries of deforestation by goats and man have transformed the landscape. The government is trying to encourage people to breed cattle rather than goats, but old habits die hard. One curiosity still to be seen in some rural areas is goats wearing bras. This is not part of an Islamic revival or even an attempt at modesty, but a purely practical way of preventing the young from suckling too often.

PRACTICAL INFORMATION

ANKARA

For most people the reason for coming to Ankara is not so much to see the Turkish capital (with the possible exception of the museum), but rather because it is the most convenient starting point (with its many daily flight connections from İstanbul and direct international flights from Amsterdam, Zürich, Munich, Vienna, Rome and Athens) for any journey into the central and eastern parts of the country. It also has excellent onward bus and train connections, as well as offices of the international car hire agencies of Avis, Hertz and Europcar. (Avis in fact has two, one at the airport, the other in the city centre).

Air. There are 7 or 8 flights a day to and from İstanbul (1 hour), one daily to Adana (1 hour), Antalya, İzmir, Trabzon, Diyarbakır and Erzurum; 4 times a week to Elazığ and Malatya; 3 times a week to Samsun; twice a week to Sivas and once a week to Kayseri. The airport is at Esenboğa, 28 km to the north on the road to Çankırı. This is why your luggage has ESB stuck on it rather than ANK. The drive into the centre from the airport takes less than half an hour. Inside the town the one-way system can be confusing and there is a complete dearth of signposts, so reference to the town plan provided is essential.

Rail. The station is shown on the town plan and there are several daily services to İstanbul (c8 hours); to İzmir and the Aegean (via Eskişehir) c13 hours; to Konya; to Adana (via Kayseri); to Sivas, Samsun, Erzurum, Malatya and Van. Make sure you get an express train, but even then it can be quicker to go by bus.

Bus. The bus station is shown on the town plan, with services to all major destinations.

Taxis. Dolmuş are often very full, but taxis are metered and cheap. No tipping is required.

Tourist Information. The office is shown on the town plan, in the Ministry of Tourism building just west of Kızılay. Tel: 173012.

Hotels. The more expensive modern hotels tend to be in Yenişehir, while the more modest places tend to be in the old town near Ulus Meydanı.

Ankara Hilton (5-star), Kavaklidere (south of Yenişehir), Tel: 1682888. 327 rooms, pool. Ankara's new luxury hotel and the most expensive.

Büyük Ankara Oteli (4-star), Tel: 344920. In Yenişehir. 208 air-conditioned rooms with a swimming pool and tennis court. Roof-top restaurant.

Dedeman Oteli (3-star), Tel: 139190. In Yenişehir. 252 rooms. It tends to be noisy with car horns blaring into the night. Indifferent and pricy international cuisine. Car parking is available under the hotel at a fee. Swimming pool.

Bulvar Palas (2-star), Tel: 342180. In Yenişehir. Older style, but still very clean and comfortable. 177 rooms.

Hitit Hotel (1-star), Tel: 114102. Well-situated for the museum and the citadel, being on the road up to the citadel. Small terrace in front. Simple but friendly. 50 rooms.

Hotel Taç (1-star), Tel: 243195. 35 rooms, simple, half the rooms with private bath. In Ulus Meydanı area.

Otel Gül Palas (1-star), Tel: 333120. 41 rooms, quiet location, in Bayındır Sok., Yenişehir.

Otel Sultan (1-star), Tel: 315980. In the same street as the Gül Palas but slightly better. 40 rooms. In Yenişehir.

If you want to stay outside the city altogether, the Marmara Köşk (2-star), Tel: 231361, with 51 rooms is set in the Atatürk Forest Farm grounds, with extensive recreational facilities.

Even further out is the Turban Elmadağ Dağevi (1-star), Tel: 344420, at Elmadağ 18 km south of Ankara; or the Angora Tur (2-star), Tel: 137537, at Gölbaşı 24 km southwest of Ankara.

Restaurants. For setting, the best is the Beyaz Saray on Atatürk Bulvarı near Sihhiye Meydanı, high up with a pleasant terrace.

For fish, the Liman Lokantasi off İzmir Caddesı near Kızılay, and the Yakamoz, more expensive, in Yenişehir.

Entertainment. There are **nightclubs** in the main Yenişehir hotels, and the **Opera House** in the Gençlik Parkı has a full season beginning in the autumn.

Climate. At 850 metres, the winters are cold with much snow and last from late November to the end of April. January is the coldest month with an average of −0.2°C. Spring is very short and the hot weather begins at the end of May. July is the hottest month with an average of 23.2°C. Nights are generally cool even in summer because of the altitude. The city is at its best in spring and autumn, especially autumn, when the warm sun and blue skies continue until early November. Air pollution is a problem from mid-October to mid-April because the heating fuel, a soft brown lignite, produces a thick smoke, but from May to September the air is fine and there is less pollution than in most cities.

Average temperature (Celsius):

J	F	M	A	M	J
−0.2	1.2	5.3	11.1	16.0	19.9
J	A	S	O	N	D
23.2	23.1	18.3	12.9	7.5	2.3

Maximum temperature:

J	F	M	A	M	J
16.4	20.4	28.5	31.6	34.4	36.4
J	A	S	O	N	D
38.8	40.0	35.7	33.3	25.3	20.4

Minimum temperature:

J	F	M	A	M	J
−24.9	−24.2	−16.3	−7.2	−1.6	3.8
J	A	S	O	N	D
4.5	5.5	−1.5	−5.3	−17.5	−24.2

ESKİŞEHİR

A modern town, not living up to its name (Old Town), which is Turkey's meerschaum mining centre. Meerschaum (literally foam of the sea) is a soft white mineral which hardens on exposure to the air and looks like ivory. Turkish craftsmen have long used it for pipes and cigarette holders.

Büyük Hotel (1-star), Tel: 12162. 56 rooms.

Haş Termal (1-star), Tel: 17819. 48 rooms.

Sultan Termal (1-star), Tel: 183371.

Both the Haş and Sultan have thermal baths and are next to each other so you can compare and contrast before deciding.

Average temperature (Celsius):

J	F	M	A	M	J
−0.3	1.3	4.9	10.2	15.2	18.8
J	A	S	O	N	D
21.5	21.2	16.9	12.0	6.9	2.2

Maximum temperature:

J	F	M	A	M	J
16.5	20.8	29.1	30.7	34.3	36.0
J	A	S	O	N	D
39.1	38.7	35.8	32.8	25.6	21.1

Minimum temperature:

J	F	M	A	M	J
−23.6	−23.8	−15.5	−7.2	−2.0	2.6
J	A	S	O	N	D
5.0	2.2	−3.7	−7.1	−16.7	−26.3

KÜTAHYA

Gönen Otel (1-star), Tel: 1751. 42 rooms. Harlek Moteli (2-star), Tel: 1. At Ilıca, 27 km from Kütahya on the road to Eskişehir. 33 rooms. Pool and thermal baths.

Average temperature (Celsius):

J	F	M	A	M	J
0.1	1.6	4.7	9.8	14.4	17.9
J	A	S	O	N	D
20.4	20.2	16.2	11.8	7.1	2.5

Maximum temperature:

J	F	M	A	M	J
17.1	19.8	27.0	29.3	33.8	35.0
J	A	S	O	N	D
38.2	38.8	34.6	31.6	24.3	19.0

Minimum temperature:

J	F	M	A	M	J
−26.3	−27.4	−16.6	−7.0	−2.8	0.5
J	A	S	O	N	D
2.6	−0.2	−3.9	−6.9	−18.3	−28.1

CENTRAL ANATOLIA

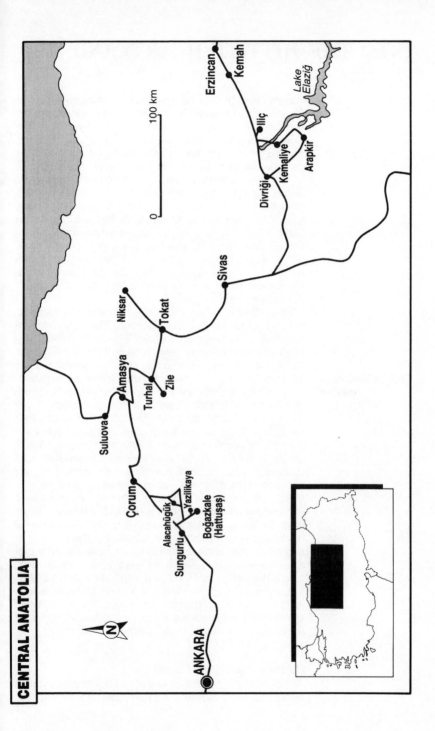

INTO THE HITTITE HEARTLAND

Having spent the morning in Ankara visiting the Museum of Anatolian Civilisations and Atatürk's Mausoleum, you can drive on after lunch to the Hittite heartlands of Boğazkale, the modern name for the Hittite capital Hattuşaş. The distance is 206 km but the roads are good and the drive can be done in two and a half hours. The landscape on the way is unusual, changing very suddenly from green lush valleys to barren bleak hills. For the ascents and descents the road becomes dual carriageway and traffic is very light. After one descent you cross the fine Kızılırmak river (Red River) whose source is in the mountains north of Divriği. From here it flows south through Avanos in Cappadocia where its waters are very red before bending back north to run into the Black Sea. To the Greeks it was the ancient Halys, a name famous from the campaigns of Alexander and Xenophon.

In the fertile valleys many cows graze at the roadside, fewer sheep and only a very few goats. The barren treeless stretches make stopping to relieve yourself difficult and any isolated clusters of trees tend to have attracted the odd person already. Among the mountain stretches there **Striking landscape** are some very curious rock colourings with mineral greens: **colours** Turkey has a rich diversity of mineral resources but much of it remains unexploited due to lack of investment. Later on the soil changes to a rich reddish brown contrasting strongly with the vibrant green crops and grass. There are a couple of pleasantly situated restaurants enroute which are probably a better bet than Ankara and certainly a lot cheaper if you can hold out for a late lunch. The one attached to the BP petrol station is especially attractive.

After about two and a quarter hours you reach the town of Sungurlu on the far outskirts of which, set back slightly from the road, stands the pretty little Hitit Motel on the right-hand side. From here it is another 30 km detour to Boğazkale but you can always check in on the way past and return to the hotel in the evening for dinner. 2 km beyond the motel a yellow sign points right 27 km to Boğazkale and a pleasant drive leads off through green landscape. At the side of the road storks can be seen with the occasional bright yellow bird by the water and the distinctive powerfully built black water buffalo with beards and horns.

Hattuşaş: the Hittite Capital

As you arrive in the **village of Boğazkale** you pass a simple motel (no hot water) and camping area on the right and, shortly after, the small local **museum** on the left which you can enter on the same ticket as the Boğazkale site.

There are no more signposts on arrival: you must proceed straight on through the village, climbing up to an open square area, then following the road as it winds through the village veering slightly to the left. It is a colourful place and if you have come from Ankara in the same day the contrast between the city and village lifestyles will strike you forcibly. Geese meander across the dirt street and circular dung cakes, later to be used as fuel, lie in heaps drying in the sun next to the simple houses.

Village life

As you clear the village the entrance to the Boğazkale site (ancient **Hattuşaş**) comes into view with a ticket kiosk at the gate to the huge fenced-in area. The site stays open till dusk, as late as 7.30 or even 8pm in summer. A tour of the site with a car takes one and a half hours. On foot it would take more like three to four hours. Distances between the various areas are long with steep climbs, so a car is an advantage.

The site is a three-cornered rocky plateau bordered by two valleys; it did not lend itself to building because of the uneven rocky surfaces. The modern name Boğazkale, 'fortress of the narrow mountain pass', reflects this topography and to overcome these problems the planners had often to build up artificial terraces. The advantages of its location however and the reason it was chosen by the militarily-minded Hittites are twofold: first the location between two valleys was well-suited to building fortifications since the natural slopes could be incorporated as part of the defence system, and second, compared to other areas of central Anatolia, it is blessed with an unusual number of brooks and springs. The land to the north of the settlement was also very fertile and well-suited for agriculture.

Natural fortifications

Hattuşaş became the Hittite capital in the 17th C BC, and the first Hittite king called himself Hattusili, 'the one from Hattusa'. It remained the Hittite capital, with kings with wonderful names like Suppiliuma and Muwatalli, until c1200 BC when the city was invaded by hostile forces thought to be from the Black Sea area, burnt down and ransacked.

Mystery of the Hittites

Three thousand years ago the Hittites rivalled the Egyptians as the greatest power on earth. Yet until a century ago the ancient Hittites were a mystery race, our only documentary evidence of their existence being in the Old Testament where they were mentioned as a tribe living in Palestine: King David married Bathsheba, widow of Uriah the Hittite. When Egyptian hieroglyphs were later deciphered, an inscription on the wall of the Temple of Amun at Karnak was found to set out the terms of a mutual defence treaty between Ramses II and the king of the Hittites, Hattusilis. Ramses II later married the Hittite king's daughter to cement the treaty.

No clue was found in the mystery of the lost Hittite empire until a Frenchman, Charles Texier, discovered in 1834 here at Boğazkale the ruins of extraordinary and puzzling rock palaces and monumental rock sculptures which he was unable to identify. German excavations in 1906 revealed thousands of cuneiform tablets which, once deciphered in the 1940s, uncovered the full history of the Hittite kingdom which ruled Anatolia from the 19th to the 13th C BC. The tablets show they were an advanced civilisation, with a body of 200 laws covering every crime they could imagine. Intriguingly, the only capital offences were defiance of the state, rape and sexual intercourse with animals. Murder, black magic and theft could all be compounded by a money payment or by restitution of property. They were skilled in the making of bronze artefacts, jewellery and pottery in black or reddish brown. They used silver bars or rings for currency, with lead for smaller amounts. Much of their culture was taken over from the indigenous Hatti peoples, on whom the Hittites, when they arrived in Anatolia from the northeast, imposed themselves.

Discovering a lost civilisation

Their most memorable relics, however, are the simple but powerful sculptures cut into the rock at their settlements or their temples, often depicting their ceremonies and their weather god whose sacred animal was the bull. The figures are broad, squat and heavy, with none of the grace and subtlety associated with Egyptian or Babylonian art. They represent a tough mountain people, accustomed to a harsh climate and conditions, constantly prepared for war and attack, contrasting with the valley cultures of Mesopotamia and Egypt where man had peacefully pastured his flocks alongside great rivers with no need for defence fortifications.

Mountain culture

The Hittities were the only ancient civilisation to exist and develop in inhospitable mountainous country. Their military strength, necessary to their survival, was awesome, but they were humane in the treatment of their conquered enemies (unlike the later Assyrians) and in peacetime they were governed by statesmen with sound and well-developed imperial policies. A practical and intellectually unpretentious people, they lacked the sophistication and finer graces of their Near Eastern neighbours. One touching account tells of a campaign by Mursilis I who penetrated into Mesopotamia as far as the walls of Babylon. Finding its defences unprepared he entered the city and slew its king. Suddenly Mursilis and his simple highlanders were

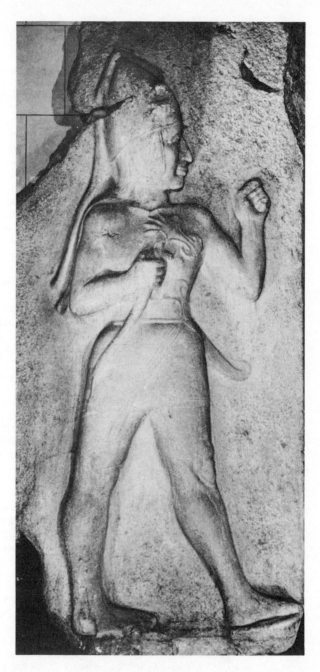

Hittite warrior relief from the King's Gate at Hattuşaş

masters in this great world centre of civilisation amid its pomp and luxury. Feeling out of place and abashed, they soon withdrew to more familiar lands.

One of the clay tablets found at Boğazkale curiously links the Hittites with the Egyptian boy-king Tutankhamun. The Hittite king, Shubbililiuma, was camped near the Euphrates, when a messenger arrived from the queen of Egypt pleading with him to send one of his many sons to marry her, for her husband had died. Shubbililiuma was puzzled and sent the messenger back for further information. She again sent the envoy, begging him to send one of his sons quickly, for she had heard that he had many sons. Egyptologists have confirmed that the Egyptian queen who sent this plea was the widow of Tutankhamun. In Egypt, with its earlier tradition of matrilineal succession to the throne, marriage to the widowed queen would enhance any claim to be pharaoh. A powerful but elderly courtier, Ay, was eager to achieve this power, though the queen was evidently not disposed towards it. Her objection would not have been a May–December marriage: her father Akhenaton and her husband had turned away from the old polytheistic worship of Amun and the other gods in favour of a new monotheist religion based on the Aton— the sun's disc. The forces of reaction now wanted a return to Amun-worship, and Tutankhamun's widow was clearly seeking allies abroad to counter opposition at home. Shubbililiuma eventually sent one of his sons, but he was put to death on arrival in Egypt at Ay's order, and Ay then legitimised his succession by marrying Tutankhamun's widow.

Scholars have recently also found much to suggest a link between ancient Troy and the Hittite kingdom. The fall of Troy roughly coincides with the disintegration of the Hittite empire.

Touring the Site of Ancient Hattuşaş

None of the remains at Boğazkale today stand very high: you will not see here tall pillars, magnificent theatres and imposing façades. Most of what remains are foundations and low walls, but what cannot fail to impress is the size and scale of the conception. Hattuşaş covered an enormous area, at least 3 km square, and the scale of all its buildings was vast. The defence walls were 6.5 km long with nearly 200 towers: one of the earliest surviving examples of a walled city. It is best to drive first up to the highest point of the settlement where you will find the three city gates— the Lion Gate, the Sphinx Gate and the King's Gate—at each of the three corners of the top plateau set about 500 metres from each other. From here you gain a sense of

Tutankhamun link

View from the gates

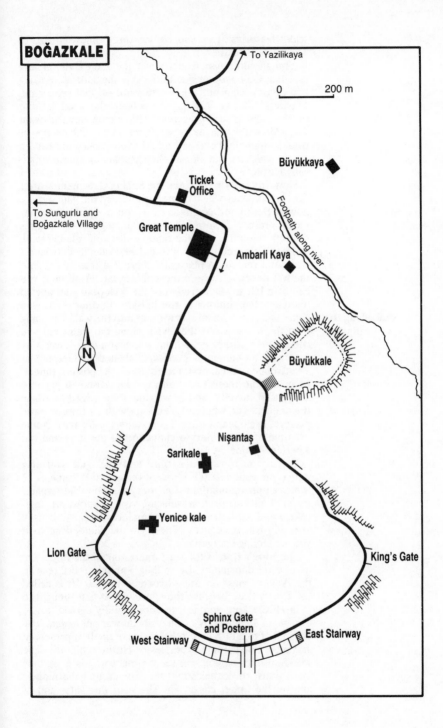

BOĞAZKALE

To Yazilikaya

0   200 m

Büyükkaya

Ticket Office

Footpath along river

To Sungurlu and
Boğazkale Village

Great Temple

Ambarli Kaya

Büyükkale

N

Nişantaş

Sarikale

Yenice kale

Lion Gate

King's Gate

Sphinx Gate
and Postern

West Stairway

East Stairway

scale: Hattuşaş at its apogee was three times the size of Themistocles' Athens.

You should begin your tour at the **Lion Gate**, clearly labelled. On the outer side of the gate the doorjambs carry two *lions* jutting out fullface to ward off evil spirits and to defend the city. The left one is badly damaged but that on the right is well-preserved with mouth open in what was presumably meant to be a fierce growl. The deep eyes would originally have had inlaid white stone; the carved mane, whiskers and hair on the chest are all characteristically Hittite.

Now drive on to Yer Kapı, the **Sphinx Gate**, named after the two sphinxes which originally guarded the gate but are now in Berlin and İstanbul. Here you can climb to a perfectly preserved *postern tunnel* running for 70 metres through the hillside to the outer walls; you can still walk down this quite comfortably. On the far side the doorjambs and lintel remain in place and there is a *seat* carved into the left doorjamb where the sentinel sat. From here you can turn left to see a **section of the cyclopean wall** angled to follow the contour of the hillside. Further along you come to a fine colossal *stairway* cut into the wall. Climbing it to the top you can then walk along the wall until you come to the corner edge from which you can descend by a second monumental *stairway*, labelled in German as Westtreppe (west stairs), returning via the postern tunnel. In peacetime these two stairways were used to get into and out of the city, and in wartime they served to attack the enemy. The whole of Yer Kapı with its towers, gate, postern, cyclopean wall and two stairways is a remarkable example of the military architecture of the time and has a perfect symmetry.

A walk along the cyclopean walls

Driving on towards the third and final gate you may notice on your left the scarcely recognisable remains of some **temple foundations**. On rocky outcrops the remains of well-built fortification walls are visible, known as Yenicekale and Sarıkale; both were small **castles** possibly used also as royal residences. These can be climbed up to if you are feeling energetic.

The **King's Gate** is the least interesting of the three. On its outside doorjambs the smiling **war god relief** seen in the Ankara museum was discovered in 1907. It is called the King's Gate because the figure was at first thought to be a Hittite king and not, as subsequently agreed, a god of war. In 1968 a copy of the original was put *in situ*. The original of this 14th C BC relief is one of the best preserved and most outstanding examples of Hittite sculpture. The workmanship, as you can see on this copy, is extremely fine: notice the cuticles and the hair around the nipples and on the upper chest. The shape of this gate, and of the Lions' Gate, which originally formed a parabolic arch, is distinctively Hittite and is also reminiscent of the Lycian tombs in southern Turkey.

You now continue on downhill past the poorly preserved Nişantaş (a 13th C BC castle) with a long inscription in **The royal palace** Hittite hieroglyphs cut into the rocky hill. A few metres further on you reach the clearly signposted **Büyükkale** (Great Fortress) which was the residential palace of the Hittite kings in the 13th C BC. It was a fortified citadel within the outer fortification walls of the city and was protected by the steep drops on all sides. You reach it from the road now by a modern flight of steps which replace a lost Hittite ramp and lead to a poorly preserved citadel gate. Inside the once strong walls are the foundations of a series of large courtyards at different levels. In one of the rooms identified as an *archive* 300 cuneiform tablets were found in 1906, including the famous treaty of 1279 BC between King Hattusili III and Ramses II of Egypt. One of the other buildings was thought by the excavators to have been a great *audience hall* of the Hittite kings. The area on the *highest terrace* is believed to have accommodated the houses of the royal family, but only the magnificent setting can be appreciated today, so fragmentary are the remains. Two cylindrical rainwater cisterns can be seen carved in the rock.

The road winds down to the **Great Temple of the Weather** **The largest Hittite** **God**, clearly signposted. Built of limestone and some gra- **temple** nite, it is the largest and best preserved Hittite temple. Its precincts are entered via the *processional gate* through which the Hittite Great King and his Great Queen would have passed as they went to worship as priest and priestess, accompanied by their entourage. Before the gate you pass a great *water basin*, now fractured, originally made from one colossal limestone block, with two lion heads and forepaws on one side. Once through the gateway a street leads straight ahead with its *drainage system* visible beneath the collapsed paving. The street turns right and in the corner is another large limestone water basin which was clearly connected to the drainage system. To the left of the basin, standing by itself in one of the temple rooms some 20 metres away, your eye will be caught by the enormous *green marble stone*, polished and smooth. The stone is a mystery; archaeologists who have devoted years of their life to excavations here choose never even to mention it, so its purpose remains unknown. It is tempting to think that like the meteorite Black Stone of the Kaaba at Mecca it may have had a religious significance as it is so different from the limestone blocks all around.

Following the street to the right from the basin you come to the *temple proper*. Its outer courtyard walls would originally have been finished with plaster, possibly painted in several colours. The temple itself would have been covered by a flat roof. There is a lot for the imagination to supply here, but the first and abiding impression is of its great size. It was probably built in the 14th or 13th C BC and can be compared with the great sanctuaries of 19th Dynasty Egypt. It was destroyed around 1200 BC at the same time as the royal citadel.

Surrounding the temple are *storerooms*, 78 in all, in some of which more cuneiform tablets were found. The colossal *storage jars* are set into the ground and were not designed to be moved. The smaller ones held up to 900 litres while the largest held almost 3000 litres. It is probable that they contained liquids, probably wine and oil.

The Rock-cut Sanctuary

From Boğazkale it is only a further 3 km on to Yazılıkaya (Carved Rock), the 13th C BC rock-cut sanctuary of the Hittite capital. Within a kilometre from Boğazkale the narrow tarmac road crosses a little bridge over a river from where you can have a very pleasant stroll along the river banks between the rocky hills rising either side. The path leads to the foot of Büyükkaya, a rocky outcrop on the left of the river. At the point where this comes closest to the rock of Ambarlıkaya on the western (Hattuşaş) side, **Hittite bridge and** the Hittites ingeniously built a bridge and walkway gallery **portcullis** over the gorge to make the city fortifications continuous. Under the bridge they built a portcullis which blocked access through the ravine in times of danger: the three pairs of *perpendicular grooves* down which it was lowered are still visible hewn into the canyon wall.

The rest of the drive to **Yazılıkaya** climbs quite steeply uphill all the way to reach a striking setting in a group of natural rock clefts set among pine trees. Apart from the Neo-Hittite site at Karatepe near Adana, this is the only Hittite site to have its rock reliefs *in situ* and the only open-air temple to have survived to the present day. All the more tragic then is the fate that befell it recently as a result of a French archaeologist's work.

Formed of two natural rock galleries whose inner faces are carved with reliefs of the gods and goddesses of the Hittite pantheon, the Yazılıkaya **temple** was built between 1250 and 1220 BC. Over the years it has provided a wealth of information for archaeologists, the latest of whom, the Frenchwoman Smilia Masson, began her work here in 1976, publishing her findings in a book entitled *New Inscriptions at Yazılıkaya Temple* which was well received.

After Madame Masson returned home it was discovered **An archaeologist** that some of the reliefs and inscriptions had been damaged **ruins the ruins** and the watchmen employed to guard the temple were accused of negligence. The finger was first pointed at Madame Masson by a professor at Chicago University who produced a study casting doubt on her working techniques, with photographs to prove how her methods had damaged the rock carving. Similar accusations were subsequently levelled by Hittitology experts attached to London and Oxford universities. The damage was apparently caused by Madame Masson using latex on the rock surface to obtain an impression, which resulted in the removal of the centuries-old patina and exposed the inscriptions to air and erosion. The use of latex for this purpose is common in archaeology, but for indoor areas only—it had never been used outdoors.

Looking at photos taken before 1976 and comparing them with what you see today, there is unquestionably a deterioration, a fading of the relief contours. If the deterioration has been this marked in ten years, in 20 years' time there may be little left to see at all.

In the first, that is the *main gallery*, of the temple the left rock face shows the 42 warrior-like gods walking in sideways relief towards the right, while the right rock face shows 21 goddesses walking in a row towards the left to meet the gods in the middle. The gods are in their characteristic short kilts, conical helmets and Ali Baba shoes and carry either a mace or a scythe-shaped scimitar. Many wear earrings, though since the relief is sideways-on, it is not possible to say whether they are à la punk in one ear only. The rank of gods is indicated by the number of horns decorating the conical helmet, from one for a junior god up to five for a real superstar. The female deities are all wearing trailing gowns with tall cylindrical headresses and long braids of hair down their backs. Most of the reliefs carry the names of the deities in hieroglyphs always written above the uplifted hand. The two most important are the two biggest, where the male queue meets the female queue. Here we have on the left *Teshub the weather god* standing on the shoulders of two mountain gods with heads bowed forward and *Hepatu the sun goddess* and wife of Teshub standing on a panther, which is in turn standing with each foot on a mountain. It is interesting to note the extent to which the Hittites depicted themselves as a mountain culture. Evidence is mounting now to indicate that this main gallery was used for the Spring Festival, which marked the beginning of the new year and lasted for many days with sumptuous feasts.

A cleft in the rock leads from the main gallery through into the long narrow *smaller gallery*. The floor was originally paved in stone slabs which have long since disappeared. The four reliefs however are better preserved than those in the large gallery, but consist of isolated figures

Gods meet goddesses

Spring festival chamber

instead of a single unit. 'The Twelve' identikit warrior gods here, like the ones in the main gallery, were *gods of the underworld*. Nearby the intriguing *sword god* is also

thought to be a god of the underworld, though he is by no means fully understood by scholars. He has a man's head with conical helmet, denoting his god status, but his torso is made up of a composite of four lions tapering down to a sword blade. On the opposite side is a large relief of the deity *Sarumna*, son of the sun goddess and Teshub, with his arm protectively round a smaller figure known from the hieroglyph to be *Tuthalia*, a Hittite Great King. From the themes of these reliefs it has been speculated that this narrow chamber was used in funeral rites for the Hittite kings.

A Feeling for Past and Place

The 14th C BC Hittite site of **Alacahüyük** lies somewhat apart from the Boğazkale/Yazılıkaya cluster and as a result is often missed off the traveller's itinerary. This is a shame as it is in many ways the most attractive of the three and conveys most clearly the feel of a fortified Hittite city. The fact that the stupendous finds at the royal tombs here will still be fresh in your mind from the museum at Ankara also helps to lend the site a special significance.

If you have spent the night at Sungurlu you again take the right hand fork towards Boğazkale but after about 8 km a yellow sign points off 22 km to the left to Alacahüyük. About 12 km after this turn-off there is a second turn-off suddenly to the left. A further 10 km brings you to the pretty village of Alacahüyük; the site lies on the near side. There is a well laid-out and pretty site musuem where you buy your ticket. The site is open every day from 8am to noon and 1.30 to 5.30pm

The whole city at Alacahüyük was protected by an inner city wall; you enter through its monumental gateway today. It is called the **Sphinx Gate** from the massive female sphinxes facing outwards from the door jambs. To the left are colossal stone slabs with a series of **reliefs** describing scenes from the cult of the thunder god. Particularly striking is the double eagle which has caught two hares in its talons, and there are also three priests in ritual gowns, a priest with four rams and the king and queen worshipping a bull with the king carrying a long crook. The sculptor evidently started to work on the crook from both ends and had some difficulty in making them meet. The royal sun discs found in the royal tombs here at Alacahüyük

were carried on the top of such crooks. Also noteworthy are the attendant musicians, one playing a lute-like instrument, and on the next slab an entertainer either playing a wind instrument or doing a sword swallowing act. On his right are two acrobats, one, his head shaven but for a lock, is climbing a free-standing ladder while the other is ready to catch him. When compared to acrobats like the bull vaulters of Minoan Crete in the Palace of Knossos, these rather stumpy Hittite acrobats lack conviction.

From the gateway you enter the **main street** with the drainage system underneath still clearly visible. The street helps very much to give Alacahüyük the feel of a real town, a feel it is difficult to get at Hattuşaş. Those parts of the town that have been excavated are clearly labelled. In a hollow near the centre are the royal tombs where the treasure displayed in the Ankara museum was found. The finds dated to the Early Bronze Age before the Hittite town you see today was built on top of the tombs.

The **postern** is especially impressive but is difficult to find unless you know where to look. From the raised watchtower area to the left of the Sphinx Gate you must walk off to the west beyond the excavations for about 300 metres until you suddenly come on a signpost announcing it. Steps lead down and continue underground in a tunnel for 5 metres or so; then the tunnel turns sharply right and continues for a further 20 metres to come up outside the walls.

The **museum** shows some impressive reconstructions of the city and some fine Hittite sun discs and pottery. Some of the pots are for all the world like modern teapots with lids. One particularly intriguing exhibit is the large free-standing Hittite clay bath, possibly the earliest manufactured bath in the world. Downstairs is a colourful ethnographic section with costumes, carpets and weapons.

Recognition of a once obscure civilisation

The emergence of the Hittities from almost total obscurity has been one of the great achievements of archaeology this century. In the English-speaking world the significance of the discovery of the lost Hittite empire has still not been fully recognised, probably because the bulk of the literature has been in German and the Hittite language was deciphered by Germans and a Czech. Yet this was one of the greatest Bronze Age civilisations, speaking the earliest Indo-European language known.

The road continues on through the slightly primitive village of Alacahüyük itself. Geese run all over the street but the local people keep themselves pleasantly to themselves, content to wave from a distance. There is a very simple hotel where a night could be spent if necessary, though most people will prefer to drive on to Amasya, an interesting town with Pontic rock tombs and Seljuk monuments. This lies a further hour and 45 minutes' drive away and you can therefore reach it in time for lunch after visiting Alacahüyük in the morning from Sungurlu.

AMASYA

To reach Amasya from Alacahüyük you drive through the village and continue for some 7 km until you reach a T-junction where you turn left toward Çorum and Samsun. The countryside is very rural and with the soil appearing so rich and fertile you find yourself constantly wondering why there are no trees. A drive on of some 100 km brings you via **Çorum**, a faceless modern town, to **Amasya**.

Strabo, the famous geographer of the ancient world, was born in Amasya in 64 BC when it was the capital of the Pontic Kingdom. He describes his birthplace in grand terms: 'My native town is situated in a deep and large valley through which flows the river Iris. It has been provided in a surprising manner by art and nature for answering the purpose of a city and a fortress. For there is a lofty and perpendicular rock which overhangs the river, having on one side a wall erected close to the bank where the town has been built, while on the other it runs up on either hand to the summits of the hill. These two are connected to each other and well fortified with towers. Within this enclosure are the royal residence and the tombs of the

Expectation and reality

kings'. Having thus formed certain expectations of Amasya's magnificent setting and perhaps having read in another guide book that it is 'one of the loveliest of all Anatolian towns', your first sight of it cannot but be a disappointment. The approach road leads through a messy industrial zone with half-finished buildings and telegraph wires everywhere. One description, written only 15 years ago, reveals how recent this deterioration has been: 'The evident care taken in the apperance of the town and the good condition of so many of the houses is a hopeful sign that Amasya will not too soon lose itself in a welter of concrete'.

Fortunately the town improves once you have reached the centre, left the car and begun to walk along the river frontage to explore. The river is in spring a muddy reddish colour in defiance of its name 'Yeşilırmak', Green River. The left bank which you walk along first is lined with a series of pretty cafés where it is pleasant to linger over tea or coffee while looking across the river to the rock tombs cut into the cliff face opposite. On the far bank

Overhanging balconies

stand beautiful timbered **houses** with balconies overhanging the river. Two disasters, the great fire of 1915 and the Erzincan earthquake of 1939, together with the periodic floods which sweep the valley have reduced the number of these houses; many of those remaining are delapidated. No food is on offer at the river cafés; the best place for a meal is the Turban Amasya Hotel restaurant which prides

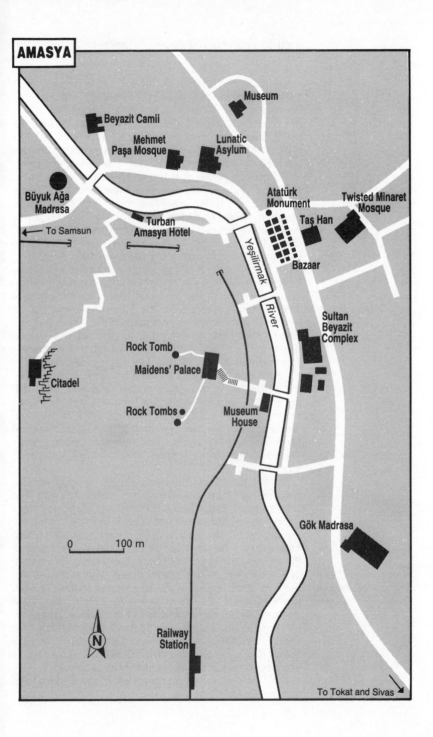

AMASYA

Museum

Beyazit Camii

Mehmet
Paşa Mosque

Lunatic
Asylum

Büyuk Ağa
Madrasa

Atatürk
Monument

Twisted Minaret
Mosque

Taş Han

← To Samsun

Turban
Amasya Hotel

Yeşilirmak
River

Bazaar

Sultan
Beyazit
Complex

Rock Tomb

Maidens' Palace

Citadel

Rock Tombs

Museum
House

0   100 m

Gök Madrasa

N

Railway
Station

To Tokat and Sivas →

itself on its cuisine and where you may even get some local
fish.

Climbing up to the Palace of the Pontic Kings

To explore the town the best bet is to leave the car on
the river bank street between the main square with the
inevitable equestrian statue and the Ottoman mosque, then
walk on to the bridge which crosses the river and up towards
the rock tombs set in the cliff face overlooking the town.
A yellow sign points over the bridge to the Kızlar Sarayı
(Maidens' Palace) and the **Hazeranlar Konağı** (Museum
House). The latter is a beautifully restored 19th C Ottoman
house in white and brown timber on the river converted
very recently into an ethanographic museum (closed Mondays). It stands out by its superb condition in contrast to
its decaying neighbours along the river bank. From here
a sign points to the **Kralkaya** (King's Rock) up some steps
between the old houses. The ascent takes only ten minutes,
but is quite steep and can seem like a huge effort after
a heavy lunch and wine at the Turban Amasya. Strabo
tells us that the town was founded by the Amazon queen
Amasis, but however early the original settlement here
it was as the capital of the Pontic kingdom that Amasya
rose to prominence. This kingdom was founded in the third
C BC by an adventurer called Mithradates, whose uncle,
one of the last of the Greek tyrants, had been executed.
Mithradates escaped with a few followers into the Pontus
mountains and finally established himself at Amasya,
where he built his palace and citadel. The kingdom survived
for more than two centuries of turbulent history, finally
being crushed by the Romans under Julius Caesar in 47
BC.

Of the palace of the Pontic kings virtually nothing
remains today but the terrace on which it stood. The
modern name **Kızlar Sarayı** (Maidens' Palace) presumably
refers to the Ottoman harem. The Seljuks and Ottomans
rebuilt, but all that remains of their work is a little Turkish
bath over on the far right of the terrace. The **tombs of
the Mithraditic kings** are above the terrace, carved out
of hard basalt. A remarkable **tunnel** with steps cut into
the rock leads round to the two largest tombs. The left
tomb was used as a chapel during Byzantine times. Near
the tombs is the entrance to one of the three puzzling tunnels supposedly leading down to the river or to wells. One
theory is that they were used in religious rituals, but the
theory that they were sally ports for surprise attacks seems
unlikely, as no exit for them has ever been found.

From here there is a pleasant view of the Turkish town
and its monuments below.

**Tombs and
tunnels**

Amasya on the Yeşilırmak and above it the ancient citadel

The Seljuk and Ottoman Town

The Seljuks took Amasya in 1071; it fell to the Ottomans under Beyazıt I in 1392. Amasya's decline in the 18th and 19th C was hastened by serious earthquakes and the great fire of 1915.

Medieval monuments

Along the main street is the **Gök Madrasa**, a Seljuk building of 1266. You have to look hard at the exterior to see any of the turquoise tiles which gave it its name gök, sky-blue. On the river bank set among trees and gardens is the **Mosque of Sultan Beyazıt** built in 1486. Further along the dusty main street you come to the 17th C **Taş Han** (Stone Caravanserai), used as metal workshops. Behind it is the Twisted Minaret Mosque, **Burmalı Minare Camii.** Built in 1242 it was heavily restored in the 18th C after a fire. Inside are wooden galleries on the three sides facing the mihrab. Further uphill, away from the river, stands the **Fethiye Camii**, originally a 7th C Byzantine church.

Along the town side of the river bank you come to the **lunatic asylum** built in 1308 by the Mongols with a fine oriental-flavour portal, now an abandoned ruin. This building is an apt introduction to the history of destruction of these warrior horsemen, whose raids throughout the 13th and 14th C spelt the end for many rulers in the Near and Middle East.

Mongol scourge

The first wave of Mongols was led by Ghengis Khan in 1243; he and his successors were responsible for the downfall of the Seljuk Sultanate of Rum, the Crusader kingdoms in southeast Anatolia and, in 1258, the Abbasid caliphate in Baghdad, a date Oxford university until recently regarded as the end of Arab history. Ghengis Khan described himself as 'the scourge of god sent to men as a punishment for their sins'. Tamerlane, leader of the second Mongol wave, swept into eastern Anatolia in 1401, having already overrun Central Asia, India, Persia, Iraq and Syria, leaving a trail of destruction behind him. Exceptionally aggressive and warlike, the Mongols specialised in slaughtering wholesale anyone they came across, virtually wiping out the populations of the cities they took, and then building pyramids of the victims' heads. They destroyed the priceless palaces and libraries of the East, while the revered mosques of Bukhara served them as stables. Any skilled craftsmen were carried away to Tamerlane's capital in Samarkand. Among the Mongols' more charming habits were drinking the blood of their horses by cutting a hole in the leg and having themselves buried surrounded by beautiful young maidens. Tamerlane

Tamerlane

(Timur Lenk), claiming descent from and modelling himself on Ghengis Khan, crushed the chief Ottoman cities of Ankara, İznik, Bursa and İzmir. He then returned to his native steppeland without consolidating his victories, but leaving behind him a devastation from which it took the Ottomans 50 years to recover. In his avowed aim to conquer the world and establish an empire, Tamerlane failed, for, bringing with him no religion or culture, he could offer nothing on which to base his power except destruction. His reputation today therefore is not as a founder of a great dynasty, but as the most comprehensively destructive ruler in history. With these associations it is surprising, to say the least, that Timur is a popular boys' name in Turkey today. Many Turkish girls' names are, by contrast, derived from flowers.

Beyond the Mongol asylum there is a pleasant walk over a little footbridge to the early Ottoman **Mehmet Paşa Mosque** built in 1486, prettily set among tall trees along the river's edge. A short walk from the river takes you to Amasya's new **museum** set in pretty gardens strewn with sculp-

Decaying mummies

tures from the town's past. Apart from various Pontic, Roman, Byzantine, Seljuk and Ottoman artefacts, including a fine bath tub, the major attractions are the gently decaying mummies of two Mongol governors and a Seljuk family displayed in glass cases in the adjacent Seljuk **türbe**

of Sultan Mesut. You will notice several türbes scattered in con-gruously round the town.

The other two Moslem buildings of note are on opposite sides of the river at the Samsun end of town. The fine early 15th C **Beyazıt Camii** stands just to the right of the main road bridge that crosses the Yeşilırmak towards Samsun. On the far side, also to the right of the road, is the unusual eight-sided **Büyük Ağa Madrasa**, with a lovely interior arcade and courtyard. It was founded in 1488 by the Chief White Eunuch of Beyazıt II.

Ascent to the Citadel

A little outside the town you can drive up to the citadel. A yellow sign indicates Kale 2 km a short way beyond the Turban Amasya Hotel. The road is unmade and rough but perfectly all right for a saloon car and very well signposted at each turn.

From where the road ends there is a ten-minute scramble up through the walls to the highest point for the best views. The area of the **castle** is surprisingly large and the walls and towers are extensive but heavily ruined. Two of the towers are thought to be from the Pontic days, but most of the walls are of Byzantine or Turkish reconstruction. From the highest point, where there is a flagpole, the view down to the river and town below is superb, and the grassy summit makes a lovely place for a picnic. During Ramadan an old Russian cannon is fired from here at sundown.

EAST TO TOKAT

From Amasya there are two options open to you, either to drive north to Samsun on the Black Sea and maybe begin a huge circuit of the east going inland at Trabzon or Hopa, or to stay inland and continue visiting the Seljuk monuments of central Anatolia. This section continues with the latter route, but see the later *Black Sea Coast* chapter for the alternative route.

Seljuk Civilisation

Origins The Seljuks were originally nomads from the region of Samarkand and Bukhara descended from the Tu-Kin people in the steppes of Mongolia, and this Chinese name evolved to give us the modern name Turk. They worshipped their own weather gods and were renowned for their physical prowess. In the 11th C a wave of Seljuks surged out from their homeland, through Persia, Iraq, Syria and Palestine. Here they were converted to Islam and brought their new religion with them when, in 1067, under the leadership of Alp Arslan, they pushed up from Antioch (modern Antakya) into Anatolia to Konya.

Although the Seljuks were effective fighters, once they had established themselves and the fighting was over, their greatest sultans, notably Alp Arslan, Malik Shah, Keykavus I and Keykubad I (Alaeddin), were enlightened rulers, laying down the foundations for commercial prosperity, education and the arts. Alp Arslan introduced the appointment of viziers (ministers or advisors), and his first vizier, Nizam Al-Mulk, was responsible for founding universities, observatories, hospitals and mosques. Over the two centuries of their rule, the Seljuks evolved a remarkable welfare state where medical schools were linked with hospitals, orphanages, poor-houses, mental homes, baths and religious schools, all offering their services to the needy free of charge. Many of these institutions are still in existence.

Caravanserais along the trade routes The system of caravanserais they built facilitated trade and concentrated the trade routes; they were usually built a day's journey apart. The services they offered for the travelling merchants were remarkable for their time, with the central mosque and ablution fountain, the range of sleeping quarters, the baths to revive aching limbs, the cafés for refreshment, the blacksmith and leatherworker ready to do repairs, and musicians to relax and entertain. Stabling was offered for donkeys, horses and camels, with the doors varying in height to suit the height of each animal.

Most remarkable of all, however, was that these services were offered free by the state, which funded the system through taxation.

In Seljuk architecture the elaborate tiles and carving distantly reflect Persian influence, and in the strength and power of their castles and minarets there are traces of Syrian Arab influence. But whereas the later Ottomans often converted churches to use as mosques, not a single Seljuk mosque was converted from a church or even raised on the ruins of a church. Without exception they built on new foundations. The Seljuks developed their own distinctive forms, such as the cylindrical mausoleum (türbe) on a square base with a conical roof (the most famous example being the Mevlana Tomb in Konya). It has been suggested that this shape was meant to recall the pointed tents of the Seljuks' nomadic origins. The double-headed eagle, symbol of the Seljuk state, can be seen on many of their buildings, which were usually constructed in red brick with plain high walls contrasting with the very elaborate decorations and carving in niches and doorways. The main entrance was always highly elaborate with honeycomb (or stalactite) carving, as can be seen in the extant caravanserais and madrasas.

Madrasas for body, mind and spirit Madrasas were generally charitable foundations and taught, besides the Koran, Islamic jurisprudence, languages, mathematics, geometry, astronomy, medicine and music. Sports were also practised, and famous wrestlers often came from these schools. In many ways, madrasas were the Islamic version of the gymnasiums of the ancient world, as gymnasiums were as much for teaching as for sport, and frequently had schools and libraries attached. Their layouts too were similar, with buildings arranged round a courtyard.

The Seljuks were also prolific bridge builders. Built solidly in stone with a single pointed arch, many remain in use today. The pointed arch, also used to great effect in windows and doorways, was possibly the inspiration for the later Gothic arch, taken back to Europe by the Crusaders.

Tiles and carpets Tilework was something the Greeks and Romans never learnt, but the Seljuks brought this exquisite art with them from Persia. They evolved the Persian style into their own form of tile mosaics in plain colours and geometric designs, which so often embellish their mosques, tombs and madrasas. The best examples of tilework in Turkey are on display in the Karatay Madrasa museum in Konya. Carpet weaving was the other great Seljuk art. Their colours are rich: blues, brick red, soft green, with sand and earth backgrounds. The motifs are geometric often with stylised animal, bird or tree forms. Like the türbe's roof, this art recalled their nomadic background, for the carpet is the essential piece of tent furniture.

The Seljuks' most important contribution to religion was the foundation of the Mevlana order of Whirling Dervishes at Konya, the Seljuk capital. This form of Islamic mysticism continues today despite Atatürk's dissolution of the order in 1925 in his attempts to secularise modern Turkey.

The Madrasa and Ma

The drive from Amasya to Tokat takes one and a quarter hours through pleasant though unexciting landscapes, with rural villages and fertile valleys. You pass at **Ezinepazar** the ruins of a Seljuk caravanserai, once the last stop on the road from Sivas to Amasya: at that time Ezinepazar was a day's journey by camel from Amasya, whereas today it is less than half an hour by car. 26 km before Tokat a short detour to the village of **Pazar** will show you a particularly fine Seljuk caravanserai, the **Hatun Han**, built in 1238.

In **Tokat** there is really only one monument to see and
Turquoise that is the **Gök Madrasa** (Turquoise Madrasa), named for its tiles. Blue is a holy colour in Turkey, and our word turquoise is derived from Turkey. The madrasa is indicated as 'Müze' by a yellow sign pointing right at a roundabout on the edge of town: the road straight on continues to Sivas. Built in 1275, the madrasa was closed for extensive repairs in 1974, only reopening in 1982. In fact the restoration has been so exhaustive that very few blue tiles remain. In the courtyard are Seljuk tombstones, inscriptions, Roman column pedestals and capitals from Comana Pontica. In an upstairs room are exhibits of the patterned cloth called 'yamas', made by using wooden stamping patterns on the cloth, a craft for which both Tokat and Sivas are famous. In a downstairs room are the 40 tombs of the founders, though tradition refers to them as the 40 maidens.

The first known madrasa was built in Nişapur, Iraq, in 1027 by Nizam Al-Mulk. Students in all these Seljuk institutions were provided with free board and lodging and given a monthly cash allowance. To provide for the students'
Madrasa life lodging and their studies, rooms with fireplaces and cupboards, a communal classroom, a mescit (prayer room), a professor's room, a library and wash rooms were installed on two storeys round a courtyard: it was these arrangements which determined the form of the building. The plan did not include a kitchen as meals were obtained from a public cookhouse. Another common feature was a small mosque for public use often containing the mausoleum of the founder.

Next to the Gök Madrasa is the **Voyvoda Han**, a large market building built in 1631 for the Armenian merchants who had traded here since the early days of the city. Tokat, Sivas and Kayseri all had large Armenian communities till the 1920s, but now only a few remain. In the old market quarter of Tokat, back up towards the main square, you can still buy the fine copperware for which Tokat has been famous for centuries.

At the roundabout along the main road a yellow sign points up to the **Kale** (citadel) dominating the town, but the road is not signposted again and you have to find the way by asking. The remains on the spectacular twin-peaked rock today are of Byzantine date, repaired by the Ottomans and still with a total of 28 towers. At the time of the Pontic kingdom where modern Tokat stands was ancient **Dazimon**, and its fortress guarded the approach to the temple-city of **Comana Pontica**, 10 km away to the north. Nothing of this great sanctuary remains today, where the Anatolian

Ma and her girls

earth mother was worshipped under the apt name of Ma. The high priests of the sanctuary ruled over a community of serfs with handmaidens of the goddess serving as temple prostitutes. Every two years a festival was held to worship the mother goddess, a very popular and well-attended kind of market fair cum orgiastic feast in which a statue of the goddess, said to be the image of Artemis, was carried about in procession accompanied by frenzied worshippers practicing flagellation.

Pax Anatolia

At nearby **Zile** (ancient **Zele**) in 47 BC Julius Caesar put an end to the upstart Pontic kings in a battle lasting only four hours. The speed of his victory led Caesar to pronounce his famous one-liner, 'Veni, vidi, vici', I came, I

'I came, I saw, etc.'

saw, I conquered. The Roman age was in many ways a continuation and development of the Hellenistic. Rome was at first drawn reluctantly into Asia Minor, crossing the Hellespont in 190 BC to crush the ambitious Seleucid King Antiochus III at Magnesia, today's Manisa. When however the king of Pergamum died in 133 BC, bequeathing his entire kingdom to Rome, the Romans of necessity organised western Asia Minor into the province of Asia. Later problems with the troublesome Cilician pirates and the Pontic kingdom of Mithradates in the 1st C BC drew Rome eastwards to take over the whole of Anatolia and Syria. By and large, Roman rule brought 200 years of peace and prosperity to Anatolia.

At Sulusaray, a village 48 km from Tokat, a major archaeological discovery was made in summer 1988. This

Another Ephesus

was **Sebastopolis**, a Roman city whose state of preservation promises to rival Ephesus, Turkey's greatest Graeco-

Roman city, on the Aegean coast. The first relics of the city, marble columns and inscriptions, were uncovered by a flood. The Emperor Augustus is thought to have been the city's founder, in the 1st C BC.

Work at Sebastopolis is pressing ahead under both Turkish and European archaeologists, and so far large sections of marble flooring and a gymnasium have been unearthed. It will of course be many years before the city is sufficiently uncovered to make it a real tourist attraction, but the entrepreneurial element in Tokat's population is building a 4-star hotel in anticipation.

From Tokat or Amasya an alternative route to the Black Sea can be via Niksar to Ünye. The drive is attractive through pleasant mountain scenery and **Niksar** is an old Pontic town with a Pontic fortress. In the town there is also the fine Ulu Cami with a magnificent gateway. Most will prefer however to continue inland looking at the impressive Seljuk monuments of Sivas, and then the unique mosque-madrasa complex at Divriği.

FOLLOWING THE CARAVANSERAIS TO SIVAS

From Tokat the road to Sivas climbs through low hills of about 700 metres to a plateau with snow-topped peaks in the distance. There is a dearth of petrol stations between Tokat and Sivas so it is as well to check that your tank has sufficient to last for the 103 km (one and a quarter hours') drive. Some 10 km before the village of Çamlıbel there is a ruined Seljuk caravanserai on the right of the road, and just before the village is another, again on the right. These, like those at Pazar and Ezinepazar, were part of the series linking Amasya with Sivas.

During the Sultanate of Rum **Sivas** was one of the principal Seljuk cities and so was adorned with an abundance of beautiful Seljuk buildings. On arrival you follow signs into the town centre and there is no mistaking your arrival in the main square. To the right is a large open grassy area with the famous Çifte Minare Madrasa (Twin Minaret Madrasa) rising above the trees. It is best to stop and park the car in a side street nearby rather than going on to the main roundabout where the yellow sign to the Müze points off in totally the wrong direction. Changes in the last few years mean that the **museum**, such as it is, is now in the **Buruciye Madrasa** (1271), behind the Çifte Minare Madrasa. The exhibits are largely confined to more of the patterned cloth already seen in Tokat's Gök Madrasa.

Seljuk jewel   The **Çifte Minare Madrasa** (also 1271), the most attractive of Sivas' Seljuk monuments, is set among the pretty gardens of the small municipal park. The notion of twin minarets flanking the entrance as found here and at Erzurum was brought by the Seljuks from Persia. The ruins lie among the flowers and grassy banks with birds singing in the trees and local people lingering on the benches in the pleasant atmosphere. The curious thing is that on walking up to the façade expecting to enter, you discover that this is in fact all that remains of it. Like some film set it is very convincing seen from head on, but the illusion crumbles when seen from any other angle.

The **Şifahiye Madrasa** (also called the Darüşşifa of Keykavus I), built earlier than the other monuments, in 1217, lies immediately across the alley from the Çifte Minare and is being carefully restored. An attractive building to walk round today, it is the largest and most elaborate medical institution ever built by the Seljuks, a combined hospital and medical school, also looking after mental patients. Music and hypnosis were the favoured methods of treat-

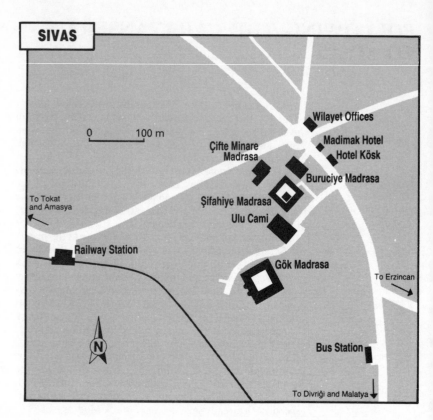

ment for these. On the *türbe of Keykavus* inside, the decorative motifs of the glazed tilework include the age-old swastika motif, eight-pointed stars and Kufic inscriptions. Of the various styles of Arabic writing the square Kufic script, being particularly well adapted for mosaic, was found the most appropriate for Seljuk faience. There are also Hittite throwbacks in the tilework, with marching lions in relief.

From the back of this area of parkland round the Çifte Minare, you can walk off towards the **Gök Madrasa**, often considered the masterpiece of Sivas' monuments, and formerly the museum. Turning first right from the parkland and then left, you will see it signposted at a small roundabout. A five-minute walk brings you there. Kept shut now, it has an abandoned air with grass growing over the walls and courtyard. Built in 1271 (the same date as the Çifte Minare) by the famous architect Sahip Ata, whose work is also prominent in Konya and Kayseri, this madrasa is

Neglected masterpiece

reckoned to be the most beautiful madrasa built by the Seljuks. This is by virtue of its design, the delicate stone-work on the porch and façade, and the lovely mosaics of brick and tile in the mescit (prayer room) and the two iwans (three-sided niche-like rooms). As with the Gök Madrasa in Amasya, it looks incongruous today among the modern buildings with washing hanging from the balco-nies, almost as if it is an oversight which someone forgot to knock down.

On the walk back towards the park you pass the **Ulu Cami** which you may well not even have noticed on the way past the first time. This thoroughly inconspicuous building is the oldest Turkish building in Sivas. With its leaning austere minaret and its corrugated iron roof it looks from the outside more like a factory than a mosque. Inside it is of the forest-of-pillars variety.

The Tourist Office in Sivas is inside the Wilayet building on the main roundabout square, and the hotels and restaur-ants are on the main street near the roundabout end. With a population of 200,000 Sivas is three times bigger than Tokat, and is quite a thriving agricultural centre today. In modern times the town is proud to have served as the **Atatürk's call** location for the Sivas Congress in 1919 where Atatürk first announced that Turkey would be independent and that a national assembly would be called. This was therefore the start of the War of Independence that would lead to the emergence of Turkey as we know it today.

OUT OF THE WAY TO DIVRIĞI

From Sivas, those with an interest in Islamic architecture usually feel it is imperative to make the journey to **Divriği**, 174 km away in a remote valley. The reason is the mosque-madrasa which is certainly unique in Turkey with its highly ornate portals and façades looking like something from the Indian Mogul empire.

Divriği dilemma

The problem with a visit to Divriği is where to go next. It takes two and a quarter hours to drive there from Sivas and the scenery is not exactly great enroute. The hillsides and landscape are barren with snow-topped mountains in the background. The road is mainly tarmac but those parts which are not are hard packed gravel which, though easy enough to drive on, are good puncture material. Roads leading out are bad, so that by and large people tend to drive all the way back to Sivas to spend the night: a lot of driving to see just one building. The alternatives are not to bother, but to go from Sivas south to Kayseri and Cappadocia, or north to Tokat and Amasya, or to take one of the bad routes leading out. Because of its remoteness and dearth of suitable hotels, Divriği is not included on coach tour itineraries.

Originally a Byzantine stronghold, Divriği was taken by the Seljuks after the Turkish victory at Malazgirt and held until 1251. During this time it was beautified with some of the most lovely and unusual of Seljuk buildings, which, uncharacteristically, the Mongols spared when they took the town in the 13th C, though they dismantled the citadel.

The Mosque-Madrasa

The altitude at Divriği is 1250 metres. The town is unremarkable, with a fair degree of building work going on. As the road drops into it you must look for the pointed dome and the minaret of the mosque in sand-coloured stone. The madrasa shares the qibla wall (that facing Mecca) with the mosque, making the whole appear like one large building from the outside. The mosque-madrasa was commissioned in 1228 by the local emir and his wife. There is no signpost, so you must simply fork off to the right and head in that direction.

Mogul and pre-Islamic influences

The lavishly carved **portals** are abundantly decorated with huge floral and geometric motifs and owe much to Mogul examples. You almost expect to see on closer inspection representations of elephants decorated with elaborate trappings. There is in fact the occasional bird and animal hidden in the garlanded fronds. The central Asiatic Turks had always used animal figures, scrolls and fronds in their decoration. After the conversion of the Seljuks to Islam, abstract geometric patterns were incorporated as well. The carved animal and human figures on the Şifahiye Madrasa and Gök Madrasa at Sivas, the türbes of Niğde and Kayseri, the walls of Diyarbakır and these portals at Divriği are all a continuation of the animal style employed by the old Turkish tribes of central Asia.

The **madrasa**, originally a hospital, is now derelict, but a guardian is usually nearby to open it for you and will proudly produce his visitors book for you to sign. The second portal leads into the **mosque**. Some of its carpets are virtually museum pieces, and the minbar is one of the most beautiful in Turkey. In the middle of the mosque is a rectagonal water basin above which is a dome open to the sky. The most elaborate of the three portals is round the corner on the far side of the mosque; this is the most reminiscent of Mogul art. Craftsmen from Tiflis in Georgia and Ahlat in Armenia are known to have worked on both buildings.

The mosque-madrasa is spectacular, but its setting does much to detract from its beauty. Were it situated on a lovely hillside terrace surrounded by trees and gardens, a visit to it would be much more enjoyable and memorable.

PRACTICAL INFORMATION

Enroute from Ankara after a 45-minute drive on the road to Sungurlu a BP station **restaurant** stands by the roadside in a pleasant setting among some trees.

BOĞAZKALE
Hitit Motel (1-star), Tel: 42409, at Sungurlu (30 km from Boğazkale). Prettily laid out round a swimming pool which functions from June until September. The motel itself is open all the year round. 20 rooms, all carpeted and with private bathroom, and balconies onto the gardens and pool. The motel is linked to the nearby **restaurant**, used by coaches, where dinner and breakfast are taken and paid for separately. The food is good and service almost too efficient. Good value.

There is also a very simple **motel** at the entrance to Boğazkale village itself. Its setting is excellent and it has a **restaurant** but no hot water. There is **camping** next door.

ÇORUM
Turban Çorum (1-star), Tel: 5311. One of the lowliest in the Turban chain of hotels.

AMASYA
Turban Amasya (2-star), Tel: 3134. The only place to consider unless you crave squalor. 36 rooms, situated on the rock-tomb side of the river towards the northern outskirts of town; the front rooms have balconies overlooking the river. It forms a haven of civilisation and cleanliness after a few hours walking round the dusty town. Attentive service in the **restaurant**, and the food is very good.

SULUOVA

If the Turban Amasya is full, the Sara-
çoğlu Muzaffer Turistik Tesisleri (2-star),
Tel: 783, is the only other option, on the
Samsun road 30 km away. It is adequate
but not as good as the Turban. 15 rooms.

SIVAS

Hotel Kösk (1-star), Tel: 1150. 44 rooms,
fairly basic.

The Şadrivan **restaurant** near the Madi-
mak Oteli (see map) is the best in town
and is surprisingly classy.

Sivas has 2 **flights** a week to Ankara
(Wednesday and Sunday, 45 minutes),
connecting to İstanbul (3½ hours including
transfer).

Average Temperature (Celsius):

J	F	M	A	M	J
—4.0	—2.4	2.1	8.5	13.3	16.7
J	A	S	O	N	D
19.6	19.6	15.6	10.6	4.8	—1.0

Maximum Temperature:

J	F	M	A	M	J
11.8	17.5	25.2	28.4	31.0	34.5
J	A	S	O	N	D
38.3	37.6	33.7	30.5	24.0	15.5

Minimum temperature:

J	F	M	A	M	J
—34.6	—34.4	—24.0	—11.0	—5.5	—0.6
J	A	S	O	N	D
3.0	3.2	—3.8	—9.0	—24.4	—30.2

CENTRAL EASTERN TURKEY

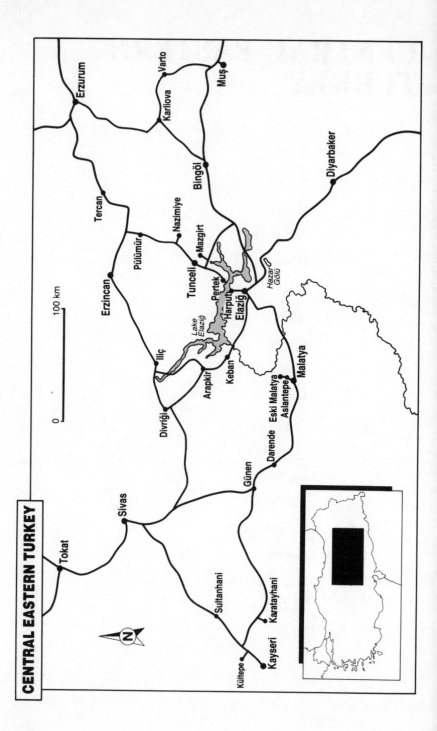

CENTRAL EASTERN TURKEY

100 km

0

N

Tokat
Sivas
Erzurum
Tercan
Erzincan
Ilıç
Arapkir
Divriği
Günen
Sultanhani
Karatayhani
Kültepe
Kayseri
Darende
Eski Malatya
Aslantepe
Malatya
Keban
Harput
Elazığ
Pertek
Tunceli
Pülümür
Nazimiye
Mazgirt
Bingöl
Karliova
Varto
Muş
Diyarbaker
Lake Elazığ
Hazar Gölü

TO KEBAN AND ELAZIĞ

Southeast of Divriği is **Keban**, a new town built as a result of the **Keban Dam**. The dam is guarded and access is forbidden. This colossal engineering project was the first of a series of dams on the Euphrates designed to bring electricity and irrigation to the underprivileged parts of the country, a series to culminate in the even more colossal Atatürk Dam near Urfa, due for completion in 1990.

Salvaging the Early Bronze Age

The Keban Dam meant the flooding of 50 known archaeological sites. Most of the sites were early Bronze Age settlements, important for contributing evidence to man's first settled existence in Anatolia after he had stopped his nomadic wandering and hunting. Five foreign archaeological teams, two British, two American and one German, all self-financed, set to work to excavate as many of these sites as they could before the flooding in 1974. What they salvaged is on display in the new museum at Elazığ.

Water disputes   One curious side effect of the dam has been on the carp which used to breed in the upper stretches of the Euphrates. They now collect in confusion before the dam, creating a fisherman's paradise. The waters are not entirely for Turkish use; Turkey insists it will honour its international obligations in the use of Euphrates water, but downstream, Syria and Iraq remain worried. Whenever a water or electricity shortage occurs in Syria, the Syrians accuse the Turks of turning off the tap upstream.

From Keban the road winds on southwards to **Elazığ**, founded only in 1862 by Sultan Abdel Aziz. Flights link it to Ankara and Istanbul four times a week. The approach is on enormously wide, endless and straight boulevards, almost empty of traffic. An unremarkable place, Elazığ does offer a convenient overnight stop at the large and comfortable Büyük Elazığ Hotel, used largely by local businessmen. Tourists are a rarity in Elazığ and this at least is a point in its favour. As yet little known, Elazığ does in fact have one remarkable sight to offer, and this **A remarkable** is the new **museum** on the campus of the Euphrates Univer-**museum . . .** sity outside the town, which now houses the items salvaged from the Keban excavations before the flooding. It is a surprisingly large museum, and the collection of Urartian objects on display here— gold belts, ivories and jewellery— is even more magnificent than that at the Ankara museum. Upstairs there is an ethnographic section with costumes and carpets.

The town's other distinction is its grapes, the long white kecik memesi (goat's teat) and the okuzgözü (ox-eye), a full midnight blue grape from which the famous full-bodied red Buzbağ wine is made. Buzbağ means 'ice vineyard', not bagpipe as one somehow feels it should. If this area was in fact where Anatolian man had his first settlements, it could well have been here too that he first cultivated the grape, an accomplishment thought by some to have originated in Eastern Turkey.

. . . and superb grapes

Abandoned Town by the Lake

Elazığ is not on the lake, but by driving 5 km to the north you can visit the old fortress city of **Harput** on a hill from where you can at least see the water. Now almost derelict, its population moved down to Elazığ when the new town was built. The road out of town to it leads through a heavily militarised area with army camp after army camp, presumably stationed here to guard the dam. This road is a dead end leading to Harput only, and after the military camps it climbs a hill past a modern housing development into the old ruinous town of Harput. Inside is a maze of yellow signs pointing to various mosques scattered over the hilltop.

Follow the sign to the kale and you will pass the 12th C **Ulu Cami**, with a severely leaning red brick minaret; from here you have a first view of the **castle** and the most impressive, as the walls have real height from this vantage point. On entering the gateway round the side, however, there is virtually nothing to be seen except a grassy mound and a few crumbling remains of walls. Originally a Byzantine fortress, restored by the Turcoman Artukid rulers of the 13th C, it was built on a group outcrop of rock towering over the valley to the east. It appears impregnable yet was taken by Tamerlane, by a Persian shah and finally in 1515 by the Ottoman Selim the Grim. Down below are the remains of a ruined han, Dabakhane, and a crumbling bath. On the castle hilltop you can visit the 13th C **tomb of Arap Baba**, Father Arab, much revered locally. After removing your shoes and entering through a low door, a plain wooden coffin lies before you. The guardian may raise the lid and pull aside the clean grave clothes to reveal the embalmed naked and hairless body, brown like leather, with the back of its head bashed in — not a sight for the squeamish. Only 100 years ago Harput had 800 shops, ten mosques, ten religious schools, eight churches, eight libraries, 12 hans and 90 baths. Earthquakes helped with the destruction and precipitated the move to the new town of Elazığ.

Dead saint

Amphibious Excursion

From Elazığ the road on to **Pertek**, site of a superb medieval castle, is no longer marked. Setting off towards the northwest from Elazığ it is quite a narrow tarmac road, evidently no longer maintained. It winds through pleasant countryside, reaching the lake after some 20 km. Before the creation of the Keban reservoir this was the main Erzurum road, but now it runs straight into the lake, eerie and unannounced. Road maps more often than not show the road as continuing across the lake, but in practice you would need an amphibious vehicle to follow it along the lake bed to reach Pertek village on the other side. A car ferry is in service, but traffic is very light indeed.

Island castle

It is a tragedy that this magnificent **castle** (1367) **of Eski Pertek** that once stood on its hill proudly guarding the river valley of the Euphrates is now an indignant rocky island outcrop, cut off in the middle of the lake. Previously accessible by simply scaling the hill from the roadside, the superbly preserved castle is now impossible to reach except by swimming (not a feat to be undertaken lightly), or by hiring a boat privately from Pertek (not straightforward as boats have some difficulty in mooring at the steep rocky slopes).

ROUTES FROM ELAZIĞ

The Way South

From Elazığ you can drive south to Diyarbakır on a pleasant route if you have already seen or want to by-pass Malatya or Nemrut Dağ. This route takes you past **Hazar Gölü** 25 km on, the lake source of the Tigris. From here the river flows south through Turkey, into Iraq through Baghdad and out into the Persian Gulf, 1840 km away.

Source of the Tigris

Near the shore is a simple restaurant serving fish from the lake. Large and white, they are like freshwater mackerel and are very cheap. Lake eels are sometimes on offer. The restaurant has a few tables laid outside, and across the road on the shore is a row of bathing huts, clearly a spot frequented by locals for summer bathing. Unless you are extremely hardy you would have to wait until late June before the slightly salty water is warm enough for a swim, as the altitude is 1220 metres and the lake is 90 metres deep in the middle.

The Way North

One unusual route rarely tried by travellers is via Tunceli and Erzincan to Erzurum. A lot of the route, though highly picturesque, is difficult and there is one 25 km stretch of bad unsurfaced road. Accommodation is very scarce, especially in **Tunceli**. The village is surrounded by a high wall of mountains and the region is one of wild charm and great natural beauty with many mountain lakes and excellent hunting in the hills.

How to catch a bear

Among the animals found here are bears, and the locals will tell you that they have a special method of catching them. Bears, it would appear, are frightened by two things: fire and human nudity. The villagers hunt them for their skins, tracking the bear through the snow to the cave where he lives. A man then takes off his clothes, binds his forearm with thick material and goes into the cave. When the bear snarls, the man plunges his hand into its mouth and the bear bites on it. A bear's teeth are apparently inward curving and not very strong, so when the man pulls, the bear follows so as not to break its teeth. Once pulled out of the cave, the other villagers can shoot him.

Some of the prettiest places to visit are the waterfalls at **Karapğlan** and **Nazimiye**, the Bağın hot water springs on the banks of the Peri creek at **Mazgirt** and the mineral water springs at **Pülümür**. The mountainous landscape is also ideally suited to guerilla warfare, and several clashes between Kurdish dissidents and the Turkish army have recently taken place here.

Turning left at the T-junction towards Erzincan you come after about 20 km to a road to the right which leads to **Altıntepe** (Gold Hill), an important Urartian site. Here, since 1959, Turkish archaeologists have uncovered a wealth of objects. Tombs are built into the side of the hill in Urartian fashion, as at Van Kalesi. In one of them a man and a woman were found completely undisturbed in stone sarcophagi, the woman in all her best clothes and jewellery, her household objects in bronze, pottery and wood laid around her. The man was buried with many weapons and a beautiful gold belt. The famous bronze cauldron on three legs with bulls' head handles now in the Ankara museum was also found here. On the hilltop above, a **temple, palace** and **great hall** have been found in very good condition, better than that at Çavuştepe, one wall even having *coloured murals*. On terraces below are the foundations of spacious **houses** with three to six rooms. The richness of the finds here when compared to those at Van Kalesi, Çavuştepe and other Urartian sites indicates just how much must have been stolen and illegally exported from these other sites before proper precautions were taken by the government to clamp down on such activities.

A further 16 km brings you into **Erzincan**, rebuilt after the terrible earthquake of 1939. Its name is said to mean 'life crusher', graphically describing the havoc earthquakes have wrought here. The destruction has been especially sad, as in the 19th C Erzincan was considered one of the most beautiful cities of Asia with over 79 mosques. The region fell under the rule of Armenia in the 4th C AD and even until the end of the 19th C the Armenians accounted for around one-sixth of the population. During the First World War the Russians occupied the city for 18 months.

Life crusher

On the route from Erzincan to Erzurum you pass after 90 km the village of Tercan, near which stands the distinctive conical **türbe of Mama Hatun** built in the 13th C. This magnificent türbe stands in the middle of a circular walled courtyard entered through a large stalactite portal. Close by is a **caravanserai**. The tallest stable was for camels, the middle one for horses and the smallest for donkeys and mules. This and the türbe were built by the Saltuklu emir of Erzurum in 1192 and are more restrained than Seljuk architecture. The nearby Mama Hatun **bridge** is also from the late 12th C.

The road leads on through attractive mountain scenery to Aşkale, where it joins with the route from Trabzon to Erzurum described later.

The Way East from Elazığ

Continuing east from the Tunceli fork you can pass through Bingöl and Muş, eventually reaching Bitlis and Lake Van, a drive of 325 km, possible in a day. **Bingöl** (a thousand lakes), a Kurdish town set in the mountains, was destroyed by an earthquake in 1966. An earthquake belt runs north-east from here to Varto and southwest to Malatya, where a minor earthquake claimed nine victims as recently as May 1986. The region is rich in lakes and streams and is an area for pasturing sheep, goats and cattle. Much of the population is semi-nomadic.

Just after Bingöl a spectacular road forks off left and runs north through the mountains to Karlıova and then to Erzurum. It is motorable but difficult and should be driven with care.

The road on eastward crosses a pass at 1640 metres before dropping to reach **Muş**. A town with little to offer the tourist today, Muş was till the end of the 19th C lived in by poverty stricken Armenians, with Kurds in the mountains and on the edges of the plain. The Armenian **castle** above the plain is a sorry ruin. In the hills around, reachable with difficulty and a guide, are several ruined Armenian **monasteries**, notably Surp Karapet, known locally as Çanlı Kilise, with fine stone carvings. To reach Surp Karapet you fork (left) towards Varto 45 km to the north. Enroute near the village of Tepeköy on the steep bank of the Murat Nehri are the ruins of the Urartian castle, **Kayalıdere Kalesi**, excavated under Seton Lloyd, where many rich individual finds were made in an Urartian temple. Near the village of Yaygın a track leads off right 4 km to the village of Ziyaret. Here you must take a guide and walk two hours in a north-northeast direction to reach **Surp Karapet** (also known as the Church of John the Baptist). Taxis which know the route will also drive there. Little remains of the once large monastery, as the stones are being systematically carried off by the local Kurds for their own building purposes.

Armenian monasteries

On the Way West

If, from Elazığ, you want to go to Cappadocia, the region of weird lunar landscapes and rock-cut churches, the drive can be done in one long and boring day via Malatya to Kayseri. The route to Malatya takes one and a half hours through featureless dull landscapes of barren hills. The high point comes shortly after halfway there, where the road begins a steep descent off the central Anatolian plateau, often leaving the cloud and rain behind as you drop down into the plain of the **Euphrates**. The first sight of this colossal river is awe-inspiring: even diminished by the Keban Dam upstream, it still has a power and a majesty unlike other large rivers. Much of this is obviously association, but one can readily imagine life and early civilisation growing up on its banks. The water is a deep green as it flows

Majestic river

through the serene and fertile valley. The road crosses high above it on the old bridge, but even higher, a new suspension bridge is nearing completion. Below on the bank is a heavily ruined Ottoman caravanserai, built by Sultan Murad.

The road now remains flat all the way to Malatya. Traffic is light and so speeds can be high. On the outskirts of Malatya as you approach from Elazığ a yellow sign points off right to Aslantepe and a blue sign to Eski Malatya. The colours are significant because Aslantepe, a Neo-Hittite site, is a ruin, whereas Eski Malatya despite its name (old Malatya) is now an inhabited village again on the site of the old Seljuk town. 3 km after this turn-off the road splits with no signposts. Veer right for Aslantepe which you then reach after about 5 km near the village of Ordusu.

Lion Hill

The name **Aslantepe**, Lion Hill, is so called because of the stone lions found here guarding the north gate to the Hittite city. This gate, reconstructed with the lions, is now in the vast central hall of sculptures at the Ankara museum. The Hittite name of this site is Kammanu, later Milid (the original name of Malatya), and was the capital of a new Hittite kingdom after the fall of Hattuşaş. The lions, with beautifully stylised manes, are thought to be 11th C BC. The figure of a king cut from a vast limestone block over 3 metres high was found near the gate, and is now also in the museum. This colossal handsome figure with a curly beard is thought to be 8th C BC and shows much Assyrian influence in his hairstyle and dress. Also found on site and likewise removed to the Ankara museum were a series of five reliefs depicting a king pouring a libation of wine to the weather god, the weather god attacking the flaming dragon and scenes from lion and stag hunting. These hunting scenes again show Assyrian influence with the hunters riding in chariots.

Italian archaeologists have been working regularly each summer at Aslantepe and the excavations on site are confusing for the uninitiated and not very exciting. The setting, however, overlooking the green valley of a Euphrates tributary, is attractive. It was not, like Hattuşaş, a natural fortress, but the Neo-Hittites brought with them from their Hattuşaş ancestors their superb wall-building techniques and so the place was adequately fortified against the Urartians and Assyrians, serving for some while as the regional capital until it finally disappeared from history. Before the excavations could begin in 1932, a ruined 16th C Turkish palace standing on top of the tumulus had to be laboriously removed.

For **Eski Malatya** you continue straight on for about 7 km after the fork to Aslantepe. On arrival the walls are visible to the right of the road, but very little remains inside them.

Ruins re-inhabited A newish village of 2000 people has grown up scattered among the ruins and open spaces. Originally a Roman and then a Byzantine town with 53 churches and numerous monasteries, it has suffered from systematic re-use of its masonry. Add to that sacking by Byzantine emperors, Arab armies and a visit from the ubiquitous Mongol Tamerlane, and you begin to understand why so little is left above ground.

The **walls** cover an extensive area and you can drive round large sections of it, but it is difficult to drive right inside. The best approach is through the south wall. Once you have spotted the distinctive red brick minaret of the **Ulu Cami**, you should to stop and walk to it along the narrow paths winding round inside the walled area. There are newly built houses here, with a large new primary school near the Ulu Cami. The mosque itself, as so often with Ulu Camiler, looks totally unprepossessing from the outside with its new corrugated iron roof. it is still very much in use. Inside, however, it is worth a look for its open arched courtyard with abstract blue tile decoration and graceful lettering on the tiles. From the school a road runs north along a narrow street to the present village square. 100 metres to the right of the square and set down at a lower level is a fine 17th C Ottoman **caravanserai** which has been largely restored. Along the outside wall facing the village was a line of little shops to supply the needs of the travellers. Inside there are fireplaces with their tapering stone canopies, one for each of the parties staying the night. The han does not have the beauty and ornamentation of the earlier Seljuk ones to be seen in central Anatolia, but its size and preservation nevertheless make it impressive and interesting to imagine with Ottoman travellers warming themselves in front of their fires in the cold nights of the plateau.

ALONG THE ROAD FROM MALATYA TO KAYSERI

Malatya, like Elazığ, is a new town of the 19th C that grew up when the old town of Eski Malatya declined. A large sprawling and ugly city, it is quite a centre of commerce for the area, with a fast-growing population of 250,000. However, it offers quite sophisticated shopping, and surprisingly good food at the Melita restaurant. Capital of the province of the same name, Malatya has its own airport with daily flights to Ankara with connections to Istanbul. Fruit has long been one of its specialities, and today dried

Apricots and apples

apricots are its main export. In the past it was famous too for the quality of its apples, but today it is impossible to buy a true Malatya apple because the only trees remaining are in the garden of a local family which keeps them all for private consumption, a sure sign that they must be good.

On the Road

The road on towards Kayseri climbs over many ranges, reaching 2000 metres at its highest point. The road condition is good and high speeds can be averaged but there is a dearth of petrol stations en route so it is worth filling up in Malatya. The drive of 351 km takes four hours with no stops.

The best han in central Anatolia

Some 60 km before Kayseri a yellow sign points off left 12 km to **Karatay Hanı**. If you are not intending to see either of the two Sultanhanı (one near Aksaray, the other near Kayseri), this is a detour you should make if you have the time, as it is a fine and well-preserved han, in many ways the most rewarding han to visit in central Anatolia. The drive also takes you through some interesting Turkish villages. Karatay Hanı was built by the great Seljuk vizir Celalettin Karatay in 1240; the quality of the stonework throughout is very high, and the whole was carefully restored in 1964. On the impressive *outside walls*, human and animal shapes are used as water spouts. To the right of the entrance is the *hazine* or treasury (corresponding to a modern reception desk and safe area) with a small door leading to the inner treasury for the valuables. To the left of the entrance were the *kitchen and dining room*. On the right side of the open courtyard were the series of *bedrooms* for the guests, with the three rooms nearest the entrance forming the *bath* with openings in the vaulted roof. The vaulted arcade on the left of the courtyard was used as a *depot*, a *bazaar* and as *stabling* for the animals.

117

Steps near the kitchen area lead up onto the roof where you can see deep water tanks above the hazine and the kitchen for use in the kitchen and baths. There are also two *mosques*. The high main *hall* at the end of the courtyard was used as the winter quarters and has a fine conical dome.

Assyrian traders 20 km before Kayseri, after the road from Sivas joins in from the right, there is a yellow sign to the right to **Kültepe Karum**, the site of the Assyrian trading colony which has yielded so many of the displays in the Assyrian section of the Ankara museum. Like so many very ancient sites, it is interesting for its history rather than its visible remains today, and a visit here does more for the expert than the interested amateur. Excavated since 1948 by a Turkish professor, it was here that he found the earliest Anatolian written documents in cuneiform script. In the megaron-style of buildings found here, archaeologists have also noticed a striking resemblance to the Mycenaean palaces of a thousand years later. Long before they built an empire of their own, the Assyrians of northern Mesopotamia established great trading colonies in Anatolia to reap the rewards of the prosperity of the times (2nd millenium BC), and they called these trading colonies 'karums', the one here at Kültepe (Kanesh to the Assyrians) being the chief of these to which all the others were subordinate. They imported tin, garments and cloth using caravans of 200 to 250 donkeys (the black donkeys of Cappadocia), in exchange for gold and silver.

Access to this centre at Kültepe was by way of Carchemish or Harran to Birecik, Maraş and Elbistan, and this became a great corridor for cultural as well as commercial exchange. It is perhaps the most ancient and important route of cultural exchange in the world, following either the Euphrates up into the heart of eastern Anatolia, or westwards along tributaries through the Taurus mountains to central Anatolia and the West.

The Assyrians had no desire to exercise political power in Anatolia but confined themselves to purely commercial affairs. Their cuneiform tablets did not therefore concern themselves with weighty political treaties, but with dull **Trade marks** records of their business transactions. They introduced too the habit of using cylindrical seals, already widespread in Mesopotamia; just as had happened in Mesopotamia, their manufacture and use developed into an art in its own right. The appeal of marking something with your own stamp has always been universal: today's equivalent can be seen in the designs of company logos, seeking to project a particular image.

On reaching the junction with the main Sivas road from the right, you can make a detour of 30 km north towards Sivas to see the great caravanserai called **Sultanhanı** (45 km

The Sultanhanı near Kayseri

north of Kayseri), built in 1236. It is on a slightly smaller scale than that of its namesake near Aksaray, but is otherwise very similar in design and appearance. It too has been carefully restored. It does not warrant a special detour unless you are not able to see the other Sultanhanı or the Karatay Hanı.

PRACTICAL INFORMATION

ELAZIĞ

Büyük Elazığ (2-star), Tel: 22001. 150 adequate rooms with private bathrooms, opened in 1982. Fine **restaurant** on the first floor, and on the roof in summer. Much used by Turkish businessmen. Breakfast is taken in the lounge cum salon area in armchairs, Middle Eastern-style.

The Akar and the Erdem Hotels are both poor to basic, with no restaurant.

There are **flights** to Ankara every Monday, Wednesday, Friday and Sunday (1 hour 25 minutes) with connections to İstanbul ($4\frac{1}{2}$ hours including transfer).

HAZAR GÖLÜ
Restaurant on the lakeshore offering the lake fish, like a freshwater mackerel. Very simple but pleasant and cheap. In summer months you can sit outdoors and even swim in the lake if you are hardy.

ERZINCAN
Urartu Hotel (1-star), Tel: 1561. 58 rooms.

Average temperature (Celsius):

J	F	M	A	M	J
-3.7	-1.8	3.4	10.3	15.6	19.7
J	A	S	O	N	D
23.7	23.9	18.9	12.1	5.6	-0.6

Maximum temperature:

J	F	M	A	M	J
12.6	17.2	23.4	29.5	31.6	35.6
J	A	S	O	N	D
40.0	40.5	36.4	31.4	24.9	16.7

Minimum temperature:

J	F	M	A	M	J
-32.5	-32.4	-21.1	-11.1	-4.2	3.1
J	A	S	O	N	D
5.7	5.9	0.4	-6.8	-17.4	-25.9

MUŞ
Zengök Hotel, Tel: 511. 42 rooms, very basic.

MALATYA
Kent Hotel (1-star), Tel: 12175. 51 rooms, and the Sinan (1-star), Tel: 12907, are both about the same.

The Melita **restaurant**, round the corner from the Sinan Hotel, offers excellent food and presentation, and is much frequented by its business clientele. Even coffee comes swathed in rose petals, with a complimentary rose petal liqueur.

There are daily **flights** to Ankara (1 hour 30 minutes), with connections five times a week to İstanbul ($3\frac{1}{2}$ hours including transfer).

Average temperature (Celsius):

J	F	M	A	M	J
-1.1	0.9	6.4	13.0	18.4	23.1
J	A	S	O	N	D
27.2	27.2	22.4	15.5	8.1	1.8

Maximum temperature:

J	F	M	A	M	J
15.4	17.7	25.4	29.6	35.0	37.2
J	A	S	O	N	D
41.8	40.6	36.7	34.4	24.0	15.8

Minimum temperature:

J	F	M	A	M	J
-25.1	-21.2	-11.8	-6.6	1.9	5.8
J	A	S	O	N	D
10.1	9.3	3.2	-1.1	-9.0	-22.2

CAPPADOCIA, KONYA AND SOUTH TO THE COAST

Kayseri

Cappadocia Proper
  Ürgüp
  Ortahisar
  Üçhisar
  Göreme
  Çavuşin
  Zilve
  Sarıhan
  Avanos
  Özkonak
  Soğanlı
  Derinkuyu
  Kaymaklı
  Nevşehir
  Hacıbektaş
  Ihlara
  Sultanhanı

Konya

South to the coast at Silifke
  Karaman
  Çatalhüyük
  Alahan
  Mut
  Silifke
  Diocaesarea
  Kız Kalesi
  Heaven and Hell
  Pompeopolis
  Mersin

South to the coast at Tarsus
  Eski Gümüş
  Niğde

Practical Information

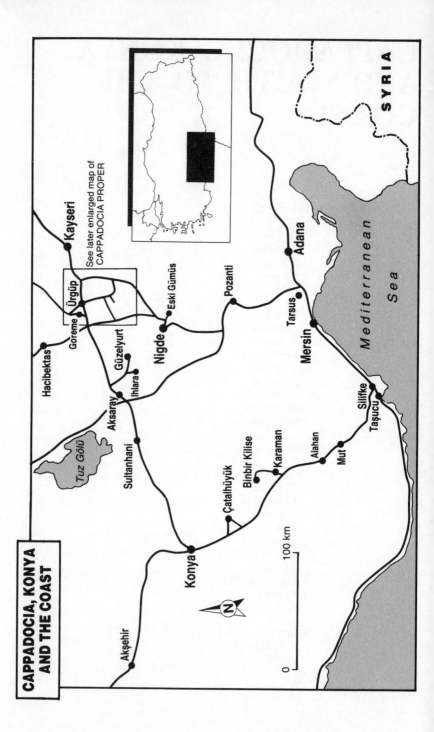

CAPPADOCIA, KONYA AND THE COAST

See later enlarged map of CAPPADOCIA PROPER

SYRIA

Mediterranean Sea

Kayseri
Hacibektas
Göreme
Ürgüp
Güzelyurt
Ihlara
Aksaray
Tuz Gölü
Sultanhani
Eski Gümüş
Nigde
Pozanti
Tarsus
Adana
Mersin
Silifke
Taşucu
Mut
Alahan
Karaman
Binbir Kilise
Çatalhüyük
Konya
Akşehir

N

0   100 km

KAYSERI

Legacy of a volcano

Kayseri lies on the eastern fringes of Cappadocia, but there is no sign here of the famous Cappadocian landscapes. Their creator however is here, in the form of the now extinct volcano, **Mt Erciyes**, rising behind the town though visible only in fine weather. Its eruptions eons ago spewed out the volcanic tufa which was to be moulded by wind, rain and man into fantastical shapes. At 3916 metres it is snow-capped all the year round and is a minor ski resort in winter. A road leads quite a long way up it to a mountain hut, and you can go for summer walks here in the mountain air.

The approach to **Kayseri** from Malatya is, as so often with the towns of Eastern Turkey, somewhat unsalubrious. A wide approach road leads through scruffy suburbs and eventually brings you to the main central square with the inevitable equestrian Atatürk, and the black walls of the citadel looming just off to the left.

The modern name Kayseri is an adaptation of the name Caesarea given to the town in honour of Caesar Augustus when this was the capital of the Roman province of Cappadocia Prima. As the main town of Cappadocia, Kayseri owes its importance to the fact that it stands astride the major trade routes east from the Aegean and north and south between the Mediterranean and the Black Sea. But its exposed position on the high plateau made it easy prey for all the invading armies which poured to and fro across Anatolia in medieval times, including Arabs, Turcomans, Seljuks, Mongols, Mamelukes and finally Ottomans in 1515. Today the monuments which have survived and which are the town's 'tourist attractions' are the 13th and 14th C Islamic buildings, built either by the Seljuks or by the later Turcoman emirs, first the Danishmends, then the Karamanids, who ruled the area after the collapse of Seljuk power. Their settings are uninspiring, on flat ground surrounded by ugly modern buildings which always manage to look half-finished. Even more unfortunate is the black basalt used in the older constructions, a colour so dingy and depressing, especially when wet, that it is hard to find the architecture beautiful.

Basalt architecture

The **Sahibiye Madrasa** off the main square, built by the Seljuks in 1268, is now a parade of shops selling plastic knick-knacks and newspapers. There were plans in the 1970s to convert it into a medical clinic or student residence, in line with its original function. Sahip Ata, the famous Seljuk architect who designed it, would wince if he could see it now.

Built between 1210 and 1226, the **citadel** is undergoing extensive 'renovation' and is closed to the public while it is being turned into a shopping precinct with jewellery shops for tourists. From the outside it is well-preserved with all 19 of its black basalt towers standing, and is considered one of the finest extant examples of Seljuk military architecture. This is difficult to appreciate today because on the dead flat ground the walls scarcely rise above the encroaching modern buildings.

Caveat emptor

Behind the citadel, the **bazaar** area of the town is also being restored, and much of it is therefore closed off. There are still shops you can look at in the area however, though you will probably be persecuted by determined carpet dealers. All Kayseri traders are notoriously shrewd: one story tells of a merchant who sold a neighbour a white donkey and then stole it from him in the night and painted it black. The next morning, the neighbour told his tale of woe to the merchant, who sympathised with him and promptly sold it back to him. Maybe it was the Kayseri merchants who first coined the Turkish proverb: 'If God wants to make a poor man happy, he makes him lose his ass and then find it again'. Beware of 'Kayseri silk' which is rayon in most people's vocabulary. In the food shops you can try the local speciality 'pastırma', thin-sliced beef dried in the sun and rolled in garlic and herbs, with a slightly aniseed flavour. It is a sort of Turkish version of Parma ham with none of the subtlety but you may well find yourself addicted. It is also found in many other parts of Eastern Turkey and is good for picnics as it lasts well.

Opposite the citadel, just off a small open area at the back of which is the tourist Office, stands the **Huant Foundation**, the first mosque complex to be built by the Seljuks in Anatolia. Now an ethnographic museum of local crafts, it has a fine Turcoman tent decked out with all the nomadic paraphernalia. The complex consists of the mosque itself, its madrasa, a türbe, a bath and a çeşme (fountain). Founded in 1238, the name comes from the founder, a Greek woman, Mahperi Huant Hatun, wife of Alaeddin Keykubad I. The large building with the huge outer façade is the mosque, and the smaller building to the left is the madrasa—until recently the archaeological museum, now in a modern building on the outskirts of town.

Tent-like tombs

On the way down to the museum you pass a number of Seljuk turret tombs with a high drum and conical dome, called 'kümbet' in Turkish. These were a distinctively Seljuk innovation introduced into Turkey from Persia, and with their conical shape are thought to hark back to tents. The style was later copied by the Danishmends and Karamanids. Mummified bodies were put in the crypt and above this on the main floor was a cenotaph and prayer room

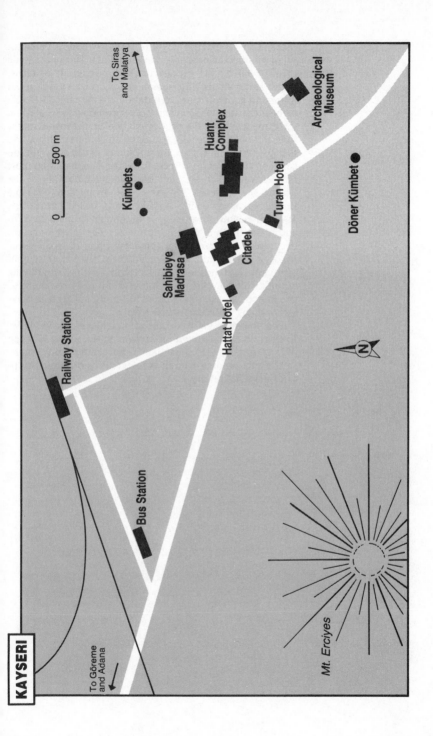

KAYSERI

To Siras
and Malatya

500 m

0

Kümbets

Huant
Complex

Archaeological
Museum

Sahibieye
Madrasa

Citadel

Turan Hotel

Döner Kümbet

Hattat Hotel

Railway Station

Bus Station

N

Mt. Erciyes

To Göreme
and Adana

reached by an external flight of steps. The most beautiful of all kümbets is probably the Hudabend Hatun at Niğde (1312) built by the Mongols, which has reliefs of birds, stages and animals with human heads, as well as the usual floral and geometric ornamentation. In the later Ottoman türbes, the sarcophagus and prayer room were located on the same level and the decoration was on the inside rather than the out and usually restricted to coloured glazed tile facings. Ottoman türbes are not found in the east, but are concentrated around Bursa, İznik and İstanbul. The most famous kümbet in Kayseri, the **Döner Kümbet**, is on the way to the museum. Its name, Revolving Kümbet (like the döner or revolving, kebab), is so called because its 12 sides suggest revolving. It is thought to date to 1276 and is the tomb of a Seljuk princess. The outer walls are decorated with tree of life symbols, a pair of winged leopards, a griffin and a two-headed eagle, the Seljuk symbol of royalty. It stands now, neglected and with grass growing out of its roof, looking faintly lost as if it had been dumped in someone's back yard. There are more kümbets in Kayseri than in any other Turkish town.

The new **museum** down the main street out towards Mt Erciyes houses many major finds from the site of Kültepe (47 km to the north), including pottery and cylinder seals. In the surrounding garden are several Neo-Hittite sculptures from Aslantepe.

CAPPADOCIA PROPER: GETTING YOUR BEARINGS

Approaches

From Kayseri the road onwards to Niğde passes through what must be one of the bleakest landscapes in Turkey, a flat featureless, treeless waste, with no hills, no contours at all. A yellow sign points off to the right 41 km to Göreme, opposite a flat lake just by a petrol station: this is the most direct approach to the fairy chimney landscape we think of as Cappadocia proper. If you reckon you will continue south and turn up the road through Derinkuyu and Kaymaklı (the underground cities), be warned that you are sentencing yourself to a further 120 km of bleak landscapes.

The first route is the best one to approach the Göreme region, soon becoming pleasantly hilly as it winds over the beginnings of the Cappadocian landscape. A third route, currently being built, will eventually be the best approach of all from the east, shortening the distance from the present 88 km to 50 km from Kayseri, and leading through Aksalar.

All these roads approaching from the east bring you into Ürgüp over a small bridge. Most buses and coaches in fact follow the dull route from Kayseri towards Ankara, then turning south to Avanos to aproach Ürgüp.

Suggested Excursions

Cappadocia covers a large area and the sheer number and variety of places to visit can be a little bewildering on first arrival. To help plan your stay, the following is a table of half-day excursions which can all be done from Ürgüp (or for that matter from Nevşehir or Avanos if you prefer).
(1) Ortahisar, Üçhisar (lunch), Göreme
(2) Çavuşin, Zilve (lunch), Avanos, Sarıhan, Özkonak, Peribacalar Valley
(3) Ürgüp, Mustafapaşa, Soğănlı (lunch), Derinkuyu, Kaymaklı, Nevşehir
(4) Ürgüp, Avanos (lunch), Hacıbektaş, Gülşehir, Nevşehir
(5) Nevşehir, Ihlara (lunch), Güzelyurt, (Sultanhanı if you are going on to Konya)
(6) Ürgüp, Mustafapaşa, Soğanlı (lunch), Eski Gümüş, Niğde (on to Adana the same day)

Base at Ürgüp

On arrival you can look over the hotels, as Ürgüp offers the fullest range of accommodation and is a good base from which to explore the region. The Kaya Motel in nearby Üçhisar village is probably the best place of all to stay, though it is only open from June to September.

Ürgüp is an attractive rural town situated in the heart of the main Cappadocian valleys, unlike Nevşehir 22 km to the west which is on the edge. A hilly place, the winding cobbled streets are lined with many grand **Greek houses** with fine loggias and carved decoration round the doors and windows. Many of the houses are set partly into the cave-riddled cliff faces, and the locals still use these caves where their predecessors lived, as garages, storage and stabling. The town's atmosphere is pleasant and calm, with only 7900 inhabitants. In the main street from the Büyük Hotel past the Tourist Information Park and Museum on the right and up the cobbled street past the banks, there are a series of very good shops for souvenirs. There is a vast selection of silver jewellery with a range of semi-precious stones like amethysts, lapis lazuli, jade, ivory, amber and garnet, good carpets, elaborate woodwork, boxes and metalwork. There is also a shop selling colourful woollen gloves and socks at government regulated prices, which are half what the children selling them to you in the street will try to charge. One genuine curiosity of the Ürgüp region is the travelling library on the back of a donkey, to tour the far flung areas of town. The inventive director of the local library, who first thought of this sensible idea in 1963, was voted Librarian of the Year in 1969.

Good shopping

Cappadocia, this region of weird volcanic landscapes and rock-carved churches, was largely forgotten by the Western world until 1907, when a visiting French priest, Guillaume de Jerphanion, decided to devote the rest of his life to the study of its churches, publishing his vast research in the 1930s and 1940s. Since then, and especially in the last five years, the renown of the area has spread worldwide and Cappadocia has become one of the most visited and most photographed areas of Turkey. Be warned therefore that the invasion of tourists, almost all in organised coach tours from all parts of Europe may mar your enjoyment of the region. The Göreme heartlands have been particularly hit by tourist development, with forests of signs and billboards advertising hotels and restaurants almost competing with the forests of fairy chimneys for your attention. It is possible, however, as an independent traveller, to get off the coach tour routes and visit some of the lesser known valleys like Soğanlı and Ihlara, where you can still enjoy untouched Cappadocian landscapes and churches. These are described later.

Tourist invasion . . .

. . . and how to avoid it

In winter the whole of Cappadocia is covered in snow and in many ways this is the best time to see it. The rock formations look more curious and unreal and above all there are no coach tours: all the sites stay open but the

Rock-cut pigeon cotes at Ürgüp

place is deserted. The tourist season begins in earnest in April and continues until the end of November. In spring Cappadocia remains remarkably cold and it is not unusual to have snowfalls early in May. The swimming pools of most of the hotels do not function until June when the real hot weather starts. August and September, though crowded, have the advantage of being the season when the local grapes, apples, pears, plums, apricots and walnuts ripen. The Wine Festival begins in Ürgüp in early September each year. Autumn is probably the most colourful season, when the apricot and poplar trees turn to lovely yellows, reds and greens under clear blue skies.

Formation of the Fairy Chimneys

Following the eruptions of 4000-metre Mt Erciyes near Kayseri over 30 million years ago, its volcanic ash consolidated into a soft porous rock called tufa, which covered an area of about 4000 square km. The soft tufa eroded during millenia of wind, snow and rain, but where it was protected by a harder block of stone above, the result was the curiously shaped fairy chimneys (or cones) seen today, some standing as much as 50 metres high and often still capped by the protecting fragment of hard stone. They are called 'fairy' partly because of their unreal appearance, but also because local folklore talks of men being carried off by 'peris' or fairies after venturing into old churches in the rocks. The greatest concentration of chimneys is in the Zilve valley and in the Peribacalar valley between Avanos and Ürgüp. Unlike the usual harsh greys and blacks of most volcanic landscapes, the rocks here are soft shades of pale grey, yellow, mauve, pink and umber. This variation in colour is due to the variety of metals and minerals spewed out during different eruptions. Where, in the cones, you appear to be looking into open caves or terraces, these were originally rooms, now exposed as the façades have eroded away. Some were also dovecotes, and the fallen façades expose the nests, rows of little holes in the rock face. A constant battle is waged between the tourist authorities and the local farmers, who like to block up the cave entrances and use the churches as pigeon-cotes. The pigeons are highly prized for their droppings which are used as fertiliser, perhaps accounting for the distinctive taste and bouquet of the local wine.

It is probable that even in pre-Christian times the rural population of Cappadocia made use of natural caves and the ease of extending them, and early Christians may have resorted to them to avoid pagan persecution. The area became an important frontier province during the 7th C AD when the Arab raids on the Byzantine Empire began. By now the soft tufa had been tunnelled and chambered to provide underground cities where a settled if cautious life could continue during difficult times. When the Byzantines re-established secure control between the 7th and 11th C, the troglodytic population surfaced, now carving their churches into rock faces and cliffs in the Göreme and Soğanlı areas, giving Cappadocia its fame today. Their churches and monasteries were many and small: the landscape was suitable for recluses in search of the spiritual life, and the region distant from the contending doctrines

of orthodox Constantinople and monophysite Syria. St Basil, a 4th C Father of the Church from Caesarea (Kayseri), opined that small and intimate disciplined communities were most conducive to religious feeling. At any rate, here they flourished, remarkable for being cut into the rock, but especially interesting for the church paintings, relatively well preserved, rich in colouring, and with an emotional intensity lacking in the formalism of Constantinople—and one of the few places where paintings from the Pre-Iconoclastic period have survived. Icons continued to be painted after the Seljuk conquest of the province in the 11th C, nor did the Ottoman conquest interfere with Christian practices in Cappadocia, where the countryside

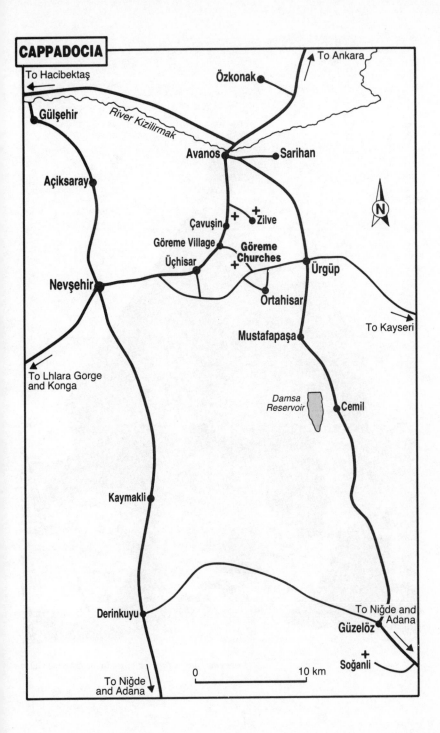

Storks nest atop a fairy chimney in the Göreme valley

remained largely Greek, with some Armenians. But decline set in and Göreme, Ihlara and Soğanlı lost their early importance. The Greeks finally ended their long history here with the mass exchange of populations between Greece and Turkey in 1923.

TOURING CAPPADOCIA

From Ürgüp you drive up out of the town uphill westwards, passing the vast coach tour haunt of the Turban Ürgüp Motel. After 5 km you follow the sign left 2 km to Ortahisar, a small village up a dead end valley.

Ortahisar and Uçhisar

The main attraction of **Ortahisar** is a huge honey-combed cone **fortress**. In the village are the **Harın Church** with huge columns and the **Sarıca Church**, ruined but with a good fresco of the Annunciation. A brief look round Ortahisar need detain you no longer then half an hour or so, but if you want to explore fully and do some walking, you can visit the 13th C **Halaşdere Church** (meaning hospital because it was used as such in the past), 1.5 km away, a vast monastic ensemble on several floors thought to have been carved by Armenian stonemasons; the **Tavşanlı** (Rabbit) **Church**, 3 km away, with fine frecoes and a lot of unusual green painting; the **Balkan churches**, 2 km away, a monastic ensemble with a few frescoes; the **Kepez churches**, 3 km away; the **Uzun** (Grape) **Church**; and finally the **Pancarlı** (Beet) **Church**, still in use till 1923 and with 11th C frescoes. You will need a guide to find these churches, unless you want to spend the entire day wandering about the valleys in the hope that you will stumble on them.

From Ortahisar you return to the main Ürgüp road and continue west towards Nevşehir, forking left after 6 km towards Üçhisar and Göreme.

Üçhisar is a scruffy village, dominated by a tall fortress cone similar to that at Ortahisar. The Kaya Motel and Bindallı Restaurant are in the first parts of the town, to the right of the road, and are quite difficult to spot from above as they are tucked slightly under the cliff: the coaches are usually the clue. The Kaya is the best place to stay in the area, with lovely views over a white valley of fairy chimneys. The impressive looking façades cut out of the rock opposite are in fact pigeon cotes.

Further on in the main square a yellow sign saying 'Kale' points towards the tall honey-combed cone, and you can leave the car and walk on to it through the houses. You can climb right to the top of the **citadel cone**, from where there is an impressive view of the whole Göreme valley. At night the cone is illuminated, looking like some colossal hollowed-out gourd for Hallowe'en.

View of the
Göreme valley

You now return to the main road and follow the signs to Göreme. The road suddenly swoops down into the valley below the Üçhisar citadel with a fine view across.

The Göreme Valley

Continuing along the road to Göreme, do not make the mistake of stopping at the first yellow sign announcing 'Churches'. There is a large open parking area to the right of the road and a restaurant built into a free-standing cone. This is not the famous Göreme open-air museum, but simply a coach-stopping place, a distraction to fool you. If you follow the paths off behind the restaurant here into the vineyards and potato fields of the valley, you will probably eventually be picked up by a peasant woman who lures you back to her troglodyte home in the promise of showing you a 'kilise' or church. Sometimes, in fact, the local farmers' houses will have a church, but you will only be shown it after first being shown postcards and headscarves which you feel compelled to buy whether you want them or not.

To reach the Göreme valley proper you must continue another 2 km on the road, passing through Göreme village. As the road from Göreme village begins to climb uphill you will notice another small sign saying 'Churches' to the right. This again is not the main Göreme park, but leads to the El Nazar valley where you can find the **El Nazar Church** carved out of a free-standing cone with fine arches and frescoes, and closer to the road, the **Saklı** (Hidden) **Church** with fine frescoes, so-called because its entrance stayed hidden for centuries as a result of a landslip. The whole valley of El Nazar (aptly meaning 'the view') has good Cappadocian views with dozens of the cone-shaped fairy chimneys.

View of the El Nazar valley

The main road continues to climb up the other side of the valley, and then some 500 metres later **Göreme** announces itself unmistakably with large signs. This whole valley area is now full of new motel and camping sites galore in the midst of all the cones.

Leaving the car in the large space on the right, a car park attendant rushes to sell you your parking ticket on top of the relatively expensive entry fee to the valley itself. There is even a parade of shops near the entrance with a bank for changing money, and a refreshments kiosk cut into the rock.

The tour of the churches at Göreme only takes about an hour as there are not that many to see and the route round is carefully arrowed and labelled. Göreme was one of the great centres of Christianity from the 6th to the

10th C and the valleys around Zilve, Mustafa Paşa, Üçhisar, Ortahisar and Çavuşin contain almost 400 churches. The entire area is a network of valleys close together, all of which are considered to form the core of Cappadocia.

Frescoes, graffiti and a miraculous brew

The frescoes in Cappadocia were executed largely by local monks, and the majority of the Cappadocian frescoes reflect the comparatively primitive provincial style when compared to the contemporary frescoes at Constantinople where the great artists of the time were at work. The flowering of Byzantine art here was brought to an abrupt end by the Mongol invasions of the 14th C, but though they normally left a trail of destruction behind them, it is not the Mongols who are to blame for the defacement of the Göreme frescoes. Much of the damage was in fact carried out by the Greeks themselves: they apparently believed in the miraculous medicinal powers of a brew made by adding broken fragments of the frescoes to water. The custom was then for the Christian to carve his name and the date beside the chunk he had chiselled out, just to make sure God had registered who he was. The Turkish graffiti on the frescoes are mainly post-1923, and certainly the defacement, literally, of Christ, Mary and the saints was carried out by local Moslem villagers for whom representation of the human form was impious, as you are creating man, which only God is permitted to do. Having scratched off their faces, they were considered dead.

The graffiti of centuries cut deeply in the **Elmalı Kilise**, the first painted church on the Göreme circuit. The entrance to this, the Apple Church, is through a narrow arcade tunnel suitable for one way entry and exit only, then opening up into a dome over four pillars. If you get a chance to look at the *frescoes* through the crowds, you can make out the baptism of Jesus, his migration to Jerusalem, the Last Supper, the Crucifixion and the Betrayal by Judas, all 11th C. You may wonder where the apple comes in, and there is in fact some dispute about this. It is either because of the dwarf apple trees growing near the entrance, or else Jesus, in one of the illustrations, is holding a round object in his hand thought to be an apple, though more likely it symbolises the earth.

You come next to the **Church of St Barbara**, cut into the back of the same rock as the Apple Church. Decorated with the geometric red lines of the Iconoclastic period when the use of images was forbidden (726–842), the church seems plain by comparison. The red dye used was made from the local red clay.

Iconoclastic church

The dating of these churches and monasteries is in most cases very difficult. Most were pre-11th C with just a few after the 13th C. The architectural design of the church tended to follow the accepted Byzantine patterns, with arches, pillars and dome. The pillars of course were not at all necessary to the soundness of the structure, and sometimes the column can be seen not quite to reach the arch, or the dome the pendentive. Their curious smallness, as already mentioned, was in line with St Basil's views on the importance of small monastic units. The paintings of the churches are generally considered far more significant than their architecture. The Iconoclastic paintings are dull in their geometric designs of red or ochre, but the symbols used are slightly more interesting, mostly of the cross, but also fish and various animals all of which had secret meanings. The following list is interesting to bear in mind when looking at all the churches of the region.

Symbolic painting *pigeon or dove:* representing fertility, peace, goodwill, purity, love and innocence
cock: alertness, prophecy, a white one is good luck, while a black one is the devil
peacock: the resurrection and transfiguration of the body after death
lion: victory and salvation
rabbit: prophecy, sexuality, the devil and magic
deer: eternal being and healing
bull: a sacred animal
fish: the pious followers
vine: the symbol of Jesus
fir: fertility and healing
palm: heaven and eternal life

You come next to the **Yilanlı** (Snake) **Church**, one of the most interesting churches in Göreme. It does not have pillars and domes, but an arch-shaped ceiling with the frescoes on its sides. The name comes from the scene of St George on horseback fighting the dragon represented here as a serpent, in whose coils the damned are wrapped.

Continuing on, you pass a series of rooms and refectories, part of a monastery complex, cut in the rock before reaching the **Karanlık** (Dark) **Church**. The façade has now fallen away, exposing the interior, but originally it had only one window, making it very gloomy inside, whence its name. Because little light has got in, the 11th C *frescoes* are still very colourful with no fading. There are scenes of the Last Supper, the Three Kings bearing gifts to the infant Jesus and the Betrayal by Judas.

You then come to the **Çarıklı Church** (Church with the Shoes), reached by an iron staircase. The name comes from the shoe-prints visible at the bottom of one of the pictures of Christ. Çarık is a kind of moccasin. Returning towards the exit, the last area on your right is the **Kızlar Kilise** or convent, with steps leading up to it. It is on three levels, with a refectory and kitchen. Remarkably, some 300 nuns are thought to have lived here. On the other side of the site entrance, opposite the convent, is the monastery, similar in concept.

Discovering the most beautiful church

The loveliest of the churches by far is the **Tokalı** (Buckled) **Church** which is not even in the main area at all. In fact, unless you ask the ticket collector where it is, it will often be locked, as they cannot be bothered to keep someone on duty there. It lies on the opposite side of the road from the car park, back down the hill about 200 metres, and the guardian will come with you to open the door and turn the lights on. Inside it is magnificent. The *frescoes* are only slightly damaged, and for the most part the colours and quality are superb, with an exquisite deep blue background and pillars covered in frescoes, and a small crypt underneath. Many of the frescoes depict the miracles of Christ, including the Marriage at Cana where water was changed into wine, the Feeding of the Five Thousand and the Raising of Lazarus. Other scenes are the Annunciation, the Journey to Bethlehem, the Nativity, the Flight into Egypt, the Entry into Jerusalem and the Last Supper. The artistic style here is among the most sophisticated of any of the Cappadocian churches. It is also the biggest of the Göreme churches by far. The name comes from a buckle which once adorned the ceiling, now vanished. The design, with transverse nave, shows north Syrian influence.

Near the Tokalı Church you can visit several other churches cut in the same group of rocks. The first is **St Eustachius**, 12th C, and reached by an iron staircase. With Iconoclastic symbols in red and green representing the saints, it is thought to be the work of Armenian Christians. Note also the 12th C graffiti near the robe of the angel.

Also to the left of the road, behind the ridge, is the **Kılıçlar** (Swords) **Valley**, so called because of the blade-like cones. Here stands the **Kılıçlar Church** with four columns, simply decorated with the fine frescoes. Lower down the road from the Tokalı, in the cones behind on the same side of the road, you can find the **St Daniel Chapel** with a picture of Daniel in a lion ditch, and, at the end of the road, the **Church of the Virgin Mary**, with columns and very well-preserved frescoes in fine blues, reds and yellows, from the life of Christ and the Virgin.

You can now return to Üçhisar to have lunch at the Bindallı, and after lunch go on to do a half-day circuit of Çavuşin, Zilve, Avanos, Sarıhan, Özkonak and return to Ürgüp via the famous Peribacalar Valley.

Çavuşin and the Zilve Valley

Returning to Göreme village and forking along the valley on the flat towards Avanos, the landscape soon opens out and you reach the **Çavuşin Church**, slightly set back to the right of the road. After paying your entrance fee you climb up the right hand iron steps. The front section has been worn away by erosion, exposing frescoes of the archangels Gabriel and Michael guarding the entrance to the church. Inside, the frescoes are rather different to those at Göreme, in unattractive orange and yellow colours. Some experts believe they are the work of Armenians. The left-hand steps lead up to the monastery next door with four carved graves inside. This church was in fact till quite recently a pigeon-cote, which helped preserve it from the attentions of irreverent visitors. In the village of **Çavuşin** itself, some 400 metres before this church but also on the right, is the church that is generally regarded as one of the oldest in the region, that of **St John the Baptist**, with parts of it as early as 8th C. Its façade has recently collapsed and it is now heavily ruined, but the interior still has fine paintings. The whole village is frequently subject to landslips.

Soon beyond Çavuşin there is a fork off to the right, reaching in 3 km **Zilve**, a pretty series of three valleys dug out with troglodyte dwellings. There is no village here anymore, as the local Turks who moved in after the Greeks left in 1923 also had to leave in 1950–55 because of the danger of landslips and the effects of erosion. Just a simple restaurant stands here at the head of the triple valley, where, when the weather is warm enough, the tables are all spread out under the trees. In May it is usually still too cold to sit out.

The Zilve valley is one of the most enjoyable areas of Cappadocia to walk round and also boasts the most interesting and numerous fairy chimneys. Although much frequented by tours, these generally only take 20 minutes to go to the main part and then return, leaving the best parts of the valley untouched: it takes at least an hour for even an energetic individual to do the circuit of the three valleys.

Exploring the triple valley

Set off first into the right hand valley, the main one, where the path leads after a little while past a charming little **rock-cut mosque**, the only one of its kind. The most spectacular part however is the **monastery complex**, cut in the right hand cliff face, a huge bowl cut out of the rock with a gallery running round half way up from which a tunnel leads off up steep steps to the very ceiling of the dome. You begin by clambering up the rickety metal steps and then up earth steps with handholes in the walls to reach the gallery, about 15 metres above the ground. To clamber on up one of the tunnels you really need a flashlight as it is pitch black and you cannot find the handholes to pull yourself up. On the opposite side of the valley a flight of metal steps leads up to a rock-cut complex from which a **tunnel** links up with the second valley. With a flashlight this is fun to do, and there are steps to get you down on the far side.

Scattered around in the second and third valleys are more churches and even a **rock-cut mill** with a grinding stone. The whole area is overrun with myriad little footpaths dashing up and down the hillsides which you can skip along mountain-goat style. About 1 km from the valley entrance on the road back to rejoin the main Avanos road, there is often a group of youths selling a good selection of colourful wares including woollen socks and gloves.

Around Avanos

You come next to **Avanos**, 7 km on from Zilve. Just on the outskirts of town, before crossing the river, a yellow sign points off 5 km right to **Sarıhan**, the Yellow Caravanserai, accessible now on a narrow tarmac road, built specially to it. The han itself is remarkable for the soft colour of the stone which coated its exterior, and for its very small proportions: it cannot have held many travellers. Its state of preservation today is rather poor, as locals have run off with the large exterior facing stones, but it is being restored. Its setting is pleasant, in a slight dip, with no village nearby, a most unusual phenomenon.

Avanos is a pretty little town on the banks of the Red River, the Kızılırmak, the longest river in Anatolia. Just over the bridge stands the Hotel Venessa (an old name meaning 'city on the river' in Latin). The distinctive deep red soil which colours the water is much in evidence all around and on a rainy day you and your car are soon covered in it. From this local clay the famous pottery is made, exported from earliest times to Greece and Rome.

From Avanos you can drive the main road 11 km north towards Kayseri and fork off left 9 km on a small road to **Özkonak**, the most recently opened and largest of the Cappadocian underground cities, once housing 60,000 people. Here you stand your best chance of seeing an underground city without the coach tours, but the descriptions of underground cities given later still apply. (See Derinkuyu and Kaymaklı for background on the underground cities.)

Returning to Avanos you drive on to Ürgüp via the much-inflated **Peribacalar valley**. The road takes you along the crest of the hills and you look down into the forest of red earth cones from above: it does not look particularly spectacular. As a rule, the Cappadocian landscapes seen from above, as they often are since the roads tend to run along the crests, are unimpressive. It is only when you are down in the valley amongst them that they become more interesting.

Yellow ...

... and red

**Least visited
underground city**

Soğanli: Unspoilt Cappadocia

To escape the crowds of downtown Cappadocia a pleasant excursion is to the Soğanlı valley 33 km away to the south. In a half-day it can also be combined with a round trip to Derinkuyu and Kaymaklı, the other two underground cities, besides Özkonak, that are open to the public.

From Ürgüp you follow the road south marked with a yellow sign to Mustafapaşa. The drive for this stretch is more picturesque than usual, through treed valleys and colourful villages, and passing by the lovely blue-green reservoir of Damsa. **Mustafapaşa** is an attractive rural village with houses richly decorated round the doors and windows. It was Greek until the 1920s since when the Turks **Whitewashed** have whitewashed over the paintings in its churches. One **paintings** two-storey monastry, however, still preserves its frescoes and now serves as a hotel.

At Güzelöz you follow the turn-off left to Yeşilhisar and continue a further 9 km until you see the yellow sign pointing off right 5 km for Soğanlı. An attractive drive winds through the valley passing signs to the Church with a Buckle and the Church with Sky, up paths to the right of the road. Some 3 km further on you come to the pretty troglodyte village of **Soğanlı** itself set into a huge table-topped mountain, with the road forking to either side of it. A map on a large metal sign stands at the fork marking all the churches. In the cones above the village the white squares mark the pigeon-cotes, painted to attract the birds' attention. The villagers keep them to produce manure for their fields.

Take the left fork first, past the prettily laid-out restaurant with tables on terraces out of doors, to the terminus of the road. A sign points off to the Church with the Deer which you can scramble up to on the left, and various other churches lie on the right hand side of the road. A guardian will offer to take you on a guided tour of the major churches, but you can find them yourself if you prefer.

The whole setting of Soğanlı is far more attractive as a village and valley than the more famous Göreme: it is **Escape from the** closer to the original setting and is still unspoilt by the **crowds** mushrooming motels and billborads that ruin the landscapes of the Cappadocian heartlands. There is still just one restaurant, an attractive place to pause. The frescoes are generally less impressive and more fragmentary, so that in the Church with the Deer for example, the deer are difficult, not to say impossible, to spot.

There are some 60 churches in all in the Soğanlı valley, but many are filled up with earth or have been turned into pigeon-cotes by the villagers. The most interesting ones are along the right-hand side of the valley, and particularly noteworthy are **Yilanlıkilise** (Church with a Snake), **Saklı**

Kilise (Hidden Church), **Meryem Ana Kilise** (Church of the Virgin Mary), **Karanlık Kilise** (Dark Church) and the extraordinary three-storeyed **Kubbeli Kilise** (Domed Church or Church with a Beret) in its own curious domed rock formation just to the right of the road.

Underground Cities

Returning to Güzelöz and turning left, a drive of 21 km will bring you to the dirty little village of **Derinkuyu**. A yellow sign announces the underground city and you then turn left into the huge area with coaches parked. The entrance to the underground city here, one of three open to the public (see also Özkonak and Kaymaklı), could hardly be less prepossessing. It is a little hut like a public convenience from which steps lead down, with no clue from the outside as to its extent underground. There is no compulsory guided tour; you can hire a guide, but the way is marked by arrows and signs, and after buying your ticket you can simply descend into the city which is fully illuminated by electric lights. It is open daily from 8am to 6pm.

History of the cities

Throughout history the local people used the underground cities as retreats to escape the invading hordes of armies which poured across the Anatolian plain. They were used as a place of retreat as recently as 1839 to hide from the invading Egyptian army under Ibrahim Paşa. Today, unfortunately, they are no longer a retreat from the armies of tourists pouring over Cappadocia, who now pour right underground by the busload. Tours wreak havoc in these cities: Derinkuyu has open eight storeys (Turkish 'kat') and there is only one single-file stairway to the bottom. If you encounter a tour on Kat 2 you have no hope of reaching Kat 8 for hours, and if two tours encounter each other on the stairs then you have a total blockage.

The underground city at Derinkuyu came to light by accident only in 1963. There is controversy over who were its original builders, but it is thought likely by Turkish experts that the first level was built by the Hittites and used as a store area: Hittite seals have been found by local inhabitants digging new foundations for their houses, and certainly the Hittites built a surface city at Göllü Dağı, 20 km southwest of Derinkuyu. The full number of storeys at Derinkuyu is still not known, but is thought to be as many as 18 or 20, only the top eight of which are open. At least 20,000 people are thought to have lived here, and 36 other underground cities have been found in the vicinity.

Cutting into the rock

It is thought the first step would have been to dig the air chimneys, 70 to 80 metres deep, until water was reached and then to cut sideways until reaching the next air chimney. The volcanic tufa was very soft to cut out, only hardening on contact with air, which is why its surface feels hard

142

to the touch. It is still used today for building, cut into regular-shaped blocks. One theory is that rubble from the digging was emptied into streams and carried away by the current. Both above and below ground, the tufa chambers make very agreeable living areas, with good air circulation, constant temperatures, year round humidity and above all no insects.

The cities are an elaborate network of tunnels, stairways and chambers hollowed out of the rock, but totally bare, with no carved benches or bed areas and therefore very little to help you identify the rooms. Scholars have nevertheless concluded that at Derinkuyu the first two storeys contained kitchens (clearly communal, as relatively few exist), storage chambers, bedrooms, dining halls, wine cellars, stables and toilets, whereas the lower levels were hiding places with wells (Derinkuyu means Deep Well), churches, armouries, dungeons, graves and a meeting hall. Illumination was by oil lamps. It would help today's visitor to have a few of the rooms furnished with carpets, furs and pottery to encourage the imagination to visualise what it was like to live here. The inhabitants must have had an excellent sense of direction to find their way round inside the maze of tunnels. Tunnels are never so low that you cannot stand upright, but the steps and stairways are somewhat claustrophobic: the thought of 20,000 people living down here is still enough to make a sensitive mortal shudder. In the lower levels, several of the tunnels could be sealed off from the inside by large circular cartwheel-shaped stones. Some of the tunnels even link up with other underground cities in the area, to serve as escape routes, and one of them is known to link up with Kaymaklı, 9 km away. This astonishing **tunnel**, provided with ventilation ducts, is broad enough for three or four people to walk abreast.

On the **first level** there is a large open area which was used as a *missionary school* with two long tables cut out of the earth and a baptism basin at the end. The famous Cappadocian wine was also made underground and you can still see the *wine presses*. The grapes were dropped from the surface down the appropriate ventilation shaft into the wine press area. On the **lowest level** a *church* is carved out in the form of a cross and opposite it is a hall with three central columns hewn out of the rock, thought to be a *meeting hall*. Under the modern village are many further underground chambers, some of which open up into the houses still inhabited and used by the occupants as storage space, like an elaborate basement. The villagers of Derinkuyu still depend on the wells on the bottom level for their water but have now installed motor pumps to replace the old hand-turned wheels they were still using in the 1960s.

143

9 km to the north of Derinkuyu on the road back towards Nevşehir, **Kaymaklı** is the other major underground city, discovered in 1964. The village is similarly squalid and unprepossessing but the entrance to the city is far prettier than at Derinkuyu with steps leading up to a honey-combed eminence. Around the outside are kiosks selling postcards, films, booklets and colourful woollen gloves and head-scarves. It is open from 8am to noon and from 1 to 6pm. On top of the hillock long narrow graves have been carved into the rock. Underneath it is far less extensive than Derinkuyu, with only four storeys, but more interestingly arranged. There are bedrooms, food warehouses, wine cellars, ventilation chimneys, water depots, a church with double apse and stone doors which could be rolled open or shut from the inside.

Nevşehir, 16 km north, is the main town of Cappadocia but an unexciting place with little to detain you. It was settled by the Hittites between 2000 and 1200 BC and, after the Hittite collapse, came under the protection of the Assyrians and the Phyrgians. Its name Nevşehir means New Town. It has two of the best hotels in Cappadocia but by and large they are faceless places and it is far pleasanter to stay in Ürgüp which still has some atmosphere and is closer to the main valleys anyway.

North of Nevşehir on the road to Gülşehir, a sign marks the so-called **Açıksaray** (Open Palace) where there is an interesting church with an elaborate façade cut out of the rock. There are no frescoes inside but the walls, ceilings and niches are carved with cross motifs.

The Holy Shrine of Hacı Bektaş

If you have several days in the Göreme region, another half day excursion can be made to the north, to the **Hacıbektaş Monastery**. From Ürgüp you drive up to Avanos and then a pleasant narrowish tarmac road leads north along the river banks for 20 km or so with pretty rural views until it joins up with the main road from Nevşehir at Gülşehir. From here a yellow sign points to the right to Hacıbektaş, 25 km, the monastery of the 14th C dervish of the same name. The Bektaşi order he founded was closely connected to the Janissaries. The order survived the extermination of the Janissaries in 1826 and was dissolved only in 1926 along with the Mevlevis of Konya and all the other dervish orders. The Bektaşis were much concerned with the villages and the rural poor. They had a reputation for free-thinking and loose ways and also retained the old Turkish tradition of allowing the participation of women, unveiled, in their ceremonies.

The monastery is prettily set among gardens and was opened as a museum in 1964. It is visited more by Turks as a holy shrine and by school children on educational outings than by coach tours. In the *main courtyard* there is the soothing sound of constantly running water, and around it are living rooms and a kitchen. Beyond the courtyard you come to the *mosque* and two *türbe shrines*. The smaller türbe, with rags tied in the trees outside, is that of Sultan Belim, the secondary founder, while the larger contains Hacı Bektaş himself. The domed ceilings are lavishly painted and in the larger türbe are also displays of clothing, purses, belts and earrings worn by the dervishes. Shoes are taken off during the visit and the most interesting thing is watching the Turks and the children peering reverently at the displays with awed whispers and kissing every tomb in sight. The stairs in the main courtyard lead up to a library which is still used as a children's classroom.

The Ihlara Gorge

If you are tired of tripping over coach tours and of being
Getting off the beaten path unable to enjoy Cappadocia for the crowds, then one trip you should make as an independent traveller is to the splendid Ihlara Gorge, formerly called the Peristrema valley by the Greeks. The trip can take a full afternoon, or an entire day if you want to do some extra walking.

The drive is scenic and takes $1\frac{1}{2}$ hours from Nevşehir. About 14 km before Aksaray and c 4 km before reaching the turn-off to Ihlara and Güzelyurt, the road passes through **Ağzıkarahan** village, named after the **caravanserai** immediately to the left of the road. It is on huge proportions, its main gate facing west and the whole in a lovely soft reddish coloured stone. The *facade* is elaborately worked. Inside in the open courtyard is a *mosque*, its colossal interior section like a cathedral with high vaulted ceilings.

The fork off to Ihlara and Güzelyurt, 10 km before Aksaray, follows for the first 19 km a narrow tarmac road across flattish landscapes dominated by the snow-covered Hasan Dağı volcano, 3268 metres high. For the final 12 km the road becomes more winding, passing through several half-troglodyte villages partly built into the rock face and partly in primitive houses with flat-topped roofs. The last of these is **Selime**, at the entrance to the gorge, recognisable by the fine conical türbe which you pass here on the bank of the Melendiz river. From here the road crosses the river and continues on the main road for the final 6 km to Ihlara.

On arrival at the edge of **Ihlara village** there is a confusing
Unexpected resthouse sign indicating the Ihlara Hotel which seems to be pointing straight down the hill into the village. This is misleading and you in fact turn left at this junction and follow the tarmac road for about 1 km to then suddenly reach a splendid modern resthouse with superb open terraces laid

out with wooden tables and benches overlooking the canyon: a most unlikely but welcome discovery in the midst of otherwise primitive surroundings. The resthouse here can offer six simple rooms as a pension for keen walkers and has a good restaurant and snack bar. It is open from mid-May to Mid-November. A few coach tours do penetrate here but they tend to be smaller and more adventurous groups as the walking is fairly energetic.

Suitably refreshed from the resthouse you can now make the descent into the **Ihlara gorge** down the specially-built wide concrete steps. The 150-metre deep canyon was formed thousands of years ago by erosion from the Melendiz river, flowing north into the Tuz Gölü (the Great Salt Lake). The river is the product of melting snow from the Hasan Dağı volcano and the Melendiz mountains. While the steep descent takes only 5 minutes or so, the ascent takes more like double that.

Down the gorge: butterflies and churches

The major churches are indicated by signs, but it is fun to go a little further afield to the more distant churches as the walking along the canyon bed is extremely pleasant with the sound of the rushing river and the wind in the tall poplar trees. Wildlife is exuberant with birds, frogs and lizards, and there are far more butterflies to be seen here than almost anywhere else east of Ankara, including Blues, Large Coppers and Painted Ladies. After the bleak and featureless wastelands of the plateau this is indeed a sight for sore eyes.

Just before the bottom you come to the first church, the **Ağaçlı Kilise** (Church under a Tree). Carved out of the cliff, it is cross-shaped and older than the other churches, but its frescoes have been quite well-preserved. On the wall facing the door is a frescoe of Daniel between two lions and on the ceiling is a dragon.

Turning right at the bottom and following the path along, you come after a few minutes to the **Purenliseki Kilise** (Church with a Terrace) which has fragmentary frescoes. Continuing along the path round the cliff which juts out, where a colossal landslip has recently taken place, you come, just round the corner, to the **Kokar Kilise** (Fragrant Church) with some attractive paintings on the outside window, but none inside.

Retracing your path, you continue past the bottom of the concrete steps and come soon to the lovely **Sümbüllü Kilise** (Hyacinth Church) which lies directly below the restaurant terrace 150 metres above. It has attractive arches and an elaborate façade carved in the rock, making it the loveliest of the churches from the outside. It has two storeys, and its fragmentary frescoes are 14th C. Just a few metres after the Sümbüllü Church you come to a pretty **wooden bridge** over the river, until the far end of the gorge

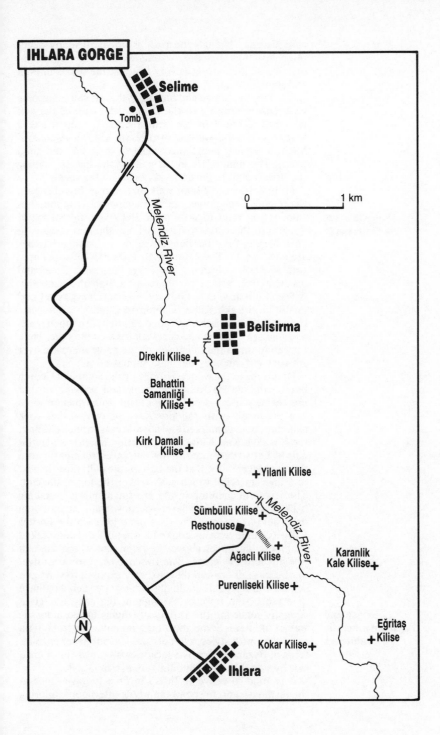

IHLARA GORGE

Selime

Tomb

Melendiz River

0   1 km

Belisirma

Direkli Kilise

Bahattin Samanliği Kilise

Kirk Damali Kilise

Yilanli Kilise

Sümbüllü Kilise

Resthouse

Melendiz River

Ağacli Kilise

Karanlik Kale Kilise

Purenliseki Kilise

Eğritaş Kilise

N

Kokar Kilise

Ihlara

at Belisırma. Though the river is not particularly deep, often less than 1 metre, wading across it is not recommended as the current is very fast and the bed is uneven and slippery.

Crossing the bridge and turning to the left you soon come to a path leading up to the right to the base of the cliff to **Yilanlı Kilise** (Church with a Snake), shaped like a long cross. On the walls are pictures showing the Archangel Michael judging people according to their sins and good deeds. The sinners are in the coils of the snakes, coming to a grizzly end. In the dome is Christ and the angels.

Walking to the end of the gorge

From here it is a 2-hour walk on a narrow brambly path to the end of the gorge, and the signposts to the churches stop. If you want to walk on to **Belisırma**, the village at the end of the gorge towards Selime, the best thing is to cross back to the other bank, as all the remaining churches are on that side. These are the **Kırk Damalı Kilise** (Church with 40 Roofs) which has St George between a Greek and his Armenian wife. Next there is the **Bahattın Samanlığı Kilise** (Church with a Granary) which is very small and finally the **Direkli Kilise** (Columned Church), a monastic church with three aisles and good paintings. You then reach a bridge at Belisırma and can walk back on the other bank for variation. In the full 16 km of the gorge there are over 100 rock-cut churches and many monasteries.

Returning to the wooden bridge by the Sümbüllü Church but continuing on the same bank and walking further upstream, you can do a very pleasant walk which rewards you ultimately with the discovery of two further rock churches, both unmarked and not that easy to find. The first, the **Karanlık Kale Kilise** (Dark Castle Church), is identifiable by its two decorated arched entrances, set high up from the river level but still at the base of the cliff, directly next to a high waterfall which gushes over the top of the cliff. The traces of painting inside are fragmentary. Climbing back down to the river level you now walk on across an open field-like part of the river bank to reach the **Eğritaş Kilise** (Church with a Crooked Stone) of large interlinked chambers, again set above the river, but where the cliff juts out into the gorge. The frescoes here are extensive, but because of erosion they are very exposed to wind and sun now and so will gradually deteriorate. Scholars have detected in the frescoes throughout the canyon a great diversity reflecting the variety of origins in the monastic way of life here. Some show oriental influence from Syria and Egypt with styles, symbols and legends never encountered in Byzantine art. The facades with round vaults lined side by side (like the Sümbüllü) are Syrian in style.

Syrian and Egyptian monastic influences

It is good to arrive at Ihlara in time to have lunch at the resthouse and to spend the whole afternoon exploring

A peaceful walk through the Ihlara gorge

in the gorge. This is a rare opportunity to do some walking in pleasant surroundings in this part of Turkey, a welcome change after so much time is necessarily spent in the car. If you want to make it a full day excursion you can go from Ihlara 15 km back to the fork and on to **Güzelyurt**. This is an attractive troglodyte village (Güzelyurt means Beautiful Place) where St Gregory was born in 330. The Byzantine Church of St Gregory, now converted to a mosque, is the main thing to visit. The saint wrote a memorable passage about the difference between life in Constantinople, where everything is full of complexity and contradiction, and life in rural Cappadocia where matters are simple and straightforward: 'When I ask how many coppers I must pay, they reply with minute distinctions on the Born and the Unborn. If I ask the price of bread, I am told the Father is greater than the Son. I call to ask the servant if my bath is ready, and he replies that the Son was created from Nothing'.

A countryman's view of the metropolis

4 km beyond Güzelyurt on the road to Niğde (55 km on) you pass through the picturesque troglodyte village of **Sivrihisar** at the foot of a rocky outcrop with the ruins of a Byzantine fortress on top. 2 km beyond Sivrihisar to the left of the road is the charming little **Kızıl Kilise** (Red Church) from the 5th C, almost intact. The Güzelyurt area is also famous for its pottery made from fire-resistant soil, different in form to Avanos pottery.

A Caravanserai Fit for a Sultan

Having come this far those with an interest in caravanserais could make the 40-minute detour east of Aksaray on the Konya road to visit the famous Sultanhanı, the most colossal and best preserved caravanserai in Turkey. It is a tedious drive of 39 km beyond Aksaray through a bleak and featureless landscape and must have been deadly dull for travellers who moved at walking pace through it, and a real relief to arrive eventually at the han.

The small village of **Sultanhanı** has now grown up around the han, and a yellow sign points off in the village to the left where the han itself stands in a clearing among the houses, some 500 metres off the main road. A guardian is on hand to sell you an entry ticket, but there is no refreshments place, only a host of village children trying to sell you outrageously priced woollen socks and gloves made from the local sheep. Built between 1232 and 1236 by the great Seljuk Sultan Alaeddin Keykubad I, Sultanhanı cannot fail to impress. The two hans of this name are the most luxurious and largest of the hans in Turkey and both were on the major caravan routes. There was no charge for lodging in these, though there was a charge for the use of the hans in the cities and also for entering and leaving

Along the caravan routes

the cities. In the hans the travelling merchant would attend to the safety of his goods and wares, to the repair of his vehicles and the needs of his camels and horses, do his buying and selling, perform his ablutions and devotions, and then pursue his journey a day or so later. In time of war the buildings also served as storage for food and munitions.

These were the requirements which the plan of the building had to meet. As in the Seljuk madrasa, a strong gateway was built. This was the only external architectural feature and all the decoration was concentrated on it: the elaborate *portal* here at Sultanhanı is a fine example, its richly sculptured gateway contrasting sharply with the solid plainness of the powerful exterior walls. This use of contrast, especially effective when seen from a distance, is one of the most striking features of Seljuk architecture and is used frequently to great effect. Around the open *courtyard* are arched and vaulted storerooms for baggage, hay and oats, separate private rooms with hearths, dormitories for the less well-off, washrooms, gateway rooms for the innkeeper and janitor, a coffee-room, repair shops for the carts and vehicles, a blacksmith and stables for the animals. A stairway leads up from one side of the courtyard to the flat roof for the evening assembly, where the evening breezes blew more freshly. In the middle of the courtyard is a freestanding *mosque*. Within, the huge cathedral-like covered hall served as winter quarters, and in the middle is a dome with an opening for light and ventilation. The hubbub in here during the long cold winters must have been quite something.

Later Ottoman hans were usually built in cities and acquired a more commercial character, serving as markets as well, until they lost their lodging function altogether, this being fulfilled by hotels.

From Sultanhanı a further drive of 100 km across the steppe brings you to Konya, Turkey's most religious city.

KONYA

Mystic centre

For many people who know something of Islamic history the name **Konya** conjures up a certain magic and mystery, for this was the home of Sufism, a mystical sect of Islam, and its famous Whirling Dervishes. Their centre was the Mevlana Tekke in the heart of Konya; with its unforgettable blue-green dome, it remains the highlight of any visit. Also the city has a number of exceptionally beautiful Seljuk buildings, more or less well-preserved, all dating from the 12th and 13th C when Konya served as capital for the Seljuks of Rum and was a haven for Moslem art and culture, attracting many great men of learning.

But apart from these buildings the town today is not especially prepossessing; in fact many visitors express disappointment. It is essentially a city of the steppe, a small oasis of relative greenery surrounded on all sides by vast bleak horizons. In the summer months it is inclined, like all cities of the plateau, to be very hot and dusty, and if you have approached from the coast at Silifke it comes as something of a shock to see traffic lights and roundabouts and the hubbub of people. The best thing to do is to find a central hotel or pension where you can leave the car, and then explore the city on foot. Fortunately, the major sights are concentrated within a square kilometre of the city centre, the main square, Hükümet Meydanı. It takes the best part of a day to see them, so that two nights here is generally the minimum. Avoid Mondays as the major monuments close on that day.

Konya is Turkey's most religious city, and so in Ramadan it is one of the few places where restaurants and cafés close during the day, which can make life difficult when you have been walking in the heat and are desperate for a cold beer. Konya is also the centre of Turkey's carpet trade: you will not have to go in search of them, however, but will doubtless be invited to view.

Heart of the Holy Seljuk City

According to Phrygian tradition, Konya was the first city to emerge after the Flood: at any rate there were prehistoric, Hittite and later Roman settlements here, though none of these remain today. Rather it is the Seljuk monuments of the 13th C that have earnt Konya its fame. It owed its importance throughout its history to its location on the junction of major trade and communication routes. The Romans built ancient roads which were followed by the Seljuks and then by the Ottomans, and today's main roads follow the same course, as can be seen from the number of Seljuk caravanserais still standing at the road-sides.

Mevlana and the Whirling Dervishes

The most famous and striking monument in Konya is the conical, turquoise-tiled fluted dome of the **Mevlana Tekke**, where Celaleddin Rumi, known as Mevlana, is buried (died 1273). Mevlana, a Sufi and the founder of the Whirling Dervishes, was also a poet and philosopher, believing in ecstatic universal love, a state which he induced by the practice of whirling round and round. This ritual can now be seen only once a year in December during the Mevlana Festival. A sacred Islamic shrine and object of pilgrimage from all over Turkey, it is this tekke (monastery) which gives Konya its special status as a religious city. The tekke was the centre of mystic Sufi culture for more than six centuries until the dervish sects were banned and dissolved by Atatürk in 1925. The following year it was opened as a museum, for it is crammed full of precious works of art and opulent furnishings, even housing what purports to be a remnant of the Prophet Mohammed's beard. Awed visitors creep respectfully from one exhibit to the next, and the air of profound reverence is almost overwhelming.

The entrance leads into a small courtyard with an *ablution fountain* or şadirvan. It was around this fountain that the dervishes used to perform their whirling sema dance in remembrance of Mevlana. The heavily decorated *tombs* of Mevlana, his father, his son and other distinguished dervishes, lie in the main building draped in richly embroidered cloths and with the distinctive turban on top. Mevlana's own is an exquisitely carved sarcophagus covered in his poetry. The blue-green *dome*, patterned on the inside with stars, rises directly over his tomb. The bulging treasures, carpets, gold and silver ornaments and such like, were all gifts from the sultans and princes to the Mevlevi order. In the mosque the *mihrab* is quite magnificent, with elegant calligraphy and turquoise mosaics. Next door to the tombs is the *Semahane*, an opulent vaulted hall with fine carpets and chandeliers, where the sema dance is still performed every December and is otherwise used to exhibit dervish clothing and musical instruments.

Next to the Mevlana Tekke is the huge **Selimiye Mosque**, severe in its early Ottoman style.

Elsewhere in Konya

The other monuments of Konya are mainly grouped around the Alaeddin Park, the former acropolis of Roman Iconium. The most major is the **Alaeddin Mosque**, the largest Seljuk mosque in Konya. It took 70 years to build; the sequence of construction is uncertain and the plan is irregular. Eight Seljuk sultans are buried here. Among the park trees are pathways and cafés. In Seljuk times this hill was the site of the Sultan of Rum's palace and gardens, and one small fragment of the palace still stands. Opposite the mosque is the **Karatay Madrasa**, a theological college built in 1251, whose elaborately carved entrance *portal* is considered to be one of the best examples of Seljuk stonework. Recently refurbished, it is now a museum of Turkish tiles from the Seljuk and Ottoman periods. Even surpassing the exquisite tiles in beauty is the magnificent *domed ceiling* covered in 24-pointed stars in yellow against a deep blue background. The colours are superb and the stars appear to shine with an extraordinary brightness. The most beautiful of the tiles are from the Seljuk palace on the Alaeddin hill and the Seljuk summer palace on Lake Beyşehir, and include representations of humans, birds and animals as well as the Seljuk two-headed eagle.

Museum of exquisite tiles

On the far side of the Alaeddin Park are the **Ince Minare** (Slender Minaret) **and Madrasa** with an elaborate, almost baroque Seljuk portal. The minaret is more stubby than slender now, truncated by a lightning bolt in 1901. Nearby is the **Sırçalı** (Glazed) **Madrasa**, so called from the glazed tiles used in its decoration. Now partially ruined, it is used fittingly as a museum for Seljuk tombstones. If you have the time you can also visit the **Sahip Ata** complex of Seljuk mosque, türbe and oratory, much ruined, but still with a fine brick and stone portal, and the **Archaeological Museum**, where the only evidence of Konya's pre-Seljuk history is to be found. The most notable exhibit is a Roman sarcophagus with a bas relief showing the 12 Labours of Hercules.

Escape

Northwest of Konya is the little village of **Sille** (8 km) in a valley with an interesting series of **hermit caves** in the cliffs and some **Byzantine church ruins**. It is a pleasant place to escape from the bustle of the city. The Turkish military is in evidence here, but tends to keep itself to itself.

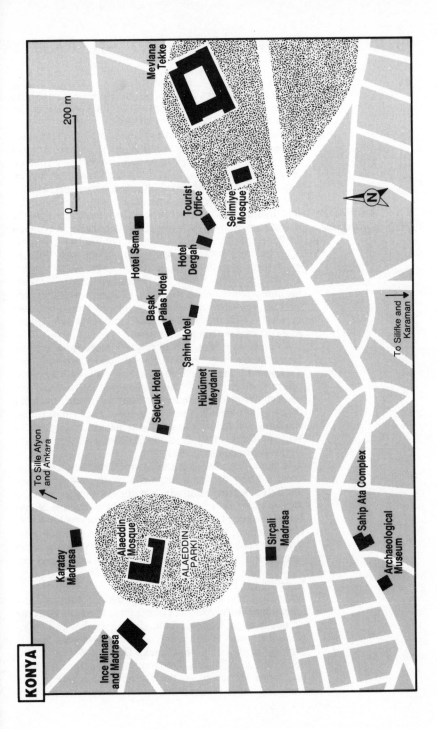

KONYA

To Sille Afyon
and Ankara

Ince Minare
and Madrasa

Karatay
Madrasa

Alaeddin
Mosque

ALAEDDIN
PARKI

Sırçalı
Madrasa

Sahip Ata Complex

Archaeological
Museum

Selçuk Hotel

Hükümet
Meydani

Şahin Hotel

Başak
Palas Hotel

Hotel
Dergah

Hotel Sema

Tourist
Office

Selimiye
Mosque

Mevlana
Tekke

To Silifke and
Karaman

N

0   200 m

155

SOUTH TO THE COAST AT SILIFKE

From Konya you can head south for the beaches at Silifke along an interesting route that can be done in a day including a number of unusual excursions on the way.

The drive starts off uneventfully with more bleak landscapes until after one and a half hours you reach the town of Karaman, a surprisingly green oasis in the barren colourlessness of the plateau. En route, some 50 km from Konya, you will have noticed a road off to the left leading in 26 km to **The world's first city?** to **Çatalhüyük**, the most ancient and important Neolithic and Bronze Age site in Turkey, and thought to be the oldest known city in the world. Discovered in 1958 by James Mellaart, the finds date back as early as 6800 BC and reveal a remarkably advanced Anatolian culture with sophisticated tools, jewellery, sculpture and above all extraordinary wall paintings which decorated their shrines. Despite the importance of the site it is, like most Neolithic and Bronze Age sites, uninspiring to look at today, not least because all the finds have been removed to the Ankara Museum of Anatolian Civilisations.

Another excursion, which requires more time, can use Karaman as a base. This is to the region called Binbir Kilise, a **Thousand and One Churches**, an important monastic centre from the 9th to 11th C. The route is fine until the nearest village of Maden Şehir, then rough dirt track for the last 8 km leads to the most impressive group of ruined churches and monasteries near the hamlet of Değler. Sir William Ramsey and Gertrude Bell made a study of these Byzantine buildings in 1905.

In **Karaman** itself you can, if you have the inclination, make a short detour to the town centre and drive past the Seljuk citadel near which is the **Ak Tekke** (1371), a former monastery of Mevlevi dervishes, and the **Yunus Emre Mosque** (1349). The Karaman region was for a long time inhabited by Turkish-speaking Orthodox Greeks who wrote Turkish in Greek script. The town is now somewhat unappealing and there is a dearth of places to stay and eat.

Leaving the Plateau

After Karaman the road crosses a pass and you suddenly enter a heavily forested belt of mountains, a most welcome change from the plateau. Soon after, in a valley just opposite a little café, a sign points off left to **Alahan** a further 2 km up a reasonable dirt track. This is a detour not to be missed, as Alahan is the remote site of a ruined Byzantine monastery complex, the like of which is rarely to be seen. The setting is magnificent, on a terrace overlooking the lovely Göksu gorge with wild mountains all around. The only other form of life you may encounter here is goats, or sometimes a site guardian.

You arrive first at the great **western basilica**, built at the end of the 5th C, with elaborate relief sculptures on its beautiful doorway of the four Evangelists. On the insides of the pillars of the main door are reliefs of the archangels Gabriel and Michael, trampling underfoot figures which represent Cybele (the Anatolian mother goddess), a bull and a priest of Isis, representing the triumph of early Christianity over paganism. From here you pass the stark **baptistry** to the **eastern church**, built some 50 years later in the early 6th C, with a simple but beautiful façade, remarkably well-preserved. Inside, the arches and slender columns give a marvellous impression of grace. The buildings backing into the cliff, some of them cut into the rock, are the refectory, kitchen, bakery and guest rows. Many carvings of animals and abstract motifs are to be seen in the complex on blocks of the softly coloured stone.

At the entrance to the complex you will notice a series of caves cut into the cliff. These were **cells** for the early monks, with little nooks carved out for cupboards.

Some 20 km after Alahan you reach **Mut**, down in a valley surrounded by mountains. A brief stop can be made here to see the sturdy 14th C Turkish fortress built on the edge of the town. The local children are particularly charming. From Mut the final 77 km down to Silifke passes through some of the most spectacularly beautiful mountain scenery in Turkey, following the gorge of the Göksu river through the Taurus mountains. At one point, just 7 km short of Silifke, you will notice a parking area on the left of the road from where there is a magnificent view of the **Göksu gorge**. A nearby plaque commemorates the drowning of the German Emperor Frederick Barbarossa in the river below here in 1190, on his way to Palestine and the Third Crusade.

Arrival at Silifke

You now approach **Silifke**, the ancient Seleuceia, founded by Seleucus I in the 3rd C BC. The town has a pleasant open feel, on the banks of the wide Göksu overlooked by the Crusader castle on the summit of the acropolis.

Of the ancient town nothing remains except the **Roman bridge** over the river and the scant remains of a Roman temple. The best thing is to head straight up to the **castle** where there are several restaurants offering wonderful panoramas. Vast, overgrown and crumbling in parts, the castle is not maintained and there is no ticket office or official entrance. Entry therefore is by a narrow path round the east side of the castle where a breach in the walls can

Christian victory over pagan gods

Spectacular mountain scenery

Vast fortress

be crossed. Once inside you can clamber all round the edge of the fortress, taking care to avoid the crumbling sections. Originally Byzantine and built in the 7th C as a defence against Arab raids, it was rebuilt by the Crusader Knights of Rhodes into this colossal structure with 23 towers and bastions. In the cellars was a cistern whose waters were reputed never to dry up. The Ottoman Beyazıt I later built a mosque inside.

Diocaesarea Detour

From Silifke a signposted road leads north 38 km to **Uzuncaburç**, the site of ancient **Diocaesarea**. Although this involves a considerable detour along a winding road, it is worth it if you have the time, for the drive itself is attractive and the site is one of the most impressive on the Cilician coast.

From about 8 km outside Silifke, the road through the mountains and pine forests is dotted about with **Roman tombs** often in the form of temples, some of which are remarkably well-preserved and still with bones inside. On the right at the entrance to Uzuncaburç, a road leads to Ura, a village identified with the ancient city of **Olba**. Here are remains of a nymphaeum, an aqueduct and several Byzantine churches.

Oldest Corinthian temple

Uzuncaburç itself is a pretty village, isolated in the mountains. Leaving your car in the village square, to the left before the square is a **theatre** dating from the 2nd C AD. Passing through a monumental Roman **arch** which crossed a colonnaded street, you come to the **Temple of Zeus Olbius**. Built at the beginning of the 3rd C BC by Seleucus I, it is the oldest known temple in the Corinthian order. It was later transformed into a Christian church at the beginning of the Byzantine era. Most of its columns are still standing.

Beyond the wall of the temple enclosure you see on the right another colonnaded street leading to a Roman gate, and beyond this the remains of the **Temple of Tyche** of the 1st C BC: a vast foundation with five Corinthian columns on high bases. Returning to the arch near the village square, turn left, and after passing the school you find a small restaurant where you can eat before or after your visit. Immediately after this a path leads to a powerful **Hellenistic tower** nearly 25 metres high which has given the village its name (Uzuncaburç meaning tallish tower). A stone has slipped, nearly blocking the entrance, so only a slight person can enter now.

The Three Graces

Crossing the marshy delta of the Göksu river east of Silifke, you come after about 15 minutes to the village of **Narlı**

Kuyu, the Pomegranate Well, where you can eat a good if expensive fish meal at one of the pretty restaurants suspended on stilts overlooking the sea. On the village square before the restaurants are the remains of a Roman baths of the 4th C AD. It is known locally as the **Baths of the Maidens** from the lovely *mosaic* flooring inside depicting the Three Graces. The fountain of the baths was reputed to endow its bathers with beauty, intelligence and long life.

Heaven and Hell

From this village also a road leads off 5 km inland to the legendary but disappointing Heaven and Hell (Cennet and Cehennem), two caves which were regarded as so different in character from each other that they earned these epithets. The **Vale of Heaven**, Cennet Deresi, is a huge natural chasm at the edge of a field of Roman and Byzantine ruins of ancient Paperon. The ruins are indifferent, the only striking one being right on the edge of the chasm, a high-walled basilica. The descent is by an easy path to the bottom of the chasm, and from here a less easy, somewhat slippery path continues down 200 metres to the cave mouth where you will see a pretty little early Christian **church**, dedicated to the Virgin in the 5th C. Bathed in a strange bluish light, the church appears to have been built from older stones from the 2nd and 3rd C BC. In the apse are traces of murals. Inside the cave you will hear the roar of an underground river, which according to tradition is the Stream of Paradise which flows out at the Fountain of Knowledge at the Roman baths at Narlı Kuyu below. The ascent is less easy, and about an hour should be allowed for the total visit. The general atmosphere of the place, with rags tied in bushes and the rubbish of picnics littering the area, is far removed from heaven.

From the parking place a second path leads off right to the **Vale of Hell**, Cehennem Deresi, a frightening narrow pit, accessible only with a guide for those with experience of potholing. According to both Christian and Moslem tradition, this was one of the entrances to Hell. Rags of clothing and pennants are tied in the trees and bushes around it by superstitious locals to ward off evil spirits who might escape from below.

Kız Kalesi

Another 5 km east beyond Narlı Kuyu brings you to the famous **Maiden's Castle**, Kız Kalesi, in fact two castles, one on the sandy beach and the other in the sea. The beach here is not well endowed with hotels, but is a very popular camping area with a BP Mocamp nearby. The castle on the shore was built in the 12th C by Armenian kings and

Disappointing heaven

A damn good hell

The snake and the maiden

was originally linked by a causeway to the Maiden's Castle itself, now apparently floating in the sea about 100 metres from the shore. Its name derives from the local legend that the king built the castle to protect his beautiful daughter after it was predicted that she would die of a snakebite. One of her admirers unwittingly sent her a basket of fruit in which a snake had hidden, and on reaching in she was bitten and died. The castle can be reached with difficulty on a small boat or air-mattress, but most locals leave it well alone, as the fatal snake is reputed to live on in the castle.

The **land castle** can be explored though it is heavily over-grown inside: particularly impressive is the water gate. On the other side of the road from the castle lie the extensive scattered remains of the city of **Korykos**, which was a pirate refuge before Pompey's campaign of elimination in 67 BC. Cicero lived here when he was governor of Cilicia from 52 to 50 BC.

East to Mersin
Continuing east between Korykos and Mersin the remains of many ancient cities can be seen, indicating how much more populous this part of Cilicia was in antiquity than it is now. None of the ruins are particularly spectacular or impressive and do not require a visit as such, but can simply be peered at from the car in passing. As so often, it is the tombs which have survived the best, and along several stretches of the road rock tombs and sarcophagi can be seen lining the sides.

Solecism

The first of these sites is **Ayas**, only 3 km beyond Kız Kalesi, noteworthy for its temple which has survived well. Further on, a road leads off 3 km to the village of Kanlidi-vane, the site of ancient **Kanytelis**, where you can see a vast Roman necropolis. At about 10 km before Mersin a road leads off one kilometre to the sea at Viranşehir, site of ancient **Soli**, occupied since the end of the 3rd C BC, later destroyed by the Armenians and rebuilt in the 1st C BC by Pompey, and thereafter named Pompeopolis in his honour. The people of Soli spoke such poor Greek that the term solecism was coined, meaning a grammatical offence. The principal remains of the city are the splendid columns of a **street** nearly 500 metres long running down to the ancient harbour. Only about 20 of the original 200 columns, with Corinthian capitals, are still standing, leading to the sandy beach. Inhabitants of Mersin come out to swim here, and reasonable accommodation is available for the traveller.

SOUTH TO THE COAST AT TARSUS

If, after visiting Cappadocia, you are driving down to the south towards Adana, there is one jewel on the edge of the Cappadocian boundary that should not be missed: this is Eski Gümüş, the 10th C rock-cut monastery, only recently discovered. If your departure point is Ürgüp you can also incorporate the Soğanlı valley (described earlier) into this drive south.

Jewel of Cappadocia

Just 1 or 2 km before Niğde a yellow sign points off left 4 km to Gümüşler. It then forks and you follow the one marked to **Eski Gümüşler Manastiri**. The narrow tarmac road climbs gradually to the village, at the far end of which you will spot a yellow sign on the left of the road announcing it. The whole complex is set behind tall trees and cut into the promontory behind, so on arrival you cannot see the entrance properly. If the gate is locked do not despair as the guardian will materialise within a few minutes.

Once opened you can pass through the arched carved entrance into a rock-cut passageway leading out into a square courtyard open to the sky, with all the rooms cut into the rock on four sides. This style of open courtyard rock-cut monastery is unique in Cappadocia. The whole complex is visited relatively rarely at the moment, so the guardian will take great pride in conducting you round each room and explaining in broken English what each room was for. The monastery was only discovered in 1963 by an English professor. Before that it was used as stabling by the villagers for their animals, and as a result the condition of the frescoes here is almost perfect, far better than those at Göreme which the guardian disparagingly calls 'bozuk', an onomatopoeic word equating to the German 'kaputt'.

Wonderful frescoes

The *main church* is quite lovely with tall fine pillars and a vaulted roof. The *frescoes* are in exquisite colours with deep blues often used as the background. The area above the main dome by the altar was damaged by damp, and this is the only damaged patch in the church, the result of natural rather than man-made causes. The pillars have cuts near the bottom where wax was collected from candles and then re-used. A shaft with handholes in the walls leads up to the higher storey which was a *bedroom* for the monks. A metal staircase has been built up from the outside to help you reach it more easily. On the walls of the bedroom are extraordinary *wall paintings* of animals, showing deer, lions, ostriches or storks and men hunting them with bows and arrows.

There is a large *refectory* which would probably have accommodated 50 to 60 monks with a rock table and benches either side still visible but set down at floor level, as the ground height has risen since. The other curious complex of rooms is the *bathroom* which even has a huge wheel-shaped stone for rolling across as a door for privacy. Inside this complex the guardian tells you there is the entrance to an underground city which is scheduled to be cleared and opened 'this year', as are all restorations.

There is also a wine press area, and above the main entrance is a slit for pouring hot oil on enemies' heads.

Seljuk and Mongol Monuments

The road continues now 2 km into **Niğde**. The modern road largely by-passes the town, but if you are interested in Seljuk and Mongol architecture you may like to make a short detour here to see some very fine buildings. You will notice on your approach the 11th C **citadel** rising above the town. It is near this that the striking **Alaeddin Mosque** (1223) stands, looking like a caravanserai with a minaret, together with the Mongolian conical **türbe of Hudabend Hatun** (1312). This superb 16-sided türbe is more beautiful in many ways than the more famous Döner Kümbet of Kayseri, with superb carvings and on a much larger scale than most türbes. Other buildings worth taking a look at are the Mongolian **Sungur Bey Mosque and Tomb** (1335) with beautiful portals, the **Ak Madrasa** (1409) now a museum containing relics of the area from Hittite times through to Ottoman times, the **Eskiciler Çeşme** (fountain) built in 1421 and the **Şah Mesciti**, a little 15th C oratory with re-used Byzantine capitals.

A more beautiful türbe

The Dramatic Descent to the Mediterranean

South of Niğde and heading for the coast the scenery on the drive is very dramatic and alpine. Snow-covered peaks rise up to 3585 metres and there are fine pine trees on the lower slopes. On joining the main E5 route from Ankara, the sudden increase in the volume of traffic comes as something of a shock. There has been so little traffic on the roads generally that the numbers of trucks transiting here seems grossly excessive. There are also many German cars towing caravans.

Snow peaks

From Pozantı southwards a toll motorway is being constructed for the final 75 km to the coast at Tarsus. So far only about 20 km or so has been completed, but you can travel on it to escape the trucks for a patch as they all seem to prefer to stay on the old road.

The road then makes a spectacular descent through the **Cilician Gates** towards the coast, passing many places to stop and eat at the roadside, ranging from very simple truck stops to prettily laid-out restaurants.

It would be worth avoiding this road from the coast inland, as the heavily laden trucks crawl up the painful climb in first gear and you have an endless series of them to overtake around the hairpin bends.

PRACTICAL INFORMATION

KAYSERI

Turan Hotel (1-star), Tel: 11968. 70 rooms, indifferent hotel, but probably the best that Kayseri has to offer. Restaurant on top floor. Heavily used by tours.

Hotel Hattat (1-star), Tel: 19331. 67 rooms, slightly more expensive than the Turan. Used by businessmen.

The best **restaurants** are in these two hotels.

Kayseri has direct **flights** to and from İstanbul on Tuesdays and Sundays from March until October only.

Average temperature (Celsius):

J	F	M	A	M	J
−2.1	0.0	4.5	10.5	15.3	19.2
J	A	S	O	N	D
22.5	22.0	17.1	11.6	5.5	0.6

Maximum temperature:

J	F	M	A	M	J
18.0	22.6	28.6	30.7	33.6	37.6
J	A	S	O	N	D
40.7	40.6	35.7	33.6	26.0	18.4

Minimum temperature:

J	F	M	A	M	J
−32.5	−31.2	−26.6	−11.6	−6.9	−0.6
J	A	S	O	N	D
2.9	1.4	−3.8	−12.2	−20.7	−28.4

ÜRGÜP

Ürgüp Turban Motel (3-star), Tel: 490. The newest and most expensive in the area, 160 rooms, bungalow-style, at the top of the hill above Ürgüp enroute to Göreme valley. Superb location, but very geared to coach tours. Good-size swimming pool.

Boydas Hotel (3-star), much used by coach tours.

Eyum Hotel (2-star), 30 rooms, well-designed and free from tours.

Büyük Hotel (2-star), Tel: 1060. In the centre of town, the second best after the Turban, and one of the few stylish hotels in this part of Turkey. 54 rooms. Good restaurant and pleasant atmosphere. Abundant almost ferociously hot water. Lovely carpets hanging on the walls of the communal areas. Quite expensive but good value.

Tepe Oteli (1-star), Tel: 1154. 36 pleasant rooms on top of the hill on the outskirts, with a swimming pool.

ÜÇHISAR

Kaya Motel (2-star). Built in 1969, this is the best and most fun place to stay in the area if you can get in. Run by the Club Mediterranée, it is luxury caves instead of grass huts with red and white wine on tap in the room. Ornamental pool on terrace overlooking a fairy-chimney valley. Open 31 May to 30 September only. 21 rooms.

Camping: Koru Mocamp opposite the fork to Üçhisar.

Bindallı **restaurant** next to the Kaya Motel: this is a new restaurant à la troglodyte opened in 1986 and functions from March to November. In May it is usually still icy cold in the cave. The most sophisticated place in the area, it is nevertheless very geared to coach tour catering and only offers a set 4-course meal. The local wine is brought in earthenware jugs and the food is served on chunky earthenware platters.

ORTAHISAR

Motel Paris (1-star), Tel: 15. Bungalow

chalets with small kitchen and own individual water heater. Good pool (July and August only). 24 rooms. **Camping** facilities.

AVANOS

Venessa Hotel (1-star), Tel: 201. 72 rooms right on the river bank by the bridge. Good views.

Tusan Kızılırmak Motel (2-star), Tel: 99. 30 rooms, pool. Open March through November.

NEVŞEHIR

Hotel Orsan Kapadokya (2-star), Tel: 1035. Newish and faceless hotel with swimming pool on the outskirts of town towards Göreme valley. 80 rooms, much used by tours.

Camping: BP Mocamp (no chalets) on the road between Nevşehir and Göreme.

Cappadocia Wine Festival, late September. Held at the same time as the grape harvest, it amounts largely to wine tasting. Cappadocian wine is justly renowned.

IHLARA

Modern resthouse with restaurant on the clifftop overlooking the gorge and 6 simple rooms for walkers. Open mid-May to mid-November.

There is a cliff top **restaurant** overlooking the gorge.

AKSARAY

Orhan Ağaçlı Motel (2-star), Tel: 49. 87 rooms on the Ankara to Adana road. Good restaurant.

Ihlara Hotel (1-star), Tel: 1842. 64 rooms in the town.

KONYA

There is no obvious candidate for the best hotel: all are fairly old-fashioned and all are 1-star.

Park Hotel, Tel: 33770, the one used by coach tours and considered to be the best. 90 air-conditioned rooms.

Yeni Sema Hotel, Tel: 13279, out of town to the east, on the road to Meram. TV and refrigerators in the room.

Başak Palas, Tel: 11338, 40 rooms on the main square. Older style.

Şahin Hotel, Tel: 13350, 44 rooms on the main street.

Otel Selçuk, Tel: 11259, 52 rooms just off the main street, in a quieter location.

Hotel Dergah, Tel: 11197, 43 rooms very close to the Mevlana Tekke, next to the tourist office. It has its own Turkish bath.

Hotel Sema, Tel: 19212, just off the Mevlana Caddesi behind the tourist office. Good, quiet and convenient location. Own Turkish bath.

Whirling Dervish Festival, 9 to 17 December, to commemorate the death of Mevlana, the Islamic mystic poet and philosopher. This internationally famous festival consists of dancing dervishes in costume in the Sema ceremony, accompanied by mystical music played on the ney, a kind of reed flute. Since the banning of the sect in the 1920s this is the only occasion the dervishes can be seen performing.

Average temperature (Celsius):

J	F	M	A	M	J
−0.3	1.6	5.4	11.0	15.9	19.8
J	A	S	O	N	D
23.2	22.9	18.1	12.4	6.6	1.8

Maximum temperature:

J	F	M	A	M	J
16.6	23.8	28.2	30.4	34.4	36.7
J	A	S	O	N	D
38.0	40.0	35.2	31.6	25.4	21.8

Minimum temperature:

J	F	M	A	M	J
−28.2	−26.5	−16.4	−6.6	−1.2	1.8
J	A	S	O	N	D
6.7	5.3	−3.0	−8.4	−19.0	−26.0

SILIFKE

There is no accommodation to speak of in Silifke itself, but there are hotels on the beach to the east and west of the town.

Taştur Motel (2-star), Tel: 290. On the beach at Taşucu with a good restaurant and fine setting. Much frequented by Turks on holiday.

Motel Olba (2-star), Tel: 222. Open April to November, 20 rooms in Taşucu, 8 km west of Silifke. Well-maintained and pleasantly situated on the sea. Pool.

Motel Boğsak (1-star), Tel: 13. 27 rooms 18 km west of Silifke. Modern and comfortable on good beach. Open April to October.

Aile Motel (1-star), 60 rooms on the beach at Korykos near Kız Kalesi, east of Silifke.

BP Mocamp near Kız Kalesi, with a few simple chalets for non-campers. Communal facilities shared with campers. Rocky beach.

Restaurants are grouped up on the citadel under Silifke castle with a fine panorama.

Car ferries from Taşucu run to Kyrenia in Turkish Cyprus on Tuesdays, Thursdays and Saturdays. Tickets can be bought at the docks or at Silifke's bus terminal. A faster **hovercraft** service runs Mondays, Wednesdays and Fridays for passengers only and takes 2 hours.

Music and folklore festival, 20–26 May.

Average temperature (Celsius):

J	F	M	A	M	J
11.5	11.7	13.6	16.9	20.8	25.0
J	A	S	O	N	D
27.9	28.0	25.1	21.1	16.7	13.1

Maximum temperature:

J	F	M	A	M	J
22.5	23.2	27.5	33.3	37.5	41.0
J	A	S	O	N	D
41.1	44.2	39.5	36.6	30.0	24.6

Minimum temperature:

J	F	M	A	M	J
−1.4	−4.7	−0.7	3.4	8.6	12.2
J	A	S	O	N	D
16.2	15.8	12.6	8.0	4.0	0.7

MERSIN

Atlıhan Otel (3-star), Tel: 24153. 93 air-conditioned rooms in the centre of town.
Mersin Oteli (2-star), Tel: 12200. 120 air-conditioned rooms on the beach.
Marti Motel (2-star), outside town, a beach hotel and restaurant.
Toros Oteli (1-star), Tel: 12201. 62 rooms in town but overlooking the sea. Pool.

From Mersin docks, Turkish Maritime Lines operate **car ferries** to Famagusta in Turkish Cyprus on Mondays, Wednesdays and Fridays in summer, and to Latakia in Syria every Friday.

NIĞDE

Otel Evim (1-star), Tel: 1860. 48 rooms, in the main square, beside the bank.

There are many **restaurants** on the route from Pozantı through the Cilician Gates to Tarsus, ranging from simple truck stops to prettily laid-out restaurants.

South Eastern Turkey

Adana

Misis

Yılanlıkale

Anazarbus

Toprakkale

The Hatay
İskenderun
Antakya (Antioch)

East via Gaziantep or Maraş
Carchemish
Birecik
Karatepe
Nemrut Dağ and Arsameia

Urfa

Harran

Diyarbakır

Mardin

The Tûr Abdin Monasteries

Nusaybin

Hasankeyf

Siirt

Bitlis

Practical Information

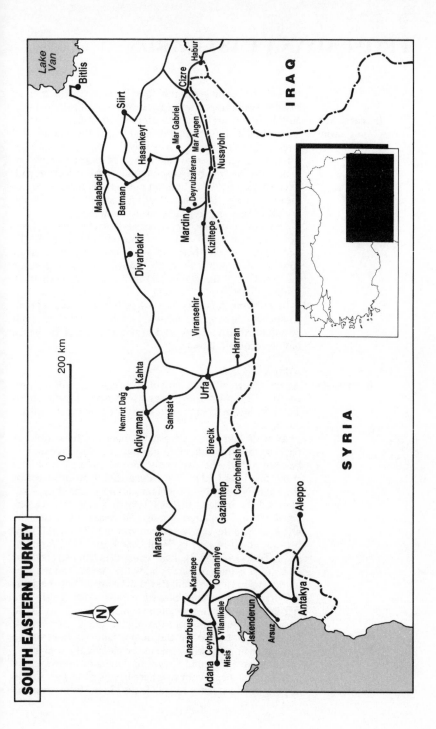

SOUTH EASTERN TURKEY

200 km

Lake Van

Bitlis
Siirt
Hasankeyf
Mar Gabriel
Malaabadi
Batman
Cizre
Habur
Deyrulzaferan Mar Augen
Nusaybin
Mardin
Kiziltepe
Diyarbakir
Viranşehir
Harran
Nemrut Dağ
Kahta
Adıyaman
Samsat
Urfa
Birecik
Carchemish
Gaziantep
Maraş
Aleppo
Karatepe
Osmaniye
Anazarbus
Ceyhan
Yılanlıkale
Misis
Adana
İskenderun
Arsuz
Antakya

IRAQ

SYRIA

167

FROM ADANA EASTWARDS

In search of a swim

If you are heading for the coast in search of a spell of rest and swimming, your experience here will not be a particularly salubrious one as the stretch from Mersin eastwards is a huge flat alluvial plain created by the three large local rivers. Lining the dual carriageway that runs between Mersin and Adana is a sprawling ribbon of industrial development with factories belching out pollution unchecked, and, beyond, rice fields and cotton plantations reach as far as the eye can see. In summer it is unpleasantly hot and sticky, far hotter than the Aegean coast to the west.

To reach a coastline that is pleasant for a few days' relaxation you must either head west beyond Mersin to Silifke and Taşucu where there are a few good beach hotels or continue east and fork south towards Antakya to reach the coast at Arsuz (Uluçınar) or Samandağ, both small fishing villages.

Inland from Adana is the **Ceyhan Dam and lake**, a popular spot for boating and picnics, and towards the sea about 30 minutes' drive away at **Karataş** is the nearest beach but no accommodation.

Adana

Boom town

As the centre of a rich agricultural region and of the prosperous cotton industry, **Adana** is growing rapidly and is Turkey's fourth most populous city after İstanbul, Ankara and İzmir.

As with Mersin and Tarsus, Adana's history stretches back to the first millenium BC, but very little remains to be seen today. The city's only ancient monument of note is the fine long bridge, **Taş Köprü** (Stone Bridge), across the Seyhan river, built by Hadrian and restored by Justinian. Of the bridge's original 21 arches only 14 have survived. It was repaired on several occasions under the Ottomans. In the centre you can visit the **Ulu Cami** (Great Mosque) built in 1507 by Halil Bey, Emir of the Ramazanoğlu Turks who ruled Cilicia before the Ottoman conquest in 1516. It is built of black and white marble and the tiles in the mosque and in Halil Bey's türbe are among the finest in Turkey. The **covered bazaars** are also worth a visit. The city has an interesting small **museum** housing many of the ancient Hittite finds from the region and a good ethnographic section showing the homes and costumes of the Turcoman nomads who came to the plain in the winter.

If you have to spend a night in Adana on your journey east, or if you begin your tour here having flown into Adana airport, the best place to stay is the Ener Motel, over the bridge and about 2 km east on the outskirts of town in a pleasant complex with camping and a pool.

Roman and Armenian Sites

Eastwards from Adana there are a number of excursions which you can make enroute to Antakya or to Adıyaman (Nemrut Dağ), some more interesting than others.

The first and least interesting comes 25 km after Adana when a sign points right to Yakapınar, the name of the modern village where the **mosaic of Misis**, such as remains of it, is to be found. The mosaic is housed in an unfinished **Dog kennel and** 'museum', but there is nothing to see except for the vaguest **columns** of fragments. The place is clearly not yet geared up for visitors and serves largely as an outsize kennel for the village dog. Scattered near the road around are various capitals and column drums which is all that remains of the ancient Roman city of **Mopseustia**, named after its founder Mopsus. The mosaic is meant to represent Noah's ark and the animals, but this is theoretical.

Some 14 km on from the Yakapınar turn-off you should start looking out for the magnificent 12th C Armenian castle of **Yılanlıkale** on a hill about 1 km to the right of the road. There is no signpost but you will notice a small tarmac road heading towards it, somewhat pothole-ridden, which takes you to within ten minutes' walk of the summit. The hill is not high but the castle dominates the flat river plain with ease, and from the top you can see the river snaking **Snakes and pigs** round the plain. It did not, however, earn its name 'Castle of the Snakes' from this, but from the armenian king who built it who was known as the King of the Snakes. Snakes still abound in the region and are eaten with relish by the local pigs whose flabby snouts protect them from bites.

As you walk closer you see the elaborate lines of the castle's defence unfold. You enter through the first gateway in the walls and proceed up through the second to the magnificent *main gate* between two powerfully-built towers. A recent landslip near the entrance now means that a bit of clambering is necessary to pass through this gateway. Its ceiling has simple vaulting as well as a slit for pouring oil on the enemy. Once inside, the castle opens before you. Stairs can still be climbed up to the main *Watch tower* by the gate, remarkably preserved and offering an excellent panorama. The *keep* is difficult to climb into as the entrance is now too high to reach without steps or a ladder. Inside are huge vaulted rooms of the royal family; in some of the lower rooms little frogs hop around in the dark. Steps lead onto the walls which can be followed for a while.

A pleasant detour can be made from Ceyhan, 6 km beyond the Yılanlıkale turn-off, to the ruins of **Anazarbus**, a Roman-Byzantine city 30 km to the north. The site is in a lovely setting on the very edge of the Cilician plain at the foot of a mountain. From Ceyhan you pass through Ayşehoca from which a road to the right takes you to the little village of Anavarza 4 km away. Founded after the 1st C BC Anazarbus flourished during the Roman period. It was destroyed and rebuilt twice at the beginning of the Byzantine era. In the 7th and 8th C it was pillaged several times by the Arabs, eventually becoming the Arab town of Ain Zarba. From the 10th to 12th C it was governed by Cilician Armenians who made it their capital. Ravaged frequently by the Mamelukes, it was finally abandoned. The 3rd C AD **triumphal arch**, Corinthian in style, is the most interesting monument left standing. From the theatre a stairway cut into the rock leads up to the upper town, passing a small **Byzantine oratory** with fragmentary paintings. The **fortress** on the top is well preserved and encloses the **funerary church of the Cilician Armenian kings** which still has some *frescoes* inside.

Continuing on the main road eastwards from Adana you come to a fork, right to İskenderun and Antakya, left to Osmaniye and Maraş. At the middle of the fork stands another 12th C Armenian fortress, **Toprakkale**, on a low hill at the outlet of the narrow valley which commands the plain of Issus. There is no road to it now, and you would have to walk across the fields to reach it; nor is it as well preserved as Yılanlıkale. So unless you are a castle fanatic there is little reward in making the effort.

Heavy traffic This fork is also where you can lose most of the heavy traffic by heading left to Osmaniye, as the trucks and oil tankers are all pushing on into Syria, making a drive on that road far more of a strain than on the normally empty roads of the interior.

THE HATAY

At the point where the road turns south towards İskenderun, you leave the Cilician Plain behind and enter the region called the Hatay or the Sanjak of Alexandretta. This is a region with a very mixed population, as one might expect from its geographical location, with large communities of Arabs, Moslems and Christians mixed in together. With the collapse of the Ottoman Empire after the First World War it was incorporated into Syria under the French Mandate, but the French gave it to Turkey in 1939 to buy Turkish support in anticipation of a new war against Germany. The Syrians have never accepted the transfer. Pleasantly hilly, it is a welcome contrast with the flat plain of Cilicia.

Towards İskenderun

On turning south towards İskenderun, you come first to the **plain of Issus**, the scene of Alexander the Great's **The battle of Issus** famous defeat of the Persians under Darius III in 333 BC, after which he was able to penetrate southwards to Syria. A little further on, at the sign to Yeşilkent, are the remains of a fine **Roman aqueduct** beside the road. Dörytol, near the coast, is the terminal of the oil pipeline from the Kirkuk oilfields in Iraq.

About 20 km before İskenderun is a short turning off to **Yakacık**, the former Payas, where you will see a huge 16th C Ottoman **carvanserai** including a mosque, a madrasa (Koranic school), a bath and a covered bazaar with spacious courtyards, leading to a bridge over a moat to a fortress on the sea, known as the Tower of the Jins. The complex was built at the order of Selim II with the advice of the great architect Sinan, famous for his many mosques, including the Süleymaniye, in İstanbul.

You now reach **İskenderun**, the former Alexandretta, founded by Alexander the Great after his defeat of the Persians. It is a busy port and commercial centre, and is a pleasant town with good hotels and restaurants along the front. In atmosphere it is an attractive combination of Mediterranean, Anatolian and Syrian. Nothing remains to be seen of its past monuments. From İskenderun a tarmac road leads 30 km south along the coast to **Arsuz** (Uluçınar), a small beach resort much favoured by Arabs crossing from Syria.

Antioch: Turkish Antakya

Leaving İskenderun for Antakya, the road heads inland winding its way up steeply through the mountains to the

Belen pass. Sometimes regarded as the Gates to Syria, **Belen** is an attractive place, becoming increasingly popular as a summer resort and famous for its spa waters which are meant to aid stomach and digestive problems. The views from the top and during the descent are spectacular over the Orontes valley and Lake Amik, an artificial lake created by blocking the Orontes river lower down. On the descent, a short detour of 4 km can be made to see the **castle at Bağras**, one of the main strongholds of the Mamelukes in the defence of northern Syria. Set up on a peak, it was built by Byzantines and Mamelukes rather than Crusaders, who captured it in 1097 during their siege of Antioch. It was abandoned after the Ottoman conquest in the 16th C.

Licentious Antioch

You now reach **Antakya**, pleasantly situated on the Orontes river, the site of ancient Antioch, the prosperous and ostentatious capital of the Seleucids. In the scramble for power that followed Alexander's death at the age of 33 from fever, four states emerged under four of Alexander's generals. Seleucus got Syria, a large portion of Asia Minor and eastward to India; Ptolemy got Egypt; the rest of Asia Minor went to Antigonus; and Antipater acquired Macedonia. Throughout the Hellenistic and Roman periods it was Antioch in Syria and Alexandria in Egypt that stood out as the most influential and enduring. In its Roman heyday Antioch's population was estimated at half a million, a heterogeneous and excitable collection of Cretans, Macedonians, native Syrians and expatriate Jews. Specialising in sumptuous games and entertainments, it became a byword for luxury and depravity, without neglecting literature, scholarship and the arts. The old city was destroyed by a series of earthquakes in the 6th C but its situation ensured its commercial prosperity throughout invasion by Armenians, Persians, Byzantines, Seljuks and Crusaders. It was held as the capital of a Frankish principality for most of the 12th and 13th C. From its capture and destruction by Sultan Baybars of Egypt and his Mamelukes, and from its long occupation by Arabs until taken by Selim the Grim in 1516, the town never recovered.

The town today is only a shadow of its former self but is still very picturesque with its narrow lanes leading down to the Orontes and its segregated districts where the various religious communities held themselves apart in Ottoman times. The outline of the ancient **city walls**, 30 km long in total, gives an indication of the extent of the city in its heyday. As a centre for licentious living, Antioch was chosen by Peter for his first mission to the gentiles, and here his converts were the first to be called Christians. St Barnabus and St Paul later stayed here.

Remnants of Antioch's colourful history are few,

amounting to the old **Roman bridge**, a picturesque **bazaar** quarter and the **Mosque of Habib Haccar**, originally a church. A little outside the town on the Aleppo road is the **Grotto of St Peter**, where Peter preached for the first time and founded the first Christian community. It had a secret tunnel which enabled the Christians who met there to escape in the event of a surprise raid. The church was erected here in the 13th C by the Crusaders, and has a fine situation under a cliff overlooking Antakya with a gorge to the south.

Splendid mosaics   The main reason, however, for a visit to modern Antakya is to see the **Hatay Museum** (8.30am to 12, 1.30 to 5pm, except Mondays), the main exhibits of which are the finest collection of Roman mosaics in the world, all discovered in the region of Antakya. These mosaics formed the floors of private houses in Roman Antioch, and in nearby Daphne, the finest ones dating from the 2nd and 3rd C AD. They are ample testimony to the luxurious lifestyle enjoyed by its citizens, many showing scenes of banqueting and dancing, as well as mythological subjects.

Marriage of   South of Antakya, 7 km, an excursion can be made to
Antony and   the crumbling **fortress** of Antioch, more for the magnificent
Cleopatra   view from the top than to see the building itself. Also south of Antakya lies Harbiye, ancient **Daphne**, the pleasure suburb where most of the lavish villas were situated. Apollo's pursuit of the nymph Daphne is reputed to have taken place here and the laurel (*daphne* in Greek) into which she was turned still grows all around. A sanctuary and oracle of Apollo was established here which became celebrated throughout the ancient world. It was in Daphne that Mark Antony married Cleopatra in 40 BC, and that the Olympic Games of Antioch, successor to the games of ancient Olympia, were held. Nothing remains of the buildings, but the gardens with their cypress and laurel trees and little waterfalls produced by the abundant springs are the favourite picnic and strolling place of the residents of modern Antakya.

If you continue on to the coast south of Antakya, a 30-minute drive brings you to the beautiful beach of Samandağ, near which are the ruins of **Seleucia ad Pieria**, the ancient port of Antioch and once one of the greatest ports on the Mediterranean. Little remains now except some ruined walls and gates, with some fine underground water tunnels and canals.

Crossing to Syria   Returning to Antakya and forking east, the Syrian border post is reached after about 50 km, from where it is a further 50 km to **Aleppo** (Haleb). The crossing, at the Bab El-Hawa frontier post, is a lengthy process taking two hours minimum. You should obtain your visa in advance.

EAST VIA GAZIANTEP OR MARAŞ

From Antakya you can head east within Turkey by retracing your steps 30 km to the north, then forking to Kirikhan and continuing via Hassa along 170 km of uneventful road to Gaziantep. From Gaziantep or from Urfa further east you can head north for Adıyaman and Nemrut Dağ, but it would be more agreeable to reach these via the Maraş route.

Gaziantep

Pistachios and buttons

The main distinction of **Gaziantep** today is its title 'town of the pistachio nuts' which which it shares with Aleppo in Syria. A town of largely modern aspect on a broad plain flanked by two hills, it is well known for its food markets and expanding textile industry which has brought recent prosperity along with hillsides of shanty towns full of rural immigrants eager to partake of it. Gaziantep is also well known for its crafts, such as carved furniture inlaid with mother of pearl, though in recent years white buttons have been found to do just as well and have the advantage of being cheaper.

The town acquired its Ghazi (warrior) prefix as an honour by Atatürk in recognition for the fight put up by the inhabitants in a ten-month seige by invading French armies in 1920–21.

Its **archaeological museum** on the north fringe of the town is in a Seljuk madrasa and contains some Hittite reliefs from Carchemish, as well as some Roman sculptures reminiscent of the art of Palmyra in Syria. From here you can climb up through the heavily defended gateway to the fortified **citadel** built by the Seljuks at the end of the 11th C on an artificial hill.

Towards Urfa

From Gaziantep you can go due east 140 km to Urfa, a fairly dull drive which also has the disadvantage of being the oil tanker transit route to Iraq and is consequently full of heavy trucks and their dust.

At 48 km there is a turn-off south to the small frontier town of Barak near **Carchemish** (Turkish Kargemiş), the site of the capital of the most powerful of the Neo-Hittite kingdoms which prospered after the collapse of the Hittite empire at Hattuşaş (Boğazkale). The city had to repel many attacks from the Assyrians before eventually being annexed in 717 BC to the Assyrian empire by Sargon II.

Because of the closeness of Carchemish to the Syrian frontier, special permission to visit must be obtained from

T E Lawrence was an archaeologist at Carchemish from 1911 to 1914

the Jandarma and a military escort then accompanies you to the site. In fact there is not much to see here today, as during the excavations just before the First World War the colossal bas-reliefs which were found here decorating the city gates were moved to Ankara and are now on display to in the Museum of Antolian Civilisations. They represent mythological scenes with processions of warriors and courtiers and are reminiscent of Assyrian art. It was this dig which contributed some of the first clues to the identity of the Hittites. Among the archaeologists involved were such luminaries as T E Lawrence, Sir Leonard Woolley and D G Hogarth, and Gertrude Bell was a visitor to the excavations. The citadel is on a 40-metre high hill overlooking the Euphrates, and the palace originally stood at the centre of it approached by a wide monumental way.

Early career of T E Lawrence

The only town of interest enroute to Urfa is **Birecik**, on the banks of the Euphrates overlooked by the ruins of a fortress perched on a rock, probably built by the Crusaders in the 12th C. Birecik's other distinction is that it is one of the world's two remaining nesting places for the bald ibis, a hideously ugly and nearly extinct bird. It leaves Birecik in July to fly to its winter home in Morocco and returns in mid-February. For as long as any one can remember its return has heralded the end of winter and the coming of spring and is celebrated by the villagers in a remarkable festival each year. Some of the oldest villagers believe that spring will not come if the bald ibis does not return; for reasons of its own the World Wildlife Fund has a project here to protect the species.

Ensuring the return of spring

From here, Urfa is another 81 km east.

The Route to Maraş

If you are not going south to Antakya and the Hatay, the best route east is to fork left at Toprakkale towards Maraş. This route takes you via Karatepe to Adıyaman (for the ascent of Nemrut Dağ), a journey that can be done in a day. But even if you are coming up from Antakya, it would be more agreeable to reach Nemrut Dağ via Maraş than via Gaziantep.

A Diversion to Karatepe

From Osmaniye, 12 km beyond Toprakkale, in the middle of the town a yellow sign points off left 34 km to Karatepe, Aslantaş and Hieropolis. Although this is a detour of some three hours in all, it is well worth it if you have the time, as the scenery enroute is very attractive and the site of Karatepe is remote and unusually beautiful. You can see here Neo-Hittite stone reliefs *in situ* in a quantity and state of preservation unique in Turkey or for that matter in the

Remote and beautiful

world. The site is still being excavated and is not yet visited by coach parties. If you have set off from Antakya or Adana that morning, it is an excellent place for a picnic in the lovely wooded setting overlooking the Ceyhan lake. The name Karatepe, Black Hill, describes the pine covered hills on which the site, once the summer palace of the Neo-Hittite king Asitawanda, stands dominating the valley and lake below. Karatepe was only discovered in 1945, having lain on the hillside covered in brambles and scrub for 27 centuries. It was under these brambles that the final key was found to the puzzle of Hittite hieroglyphics. Philologists had struggled for 50 years to master the main elements of the language's structure, but now from a bilingual text in Phoenician and Hittite hieroglyphics they could understand the meaning of the individual words for the first time.

Puzzling hieroglyphics

The route is very well signposted all the way. About 12 km from Osmaniye the road runs through pleasant open fields. From a fine castle on a hillock, columns march across the fields towards the road. This is the site of **Hieropolis Castabala**, capital from 52 BC of an independent kingdom under Tarcondimotus. He took the part of Pompey against Caesar, providing him with vessels; in 31 BC he was killed at the battle of Actium where the fleet of Cleopatra and Mark Antony was defeated. The dynasty was short-lived, coming to an end in 17 AD. The last 9 km to **Karatepe** is on a dirt road to an area now designated a Millipark (National Park). The road is perfectly all right for a private car even after heavy rain, and passes through pretty wooded hillsides and several small hamlets.

The area immediately surrounding the site has been turned into a neatly laid out forest station with a forest house serving soft drinks but no food. The hillside around has wooden tables and benches set in the trees with views down over the lake. A site slightly predating that of Karatepe was found on the hill opposite, called Domuztepe, but has now been flooded by this artificial lake, the result of a dam built on the Ceyhan river.

Being Shown Round Karatepe

Because excavations have not yet been completed, no photography is permitted at Karatepe, and a site guardian must accompany you throughout the tour. These guardians are polite and informative, so in fact their company is a pleasure rather than a bore. Until the site is completely finished, there is no fee to enter. The Archaeological Institute is responsible for the excavations: it is increasingly the case in Turkey that the excavations of genuine Anatolian civilisations like the Hittite, Urartian and Seljuk are conducted by Turks and are government funded, whereas the Greek and Roman sites are usually funded by foreigners.

None of the site is visible from the car park, and the guardian leads you up past the entrance hut along a forest path for 300 metres until you reach a double gate into the old Hittite city. On the summit of the hill is a Hittite palace inside defence fortifications laid out on a polygonal plan with 28 towers which the guardian tells you is completely 'bozuk'. In fact nothing, intriguingly, remains of the city itself, except two sets of gates, these first ones and another set on the other side of the hill. Why the gates have remained so well-preserved with such detail left on the carvings while nothing remains of the city itself is a puzzle. The same is largely true of Boğazkale, where it is the gates of the outer fortifications which have survived leaving very little inside. It certainly shows where Hittite builders concentrated their efforts. Only at Alacahüyük does the town remain with buildings still recognisable inside the walls and streets leading off.

The **gates** at Karatepe are guarded by *colossal sphinxes and lions*. Huge basalt blocks along the inside of the first gate are cut with astonishingly well-preserved *reliefs*. The scenes show hunting and fishing, a bull being killed for the king, the king seated at his meal reaching out for one of the flat loaves in a large bowl and holding a meat patty in his left hand. Two servants wave fans to keep away insects and create a breeze. There are also people riding in chariots, dancing bears and a series of particularly fine gods, notably the monkey god (with enormous erect penis), the snake god and a sun god very like the Egyptian Horus with a falcon's (or here perhaps an eagle's) head.

Reliefs for a summer palace

The reliefs on the further gate are if anything better preserved than the first one, with one of the lions still having his ivory eyes intact. The mother suckling her child by the palm tree shows strong Egyptian influence. Though not beautifully executed or particularly naturalistic, it is nevertheless a very expressive scene. The reliefs are all thought to show Assyro-Aramean influence in such things as the defined tresses of the hair, the hair styles, the style of dress with the long Assyrian tunic and tasselled sash replacing the characteristic short Hittite tunic, and the appearance of chariots. A lot of the subject matter for the reliefs is light hearted as befits a provincial summer palace. The ordinary mortals shown in these reliefs are, as Seton Lloyd observed, 'a graceless folk with sloping foreheads and receding chins, such as are known to have inhabited large areas of Anatolia at that time'.

The remains have been dated to c800 BC, long after the fall of the Hittite empire at Hattuşaş. These were the so-called Neo-Hittites, the people whom the Israelites knew and who are mentioned in the Old Testament. It seems doubtful that the Israelites knew of the mountain Hittites

David and Bathsheba of Anatolia, for when King David married Bathsheba, the widow of Uriah the Hittite in about 1000 BC, the Hittites had long been driven out of their mountain homeland. Forced southwards from the cities and pastures of the plateau towards the plains of northern Syria, they founded a series of small and disunited city states striving to retain their independence on the fringes of the Assyrian empire. The artistic style and quality of these cities of the Hittite diaspora, like Karatepe, Carchemish and Ugarit, are generally inferior to that of the earlier Hittite kingdom. The somewhat crude and hybrid style of art seen here is thought to have been executed by craftsmen from many different nations. Part of the difficulty may also lie in the hard black basalt so plentiful in the northern Syrian plain, but coarse and much more difficult to carve than the fine white limestone used for the reliefs of the old kingdom.

Back on the Road to Maraş

Returning to Osmaniye the road now continues eastwards winding up and down hills with very heavy truck traffic until you reach after 50 km a fork in the road, right to Gaziantep and left to Maraş. The truck traffic all continues towards Gaziantep for Syria and Iraq, while on the Maraş fork the road almost empties of traffic and the landscape becomes flatter with straighter roads.

A further 50 km from the fork brings you to **Maraş**, a town with a modern aspect set into a black hillface with the flatness of the river plain in front and the high mountain plateau rising behind it. It has nothing for the tourist to see except a small museum in the Ottoman citadel displaying Hittite sculptures. The town has been described by **Entry into another world?** those with over-active imaginations as marking the entrance to another world, that of oriental Turkey, where the people and landscapes become rougher and where any maritime influence has worn away. It was held by the French until 1920, and three years later its large Armenian population was expelled. Because of the resistance offered to the French by the local population in the War of Independence, Atatürk added the epithet 'Kahraman' (hero) to its name and on maps you will generally see it marked as Kahramanmaraş.

To Adıyaman: Base for Nemrut Dağ

The drive onwards to Adıyaman is through attractive hilly scenery, sometimes following the course of rivers, sometimes **Climbing back onto the plateau** climbing up and down hills, making the gradual ascent onto the Anatolian plateau. It is possible, having set out from Adana (or even Antakya) in the morning, to visit Yılanlıkale and Karatepe and drive on via Maraş to reach Adıyaman that evening. The distance from Adana to Adıyaman is 362 km.

Adıyaman is an undistinguished sprawling town of 70,000 people at an altitude of 700 metres. For the traveller it serves purely as a base from which to make the ascent to Nemrut Dağ, and for that purpose the best bet is the Arsameia Hotel, a somewhat stark, green detached building on the right-hand side of the road on the edge of town as you leave towards Kahta.

NEMRUT DAĞ

Along with Cappadocia and the Sumela Monastery, Nemrut Dağ is one of the best known sites east of Ankara, and most people will have seen photos of the large stone heads on the top of the mountain. Virtually unknown until after the Second World War and not even mentioned in the 1960 edition of the *Guide Bleu* the site was first excavated by the American School of Oriental Research in Connecticut some years after the war. Since the building of an approach road in the 1960s however the site has been regularly visited and now, with the recent upsurge in visitors to Turkey, the droves of people heading up the mountain in minibuses have taken on the proportions of a pilgrimage.

Delusions of grandeur

Nemrut Dağ has almost no significance historically, being no more than a vast funeral monument to the ruler of a small local dynasty with delusions of grandeur, but for all that — or because of that — it is astonishing, unlike anything else in the world. This kingdom, extending from Adıyaman to Gaziantep, was called Commagene, and was established in the 1st C BC by a local ruler called Mithradates. The Seleucid dynasty in Syria to the south was disintegrating and the Commagene rulers managed to rule independently until AD 72 when the Emperor Vespasian incorporated it into the Roman province of Syria.

Bizarre setting

Antiochus (62–32 BC), son of Mithradates, imagined for himself great ancestors, claiming descent on his father's side from Darius the Great of Persia and on his mother's side from Alexander the Great. This Persian and Macedonian ancestry is reflected in the statues and reliefs surrounding the tumulus where Antiochus depicts himself at home with and as an equal among the great kings and gods. The strangeness of this subject matter would be interesting but not exceptional were it not for the setting Antiochus chose for his mausoleum: Nemrut Dağ, at 2150 metres, the highest mountain in his kingdom, was extremely remote and inaccessible. It is this bizarre setting which gives the whole monument, in its isolation and unexpectedness, a surreal feel. This essentially oriental concept of gods enthroned on a mountain has its antecedents in the Hittite reliefs where the most important gods always stood on top of mountains, or even as early as the Babylonian Ziggurat of Ur, a man-made symbol of a mountain.

Getting There

You come to Kahta after a further 25 km from Adıyaman on good tarmac road and at the beginning of the town a sign points left to Nemrut Dağ. Also at this junction the locals of the Pension Kommagene will be lying in wait to try to convince hesitant travellers that the road is 'bozuk' and that they will need to be taken up in one of the pension's minibuses at exorbitant cost. In fact you can rest assured that the road is perfectly all right for a car. The intention is to tarmac the road all the way up to the top very soon, and there is a possibility that this will have been done by the time you read these words.

Planning your excursion

The drive to the top currently involves 52 km of unsurfaced road each way and takes two and a quarter hours to the top and two hours down again, with an extra one and a quarter hours to visit Arsameia, the Commagene capital. What this means is that you need only stay one night in Adıyaman or Kahta, as you have time before or after the Nemrut Dağ excursion to press on for one and a half hours' of easy driving eastwards to Urfa or Diyarbakır. There is a petrol station just after the Pension Kommagene at the beginning of the Nemrut road, where you will need to fill up if you have less than half a tank of petrol. Before the building of the road in the 1960s, the summit was accessible only by donkey and on foot and took two days. The whole trip cannot be made before the beginning of May as the snow has not melted at the summit. The hut at the top only opens then, closing again at the beginning of October when the snow returns.

The dawn crowds

A lot of nonsense is talked about the best time of day to visit Nemrut Dağ, with the popular line fed to people being that you must be up there at dawn to see it at sunrise, an exercise which involves leaving Kahta at 2am and driving up in the dark. In practice it is often too cold at sunrise to be able to get out of your car and walk up the last 15 minutes in comfort, and the other problem is that so many tour operators have got hold of this myth about the dawn viewing that the summit is at its most crowded then. The clever ones will time their arrival to miss most of the tours, which means arriving at the summit any time after 1pm. You can in fact arrive as late as 4pm and still have time to see Arsameia and the queen's burial area on the way down before dark. This will make a terrific difference to the enjoyment of your trip, and also means that if there have been any early morning mists, as is frequently the case, they will have cleared by then and you can appreciate the extraordinary setting to the full. The hut at the top serves simple meals of omelette and salad and there are several places offering food and basic accommodation on the way up, so there is no need to take a picnic.

The first 10 km or so of road from Kahta is surfaced and fine. Shortly before the tarmac runs out you pass a huge mound just to the left of the road marking the burial

The extraordinary mountain sanctuary at Nemrut Dağ

Two thousand year old bridge

place of Antiochus' wife. Then just 250 metres after the tarmac stops, you come to the fine **Roman bridge** over the river Cendere, tributary to the Euphrates, with an inscription at the centre of the arch. It is in superb condition with excellent workmanship in the stone blocks and three of the original four columns still standing. It was dedicated to the Roman Emperor Septimius Severus.

The road all the way up is clearly marked with yellow signs so there is little danger of taking a wrong turn. In the area of the bridge the scenery is made very lovely by the wide shingled river bed and the surrounding fertile slopes covered with vines and wheat. The gradient is never very steep and there is never any question of the road being undriveable — even large motorbikes manage it. The worst patches are, as ever, in the villages where the local traffic churns up the surface and creates ruts. All the children in the village are so used to the steady stream of tourists weaving their way up the mountain from May onwards that they now try and sell you knickknacks, and the daredevils among them jump in the path of the car to show off to their friends.

About 16 km before the summit you cross a modern bridge bending to the right over a stream and some 400 metres later on you fork left. There is no sign at the turn itself, rather there is a confirming sign 500 metres after you have taken the correct turn anyway. After this the road climbs up through a village where a simple house claiming to be the Apollo Motel/Pension/Camping/Restaurant apparently offers all things to all men.

The final 10 km of the climb has been laid with cobbles and is much more bumpy and bone-rattling than the loose gravel and earth of the earlier stretch. The gradient is also steeper by far and this is presumably the reason why it was necessary to cobble this upper section. In the final village before the summit there are a number of simple camping/restaurant places, and just on the way out a new low-rise modern design motel, the Motel Zeus, looks as if it might be quite plush.

At the Top of Nemrut Dağ

Arriving at the top you leave the car just below a small modern building, decked inside with local carpets on the walls and tables and outrageously priced woollen socks, gloves and souvenirs. It is always quite chilly at the summit because of the altitude, and you will need to walk about it for an hour at least, so your own woollen socks and gloves and scarves will definitely be needed. Walking up in between the two halves of this building you come to a small rocky path which leads up quite steeply; you follow **Sacrificial landing** along the right hand side of the mountain tumulus for 10 **pad** to 15 minutes before arriving at the **eastern terrace** with a large rectangular **sacrificial altar** on its edge which doubles as a helicopter landing pad for VIP visitors.

Sitting majestically with their backs to the tumulus, facing the dawn, are the five figures, from left to right, of **Apollo** representing a synthesis of Mithra, Helius and Hermes; the Commagene **fertility goddess** representing Fortuna, Tyche and elements of local goddesses; **Zeus** (also Ahura and Mazda) in pride of place in the centre; **Antiochus** himself, recognisable from his moustache and beard and **The great statues** open mouth; and finally **Hercules** (also Artagnes and Ares). On the backs of the statues long Greek inscriptions detail the descent of the Commagenes and the rites to be used in their worship, with dawn sacrifices on the altar. Each Commagene god incorporates several similar deities, following the principle known as syncretism which the Greeks used after Alexander's death to try to unite Greek, Persian **... and their** and other Near Eastern peoples. The fact that their heads **heads** are lying tumbled on the ground in front of them lends a preposterous air, and there is undeniably something ludicrous about the ego-inflated king's final resting place. Seen on a clear day from the queen's burial mound below, the reddy-brown tumulus perched on the mountain top looks

King Antiochus before the Nemrut Dağ tumulus

for all the world like a giant anthill. Given the smallness of the kingdom and the shortness of its duration, the subjects must have spent most of their lives carrying rocks up the remote mountainside. Whether it was done with slave labour and how long it took is not known. No other Commagene buildings have survived besides the capital of Arsameia where the kings had their palace, so maybe there was no time left for the Commagene citizens to build anything else after they had seen to their kings' needs.

Scattered round the terrace you can see the various parts of a **colossal eagle** which once guarded the terrace, its head and wings separated. The fine **lion** up by the side of the altar is reminiscent of the Hittite lions at Karatepe. Like them, he does not seem fierce but appears rather to smile benignly on the world, though probably he was meant to be baring his teeth.

From the eastern terrace a path leads off round the far side of the tumulus past the heavily ruined northern terrace and on to the **western terrace** which has some of the finest pieces of carving. The **five seated statues** are as on the eastern terrace, backs to the tumulus, here facing the sunset rather than the dawn. They are less imposing and in poor condition but the separated heads are in a better state of preservation. The head of the goddess Fortuna with garlands of vines, grapes and other fruits in her hair, is especially lovely and is bigger than that of the clean-shaven Apollo who looks insipid and effeminate. Some have seen **Elvis Presley** in this head the spitting image of Elvis Presley. These statues again show the stylistic mix of Greek and oriental: the seated deities, 8 to 10 metres high, have heavy static bodies, while the fallen heads show the idealised Hellenistic features, often with Persian headdress.

Around the statues here several superb **reliefs** have survived, unlike on the east terrace. Three of them show Antiochus shaking hands with Apollo, Zeus and Hercules. The finest though is the *lion relief* with a crescent moon, the planets and stars, in fact an astronomical chart which, from the conjunction of Mars, Mercury and Jupiter, suggests the date 7 July 62 or 61 BC: about the time Antiochus was set on his throne by the Roman general Pompey. Over on the far side of the terrace are reliefs of Antiochus standing with his Persian ancestors, recognisable by their long gowns.

Unfound royal tomb The tomb of the king himself has not yet been located within the tumulus, despite numerous tunnelling attempts by the American excavators since 1953.

Visiting the Commagene Capital

In **Koçtepe**, the first village you pass through on the way down, you will notice mud brick houses with grass growing

Rooftop farms on their flat roofs. These have the advantage of providing good insulation against summer heat and winter cold, while chickens and livestock can fatten themselves on the lush summer grass. Shortly after one of the lower villages you come to a major fork in the road. If you have already seen the queen's tumulus and Arsameia on the way up then it is quicker to take the left fork to return to Kahta, whereas the right fork leads you back down the way you came.

As you approach the river valley 5 km before the village of Eski Kahta, you will pass an earth road leading uphill and right, leading in 2 km to **Arsameia**, the Commagene capital. The road is a bit worse than the main Nemrut one, but it is still fine for cars, even after rain. In winter there is at least 5 metres of snow on the summit of Nemrut Dağ whereas at Arsameia the average snowfall is half a metre.

On arrival at Arsameia a guardian is usually waiting to accompany you on a tour of the ruins. He leads you first along a narrow path past a damaged relief of the Persian **Reliefs, caves and** sun god Mithra, then past a second and clearer relief of **tunnels** Mithradates with Helios-Apollo to a large cave cut in the rock of the hillside, thought to have been used as a storage area and cistern. From here the path climbs up the hill to the main area of the ruins where there is a superb relief of a naked larger than life **Hercules shaking hands with Mithradates**, the founder of the Commagene dynasty. The cult of Hercules was widespread under the Syrian Seleucids, and this relief, like the statues of the Nemrut Dağ summit, combine Hellenistic portraiture with stocky heavy forms. Cut into the enormous rock wall below the relief is an inscription, and below that is a **tunnel**; its steps can still be walked down quite a long way, but the tunnel is now blocked at the bottom with debris and fallen rock. Its purpose is not known for sure but it is thought to have been used to fetch water from the river below.

From the tunnel the path climbs a little further to the highest point of the hilltop, through a heavily ruined gateway and various wall foundations. This was the **town** of Arsameia; the ruins are scant with nothing recognisable except a cistern and a few carved column bases. But the setting at the summit is lovely and makes a marvellous picnic spot among the long grass and spring flowers. There **Superb view** is a superb view down into the valley and across to the Mameluke castle known as **Yeni Kale** (New Castle) on a lower cliff outcrop. The castle is extensive and though kept locked can be visited as the 'muhtar' or headman of Eski Kahta will open it up for you. Inside the fortification walls are various rooms and a well.

Having crossed over the river valley again and over the Roman bridge and back on the tarmac road, you pass by

the **queen of Commagene's tumulus** again. The wife of
Antiochus is buried here. The mound is called Karakuş
(black bird) which may be a local interpretation of the
clumsy eagle on top of one of the pillars.

Ferry Across the Euphrates

From Adıyaman you can make an excursion 38 km south
to Samsat on the Euphrates, or even continue by this route
for a further 61 km to Urfa by taking the ferry across the
river. The road is manageable by car throughout.

An important stronghold in Byzantine times, controlling
a strategic crossing point on the Euphrates, **Samsat** fell
to the Arabs in 640. From the early 10th C it belonged
to the Hamdanid emirate of Aleppo, then fell to the
Kurdish Ayyubids and finally to the Seljuk Turks. Its
importance declined considerably in medieval times and
today it is an insignificant little town. It was the birthplace
of the Greek sophist Lucien (125–192 AD). A few arches
remain of the 32 km-long **aqueduct** built by Septimius
Severus.

URFA AND HARRAN

From Adıyaman you can reach Urfa via Samsat (see previous chapter) or via Kahta. From Kahta it is a pleasant one and half hour's drive through fertile landscapes to reach Urfa or two hours to Diyarbakır. The road makes a gradual descent from the plateau (800 metres) down onto the plain where it crosses the Euphrates unannounced, a surprising omission as normally even the most insignificant streams are meticulously labelled.

Lowering Your Expectations

After 54 km you reach the T-junction leading left to Diyarbakır and right to Urfa. By this time you are down on the flat northern Mesopotamian plain and the drive in either direction is frankly dull. Those who are short of time could omit Urfa and Harran altogether without shedding too many tears and go straight on to Diyarbakır. With the exception of the Halil Ar-Rahman Mosque and its Pool of Abraham, there is little of any great excitement to see in Urfa. It is a town of historical associations rather than tangible reminders of the past. As the *Guide Bleu* somewhat scathingly puts it (translation from the French): 'Urfa requires of its visitors a sort of almost mystic or purely intellectual sympathy for the history of civilisations, for religions and for the lands of Genesis, as nothing spectacular awaits you here; everything will be in your powers of imagination, your ability to feel and understand'. Be that as it may, with two new comfortable hotels opening in the last five years Urfa is now firmly on the coach tour itinerary. But from May onwards these hotels can be full with as many as six tours of different nationalities passing through: be warned that if these hotels are booked up when you visit you are destined for a night in a sordid hotel high on the cockroach rating and with no hot water.

Test your powers of imagination

If you want to get a feel of the Middle East through the Arab cultures of Turkey, then a visit to Mardin via Diyarbakır gives you this far better than Urfa or Harran, and the drive to it is also far more interesting.

Glorious Urfa

Once down on the plain you will begin to notice a marked deterioration in the road surface which continues all the way to Urfa, and which unfortunately rarely leaves you from here eastwards. In Eastern Turkey conversation among strangers is not about the weather, that topic of such interest to the English, but about the state of the roads.

Urfa is a town of no great beauty, dusty in summer and muddy in winter. Many of the Arab-style houses of the 15th C with gracefully carved windows and doors have been demolished to make way for new roads and buildings with no attempt at restoration. There is a complete dearth of signposts and reference to the town plan is essential. On road signs you will see it called Şanlıurfa (Glorious Urfa) which is the epithet Atatürk gave to it after the independent Turkish Republic was declared. Kahramanmaraş (Hero Maraş) and Gaziantep (Warrior Antep) were the other two towns honoured by Atatürk for the fight all three put up against the invading French armies in 1920.

When Alexander the Great passed by here after his victory on the plain of Issus he named this town Edessa after the Macedonian city. In the 2nd C AD Edessa became the earliest Christian centre in Mesopotamia, and a school of religion and philosophy flourished here until the Arab conquest in the late 5th C. Edessa remained in Moslem hands until the 11th C when Count Baldwin detached himself from the First Crusade's march on Jerusalem and established here a small Christian state. When Saladin retook Edessa 50 years later the Pope in Rome responded by calling for a Second Crusade. And so Edessa's history has not been without incident, but like so many other once important cities it never recovered from the Mongol invasion led by Hulagu in 1260 which two years later destroyed even Baghdad.

From the two best hotels you can set off to see Abraham's Pool. On the way you can stop off at the **Ulu Cami**, slightly set back on the right of the road. A gateway leads through to a pleasant courtyard with tall trees and fine tall gravestones arranged in a small graveyard. In a corner of the courtyard there is an octagonal minaret with a clock on top. Founded by Nur Eddin in the 12th C, the Ulu Cami is patterned on the great mosque in Aleppo.

The street winds past the Arab-style **covered bazaar** and at the foot of the citadel reaches a complex of three mosques, two modern which you come to first, and further to the right the famous **Halil Ar-Rahman Mosque** with its **Pool of Abraham**. Legend has it that when passing through Urfa, Abraham was thrown on a funeral pyre by an angry Nimrod, the Assyrian king, for destroying the pagan idols in the temple. To save him, God created a lake which put out the fire. Abraham of course, whose name means Father of a great multitude, is revered not only by Jews and Christians, but by Moslems too. And so this spot attracts Moslem pilgrims, who come to gawk at the pool and its sacred carp and linger. The spot itself encourages

Christian centre and Crusader capital

Where God saved Abraham: a place of Moslem pilgrimage

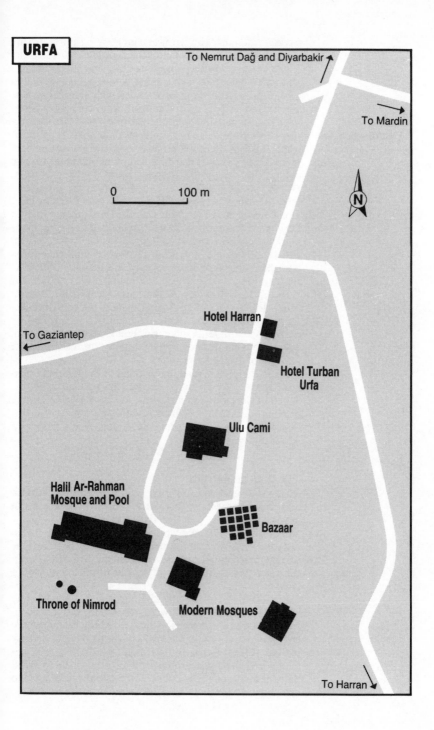

URFA

To Nemrut Dağ and Diyarbakir

To Mardin

0   100 m

N

To Gaziantep

Hotel Harran

Hotel Turban Urfa

Ulu Cami

Halil Ar-Rahman Mosque and Pool

Bazaar

Throne of Nimrod

Modern Mosques

To Harran

a certain amount of lingering as it is charming and unusually peaceful, with attractive landscaped gardens intersected by canals leading to the pool. There are several restaurants and cafés here too. The pool is a long rectangle and is a beautiful green colour surrounded with graceful arches. The sacred carp, grey and ranging from colossal salmon-sized monsters to tiny ones the size of goldfish, are severely

Cannibalistic fish overcrowded and are beginning to show signs of cannibalism. This is evidently their answer to the population problem: their sacred status forbids killing them and anyone eating them will go blind according to local superstition. At the side of the pool cooked chick peas are for sale to feed the fish, who appear in fact very bored by this fare. On occasion however, you can also buy green sprigs of herb which drive them beserk. Wherever the sprig lands immediately becomes a seething wriggling mass of carp. Either the fish are very keen on their greens or else the herb has some drug-like property and they are all frantic for their 'fix'.

In the cafés you can try the bitter local coffee, Murra-Mirr, drunk without sugar and made from local berries. During Ramadan the restaurants contrive to function by putting up cloth fences like windbreaks so that people can eat inside without offending the public outside. Avoid the *faux pas* of asking for fish.

From the park a road leads round to the right and concrete steps climb up to the **citadel** built by the Crusaders. A pair of **Corinthian columns** here are known as the Throne of Nimrod. Another version is that these are the remains of a temple of Baal. From this vantage point there is a good view over the town.

The Way to Harran

To get out of Urfa and drive south to Harran (Turkish Altınbasak) you have to retrace your steps to the north beyond the hotels, then turn right and right again to follow an appalling road, deeply pitted with holes and ruts, often crowded with the additional hazard of carts drawn by scraggy moth-eaten horses. Towards the end of the town the road passes the edge of the old fortifications with a large gate.

The drive to Harran takes 35 minutes through a totally flat and featureless plain towards the Syrian border. Reconciling this wasteland with the image of Mesopotamia where civilisation grew up on the banks of fertile rivers is no easy matter. Robert Byron in his classic '*Road to Oxiana*' evidently had the same problem: 'It is little solace to recall that Mesopotamia was once so rich, so fertile of art and invention, so hospitable to the Sumerians, the Seleucids,

Abraham's Pool at Urfa

The mud of Mesopotamia

and the Sasanids. The prime fact of Mesopotamian history is that in the thirteenth century Hulagu destroyed the irrigation system; and that from that day to this Mesopotamia has remained a land of mud deprived of mud's only possible advantage, vegetable fertility. It is a mud plain, so flat that a single heron, reposing on one leg beside some rare trickle of water in a ditch, looks as tall as a wireless aerial. From this plain rise villages of mud and cities of mud. The rivers flow with liquid mud. The air is composed of mud refined into a gas. The people are mud-coloured; they wear mud-coloured clothes, and their national hat is nothing more than a formalised mud-pie'.

The Southeast Anatolia Project, the most ambitious project ever undertaken by Turkey or by any Middle Eastern country, may however transform this wasteland back into fertile agricultural land. It consists of a series of dams on the Upper Euphrates due for completion in the 1990s. The *piece de resistance*, the massive Atatürk Dam producing 2400 megawatts being built 60 km north of Urfa, will be the fourth largest dam in the world, nearly 200 metres high, and the lake behind it will cover thousands of square kilometres. The project will transform the lives of the semi-nomadic people of the region, often sheep raisers, many of them Kurds. Already they have had to adjust to the Turkish-

Syrian border that now restricts their migration to the Syrian plain. The Turkish government estimates that work will be created for 600,000 agricultural workers once the irrigated land is planted with wheat and cotton.

After 15 km on the road south from Urfa a track forks off to the left which leads to a mound in the middle of the plain known locally as **Sultantepe**. It was here that Seton Lloyd found tablets of the Babylonian *Epic of Gilgamesh*, dated to c2000 BC, and other tablets written in Assyrian and Sumerian hieroglyphics. Some 28 km eastwards on a bad track you can reach **Eski Sumatar**, the sanctuary of the heathen Sabians who as late as the 14th C were still making human sacrifices. There is little to see here; it is of interest above all for its associations. The mystical Sabian sect was, because of its belief in one God, recognised by Islam as on a par with Christianity and Judaism. The Sabian religion united neo-Platonic philosophy with Babylonian astrology, considering the planets as embodying spiritual beings created by God as part of the universe. The Sabians had a holy script, the believers sacrificed to the sun and the moon, and they had an initiation ceremony and a kind of communion. Facing always to the north, they prayed at dawn, midday and sunset. The principal deity was worshipped in the form of a pillar or holy stone, and under him were the sun god (Helios), the moon god (Sin), Saturn (Kronos), Jupiter (Bel), Mars (Ares), Venus (Balti) and Mercury (Nabuq). The main moon god sanctuary was at Harran where the cult was practiced into the 12th C. In 830 the Caliph El-Mamun was filled with indignation at the dress, long hair and scandalous behaviour of the Sabians and gave them the choice of converting to Islam or to Christianity or facing exile or hanging. One medieval Arab chronicler wrote of their wild practices: 'There was no hill that was not moist with the blood of sacrifices, and no high place that was empty of libations. Youths in multitudes were given as sacrifices, and maidens slaughtered to female idols and to the sun and the moon and Venus and the other luminaries'.

(margin notes:) **Earliest literature**

Star-gazing blood sacrificers

Harran of the Bible
Your arrival in **Harran** after 35 km from Urfa is an uninspiring sight: a village miserably huddled round a citadel mound, living at subsistence level among the ruins. Tourists are a newly discovered source of wealth which the children have not been slow to latch on to, following visitors and pestering them for 'para' (money) and 'kalem' (pens). This is something you had best get used to as from here eastwards few and far between indeed are the places you will

visit where there is not a village among the ruins and where you will be able to walk in peace.

Most people make the journey to Harran because of its biblical associations. It was 18 centuries before Christ that Abraham (still known as Abram) was called from Ur of the Chaldees to go to Canaan. He stopped at Harran for several years until God told him to move on (*Genesis* 12: 4–5): 'So Abram departed, as the Lord had spoken unto him; and Lot went with him: and Abram was seventy and five years old when he departed out of Haran. And Abram took Sarai his wife, and Lot his brother's son, and all their substance that they had gathered, and the souls that they had gotten in Haran; and they went forth to go into the land of Canaan'. Visitors also come to see the mud brick beehive houses clustered together like a termite colony, more typical of northern Syria. These windowless cones are built as the only way to achieve a roof without timber, and so the shape is dictated by the only material to hand in abundance — mud. Life within has changed little over the centuries. Certainly they are primitive, though now electricity wires and television aerials suggest some progress.

Beehive houses

Another biblical association attaches to a well about 1 km northwest of Harran called **Bir Yakub**, Jacob's Well. Was it here that Jacob kissed Rachel and that Rebecca, later to marry Isaac, drew water for Abraham's servant?

The original settlement of Harran is indicated by a **mound** at the centre of the stone walled city, and you can make a complete **circuit of the walls** (by car if you like), though they are heavily ruined in most places. They can easily be traced, however, by ramparts and ditches that remain where the stones have vanished. You enter the city on the western side at the **Aleppo Gate**, restored by Saladin in 1192 but now much ruined. On the right is a modern concrete beehive complex calling itself Harran Tourist Coffee, selling soft drinks. Walking through the city and over the mound, coming down the other side, you come to a cluster of **beehive houses** surrounded by dung cakes drying in the sun. Beyond them, at the southeastern corner of the walls, is the most prominent monument of Harran, a large crumbling 11th C **fortress** built on the site of a moon temple. It is better preserved inside, the vaulting still intact in many of the rooms. At the centre of the city and north of the mound is the other monument of note, the vast and ruinous **Ulu Cami**. T E Lawrence, who travelled past Harran enroute from Aleppo to Urfa in 1909 when he was still an Oxford student, mistook from a distance the tall brick minaret of this mosque for a campanile. He wrote in his diary: 'The tower of Harran cathedral was in sight for four hours'. The mosque was founded in the 8th C by

Within the walled city

the Umayyads and rebuilt in the 12th C by Saladin. Within its courtyard is a pretty marble fountain, and scattered all around are carved capitals and fragments of rose-coloured columns. The mosque was part of the earliest Islamic university complex.

DİYARBAKIR

Speculations upon the wasteland

From Urfa the drive on to Diyarbakır via Siverek takes only two and a quarter hours across a flat and unexciting landscape. Along the way you have plenty of time to speculate whether it was climatic change, too many goats, Mongol destruction of irrigation works or too many centuries of armies fighting each other and foraging that have been responsible for this wasteland. The drive due east 162 km to Mardin via Viranşehir is equally unexciting and has the disadvantage of being the oil tanker transit route to Mosul in Iraq. At **Viranşehir** (City of Ruins), the Roman city of Constantina, the basalt defence walls and towers run for over 2 km, repaired in the 6th C by Justinian.

Vital City on the Tigris

The approach road to **Diyarbakır** from the west unfortunately gives you no feel for the setting of the city and its walls, and it is really only from the air that you can appreciate the great old city enclosed in its black basalt walls. In its position at the limit of navigability on the Tigris and at a convenient crossing point, Diyarbakır, backed by the eastern Taurus mountains, dominates the expanse of the northern Mesopotamian plain. Once inside the walls you are not aware of the Tigris, but perhaps because the town is concentrated within the walls, you can feel vitality humming in streets busy with confident colourful people. The produce in the shops, especially the fruit and vegetables, is better quality than anything you will find further east. It has the confidence of a place that has been important for centuries, and is still the key city of the southeast. Most people enjoy their stay here more than in other eastern cities. It has the same squalor, dust and messy unfinished building work, but also has a special identity and is arguably **Arab mood** Turkey's most Arab city. Diyarbakır is special in the same way that Avila in Spain, Aleppo in Syria and Fez in Morocco are special, all cities that have until recently been bounded within their walls. Inside it has grown up with distinctive quarters, Armenian, Christian, Kurdish and Arab, each with its own mosques, churches and community buildings, and in the narrow winding streets there is the feel of hidden courtyards behind large carved wooden doors, inward-looking, Arab-style. The city takes its present name from the Arab tribe, the Beni Bakr, who took the city in 639, Diyarbakır meaning Place of the Bakr.

Enclosed within its 5 km long walls built by the Byzantines and subsequently added to and decorated by various

Arab, Kurdish and Turkish dynasties, Diyarbakır has more
historical mosques, churches and other notable buildings
than any other Turkish city except İstanbul.

Diyarbakır today however does have its problems. Having grown up within its walls, the town has gradually
expanded to almost bursting point. In recent times it has
suffered an influx of villagers and peasants from the immediate area, about 50,000 of them each year, coming to seek
jobs in the 'big city', but finding instead overcrowding and
unemployment. Peasants armed with agricultural tools can
be seen lining up in the morning by the walls, hoping to
be chosen to pile into trucks and go off to work for the
day. The overcrowding is particularly evident in the poorest
quarters between the Saray Gate and the Yeni Kapı where
the squalid streets are full of children and flies, each family
having an average of eight offspring. There is no industry
within the walls at all, and outside the only factory of note
is the state-run plant making rakı, the equivalent of Arab
araq or Greek ouzo.

The city's young and forward-looking mayor explains
the cycle: 'Overpopulation fosters a lack of development,
which fosters ignorance, which fosters dependency on religion, which fosters overpopulation by discouraging birth
control, which results in further retarded development'.
The hope is however that in the 1990s there will be enough
work for all when the Southeast Anatolia Project with its
series of 13 dams will provide the water to convert an area of
wasteland nearly the size of England to irrigated fields.

Because of its strategically important position on the
Tigris, commanding the southeastern lowlands, the city is
an important base for the Turkish military and Nato. The
headquarters of the Seventh Army, which is responsible
for security throughout southeastern Turkey in addition
to its Nato duties, was recently moved out of the ancient
citadel to a modern building several kilometres outside
town, and the tactical wing of the Turkish air force attached
to the joint US-Turkish base has recently been bolstered
by 44 F-104 Starfighter planes donated by Canada. The
sound of low-flying jets and helicopters is such a constant
background noise to the city's bustle that no one turns
a hair in the streets any longer.

The Kurds

Diyarbakır has a predominantly Kurdish population and
until recently was a natural centre of Kurdish dissident
groups. In the Kurdish revolt of the 1920s Diyarbakır
played a major role and in 1925 a special tribunal at Diyarbakır tried the leaders and closed the 'tekkes' of the Nakşi-
bendi dervish order, which had been implicated. After

Turkey's 1980 military coup, thousands of suspected dissidents were locked up in the prison, Turkey's most notorious. Today though there is no real evidence of tension or hostility, and you can walk and talk freely in all areas of the town. No incidents have occurred in the city for years, and the flat terrain of the region does not lend itself to guerilla activity. In the neighbouring mountainous province of Siirt, however, Kurdish guerilla attacks on the army are still quite common.

Guerillas...

Recently an interesting and somewhat surprising substitute for dissident activity in Diyarbakır has developed, namely Sufism, a mystical order of Islam, and even more surprisingly, with tacit official approval. Sufism is strictly speaking illegal under the constitution introduced by Atatürk, but clearly the authorities are glad that the young unemployed Kurds living in the slums have found a fairly harmless channel for their energies. One Kurdish student admitted: 'We were all pretty wild once. I was arrested for stabbing a man a few years ago, but religion set us straight. Who needs the Kurdish Workers' Party when you've got God?'

... and mystics

Ancient and traditional enemies of the Armenians, the Kurds are a distinct racial group indigenous to the region known as Kurdistan which today straddles the modern borders of Turkey, Iran and Iraq, encroaching also on the USSR and Syria. There are in total 16 million Kurds, a very large number indeed for a 'minority': only a handful of Arab states have populations larger than this. By far the greatest number are in Turkey, some seven to eight million, with four million in Iran and three and a half million in Iraq. The Kurdish language, Indo-European like Persian, Armenian and most European languages, has several dialects, all of which are mutually unintelligible, a fact which has not helped the Kurds in their attempts to unite: there are currently seven separate Kurdish national movements. Kermanji is the purest dialect, spoken in the Hakkâri, in northern Iraq and in the Kurdish province of Iran. It employs, like Persian, the Arabic alphabet and is used officially in Kurdish schools outside Turkey. Within Turkey however the language is banned, and Kurdish children go to Turkish schools which means that they tend to be bilingual, speaking Kurdish at home and Turkish at school with their friends.

'Minority' status

Most Kurds accepted Islam in the Arab conquest of the 7th C and are Sunni Moslems, like the Turks, but unlike the Persians who are Shia. Some 50,000 Kurds are still however, even today, said to be Yazidi or Peacock-god worshippers, often unfairly known to the West as devil-worshippers. These are the ones whom the Turks and Armenians have most feared in the past. They worship the sun and water is sacred to them. For fear of the power of evil (for them the universe is a struggle between light and dark, good and bad), they never refer to Satan by name. Children are dedicated to both God and Satan. James Morier in his 19th C novel '*Ayesha*' says of them: 'The Yazidis, as a race, are one of the most cruel and sanguinary that are known in Asia. Their name is synonymous with blasphemers, barbarians and men of blood.

The Devil in a cabbage They never eat cabbage because the Devil inhabits the leaves and they abominate the colour blue'.

The Kurds have always been a nomadic mountain people and in Turkey today they are officially known as 'mountain Turks', the existence of a separate Kurdish race being studiously ignored by the authorities. By and large, throughout their history, they did not resist invaders, but were content to pack their tents and drive their animals to still higher mountains away from the main passes. Owing to these evasive tactics of non-resistance they have been nominally ruled by Arabs, Mongols, Seljuks, Ilhans and other Persian rulers, Black Sheep and White Sheep Turcoman chieftains and Ottomans, up to the time of their division between three main countries after the First World War. Under the 1920 Treaty of Sèvres drawn up by the Allies, Kurdistan was to become an autonomous state, and had it not been for Atatürk's War of Independence, this Kurdish state would now exist. Ironically however the Kurds joined Atatürk in warding off the Greek Christians and the Persians on both fronts, and then, not surprisingly, felt cheated when Atatürk declared the Turkish Republic and abandoned the Caliphate for a secular state. In the Kurdish revolts that followed in the 1920s and 1930s, hundreds of thousands of Kurds were killed or deported by the Turks. Today the Kurdish guerilla raids on the Turkish security forces continue. About 300 lives have been lost in this Kurdish war since August 1984, though no foreigners have been involved.

Though they practised a policy of evasion in the face of conquerors marching through, the Kurds have been far from unwarlike themselves and have been ready to fight in other people's wars away from their home ground. The Hasanwaghs and the Marwanids in the 19th C both established dynasties, and because they adopted Arabic as their language are often wrongly referred to as Arabs. The great

Saladin the Kurd Saladin, hero of the Crusades, was a Kurd, and the Kurds are naturally proud to have produced one of the greatest heroes of Islam and the Moslem leader most respected in the West.

The Turks have great difficulty in collecting taxes from the nomadic Kurds. Whenever they expect a visit from the tax-collector, they pack up their chattels and migrate to the mountains, only returning to the plains when their spies tell them the coast is clear. The authorities have long had a resettlement programme for the Kurds, trying to persuade them to depend less on their pastoral ways and to do some farming to become food suppliers for the big cities, rather than just follow their age-old practice of growing only what they need to survive and selling their livestock from time to time to purchase their other needs. But as Freya Stark reflects there is a set of different values at work here: 'It is easy for the peasant, and for all of us who live in civilisation and think to make the world more habitable, to point out that the nomad does very little.

The nomad's way of life He leaves things as he finds them, destroying them in a small way if it suits him. He does not spend his life as we do in altering the accidents that happen to us so as to make them more bearable — but he accepts them with gaiety and endures them with fortitude, and this is his triumph and his charm. We may think reasonably enough that we dominate circumstances more than he does, since we adapt them to our needs: but he has discovered that the meaning of life is more important than its circumstance — and this freedom of the soul, in which all things that happen come and go, makes him splendid — him and his gaunt women and dogs and horses, on the edge of starvation in the rain and the sun. His life does not allow him to forget the greater size of the world; and no amount of civilisation is worth the loss of this fundamental sense of proportion between the universe and man'.

Walking Around Diyarbakır

To go around the various quarters of Diyarbakır looking in the mosques and churches will take several hours, at least three or four, of quite strenuous and dusty walking. Although everything is on the flat and distances are not actually long at all (the length of the main street north to south straight across the town is less than 1 km), the narrow winding streets mean that you easily lose all sense of direction and seem to have to walk miles between mosques which are only 200 metres apart as the crow flies. You will sometimes spot a minaret rising up between a gap in the buildings only 50 metres away, but arriving at the mosque takes you a further ten minutes while you weave round and round in the narrow lanes. Although you will inevitably get lost, the distances are too small to make this a real problem as you soon stumble on a major monument, and all the mosques have their names up on plaques outside to help you.

The teenagers of Diyarbakır, often students at the university or local technical colleges, are unusually charming and quite sophisticated. If they offer to escort you round the town and along the walls you will spend a very informative and enjoyable couple of hours during which the teenagers are courtesy itself. They will also keep at a healthy distance any impish younger children, who tend to yell 'turist, turist!' to alert the neighbourhood of your approach.

Stupendous Walls

Having installed yourself in one of the good hotels near the Harput Gate your first priority should be to see the **walls**. These still stand more or less intact for their length of 5.5 km, except for two stretches which were demolished some 50 years ago to make way for modern roads, at the Mardin Gate and the Harput Gate. Of the original 72 **towers** all but five are still standing. By far the best way to get a feel for the extent and power of the defences is to walk along the top of them. Walking at ground level, inside or outside the walls, is actually very difficult as there is no one circuit road, so you have constantly to skirt obstacles and end up walking twice the distance. The best stretch for a walk along the top is from the **Urfa Gate** to the **Mardin Gate**: a wide grassy path allows two or three abreast; in just a couple of places it narrows to less than a metre and the drop on either side will cause a few anxious moments for those not happy with heights. At sunset especially this is an enjoyable stroll, with fine **views** from the Yedi Kardeş (Seven Brothers') Tower south across the walls to the Tigris valley. A complex of modern low buildings on the summit of a hill due south is the Shell headquarters for the region, as Turkey's oil reserves are all in the southeast, mostly near the dynamically named town of Batman.

A walk along the top of the walls

The original walls of Diyarbakır date back to AD 297 when Diyarbakır, known then as Amida the Black, was taken from the Persian Sassanids and annexed to the Roman Empire. Successive Byzantine rulers rebuilt and strengthened them. In their present form however they are the work of the Seljuk Malik Shah who rebuilt them completely when he took the city in 1088. The outsides of the walls are also rich in inscriptions and reliefs, and the **Ulu Badan** (Great Wall) and **Yedi Kardeş Tower** are two of the most interesting for the elaborate decoration outside. The lions and eagles are Seljuk. A path leads round to these from the Urfa Gate so you can view them well.

Descending the walls at the Mardin Gate is possible but difficult and should not be attempted without the help of the local teenagers. It is better to retrace your steps and make your descent at the Urfa Gate again. Inside the Urfa Gate and a little to the right as you face in towards the town is the fine **mausoleum of Sarı Saduk** with Kufic inscriptions. You can then set off to the **Melik Ahmet Paşa Mosque**

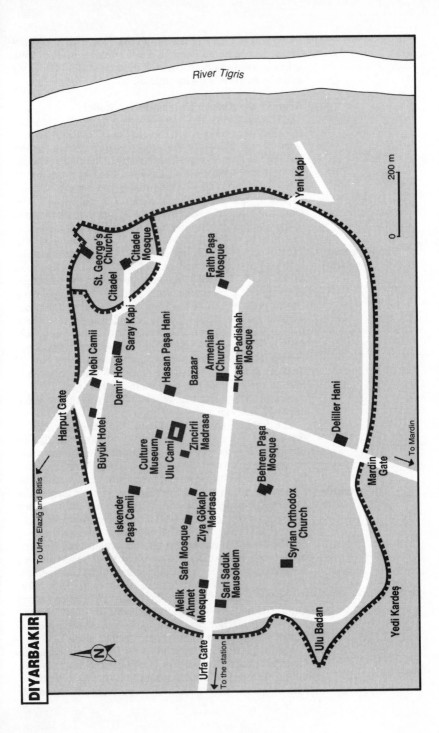

DIYARBAKIR

River Tigris

St. George's Church
Citadel
Citadel Mosque
Faith Paşa Mosque
Yeni Kapi

Nebi Camii
Saray Kapi
Hasan Paşa Hani
Bazaar
Armenian Church
Kasim Padishah Mosque

Harput Gate
Demir Hotel
Büyük Hotel
Culture Museum
Zincirli Madrasa
Ulu Camii
Behrem Paşa Mosque
Deliller Hani

To Urfa, Elazığ and Bitlis

Iskender Paşa Camii
Safa Mosque
Ziya Gökalp Madrasa
Syrian Orthodox Church
Mardin Gate
To Mardin

Melik Ahmet Mosque
Sari Saduk Mausoleum

Urfa Gate
To the station
Ulu Badan
Yedi Kardeş

N

200 m
0

203

which you will have noticed from the walls with its distinctive conical pointed dome and tall minaret. Built in 1591 it has a lovely mihrab covered in glazed tiles, the same as those on the base of its minaret.

Around the Harput Gate and the Citadel

The **Harput Gate** is the best preserved. In its slightly squat and thick-set power it can remind you of Hittite fortifications. It was known to the Arabs as Bab El-Armen, the Gate of the Armenians, either because it led to the Armenian quarter of the town or because it led to Armenia. It is enclosed by railings which mean you have to admire its reliefs and inscriptions from afar. On the corner of the main street and the street at right angles to it where most of the hotels are, you will notice a pretty little domed mosque, the **Nebi Camii** or Mosque of the Prophet, built in 1524 by the White Sheep clan. Its tall minaret is striped with alternate basalt and pale sandstone, stones common to the region, the local architects perfecting the technique of using the contrasting stones in many buildings of the city to great effect. It has even been speculated that the striping may represent the white and black totem sheep respectively of the two Turocoman.tribes, the Akkoyunlu and the Karakoyunlu (*ak*, white, *koyun*, sheep and *kara*, black) who both set up important states in this part of Turkey. Stone versions of the black and white sheep they used in their burials can be seen in the Erzurum and Van museums. Their first capital was at Erciş at the northern edge of Lake Van.

The Diyarbakır stripes

The **Saray Kapı** (Palace Gate), the main entrance to the **citadel**, is generally considered the most beautiful of the gates. It is just outside it that moth-eaten horses stand to take people on a circuit of the town. A *pointed arch* leads into a closed-off military zone where once stood the palace of the Artukids, Turcomans who governed the Diyarbakır region from the 11th to the 15th C. They encouraged the arts and were accomplished builders. They were also keen on the un-Islamic use of animals on coins and buildings; their animal embellishments can be seen on the walls here at Diyarbakır. Their most beautiful work however is at Mardin, especially in the Sultan Isa Madrasa. Above the pointed arch here in the citadel the Artukid symbol of a lion attacking a bull can still be seen carved into the stone. The bull symbolised worldly goods and the lion was the warrior strong enough to seize them, a graphic way of stating 'Unto him who hath shall be given'.

The Artukids

Inside the military area are two former churches, St George's Church and Küçük (Small) Church, but they cannot be visited. St George's is said to be in use as a prison. Just below the pointed arch a broad flight of steps leads past the impressive black basalt citadel mosque, the **Suley-maniye**, looking almost fortified itself, and with a türbe inside its courtyard. Its interior decoration is sombre and simple. It was built by the Artukids in 1160.

To the Ulu Cami
From the Harput Gate the long main (originally Roman) street cuts the city in half, leading to the Mardin Gate at the other end. As it must have been in Roman times it is full of the hubbub of markets and voices and gives you the feeling of being in a great provincial capital. Walking south along it you come after 350 metres to the main square. On the left is the 16th C striped **Hasan Paşa Hanı**, the biggest and most beautiful han in the city with a little fountain in the central courtyard. It is still in use and the whole bazaar area is behind it.

On the right a large arch leads into the open courtyard of the **Ulu Cami**. This remarkable structure was the very first of the great Seljuk mosques of Anatolia built by Malik Shah in 1091–2, just three years after he conquered Diyarbakır. It is one of the Five Holy Places of Islam and the courtyard is at all times milling with people old and young, all men. Women, especially foreign ones, are a rarity here but you should not feel intimidated by the stares. As long as you cover your head and limbs and take off your shoes you can enter the mosque without any qualms. Inside, the high *central bay* is reminiscent of a Gothic cathedral and the effect is very grand if somewhat austere. It is clearly modelled on the Great Umayyad Mosque at Damascus. Both within the mosque and in the courtyard the *columns and capitals* have clearly been reused from Byzantine buildings, with Greek inscriptions peeping out sideways and incongruously from the courtyard walls next to Arabic Kufic. The separate *minaret* is tall and square, a style typical of Diyarbakır, often with a short conical top added by the Ottomans later.

The east and west sides of the *courtyard* (the side you enter through is east) consist of elegant two-storeyed *arcades*: with their blend of classical columns, Seljuk arches and Greek and Kufic inscriptions they are strangely beautiful. In the centre of the courtyard are two free-standing conical ablution *fountains*, called şadirvans, with taps all around and stone slabs and clothes hooks provided. In Islam great value is attached to water. Among the Turks in particular water is important not only for religious and ablution purposes, but also in city and social life, in art and architecture, and many houses have central pools and ponds or even water running through in an open channel like a private river. In the far right corner of the courtyard

Damascene influence

The importance of water

an arcade of columns leads into the small dark **Masidiye Madrasa** with a **mihrab** of black basalt.

Leaving the courtyard by a door in the far left corner, you come out into a narrow street running along the side of the mosque. Turning first left and then right, you come in 50 metres to the **Zincirli Madrasa** (late 12th C) on a corner ahead of you, now an archaeological museum (temporarily closed). Nearby is the **Ziya Gökalp Museum** housed in a stark madrasa built of crude basalt blocks looking more like modern concrete and devoid of decoration. The exhibits consist of various Moslem memorabilia and the odd Turkish carpet, not desperately interesting, but the guardian shows you each one enthusiastically. Many of the rooms have photos of the famous local turn-of-the-century philosopher Gökalp who is said to have been the first person to develop the idea of Turkish nationalism. Also nearby is the home of the poet Cahit Sitki Taranca, a contemporary of Ziya Gökalp, which has been turned into an attractive **Culture Museum** with exhibits of local crafts.

Mosques and Churches
In the quarter behind this museum towards the walls you can walk through a maze of winding narrow streets in further search of Diyarbakır's many mosques and a few churches.

One of the loveliest mosques is the elegant **Safa Mosque** with its gracefully decorated white *minaret*, Persian in feel, with traces of blue geometric tilework near the bottom, still in a near perfect state. The entrance leads into an open courtyard with five graceful arches in the characteristic black and white striped stonework. Inside is an ornamented painted ceiling with blue and green tile beading. It is attributed to Uzun Hasan (1435–78), the great leader of the White Sheep.

Impossible to describe how to reach and best attempted by reference to the town plan provided are the following. The **Iskender Paşa Camii** (1551) with two corner patches of plain green tiles, set in a restful garden; the **Fatih Paşa Mosque** (1522), tastelessly colourful with mother of pearl in the mihrab and crassly painted domes in the gallery outside; and the **Behrem Paşa Cami** (1572), which is the largest mosque in Diyarbakır, with a very pleasant interior and tiling all around the walls. The minbar is in white and pink marble with an attractive green and beige conical pointed hat on top. The mihrab is attractive too, and unusually there is stained glass in the windows. This Ottoman decoration is colourful but restrained. There is a splendour in the decoration as in the mosque's proportions, within the limits of the severe local style.

Elegant white minaret

By asking, you can also find the **Syrian Orthodox Church**. From the outside it is just a large door set in the high walls like any other door in the narrow street, and you will need to bang on it for a while before the deacon comes to open it. Inside it is another world, a peaceful immaculately clean courtyard beautifully paved with fine stones leading to a complex of buildings which was once a large monastery founded here in the 7th C. The deacon will take you in to see the church, still used for services on Sundays by the 25 or so Syrian Orthodox families in Diyarbakır. The Christian buildings in Diyarbakır today do not announce themselves, unlike the mosques which always have signs, and many disused churches are now lived in by Moslem families. The only thing that gives them away from the outside is the carving of animals, usually lions, at either side of the top of the door.

The peace beyond the door

There is also the Armenian **Surp Giragos Kilesesi**, the only other Christian church still in use in Diyarbakır, equally difficult to find without help. Nearby is the **Kasım Padishah Mosque** (1512), another beautiful White Sheep construction, with its tall square *minaret* standing out in the street on four basalt pillars about 2 metres high, so that most people can walk right under it, though the locals believe that walking round the pillars seven times will make a wish come true. Its local name is 'Dört Ayaklı Minare', the Four-legged Minaret. Directly opposite is a simple restaurant serving good food where the waiters wear the red and green flashes of the Diyarbakır football team. This kind of restaurant never serves alcohol so you drink ayran, water or Coke with your meal. Near the Mardin Gate is a 17th C caravanserai, the Deliller Hanı, newly restore and now a hotel, having been derelict for many years.

Four-legged minaret

MARDIN

From Diyarbakır you can drive straight on through Silvan and Bitlis to Lake Van. This 402-km drive can be done in a day, but the first 165 km to Baykan is monotonous, passing through bare and colourless uplands, and there is also heavy traffic from the oilfields around Batman and Siirt. At **Silvan** there is a modest Ulu Cami built by the Artukids in 1228, all that remains apart from a few fragments of defensive wall, of the city that was once called Miyafarikin.

The Longer and Better Way to Van

Unless you are short of time, it is better to make the interesting trip south to Mardin, an important Syrian Christian centre with lovely Syrian-influenced architecture from where you can visit a number of monasteries on the Tûr Abdin plateau. Then you can make the spectacular drive to the impressive ruins of Hasankeyf on a cliff overlooking the Tigris, finally driving through mountainous scenery to Bitlis and Lake Van. This route will add a minimum of one, ideally two, nights to your itinerary but is well worth it.

Leaving Diyarbakır by the Mardin Gate the Mardin road seems quite narrow and minor compared to the busy main road from the west, with very little traffic. The road follows the Tigris south for the first 2 km and there is a wonderful

Looking back view back from here of the black walls of Diyarbakır rising above the river plain, a view you can never get from the city itself. A yellow sign points off to the right to **Gazi Paşa Kösk**, originally a White Sheep building in striped stone, which is another of the houses where Atatürk stayed, exhibiting some of the great man's belongings. It lies just off the road and there is a fine view from the terrace.

A few moments later you pass an elegant bridge over the Tigris with ten arches of carefully worked basalt. An inscription on it says it was built in 1065. At the Feast of the Sacrifice the locals throw slips of paper with their wishes into the river under the bridge. The road leads on through poor villages which look increasingly Arab, through a landscape that is quite hilly and fertile, with many flowers in spring. Copious potholes mark your way.

First Impressions of Mardin

After 96 km and one and a quarter hour's drive you have your first sight of Mardin, built up on a craggy rock facing south over the Syrian desert. From a distance, although its setting is striking, your first impression is not of a fine

The Sultan Isa Madrasa beneath the castle at Mardin

elevated town but rather of a hideous dingy sprawl of buildings, largely the same sandy colour as the land around. Only as you climb up to the town do you begin to catch glimpses of the beautifully decorated buildings, Arab style, which are Mardin's real attraction. Some are almost like **Decaying** palaces, now decaying, but still hinting at the past splen-**splendour** dour of the town.

There is only one hotel and that alas is not and never was a palace. The Bayraktır Hotel is on the right in the slight opening which is considered the main square, some 500 metres from entering the town. There are car parks in this area where you are well-advised to leave your car

Decoration at portal of Sultan Isa Madrasa

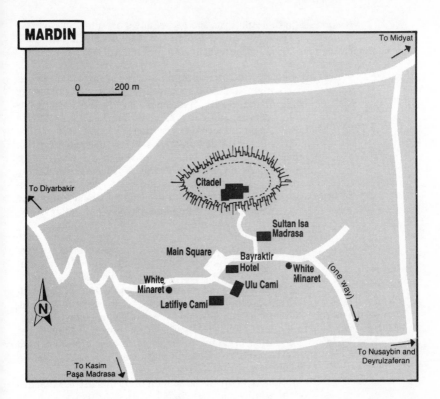

as this main road is almost the only road wide enough for motor vehicles and Mardin is therefore a place to be walked not driven round. But you will have to rise above the immediate squalor of the streets in order to enjoy the architecture. In the back streets especially there is foul-smelling rubbish littering the ground and it is definitely not the place to wear open-toed sandals. All along the main street at regular intervals futile rubbish bins are attached to posts vainly saying 'Cöp bana at', Throw the rubbish into me.

Walking up to the Citadel

You can begin by walking further east along the main street through a more salubrious part of town; after 100 metres you see on the left an exquisite large building with three arches: once a fine public building it is now the house of a fortunate Moslem family. Continuing another 200 metres, a flight of steps runs up between two buildings: climb these to reach the lovely **Sultan Isa Madrasa** at the top. Built in 1385, it is the most beautiful creation of Artukid architecture.

Passing through its beautifully carved portal to the courtyard within, you come upon the town's *museum*, containing some of the most extraordinary and interesting exhibits to be seen outside Ankara. There are a few fine Persian carpets, some enormous Urartian pots, but best of all a large number of elaborate and highly unusual Christian stone carvings from Midyat and Hasankeyf where large communities of Christians once lived. The most astonishing exhibits of all, though, are three chest-height figures in the central far chamber off the courtyard, cut out of one piece of solid stone. With haunting faces and sitting in stylised poses, they are thought to be Sumerian gods.

Returning to the entry passage, the guardian may take you up the stone steps at the back into the *madrasa proper* which is still in use as a boarding school for Koranic students. There are several *dormitories* you can peep into, extremely gaunt and primitive. From the *roof* of the madrasa there is a magnificent **view** encompassing its graceful white dome, the town and the arid plains below. Mardin, in contrast to black Diyarbakır, is sometimes called 'the White City' because of the distinctive pale limestone used here. Arnold Toynbee, no mean traveller, called Mardin 'the most beautiful town in the world'.

View of 'the most
beautiful town in
the world'

Behind you up on the summit of the hill are the remains of the sandy coloured **citadel**. A path leads up from the west side of the madrasa, though the view is just as good from the roof where you are. This hilltop citadel was originally a Roman and Byzantine fortress known in antiquity as Marida. It fell to the Arabs in 640 and after two and a half centuries of Arab rule was taken by the Sunni Kurdish Marwanids at the same time as Diyarbakır. Captured by the Seljuks in the late 11th C it was then handed over to Artukid Turcomans who made it their capital throughout the 12th, 13th and 14th C. During this period the citadel resisted the onslaughts of Saladin and then an eight-month seige by the first Mongol hordes, falling finally to Tamerlane in the second Mongol campaign in 1394. In 1431 it was captured by the White Sheep Turcoman clan, and today's ruins in the citadel date largely from this time. Inside the citadel are the *ruins of a vast palace and mosque*.

Mosques and Madrasas Worth Seeing

Returning down the main street again and turning left you could walk for 100 metres or so until you come on your right to a tall white minaret with an attractive restaurant

One of Mardin's old Arab houses

and tea area on a terrace looking on to it. Then walk back down the main street past the hotel, turning sharp left down a street running down the hill. This will bring you to the 11th C **Ulu Cami**, originally Seljuk but much restored after the various struggles to take the town. The cylindrical minaret had to be rebuilt when a mine exploded here during the Kurdish revolt of 1832. The fluted dome, like that of the Sultan Isa Madrasa, is typical of Mardin's architecture.

Nearby in the back streets at a similar height to the Ulu Cami is the 14th C **Latifiye Cami** which you should visit for its exquisitely carved entrance facade on its eastern side and for the view, from the windows inside the mosque, over the town and valley below.

There is one final building worth visiting but it is a long walk down to the bottom of the town and back up again, so you are better advised to take the car. This is the **Kasım Paşa Madrasa** built in the 15th C by the White Sheep clan. It is similar in arrangement to the Sultan Isa Madrasa.

About two and a half hours should be allowed to walk round the town and see the Sultan Isa Madrasa and main mosques, more if you include the citadel and the Kasım Paşa Madrasa. If you have even more time you can ask for directions to the **Şehidiye Mosque** built in the 13th C by the Artukids with very beautifully carved windows and portals, in the east of the town, and the 14th C **Babüssür Mosque**. It is pleasant to stroll round the town, especially in the evening, when you will be surprised at the quality of the produce on sale in the local shops. An excellent range of fruit and vegetables is found here, bananas too, a fruit never found in the more northern parts of Turkey.

Arabic spoken here Many of the shopkeepers are Arabs and Arabic can be heard spoken here more than in any other Turkish town.

THE TÛR ABDIN

The **Tûr Abdin** translates literally as the Servants' Plateau but the French phrase it more elegantly: Montagne des Serviteurs de Dieu. This highland region between Mardin and Cizre with Midyat at the centre is to the Syrian Orthodox Church what Mt Athos is to the Greek Orthodox Church. The history of Syrian Orthodoxy has been less happy in its outcome than that of Greek Orthodoxy however.

Sometimes known as Jacobites, they owe their founding to Jacob Baradai who in the 5th C was sent by the monophysite-leaning Empress Theodora, wife of Justinian, to Antioch. From there he roamed for 35 years, dressed only in a horse-hair blanket, preaching and converting across Syria and the Tûr Abdin.

From the Divine to the Distressed

In the early centuries of Christianity there was debate over the human and divine natures of Christ. Eastern theologians had decided that though born of Mary, the man in Christ had been entirely absorbed into the divine. Christ had one nature, the divine, and the adherents of this view were monophysites. However at Chalcedon, across the Bosphorus from Constantinople, it was decided by the assembled Church that Christ had two natures, unmixed and unchangeable but at the same time indistinguishable and inseparable — this is the view of the Greek Orthodox and Roman churches to this day. The issue may not seem terribly important, or even comprehensible, and really it was more a slogan by which the cultures of East and West denounced one another. But after the Council of Chalcedon monophysism became a heresy so far as Constantinople and Rome were concerned, and the churches of Egypt, Syria and Armenia, denied and denying both spiritual communion with the West and military aid, were ultimately swamped by the Islamic tide.

Heresy

Even so, in the highlands of the Tûr Abdin the Syrian Orthodox Church flourished. During the Middle Ages there were four bishoprics and 80 monasteries here, and the population was prosperous through trade and farming. Persecution came from fellow Christians, Crusaders from Edessa (Urfa) and Antioch; later the Mongols left their mark; and the last great period of suffering came in the First World War and after when Turkey's Christian minorities became involved in the Allies' intention to carve up the old Ottoman Empire. Now only 23,000 Syrian Orthodox Christians remain in Turkey, survivors of the massacres and deportations shared also by the Greeks and Armenians.

The Tûr Abdin is now classed by the Turkish government as a distressed area, to be aided by a succession of one-year plans. There is a dearth of hotels, however, making it difficult to visit many of the monasteries, and in any case only four monasteries remain active. For those prepared to put up with the meagre accommodation of Mardin or Midyat, or are prepared to stay in one of the monastery hostelries, there is more that can be seen.

Among the legends associated with the region is the one that Noah's Ark came to rest on Mt Kadur east of Cizre (rather than on Ararat, the more popular story). At any rate, Noah's grave in Cizre is a point of pilgrimage for Christians and Moslems alike.

Noah's grave

An Easy Excursion to a Monastery

From Mardin a short excursion can be undertaken to **Deyrulzaferan** (House of Saffron), a Syrian Orthodox monastery in a valley 4 km away. About 1 km after leaving the edge of the town, a yellow sign points left off the main road south to Nusaybin and you follow a small tarmac road running 3 km along the valley right up to the monastery entrance. Rising behind the monastery in the sandy cliffs are caves, at one time inhabited by monks, and the remains of a castle can be seen.

Relics

In this once thriving monastic community founded in the 5th C there is now just one monk and one nun.

Attached to the monastery is a *boarding school* for children of Syrian Orthodox families; about 30 young boys are taught here at a time. And there is a community of helpful adherents, including gardeners and cooks: one of these will greet you on arrival and take you on a little tour. First stop is usually the *church*, built at the time of the Byzantine Emperor Anastasius (491–518) above the grave, it is said, of 12,000 martyrs.

Attending Evening Service

If you are here at 6pm you will be asked to attend the evening service in Aramaic, a language known to Christ. The solitary monk with his long white beard and black robes stands chanting tunelessly from the Bible. His only assistant is a teenage boy. Between them they act out the entire ritual of the service, the boy disappearing behind the altar screen for a quick change into white robes and gold sash.

The number of these monks in Turkey has now dwindled to the extent that apart from the lone monk here at Deyrulzaferan, there is Mar Yakoub with one monk (aptly called Yakoub), Mar Malki with also one monk, and Mar Gabriel, the largest, with six monks and the bishop who is head of the Church in Turkey. Deyrulzaferan however has remained the seat of the patriarch of the Jacobean Church since 1160 when he was driven out of Antioch, though none of its patriarchs has been resident in Turkey since the 1920s.

A Place to Stay
During the remainder of the tour you will be shown the *bedroom and reception room of the bishop* (or metropolitan as bishops are called in the Eastern church). When he comes to visit he will stay here, and the reception room is decked out, Middle Eastern style, with red chairs round the walls and the metropolitan's big chair at the head. Photos of the incumbent kissing other religious dignitaries hang on the walls.

The monastery can also put up humbler folk like yourself in simple *cells* and will offer refreshments. Though the facilities are basic you may prefer the atmosphere to the squalor of Mardin's Beyraktir Hotel. But you will have to spend some time with the monk and his helpers, so it will go better if you speak some Turkish. Whether overnighting or passing through, it is customary to put a donation in the collection box inside the church.

Shadows on the Way to Nowhere
You could now drive north and east from Mardin to Midyat (see below) to visit the Monastery of Mar Gabriel and several churches, or you could first make the dead-end drive to the abandoned but most beautifully sited of the monasteries, Mar Augen, past Nusaybin. (Maps show a road running north from Nusaybin to Midyat but it is impassable for ordinary cars; nor should you go as far east as Cizre which is in unsettled Kurdish country. In other words if you visit Mar Augen you must return again to Mardin if you want to continue north or east.)

The dead flat transit route eastwards towards Nusaybin and Iraq passes through bleak featureless plains following the edge of the Syrian border, marked by barbwire fencing and guard posts. No birdwatching or photography should be indulged in here.

At **Nusaybin**, to the right of the road, all that remains of the Roman city of Nisibis is a **triumphal arch**. There is also an ancient church, **Mar Yakoub**, still in use. The town today is a mere shadow of its former self, and the most impressive monument is the **railway station**, the furthest Turkish station on the Berlin to Baghdad railway. The town became the capital of the Roman province of Mesopotamia at the beginning of the 3rd C.

Driving is difficult with the heavy dust of frequent road-works kicked up by trucks often obscuring your vision for overtaking. All along this route are a series of unlikely places to pause for a break or to stay the night, usually built round a petrol station, the Turkish equivalent to a motor transport café where truck drivers can stop. The **Unlikely haven** most unlikely place of all is the Nezirhan about 24 km beyond Nusaybin on the left of the road, where a vast complex is nearing completion in the middle of nowhere. The motel here has the dubious distinction of achieving an M1 grading from the Turkish Ministry of Tourism, and it is certainly pretty good compared to the other places along the road which merit no classification at all. Like many modern hotels it is already falling apart and the plumbing is starting to malfunction.

Suitably refreshed from your night at Nezirhan, you can make an interesting excursion to the **Monastery of Mar Augen**, derelict now but partly inhabited by a Moslem family. This is the only one of the derelict monasteries that is reachable without too much difficulty, but you should nevertheless not attempt it unless you are prepared for some bad road driving through fields and then a stiffish climb. The effort for those who do will be rewarded, for **Spectacularly** apart from its interest it is the most spectacularly situated **sited monastery** of the Tûr Abdin monasteries.

From Nezirhan you drive on eastwards for only 1 km or so to the turn off left to **Girmeli**. Nowhere is there any yellow sign indicating Mar Augen, but you take the earth road which leads about 1 km to the village. On the far side of the village the road crosses a small bridge and you come immediately after to a junction of three roads of which you take the far right. You now follow this earth road for about 3 km straight towards the hills in front of you. Although a little tricky where it is heavily overgrown, the road is fine for a car if driven slowly and carefully. It ends directly at the foot of the cliff beneath the monastery which perches about half way up.

The ascent up the rocky path is quite steep and can be taxing on a hot day; it takes around 40 minutes. As you approach you can see the lower outer walls of the monastery and remains of its former terracing where the monks once grew their produce. Several hundred monks once lived here. The Moslem family living here now have a separate house they have built at the back, under the cliff face, and only use the monastery to grow a few vegetables in its courtyard.

The monastery **church** has a large vaulted nave, now totally bare, with no frescoes or decoration left. The church is thought to date to c400. Outside in the cloister a bucket can be lowered into the deep **well** to pull up water which

Rooms with a view: a local family has moved into Mar Augen

is quite drinkable. Out on the terrace the **view** is superb down over the plain and to your tiny speck of a car just visible below.

An invitation to tea

The family will welcome you gladly if you behave politely and will almost certainly offer you tea and bread and cheese and yogurt for lunch. They seem to live quite happily alone here, the children playing with each other and the father making occasional trips down to the village of Girmeli with his donkey to get supplies.

The Midyat Route

A town in two halves

The drive from Mardin takes you through a pretty and cultivated landscape. You arrive after 70 km or 50 minutes' drive at **Midyat** which chooses not to announce itself and is a most curious place in two halves. Reaching a major junction you turn right to reach the Moslem half of the town, dirty and bustling. However there is nothing to be seen here, so returning to the T junction and continuing straight on you come after about 2 km to the other quite separate Christian half of Midyat with church bell-towers rising up above the neater and cleaner looking houses. There are five churches in Midyat and five priests to look after them. The churches are generally kept locked, though if you ring the bell the priest or some helper will come to let you in. The churches are not remarkable, but it is interesting to walk round the town comparing Christian with Moslem architecture. The best known church is Mar Philoxenos, formerly in ruins but recently restored and now called **Mar Aznoyo**.

From the Christian half you should now take the turn marked Cizre and Habur to make a visit to Mar Gabriel. This is in fact the real heart of the Syrian Orthodox community in Turkey today with a resident bishop and the giddy total of six monks and ten nuns. It was founded in the early 5th C by Simeon who came from an aristocratic family in Mardin and was the real originator of monastic life on the plateau. Under Simeon in its heyday the monastery boasted 400 monks, some coming from as far afield as Egypt.

From Midyat it is 20 km of appalling potholes, but the scenery, if you have a chance to enjoy it, is gentle hills and valleys. It is in one of these valleys in the middle of nowhere that a sign suddenly points off left to **Mar Gabriel** (also called Deyrulumur Manastiri). The specially constructed road, built by the government in 1966, leads 3 km to the monastery, and though an earth track, it is a veritable relief to get off the tarmac onto this smoother surface. Mar Gabriel is evidently prosperous for it has built a modern addition. Inside the courtyard the monastery has none of the charm and beauty of Deyrulzaferan or Mar Augen, but it is interesting to see how a living monastery functions.

A living monastery

A Chat with the Bishop
If you are here around 12.30 you will be automatically invited to join the bishop and monks in the refectory for lunch. Clad in scarlet robes, the bishop sits in the centre of the head table and three monks sit either side of him, a curious collection of faces of all types and ages, each with a beard of different length, possibly suggestive of a kind of hierarchy among them. Running at right angles from either end of the head table two further long refectory tables run down the sides of the room, one for the monastery laity, the other for any guests that may arrive. The bishop speaks good English and is quite a roguish conversationalist. He tells of his many important visitors, the British and German ambassadors plus entourage, various government officials, religious dignitaries, all of whom contact him by phone or letter in advance to give him warning of their arrival so that they can be accommodated in the new and comfortable extension. Some stay several days. Among his less distinguished visitors are some German coach tours.

A youthful lay helper will give you a tour of the monastery, starting with the *church* and moving through the *original dining room and kitchen* to a chamber with a row of tombs called the *Church of the 40 Martyrs* where St Simeon

**Burial place of the
saints**

and St Gabriel are buried. From here a vaulted arcade leads through to the lovely dark old *St Mary Church*, no longer used. Upstairs you are shown into the bishop's *reception room* with the same red chairs and whitewashed walls and pictures of the bishop and patriarch in Damascus, and you will be offered tea here if your visit does not coincide with lunch.

Churches Along the Way to Hasankeyf

A remote group of churches lies to the east on either side of the road that forks off right to Dargeçit 5 km out of Midyat on the Hasankeyf road. 10 km along this turn-off and then left 3 km along a difficult track you will reach the village of Salah with its 14th C church of **Mar Yakoub**. It was originally part of a monastery probably founded in the 4th C which was one of the most important in the Tûr Abdin. On the lintel and door jambs inside there is some fine carved decoration and the entrance to the central choir is also finely carved. The pillars which support the arches are decorated with birds and garlands. Outside, the southern facade has beautiful moulding with carefully worked stone.

5 km further on up a dirt track to the right is **Mar Kyriakos** at the entrance to the village of Arnas, now called Bağlarbası. This too used to be part of a monastery, facing a galleried courtyard. The cloister of the choir is 8th C and the church itself is probably 6th C.

Not far from Arnas is the church of **Mar Azaziel** in the village of Kefr Zeh, now called Altıntaş, built on the same plan as Mar Kyriakos, on the summit of a hill.

South of Kerburan at the end of the track, the village of Khakh (now called Anıtlı) has two churches, **Mar Sovo**,

**The most beautiful
Virgin**

now ruined, and the lovely **El Hadra** (The Virgin) at the entry to the village on the right. This graceful 7th C church with a decorated pyramid dome and two stories of elegant blind arches supported by columns with Corinthian capitals, is the most beautiful of all the Tûr Abdin churches. Around the door jambs and lintels and arches are palm tree decorations, garlands, pearls and acanthus leaves.

FROM THE TÛR ABDIN TO LAKE VAN

The road from Midyat for the first 20 km or so towards Hasankeyf is very poor indeed, riddled with the by now familiar potholes, no less trying for their familiarity. The final 20 km are slightly better and the scenery is quite interesting as you begin to make a spectacular descent off the plateau, eventually catching your first glimpse of the wide Tigris as the road winds down into the valley and Hasankeyf which marks the northern border of the Tûr Abdin. The **The reason why** visit to **Hasankeyf**, a spectacularly sited ruined town on a cliff overlooking the Tigris, is the main reason to drive this route from Diyarbakır via Mardin to Lake Van rather than heading straight to the lake.

Exploring Hasankeyf

Hasankeyf was founded by the Romans as a frontier outpost. Later it became the Byzantine bishopric of Cephe. When the Arabs took the town in 640 they called it 'Hisn Kayfa', Fortress Cephe, from which its present name has derived. It served for half a century as an Artukid capital in the 12th C, and it was the skilled Artukids who built the bridge across the Tigris here, whose crumbling supports can still be seen rising above the water. The bridge was described by early travellers as being the grandest in all Anatolia. From 1232 the town served as the capital of the Kurdish Ayyubid kings before falling to the Ottomans in 1416.

As you approach you notice in the cliffs rising up from both sides of the river numerous hollowed out caves, some inhabited by animals, some used for storage. On the left of the road you can see behind the modern ribbon development an extensive area of **ruined houses**, among which are three ruined mosques. If you have the energy and inclination later, you can spend a fruitful hour exploring this area, as many of the houses date from pre-1260, the date of the Mongol sacking of the town, and still have decorations inside with fragments of tiles. From the outside they do not appear to hold much promise, but inside you can stumble on some very attractive patterned ceilings.

First of all, however, you will probably want to drive into town and across the modern bridge from where you **Getting your** can get your bearings. On the clifftop above the town you **bearings** can see the ruins of the Artukid city you will explore, below in the modern town is the tall distinctive minaret of a red brick mosque and to your right are the remains of the once sturdy Artukid bridge, now reduced to four thick-set arches drowning in the strong river current. Just to the right of the bridge, opposite the town on a little mound, are the ruins of what was once a convent, for Hasankeyf was an important Syrian Christian centre before the Mongol invasion.

Having surveyed the scene, you can now drive back across the bridge towards the town and take the road immediately to the right after the bridge. Following this road on past the graceful sandy-coloured mosque and minaret with a stork's nest on top, you reach a narrow gully between two towering cliffs, and you leave the car here where the road deteriorates. From this point you walk up a little path towards the colossal **gateway** on the right, the entrance to the Artukid city.

The Artukid City

You walk up through this magnificent gate and along the broad stone-laid way zigzagging up the side of the cliff. The climb is not particularly steep and only takes ten minutes or so, far less than you might imagine, looking up from below. On the way up you pass more **caves** in the cliff face, many with doors and interconnecting chambers inside, used as houses until not long ago. Indeed some caves are still inhabited by troglodyte families. Your chances of avoiding being spotted by the local children are minimal, and you will probably by now find yourself surrounded by a small retinue anxious to lead you round their stamping ground. They do however have their uses, **Beware the dogs** like throwing stones at the ferocious barking dog at the top which guards the only house on the summit that is still lived in by a family. These dogs are not actually as alarming as they first seem, for they only guard a certain radius which they regard as their territory, and as long as you give them a wide berth they will bark for all they are worth but will not attack. More worrying however, are the sheepdogs sometimes to be seen with their flocks, whose collars carry sharp spikes as protection against wolves, and whose ferocity is not in doubt.

You come first to a fine ruined hall with carvings on the walls which is the 12th C **palace** of the Artukid kings. Its outer wall is perched right on the cliff edge and from the window you have a sheer drop down into the Tigris **Vertiginous view** with a fabulous and vertiginous view over the bridge and town below.

After climbing a little higher you begin to see the sheer extent of the **ruined city** on the vast cliff top. The houses extend for at least two square kilometres over the undulating slopes of the summit, and on the most prominent mounds stand the major buildings, notably a mosque and two saints' tombs with their domed roofs. The mosque is especially fine with gates leading into its grassy courtyard and the steps up its minaret still climbable. The buildings are all of a sandy mud colour, and considering they do not appear very sturdily built, it is surprising that they have survived so well through eight centuries. You could spend hours up here exploring properly but none of the houses seems to have any special feature or decoration and so the whole is exciting more for its setting and extent.

As you leave, driving along the far bank of the Tigris, you will see some 500 metres from the bridge and set all by itself across the fields near the river an unusual little red brick building with an onion-domed top. Covered on the outside in exquisite turquoise glazed tiles, this is the **Ayyubid gem** best preserved and finest example of Ayyubid architecture in Turkey, showing much Persian influence. It is the **türbe of the Ayyubid king**, Zeyn El-Abdin, a Kurdish descendant of Saladin, and though it appears quite small from a distance, you will be surprised how huge it is when you stand below it. To reach it involves a muddy tramp across 400 metres or so of ploughed field, so you may content yourself to study it through binoculars.

From Batman to Siirt

From Hasankeyf the road north soon leaves the Tigris for the superbly named town of **Batman** at the heart of Turkey's oilfields. But Turkey is not self-sufficient in oil and **A shortage of oil but no shortage of potholes** has to buy additional crude from Saudi Arabia, Iraq, Iran, Algeria and the Soviet Union. The Iraqi pipeline already produces good transit revenues and there are now plans to build an Iranian pipeline. The asphalt by-produced at Batman is said all to be sent west to resurface roads near İstanbul and Ankara, leaving Eastern Turkey's potholes crying out to be filled.

The road to the right before Batman leads off along 91 km of narrow paved surface to **Siirt**, a wild town in the Kurdish heartlands, rarely visited because it is not on a through route to anywhere, or at least only with great contrivance. The only surfaced route beyond it leads south through Şirnak to Cizre and Habur near the Iraqi border, but this area is currently very sensitive and should be avoided if at all possible. Siirt was first settled by Babylonians and Assyrians, and later flourished particularly under the Abbasid caliphate of Baghdad. Set in pastureland, the mountains which surround the town are snow-capped all the year round, though the summers are very hot. The whole region is full of rivers which are tributaries of the Tigris.

Of the town's monuments the Seljuk **Ulu Cami** built in 1129 is the most interesting, with its tall rectangular brick minaret decorated with turquoise tiling in geometric patterns, disused until recently, but now emerging from prolonged restoration. Its carved walnut minbar, superbly worked, has been removed to the Ankara Ethnographical Museum. Also worth seeing are the 13th C **Cumhuriyet Cami**, founded in the 8th C under the Abbasid caliphate, and the **Kavvan Hammam**, an 11th C Seljuk bath.

Siirt is famous for its especially warm, soft blankets made from a kind of mohair goat raised on local pastureland. Freya Stark, on her travels in these Kurdish lands, bought some of the goatswool material and had it made into a suit in Paris by Chanel 'where the the material was wondered at and admired'. Kurdish rugs and saddlebags can be cheaply bought here.

From Paris sensation ...

In some parts of the old town there are some remarkable Arab-style mud brick houses, like those found in the Arabian Gulf, very large, several storeys high, with decoration round the windows and receding plastered walls. The new town is developing at the foot of the hillside, but these tall old buildings, windowless until their upper storeys, are to be found through arches and up narrow streets. There is still much fellow feeling in this part of Turkey with the Arab world, and you will sometimes see photos of King Hussain of Jordan where you would normally expect to see the omnipresent Atatürk. Kurdish guerillas thrive in the difficult mountainous terrain around Siirt and there are frequent reports of clashes with the Turkish military.

From Batman to Bitlis

From Batman north to the Diyarbakır–Bitlis road you run alongside a large tributary of the Tigris and its broad flood plain for some kilometres. The scenery is very attractive, with unusual hill formations and the snow-covered mountains of the Van region in the background. Flocks of sheep are seen frequently accompanied by shepherds looking like giant yetis in ankle-length shaggy coats of thick felt hanging in a dead straight line from very broad shoulders. It is a curious fact that eastern Turks are quite impervious to rain. In the towns and villages the men continue to walk about in shirtsleeves, usually hatless, as if they are not even aware it is raining. The women, wrapped up in their garb with only their faces peeping out, are better protected.

... to off-the-peg yeti

On reaching the Diyarbakır–Bitlis T-junction, you could make a short detour of 4 km back towards Diyarbakır to take a quick look at the superb **bridge at Malaabadi**, which runs just next to the modern road bridge. Built in 1146 by the Artukids, it has one of the largest spans of any single-arched bridge. Near Malaabadi a road forks off north to the remote mountain village of **Sason**. In the 19th C a tribe of people were found living here who were neither Christians nor Moslems, speaking a misture of Arabic, Kurdish and Armenian. They had no churches or mosques and no institution of marriage. Women went free and unveiled but could be bought and sold.

Liberated women for sale

You now return to the junction and continue eastwards through Baykan to Bitlis, a highly picturesque road leading through gorges with rushing rivers and many unusual rock formations in the surrounding mountains, various minerals making the rocks look sometimes green, sometimes red. The scenery is semi-Alpine with poplar trees along the river valleys rustling in the stiff breeze and the white water rushing down from the distant snow-peaked mountains. Cows and the occasional flock of sheep graze peacefully near the roadsides.

At the end of this road, always climbing gradually through the valleys and mountains, you reach Bitlis, the town which is the real gateway to Turkey's eastern extremities. From here you are on the edge of the Lake Van region, the high point of any journey to Eastern Turkey.

Arrival at Bitlis

Formerly on the outer fringes of the Byzantine Empire and the Kingdom of Armenia, **Bitlis** is the gateway to a different world. You are here coming to the edge of an unknown, a blank in most people's minds, and as you approach past the filthy factories outlying the town and enter the steep black gorge with its curious houses set up on the cliffsides, you have a strange sensation of entering an alien environment. The houses have whitewash painted round their windows, contrasting sharply with the very dark chocolate-coloured stone used in all the buildings. This stone has the characteristic colour found all around the Van region. Many houses also have layers of thick wooden beams between the stonework as protective shock absorbers against earthquakes. Some of these solid old houses still have Armenian inscriptions in a band at first or second floor level, for the town was Armenian till the Seljuk conquest. The other thing that strikes you is how separate each house is, each in its own green garden.

The edge of an unknown

As you come into the town proper you can glimpse some intriguing ruins down in the gorge near the river, looking like a gateway. This river, the Bitlis Suyu, is another tributary of the Tigris.

Continuing along the main street you glimpse to your left the fine **Şerefiye Mosque** with a türbe attached. Within its courtyard you get a good impression of its powerful arches and minaret, all built in perfectly masoned blocks. It was built surprisingly late, in 1528, by a local Kurdish emir. The town remained the capital of a Kurdish beylicate until the mid-19th C. A little further up the main street is the **Ulu Cami**, a curiously malformed mosque built in 1126 by the Artukids. Its interior is exceptionally garish with a bright green carpet and foul modern blue and white kitchen tiles, and odd pieces of Koranic inscription set in the walls. The minaret stands separately with blind arcading and an odd domed roof. Also in the town is the **Şerefhan Madrasa**, the 16th C **Paşa Baths** and several türbes of the 17th C.

Bitlis today is famous for its Virginia-type tobacco and for a light-coloured honey with a lovely flavour. There used to be a very important trade route from Mesopotamia up through Siirt and Bitlis to Van, as the Bitlis valley is the only approach possible to Lake Van from the south and west, through a small break in the mountains that cut off this part of Turkey from the rest of the country. In the 19th C there was even a British consulate here. The population today is largely Kurdish, but up to the 1920s nearly half the inhabitants were Armenian.

As you leave and the road climbs up out of the gorge you can see on your left the impressive **walls of the citadel** lowering ominously above. Said to have been built originally in Alexander the Great's time (by one of Alexander's generals called Budles, from whom the town is thought to take its name) the walls today are largely Ottoman.

You are now within 150 metres of the altitude of Lake Van, and as you drive the last 25 km from Bitlis you enter the snow line even as late as May. The road is raised up above the level of the ground either side to keep it clear of the heavy waterlogging which occurs each year when the snows melt. Set down just to the right of the road **The last** at the top of the pass is a heavily ruined caravanserai, a **caravanserai** relic of the once important trade route from the south, and the last caravanserai you will see on your journey from here east and north.

PRACTICAL INFORMATION

ADANA
Divan Oteli (4-star), Tel: 22701. 116-room luxury class hotel and the price reflects it.

Büyük Surmeli (3-star), Tel: 21944. 166 air-conditioned rooms, semi-luxury class, in the centre.
Ener Motel (2-star), Tel: 11904. The best

place to spend a peaceful night at a moderate price, 2 km out of town on the main road east, by a Mobil station, on the right-hand side as you leave. You have to be looking out for it, as it is set back from the road in low bungalow chalets. There are pretty gardens and a large pool which functions from the end of May until the end of September. Its restaurant is adequate, and it has good camping facilities. 20 rooms.

Ipek Palas (1-star), Tel: 18743. 84 rooms, older style.

Avoid the Hotel Sedef, shortly after the airport turn-off in town on the main through-road. It is a rip-off place with a thin veneer of sophistication, concealing overpriced and indifferent food and service.

The turn-off to the **airport** is 2 km west of town. There are two daily flights to İstanbul, one morning, one evening (1 hour); and one daily morning flight to Ankara (1 hour).

Average temperature (Celsius):

J	F	M	A	M	J
9.3	10.4	13.1	17.0	21.4	25.2
J	A	S	O	N	D
27.6	28.0	25.3	21.0	15.7	11.1

Maximum temperature:

J	F	M	A	M	J
26.5	26.2	30.7	36.7	41.3	42.8
J	A	S	O	N	D
44.0	45.6	42.7	41.5	34.3	26.7

Minimum temperature:

J	F	M	A	M	J
−8.4	−6.6	−4.9	0.1	7.1	9.2
J	A	S	O	N	D
11.5	14.8	9.3	2.5	−4.3	−4.4

ISKENDERUN

Güney Palas (2-star), Tel: 3696. 27 rooms old-fashioned but very clean and well-run. Good restaurant.

Hitit (1-star), Tel: 3781, 40 rooms.

Kavakli (1-star), Tel: 4606, 17 rooms.

Arsuz Hotel (1-star), Tel: 12. 45 rooms, open April through November, on the beach at Uluçınar, 30 km south of Iskenderun. Very simple but clean. Heavily Arab clientele during holiday period.

Plaj **restaurant**, on the beach. Specialities are fresh fish and giant prawns.

ANTAKYA

Atahan (1-star), Tel: 1036, 28 rooms.

Divan (1-star), Tel: 1518, 22 rooms.

De Liban Hotel, Harbiye.

Restaurants: Atahan and Zumrut, with Arab specialities, notably meze (varied hors d'oevres) and hummas (chick-pea dip).

Average temperature (Celsius):

J	F	M	A	M	J
8.0	9.9	12.8	17.0	21.1	24.6
J	A	S	O	N	D
26.9	27.6	25.4	20.3	14.4	9.5

Maximum temperature:

J	F	M	A	M	J
20.2	22.3	27.7	34.4	42.5	41.5
J	A	S	O	N	D
43.4	43.9	41.0	38.0	29.4	22.6

Minimum temperature:

J	F	M	A	M	J
−14.6	−6.8	−3.9	1.7	9.0	11.6
J	A	S	O	N	D
15.9	15.5	10.3	2.0	−3.0	−6.6

GAZIANTEP

Kaleli Otel (1-star), Tel: 13417. The best in town, 70 rooms.

The **restaurants** are good by Eastern Turkey's standards; try especially the Turkish pizza, lahmacun. The best known restaurant is the Keyvanbey on Hurriyet Caddesı with an outside terrace.

Gaziantep has a military **airport** which is frequently open to commercial traffic. When it is, there is a direct flight from İstanbul on Mondays and Fridays (1½ hours) and a flight via Ankara on Wednesdays and Saturdays (4 hours including transfer time).

ADIYAMAN (NEMRUT DAĞ)

Sultan (1-star), Tel: 2122. Somewhat spartan but adequate hotel on the eastern outskirts of town (the Nemrut side), on the right hand side of the road. The main hotel is a detached green building, and attached is a camping site with a small shop for self-caterers. The rooms are very large though sparsely furnished so there is an echoing of noise especially along the corridors.

The Adıyaman **tourist office** is very basic and a complete waste of time.

At **Kahta**, 25 km closer to Nemrut and just by the turn-off for the ascent, is the Pension Kommagene (Tel: 92) a basic and slightly squalid place where the locals are well-practiced in how to fleece tourists: they will try to convince you that your car will not make it and that you therefore need to go in one of their minibuses, but they can safely be ignored. Also in Kahta is the Merhaba Hotel, closed until late May. It is not much better anyway.

On the drive up there is the Apollo Pension some 16 km before the summit, an unlikely and simple house claiming to be a motel, restaurant and camping site. Just 7 km from the summit the new Zeus Motel promises to be quite swish. There are several other basic camping/restaurant places in the final village before the top.

At the summit itself, is a simple **restaurant** where an omelette and salad style meal can be eaten in pleasant surroundings. It also sells beer and overpriced souvenirs.

URFA

Hotel Harran (2-star), Tel: 4918. 54 rooms, recently opened, the best hotel in Urfa and in the area generally, with very plush reception rooms and bar. From April until October it gets very full with coach tours, so it is worth phoning ahead. Hotel Turban Urfa (2-star), Tel: 3520. 55 rooms, the next best, slightly older and more used-looking than the Harran.

The local town **restaurants** are adequate but unexciting and many do not serve alcohol. You are better off by and large to dine at your hotel. Near Abraham's Pool there are several restaurants and cafés set in the park which are good for snacks.

Average temperature (Celsius):

J	F	M	A	M	J
5.1	6.7	10.3	15.7	21.8	27.7
J	A	S	O	N	D
31.6	31.2	26.6	20.0	13.0	7.3

Maximum temperature:

J	F	M	A	M	J
21.6	22.7	29.0	33.6	39.5	42.2
J	A	S	O	N	D
46.5	46.2	41.7	37.8	30.8	22.7

Minimum temperature:

J	F	M	A	M	J
−10.6	−12.4	−5.4	−3.2	2.5	8.3
J	A	S	O	N	D
15.0	16.0	10.0	1.9	−6.0	−6.4

HARRAN

There is nowhere to stay, and the only refreshments are in the new behive-shaped coffee house selling soft drinks near the entrance to the village.

DIYARBAKIR

Tourist Hotel (2-star), catering for Turkish tourists and businessmen. Good outdoor restaurant round a fountain. Located on the main road into town from the north, close to the old city.
Büyük Hotel (2-star), Tel: 12444. A modern hotel just inside the walls, much used by tour groups.
Demir Hotel (2-star). Rebuilt in 1990 on the site of the old run-down hotel.
The Kervanserai (2-star). Tastefully restored in 1989 from the derelict 17th C Deliller Hanı.
Saraç Hotel (1-star), Tel: 12365. 35 rooms near the Demir.
Aslan Palas (1-star), Tel: 13971. 39 rooms opposite the Büyük.

The best **restaurants** outside the hotels are the Hacı Baba, Sinan and Beş Kardeş. Food is generally good in Diyarbakır, with excellent lamb. Fruit and vegetables are also varied and good quality, and Diyarbakır is famous for its water melons, grown in the flood plain along the banks of the Tigris. Said to be the biggest in the world, some weigh up to 70 kilos so that they have to be cut using a sword. They are fertilised with pigeon dung, and pigeons are bred in special lofts in the houses for this purpose.

A **festival** is held on 5 April to celebrate Atatürk's bayram with folk dancing.

Daily afternoon **flights** to Ankara (1¼ hours) connecting to İstanbul (total 3¼ hours with transfer).

Average temperature (Celsius):

J	F	M	A	M	J
1.6	3.7	8.3	13.9	19.4	30.0
J	A	S	O	N	D
31.0	30.5	24.9	17.2	10.0	4.2

Maximum temperature:

J	F	M	A	M	J
16.9	21.1	26.0	33.0	39.8	41.8
J	A	S	O	N	D
46.2	45.9	42.0	35.4	28.4	23.1

Minimum temperature:

J	F	M	A	M	J
−24.2	−19.1	−12.2	−6.1	0.8	3.5
J	A	S	O	N	D
9.1	8.4	4.0	−8.0	−12.9	−17.7

MARDIN

Beyraktır Hotel, Tel: 338, the only one to consider in town, on the 'main square'. Largely serving the needs of local businessmen, it is not up to tourist standard. The 41 rooms, though many have their own bathrooms and balcony, are squalid and the cockroach rating is high. Old crones creep about the corridors to 'clean' the rooms with filthy old brushes, and the towels and sheets look as if they have never been clean. You would do well to come prepared with an anti-cockroach aerosol. One compensation is the pleasant restaurant and large raised terrace next door where you can sip drinks.

The **restaurants** serve the biggest range of starters you will get in Eastern Turkey, so make the most of it. The Arab influence is strong, with hummus served with hot pine kernels and a buttery sauce poured over the top. The food produce in the shops is especially good, about the best in Eastern Turkey, and the local population clearly eats well. It is also one of the few places far enough south to get bananas.

If you are a Turkish speaker, you may prefer to stay in the hostelry in the **Deyrul-zaferan Monastery**, which is certainly cleaner.

NUSAYBIN

Nezirhan Motel (1-star), Tel: 13. 24 km east of Nusaybin on the road to Iraq, an unlikely but very welcome complex in the middle of nowhere, catering for transit traffic. About 40 rooms, with pool. Make sure you get a room at the back, away from the generator.

MIDYAT

There is nowhere to stay in the town, but the **Mar Gabriel Monastery** hostelry has clean and pleasant surroundings.

SIIRT

Hotel Erdef, Tel: 1081. 30 simple rooms, 16 with showers.

Average temperature (Celsius):

J	F	M	A	M	J
2.2	3.9	7.9	13.3	19.2	25.6
J	A	S	O	N	D
30.4	29.9	24.9	17.9	10.4	4.7

Maximum temperature:

J	F	M	A	M	J
16.2	20.5	24.1	29.5	36.2	39.4
J	A	S	O	N	D
43.3	42.3	39.9	34.4	25.8	18.4

Minimum temperature:

J	F	M	A	M	J
−19.3	−16.5	−10.1	−3.3	2.4	8.2
J	A	S	O	N	D
13.1	14.5	10.3	0.3	−14.1	12.3

BITLIS

There is nowhere of tourist standard here, but should you be forced to overnight, the best bet is probably the Turist Hotel on the main road in the centre.

THE LAKE VAN REGION

Tatvan

Nemrut Dağ Crater

Lake Van

Ahlat

Adilcevaz

Akdamar

Van

Çavuştepe

Hoşap

Hakkâri

Practical Information

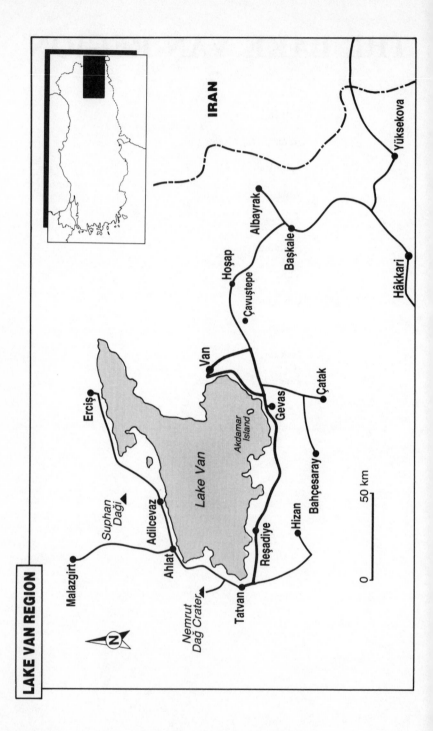

LAKE VAN REGION

IRAN

Yüksekova

Hâkkari

Albayrak

Başkale

Hoşap

Çavuştepe

Van

Çatak

Erciş

Gevaş

Akdamar Island

Lake Van

Suphan Dağı

Adilcevaz

Bahçesaray

Malazgirt

Ahlat

Hizan

Reşadiye

Nemrut Dağ Crater

Tatvan

N

0   50 km

LAKE VAN: THE NORTHWEST SHORE

Your first sight of Lake Van, for which many will have been thirsting, is impressive but somewhat marred by the ugly blot of **Tatvan** which greets you on the western shores. Arriving at the bleak, factory-ridden town you feel as if you have come to some distant outpost of Siberia and you are not too far off the mark, for the town was indeed under Russian occupation for several years until 1917. All the buildings are flat and featureless and in wet weather the streets are awash with mud. One pothole-ridden stretch of 'dual carriageway' runs the length of the town, nearly 3 km in all. The inhabitants, as throughout Eastern Turkey, seem curiously unperturbed by the filth of their potholed streets. Young girls in school uniforms of white dresses, white shoes and socks skip across the muddy streets on their way to school with little attempt at avoiding the puddles. Frederick Burnaby, travelling the region over 100 years ago, was struck by the same attitude.

'Why do you not clean the street?' he enquired of an old Turk, who had just waded across the mud to visit his friend's house.

'The mud will dry up in the summer months', he replied, 'why trouble our heads about it now?'

The Way Out

The train across the lake

At the beginning of the town you will see the small harbour with the large ships of the Denizcelik Bankası (Turkish Maritime Lines). These constitute the link from the terminus of the railway line here across the lake to Van where the railway resumes, leading eventually to Iran. The trains literally drive on board the ships, locomotive, carriages and all, to be ferried across.

North shore excursion

Just near the harbour a road to the left marked by a yellow sign reading Nemrut leads off round the northern shore of the lake. To enable a trip to this northern shore you can spend two nights in Tatvan in the comfortable hotel of the Denizcelik Bankası. The trip can be done in a relaxing and enjoyable day, beginning with the Nemrut Dağ crater (if the time of year is right), then along the lake to Ahlat with a picnic on the lake shore and on to Adilcevaz in the afternoon.

Into the Volcano

Setting off on the road marked Nemrut you come after 4 km to a second yellow sign pointing left up an earth road. From this point the road on up to the summit of **Nemrut Dağ** is the best part of 15 km and though it may look feasible to begin with, be warned that it will be closed because of snow in all months except July and August. The summit is after all over 3000 metres high, nearly 1000 metres higher than the other Nemrut Dağ further south. In those two dry months however, it is perfectly possible to drive up by car to the crater rim (ignoring the unfriendly shepherds and children who sometimes appear to be guarding the top and throwing stones at all comers), and continue down 3 km or so inside the crater. The contrast between the bleak outside of the cone and the lush vegetation inside is striking, as though another world lay sheltering there. For the energetic it is also possible to make the ascent by foot in four hours from the northeast side.

Another world

The crater, 7 km in diameter, is one of the largest complete craters in the world, and its western half holds a huge lake, about 700 metres below the rim. By the side of the lake are hot springs as well as some ice-cold ones of delicious water. No one lives inside the crater, but 'yürük' (nomad) camps can occasionally be seen here grazing their cattle in the summer months. The volcano was last active in 1441. From the top, in the clear weather that tends to accompany July and August, you have a superb view out over Lake Van and the mountains beyond.

Strange and Beautiful Lake

Turkey's biggest lake and seven times bigger than Lake Geneva, the colossal **Lake Van** has a quality that verges on the eerie, a quality born partly of its vivid and piercing blueness and partly of its magnificent setting 1750 metres above sea level and encircled with peaks rising to 3000 and even 4000 metres, snow-covered for most of the year. It is a lake you can never tire of, its aspect always changing with the different seasons and from different parts of the shoreline. Some views of it are reminiscent of the Yugoslav mountain lakes, with somewhat gaunt and treeless shores, while at other points where there are trees and flowers in the foreground it can take on an alpine look. All views, however, strangely share the pale and timeless light which is reflected from the water to the sky, and by and large you have to concede that it is unlike any other lake in the world. Its breathtaking beauty and serenity will haunt you in many a quiet moment.

Haunting sensation

Until the mid-1960s this whole region was a restricted zone which no one could enter without special permission. The roads, terrible now, were unspeakable then, and no driving of any sort could really be contemplated here in a car.

It was the eruption of Nemrut Dağ eons ago that formed Lake Van by creating a huge dam of lava and thereby blocking the flow of water out to the west. Today the lake is curious in that it still has no outflow. Several small rivers flow into it, but its level remains constant entirely through evaporation during the hot summer months. This peculiarity has resulted in the waters being highly alkaline with natural sodas. Fishermen simply trail their dirty clothes behind their boats to get a whiter than whiter wash, and the locals also insist it removes dandruff. Swimming in the lake water is like gliding through silk and it leaves a lovely smooth feeling on the skin. But immersing yourself only becomes a pleasurable experience from late May onwards, and even then it is pretty bracing. Six times saltier than the sea, it is very buoyant and even the most leaden of people can float. Pollution is almost non-existent and the water is beautifully clear. Its greatest depth is not certain, but depths of 250 metres have been recorded.

Nature and Man

The dearth of wildlife is striking. The only birds to be seen are gulls and, more rarely, cormorants and pelicans, mainly on the northern shore near Adilcevaz. The Van fish do

Dearth of wildlife

not live in the lake but are washed down from fresh water rivers when the snows melt and are then caught near the estuaries from April to June in nets and baskets. There are only two varieties, a kind of carp (called 'gögört') which can be up to 50 cm long like a large salmon in shape, and a type of grey mullet (called 'ince kefal'). The locals often do not even bother to differentiate, simply calling them all 'balık', fish. The excess catch is pickled for eating in summer.

The curiosity of Lake Van's wildlife, however, is its so-called Van cats. These fluffy white creatures, seen in kitsch postcards everywhere round Van, have one blue eye and one green eye. Their other peculiarity is that they are said to like swimming and will gaily dive into the water for the sheer pleasure of it. Some say they even dive in to catch fish if they are feeling hungry, so this must be a spring-time activity. They are also meant to be very affectionate.

Van cats

Today they are dying out, mainly because there is no systematic or careful breeding, so as time goes by their peculiar characteristics are being diluted by cross-breeding. The Agricultural Directorate of the Van Province has now begun to breed cats of the true strain so gradually its numbers may build up again.

A century ago the shoreline was much more wooded and green, but man has left his mark and only very few wooded stretches now remain. Cuneiform documents dating back to the Assyrian invasion here in the 8th C BC talk about cutting down forests as dense as rushes. 'Van in this world, Paradise in the next', is the old Armenian proverb that summed up the once legendary fertility of this region.

In some of the villages, however, like Adilcevaz, there are still excellent fruit trees, especially apricots. Van was also where the canteloup melon originated. The Pope in Rome had a farm of his own at that time called Cantalupo and he imported Van melons to grow on it. From here they spread all over the world as canteloups.

The history of the region has been a troubled one. The Hurrian ancestors of the Hittites were the first rulers here in the second millenium BC. It was the Urartians, however, coming from the south and the southeast around the great Zab valley in the Hakkâri, who created the greatest empire and period of stability, ruling from 900 to 500 BC. Their civilisation has only begun to be truly appreciated this century with the excavation of their hilltop citadels and palaces and the discovery of their beautiful gold artefacts.

Posterior Attractions

Returning from Nemrut to the shore road you continue on to **Ahlat,** once an important Armenian town on the lake shore, now a sprawl of modern houses. The Arabs took the town in the 9th C and it remained Moslem when it was ruled over by the Seljuks and the Kurdish Ayyubids. In 1245 the Mongols took the town and then the Turcoman White Sheep took it for a time before it was nominally incorporated into the Ottoman Empire in 1533. In practice, Ottoman power did not extend into these remote regions and real power was exercised by the Kurdish emirs of Bitlis.

Often referred to as a ghost town in recent accounts, Ahlat today is no such thing, and its famous extensive cemetery and distinctive kümbets rise incongrously out of cultivated fields or from among clusters of modern houses, so that they are no longer that straightforward to find. In all these kümbets (literally 'dome', but also Turkish slang for the human posterior) the body was buried in the crypt underneath, while outside steps lead to the upper chamber, a prayer room. The tall conical shape is unmistakably Armenian influenced, and Ahlat's Armenian stonemasons were in fact famous for their work. The traditional tent of the central Asiatic nomad, with its circular body and pointed conical roof is almost certainly the original inspiration for the characteristic shape of Armenian, Seljuk and Georgian building. Only Kayseri has tombs in number and variety to rival Ahlat.

The **Ulu Kümbet** (Great Kümbet) is the first you see and the largest — it is to the right of the road and set about 300 metres away in a field with a few hovels nearby. On the left of the road is the scruffy neglected graveyard extending behind the little museum where you can park and walk back to the kümbet. The **museum** is a rather feeble affair, opened in 1971, with two rooms containing

Incongruous kümbets

Urartian pottery, jewellery and bronze weapons, some Roman glassware, Ottoman costume embroidery, highly fragmentary Seljuk pottery and a few Seljuk and Byzantine coins. The museum attendant watches you uninterestedly, slightly incredulous that you can show so much interest in these old relics, and once you have gone, goes out to sit in the sun again. Such an attitude is no recent development, and Burnaby remarked in the last century how the locals in a village where he stayed could not understand his getting up so early and riding through deep snow simply to explore an old cave nearby. 'Curiosity about antiquities,' he comments, 'does not enter into a Turk's composition. He lives for the present. What has happened is finished and done with.'

Lack of curiosity

Driving further on you will spot over to your left after 1 km or so two kümbets about 400 metres from the road and known as the **Çifte** (Twin) **Kümbets.** Both date from the late 13th C. Taking the dirt road that leads off to the left here, you come to a T-junction at which you can turn right to reach them. From the outside these two are the least exciting of the kümbets, but inside the larger of the two has the remains of some coloured plaster decoration. Returning now to the T-junction and following the earth road straight on, parallel to the main road, you pass after 200 metres or so another kümbet to the right in someone's front garden and then another much prettier little kümbet just to the right of the road, calling itself **Emir Ali Kümbet,** of a different style with no steps leading up, but just an open section below.

You continue along the earth road passing a cluster of rural village houses behind walls, until after some 150 metres the road opens up into a grassy space to reveal the best preserved and prettiest of the kümbets, standing next to an oratory (mescit) which is usually kept locked. This is the **kümbet and mescit of Bayındır,** unknown in history but described as a great king and propagator of the faith in the inscription which also gives the date of 1481. This kümbet, instead of being closed in at its upper storey, has an open colonnaded arcade supporting its conical roof, so that you can look out from inside. It has been speculated that this served as a minaret for the oratory and was used for calling the faithful to prayer. All the kümbets for some reason have their entrance on the north. In the burial chambers underneath anything from one to four people were buried.

From here the earth road leads back towards the lake past the extensive **Seljuk cemetery** to the left, described in early accounts as the *pièce de résistance* of Ahlat, mournful and atmospheric, covering about two square kilometres. Today its once striking setting overlooking the lake has been spoilt by the encroachment of modern houses, telegraph wires and TV aerials which simply serve to make the huge tombstones look like neglected anachronisms. Lichen covered, leaning at drunken angles, many are 2 metres tall, carved with elaborate designs showing Armenian influence.

As you begin to leave the town behind you will notice to your right set down about 200 metres away by the lake shore the dark chocolate brown walls of the old **fortress** of Ahlat, built in the 16th C by the Ottoman Sultan Suleyman. A dirt track leads to the main gateway, where you can leave the car and walk through into the open courtyard enclosed within the walls. Walking towards the far corner of the enclosure down towards the lake, you pass through what is almost a landscaped garden with tall poplar trees and small running streams which have been channelled off to make a water system. The ruins are all covered in grass and you can walk high up along the battlements. A **ruined mosque** almost obscured by tall poplars tempts you with a climb up the steps to the top of its minaret, though the view is not as good as you might expect because you arrive at the top facing north towards the town rather than towards the lake. Like many minarets it has 99 steps, one

for each of the names of Allah. The mosque itself is now used as a potting shed, housing various gardening oddments like wheel barrows.

Where the Bell Tolled for Byzantium
From Ahlat a rough road leads north 58 km to **Malazgirt.** This was the site of the momentous **battle of Manzikert** in 1071 when the Seljuk Sultan defeated and captured the Byzantine Emperor, thereby establishing the Turks for the first time in Anatolia. The town today has little of note to offer other than the remains of the black basalt walls of its fortress, and many Armenian spoils reused in the construction of the new houses.

Lakeside Idylls
The shoreline between Ahlat and Adilcevaz has some good stretches of beach where you can find deserted areas to swim and picnic. Some parts are almost like sandy beach, others are pebbly. The dearth of wildlife contributes to the air of stillness that always seems to surround Lake Van. The occasional cow or donkey grazes on the lush meadows by the shore, and the villagers sometimes keep geese and ducks. As far as wild animals are concerned, however, there is just the occasional gull, the very occasional bird of prey and the even more occasional snake. When the weather is good there is nothing more restful than lying on the grass by the silent shores of Lake Van with a picnic

The Seljuk castle at Adilcevaz, overlooking Lake Van

or paddling in the icy clear water. The snakes, incidentally, are harmless.

At **Adilcevaz,** 25 km from Ahlat, you come to the attractive and unusual little chocolate coloured **mosque** on the lake shore. Set by itself with its tall minaret and nine cupolas it almost looks like a toy beside the vastness of the lake. Inside, its proportions are very lovely and there are none of the garish trimmings so often found in city mosques. Above it rises a Seljuk **castle** on a steep outcrop overlooking the lake. If you fancy the exercise you can climb up to it in about 30 minutes. There is not a great deal left on top beyond the walls and towers, but the views are breathtaking over the lake towards the snow covered mountains. This was the site of the discovery of the Urartian relief in polished basalt of the king standing on a bull, now erected in the garden of the Van museum and considered by some to be the finest piece of Urartian stone carving. The relief was originally from Kefkalesi, the Urartian citadel towering over the valley to the west of the village, but had evidently tumbled down and then been reused in constructing the walls of this Seljuk castle.

Climbs from Adilcevaz

Just in front of the lakeside mosque a track leads off inland into Adilcevaz proper, a most attractive village built on the hillside with water running down in channels beside the road and very green tall poplar trees separating the prosperous looking houses. The villagers have erected their own yellow signs to **Kefkalesi** which you can follow to a point just above the village where the road then deteriorates suddenly and becomes suitable only for a jeep. From this point the view back across to the Seljuk citadel on its rock framed by the lake and the snow covered mountains beyond, is one of the most lovely anywhere in the Van region. With a jeep you can drive to within 30 minutes walk of Kefkalesi at 2200 metres. At the foot of its citadel are the ruins of the 9th C Armenian **Monastery of the Wonder of Ardzgani.** On the citadel itself, Turkish archaeologists have unearthed the foundations of an Urartian **palace** with 30 recognisable rooms, some with huge storage jars and various inscribed blocks.

Urartian citadel

From Adilcevaz it is also possible to climb **Suphan Dağ,** the highest mountain in the Van region at 4058 metres and the third highest in Turkey after Ararat and Cilo Dağ in the Hakkâri. This huge volcanic peak dominates the northern shore of the lake and is snow covered all the year round. In July and August it is a two day trek with no real mountaineering problems. The views are superb in clear weather, but Nemrut Dağ, though lower, is the more exciting of the two.

Third highest mountain in Turkey

If you are a keen bird watcher, you may enjoy driving on east beyond Adilcevaz 20 km or so to **Arin Gölü** near Göldüzü, a fresh water lake where lots of birds come to fish. The northeastern corner of the lake from here on to Erciş and around to Van is scenically the least impressive section of shoreline.

AKDAMAR

Excursions to remote mountain monasteries

From Tatvan the most direct road east to Van is along the southern lakeshore. Almost immediately it heads off inland and climbs through scenic mountain stretches with abundant water flowing in bubbling streams down the hillsides and with lush yellow flowering meadows on the lower slopes. After 8 km a road forks off to the right to **Hizan,** and for the adventurous this can be the first stage of a journey to visit some extremely remote Armenian mountain monasteries. They cannot be reached without a guide and require several hours' journey from Hizan on horseback or on foot. In order of distance from Eski Hizan they are the 11th C **Gökçimen Kilise;** the **Covent of the Mother of God of Hzar** with a well-preserved 11th C church; and the 11th C **Covent of the Holy Cross of Hisan** founded by Gregory the Illuminator, the first Armenian patriarch. Today the region is inhabited solely by Kurds. Many of the churches, which were used as places of refuge when the island of Akdamar was seized, are currently in use as barns.

After 30 km a fork off to the left leads to **Reşadiye,** a town on a lovely little peninsula. On one side is a beach and on the other is a natural terrace with shady trees ending at the cliffs high above the lake.

History of the Armenians

Island in the lake

The road climbs on over a pass reaching 2250 metres, fraught with potholes. When it finally rejoins the lake after one and a quarter hours (100 km) from Tatvan, you spot for the first time the little island of **Akdamar** in the lake, a distinctive shape with a large outcrop of rock on its further side then flattening out to a small terrace on the lakeshore side. It is on this terrace that the famous Armenian Church of the Holy Cross of Akdamar stands, a masterpiece of early Armenian art and the cathedral church of the independent Armenian Kingdom of Vaspurakan.

The origins of the Armenians are not known for certain and ancient classical historians were no less confused. Herodotus calls them Phrygian colonists, while Strabo, an Anatolian, thought they were related to the Babylonians or the Syrians. Today the most probable theories are either that they came into Anatolia from the direction of the Caucasus, the same route as the Hurrians and the Hittites, or they are an original Anatolian people. Like the Hittites, their language is Indo-European.

The Armenians make their first appearance in recorded history in the annals of the Persians, c500 BC, as the people who had taken over the land of Urartu following the collapse of the Urartian State. Set free from Persian domination, like the rest of Asia Minor, by Alexander the Great in 331 BC, Armenia chose to retain its Persian-style administration, with regional satraps who were virtually independent kings running their own armies. The process of Hellenisation never reached Armenia, though Alexander's opening up of the Eastern world gave them the opportunity to extend the boundaries of their legendary commercial skills beyond Mesopotamia to Egypt, India and central Asia.

Under Tigranes the Great (95–54 BC) Armenia was a prosperous and extensive empire, but when the Romans under Lucullus invaded the country to put an end to the troublesome Pontic Kingdom, Armenia was also taken. From this time on it was to remain a client state to Rome and later to Byzantium, a useful bulwark against Persia.

In AD 280 Armenia became the first country to adopt Christianity as the state religion, when the Armenian King Tiridates, who had worshipped the Persian gods until then,
The first Christian was finally converted by his minister Gregory, later the
nation Illuminator. Together they set about the destruction of the pagan temples at Ani and Tercan and broke to pieces the golden goddess of Anahid at Erzurum. The result was war with Persia and massacres of Christians in Persia.

In 313 the Edict of Milan announced the toleration of Christianity throughout the Roman Empire, Gregory was ordained at Caesarea (Kayseri) in Cappadocia, and the Armenian Church was for a time subservient to Rome. Gregory, however, preached the new faith in the Armenian language and soon the national church developed characteristics of its own. He was given the title of Catholikos of the Armenian Church, a title which was to be inherited by the members of his family. With encouragement from the Persians, ever keen to create a rift with the West, an Armenian alphabet was developed and a school of translators into Armenian was set up in the early 5th C. Beautiful illuminated manuscripts were produced in a style which blended what had been inherited from Urartu with Persian and Syrian influences.

In 451 the Armenian Church refused to accept the verdict of the Council of Chalcedon and continued to hold its monophysite doctrine. Like the Syrian Jacobites and the Egyptian Copts, this meant they believed that the human nature of Christ was absorbed in the divine, a view which alienated them from other Christians including their neighbours the Nestorians and the Georgians, and above all the

Greeks. Their links with Syria and the Jacobite Church soon became stronger than with Byzantium, and it was the mutual antipathy of the Greeks and the Armenians that finally exposed Asia Minor to the Moslem takeover. Once more, a religious division was used as an excuse for a political and racial one.

Armenian diaspora The Arab outsurge in the 7th C flowed over Armenia too, and it remained for centuries under Islamic control. There is no evidence of persecution by the Arabs, but at this time many Armenian families left, usually the wealthier ones. It was in fact the Byzantines who were the first forcibly to send the Armenians away, when in 578, 10,000 Armenians were taken from their homes to be settled in Cyprus to till the soil and to provide soldiers. Others were settled in Crete, Thrace and Calabria. Though many Armenian soldiers became prominent in the Byzantine army, they retained, even in their exile, their nationality and insisted on their descent.

Armenia asserted itself again in the late 9th C under the Bagratid family. A branch of this family continued to rule Georgia until the 18th C. Claims from rival families, however, helped to weaken the country, and it was one of these rivals, King Gagik I of the Artsuni family, who retired from war and administration to the serenity of Akdamar Island on Lake Van. Here in the 10th C Gagik built his golden-domed palace and his cathedral church with a monastery beside it. As late as the 1890s some of the monastery buildings were still being used by a handful of monks, scarcely literate, living at subsistence level. Of the palace no trace remains today and of the monastery only a few walls are left. The church, however, built between 915 and 921, is in astonishingly good condition, all the more remarkable as it receives no maintenance from the authorities and has never been restored. All its exterior walls are covered with Brueghel-like reliefs cut into the stone of various famous Old Testament scenes as well as some Armenian fantasy tales. The shape of the church is typically Armenian, small in plan, only 15 by 12 metres, but very tall with the dome reaching a height of over 20 metres. It must be one of the smallest cathedrals in the world.

Throughout the 11th, 12th, and 13th C Armenian towns, notably Kars, Muş and Malatya, were sporadically attacked by Turcoman hordes and in 1239, Ani itself, their capital, was sacked by Genghis Khan and his Tartar Mongols. From this point on, the Armenians were ruled by Arabs, Kurds, Persians, Seljuks and eventually by the Ottoman Sultans who took over their land in the 16th C. Throughout this troubled history, Armenians continued to emigrate, some to Russian and Poland, some to the Near East and, most recently, to North America. During the First World War the Turks caused the deaths, either by slaughter or deportation, of at least one million Armenians.

Visiting Akdamar

As you round a bend in the road on a promontory which seems to be the closest point to the island, you come to the little ferry landing stage, with a restaurant and picnic area laid out to the right of the road. No yellow sign announces Akdamar from this direction, though there is one if you are coming from Van, this being the more common approach. Boats which can carry anything up to a bursting point of 50 people with men dangling their legs over the sides are waiting here from early May onwards to ferry people across the 2 km to the island. Out of season, ie before May, you will have to hire a boat for yourself, but the cost is not too exorbitant. In season they leave whenever the passengers are agreed that there are enough to make the cost reasonable, usually about ten people, but obviously you can go with less if you are prepared to pay. You should always arrive at some time in the morning, as after 2pm you may be risking that no more boats will go. For Turks, especially at the weekends, it is very popular as a picnic outing for all the family, and they pile on the boat laden with barbecues, food and water, chattering incessantly and trying to organise one another. Coach tours have followed this example and many now get taken across for a simple barbecue lunch. The ferry moors at a stone quayside from which a stepped path leads up to the church through terraces which were once the gardens of the monastery. On a little rock, separated from the island as you approach, stand the remains of a tiny **chapel,** maybe the private chapel of King Gagik.

In May the island is ablaze with flowers and shrubs, growing where once were gardens and orchards. The side of the **Church of the Holy Cross of Akdamar** you see first from the path is best viewed by climbing up onto the grassy roof of the forechurch building. From here you have a superb close-up view not only of the side immediately facing you, but also of the side facing the lakeshore up as far as the porch, itself a later 18th C addition. The *relief of Jonah and the Whale* is one of the most impressive, a highly ludicrous series of three in which it looks as if Jonah is being fed to the whale by men in a boat; the whale resembles an elongated pig with ears and teeth; and Jonah spewed out onto the land looks like a man reclining on the tree tops. The Armenian use of perspective lends an unintentionally comic air to all the scenes. The *Abraham and Isaac reliefs* just before the porch can also be seen well from this vantage point. Abraham has hold of Isaac,

Boat procedure

Biblical tales carved on the church

The David and Goliath relief at Akdamar

about half his size, by the hair as though about to thrash him. To the left of them, half way up a vine, is a happy-looking goat, evidently thinking 'There but for the grace of God go I'. On the west wall a faintly cross-eyed *Gagik* carries a model of the church looking like a birdcage. All over the walls are reliefs of vines and bunches of grapes, often intertwined with curious bear-like creatures. The Armenians had a particular weakness for fanciful animals, preferably fighting or devouring each other, and griffins, lions and dragons can be seen all over the church.

Climbing back down now to the ground level and looking at the carvings on the far side of the porch, you will spot a fine *relief of David and Goliath*. David has the cheeky grin of a real young upstart. On the rear facade of the church is an *Adam and Eve relief*, heavily defaced with graffiti and much of their faces missing.

Inside, the church is a total wreck, heavily defaced with graffiti and fire smoke. The 10th C murals which once adorned the walls have the appearance now of unfinished drawings.

Picnicking

The island could hardly be a more charming spot for a picnic. There is no stall or stand here, so you must come fully supplied with all your needs. There are numerous shady spots to sit under the trees, many of them almond, where you can catch the breeze and enjoy a lovely view down over the church, with colourful flowers in the grassy foreground, the blue shimmering lake and the permanently snow-topped mountains beyond. Spring comes earlier to Akdamar than to other parts of Van, so at mid-May it is at its most colourful. By late June and July it is already quite yellow and dry-looking. Stone tables are laid out in some areas, but despite the large numbers of people pouring across the island, they all seem to disperse surprisingly quickly and you can always find a secluded spot. The picnicking Turks *en famille* devote all their concentration to the preparation of their barbecues and scarcely give the church a second glance as they stagger past laden with pots and pans. Scattered round the church are gravestones of Armenian Christians who wished to attain saintliness. These rich floral designs contrast with the abstract Seljuk tombstones in the cemetery at Ahlat. One tradition claims that the grave of Simon, one of the disciples of Christ, is on the island somewhere.

Swiming in the lake

In the hottest months of July and August you can find spots to swim, notably on a pebbly beach on the north side of the island, though your chances of being unobserved by Turks are slim. In good weather it is certainly a very pleasant place to wile away three or four hours with a bottle of wine and a little doze in the sun.

Attached to the island is a particularly trite story about how it got its name, handed down through generations. One of the priests on the island had a daughter called Tamara who fell in love with a Turkish shepherd on the shore. They could not meet openly so the shepherd had to swim across to the island at night, directed by a light Tamara held out for him. You have to admire this shepherd's stamina to swim across 2 km of icy water, have a night of revellry, and still have the energy to swim all the way back again. The priest however smelt a rat and locking Tamara up in her room went out himself the next night with the light. The shepherd swam towards it, but it then moved to a different place, so he changed course. Again and again the light moved until the shepherd was exhausted with following it. Finally managing to swim to the place where the light was, he emerged to find a group of priests waiting for him brandishing sticks. He was too tired to struggle and as he sank beneath the waves his final words were 'Ah . . . Tamara'.

Boats begin returning from 2pm. There is no question of having to return on the same boat you came on. When you want to leave you simply stroll down to the quayside and sit on one of the waiting boats until it fills up sufficiently for the owner to feel it is worth a trip back. No one wants to see your ticket.

VAN

The whole Van area was closed to visitors till 1960, though looking at it now it is hard to believe it has only so recently opened its doors to the outside world. Approached from Akdamar, **Van** is unprepossessing, with a sprawl of modern building heralding the outskirts and the university on the right. Atatürk had wanted to establish the main university for Eastern Turkey here, but on his death Erzurum was substituted; wrongly, people now agree. Van today is the most forward-looking town of Eastern Turkey, with a large mixed grammar school, a Girls' Teachers' Training School and a Boys' Commercial Training School. Competition for places in the secondary schools and institutes is intense and the desire to be educated is strong.

You reach a crossroads where a yellow sign points off left towards the lakeshore 3 km to Van Kalesi, while right takes you into the centre of modern Van.

Disappointing Van

Modern Van, dating totally post-1918, as a town is rather a disappointment generally. The first surprise is that contrary to expectation it is not built on the lakeshore but is set back about 4 km on flat ground with no views to the lake at all. The second surprise is its smallness. As the main town on the shores of a lake seven times the size of Lake Geneva, it is natural to expect something, however remotely, approximating to Geneva. Yet with a population of 92,000, it has less than half the inhabitants of Urfa. It has none of the sophistication and hum of Diyarbakır, none of the beautiful architecture of Mardin, none of the atmosphere and fascination of Bitlis. Having thus reduced your expectations, you can enjoy Van for what it is —

A base for further explorations
a comfortable base from which to explore the surrounding area, where you can stay in two of the best hotels in Eastern Turkey, the Hotel Akdamar and the Büyük Urartu. Their restaurants, however, are disappointing with a poor range of food and not a sign of the famous Van fish.

One place you must visit is the **museum,** (open 9am to noon, 1 to 6.30pm, closed Mondays). Though small, it is extremely well laid-out and everything in it is worthy of scrutiny. Loveliest of all is the magnificent Urartian gold jewellery and a finely worked bronze Urartian lion.

The Land of Urartu

In the period 1900 to 1260 BC, contemporary with the Hittites, a warlike and aggressive people, the Hurrians, established a kingdom stretching as far south as Nusaybin with

Van as its capital. The Hurrians struggled with their Hittite neighbours to the west, and in 1400 BC they suffered a humiliating defeat at the hands of the famous Hittite King Shuppiluliuma. Dispersed in small tribes after their defeat, they gradually grew strong again and, reunited, called their empire Uratu, taken from the mountain of Ararat. They retained Van as their capital, calling it Tushpa (from the storm god Teshub), and in the 300 years that their empire flourished, they extended east to Lake Urmia in Iran, west to Malatya, north to Kars and Erzurum and south to Diyarbakır, Mardin and Hakkâri, and even to Aleppo in northern Syria and to Mosul in Iraq.

The Urartians unearthed

The first scientific excavation of an Urartian fortress city was undertaken from 1936 by Russian archaeologists at a site called Karmir Blur, overlooking the river Zanga near Erivan in Russian Armenia. No reports of the results were available in English until 1953, but the findings formed the basis of knowledge of Urartian civilisation, subsequently added to by work which Turkish archaeologists have undertaken at Altıntepe near Erzincan, at Patnos and at Çavuştepe.

In the Assyrian reliefs found at Van, the Urartians are shown as similar in appearance to the Hurrians and the Hittites, with a short stocky build, belted waists with daggers and wearing earrings and bracelets. Like the Hittites, their symbol was a lion. Their cuneiform script, taken from the Assyrians, found carved in their fortresses and temples, has been deciphered and tells us much about their kings and their achievements. Grammatically the Urartian language is close to the Hurrian and Hittite. Like the Assyrian kings the Urartian monarchs took on grandiose titles and prided themselves on their battle tactics, usually demolishing a fort when they captured it and sending all the booty back to the palace at Van.

Impressive builders ...

Their skill as builders was noteworthy. They favoured long thin spurs as sites for their fortress cities, and scattered all over their empire are over 30 such fortresses, large and small. The largest are Van Kalesi, Toprakkale and Çavuştepe, built with colossal blocks of carefully dressed stone, each block often weighing up to 27,000 kilos. They also built elaborate water systems of canals and dams, the most impressive being the Menua Canal (today called Şemiran Canal) which brought water from 65 km away to the foot of Van Kalesi, a remarkable feat of engineering.

As a result of their constant battles with the Assyrians and the Cimmerians (barbarous Europeans who had come in by a land route north of the Black Sea), Urartu suffered a loss of manpower, and so the necessary population to remedy the situation was secured from neighbouring lands, with 'men from the Halitu region and women from Manna' brought in to be resettled in Urartian domains.

Using their advanced irrigation channels they became expert at growing crops, and some historians claim to have evidence that the cultivation of wheat first began here, then spreading to other parts of the world. They also developed animal husbandry, breeding horses around Lake Urmia in Iran which became famous throughout Asia Minor.

... and skilled
metalworkers

Their most impressive accomplishment, however, was their metalwork, a field in which they were more advanced than the Assyrians or any other people of their time. Urartian metalwork in gold, silver and bronze was highly prized and exported to Greece and Italy. Evidence is mounting for the fact that the ancient Greeks and Etruscans copied heavily from Urartian objects in their own work. Many objects found at Crete, Delphi and Olympia, and the Etruscan tomb finds, show close resemblance to Urartian origi-

Origins of classical
architecture?

nals. An Assyrian relief in the Yuksekova district shows an Urartian temple inside and out full of valuable metalwork objects. The style of this building, with its gabled roof and pillared façade, has close affinities with the architectural orders we now think of as Greek Doric and Ionian.

As potters, they were competent but not exceptional, making the standard glazed red earthenware vessels.

Like the Hittites, the Urartians believed in a variety of gods, the chief ones being the storm (or weather) god and the sun god. In their inscriptions the kings recorded that all their deeds in peace and war were done in the name of the gods, and they performed sacrifices of animals to their deities at propitious times of year.

Waves of Conquerors

In the 7th C BC the Persian Medes, having overthrown the Assyrian Empire with the fall of Nineveh in 612 BC, spread into the Van region and displaced the Urartian culture

Persians and
Greeks

which had been weakened through years of rivalry with the Assyrians. In the 5th C BC the area was the scene of several great battles during the retreat of the Ten Thousand led by the Greek general Xenophon. Greek resistance to Persian power was to continue, finally culminating in the victories of Alexander the Great. In 331 BC on his way to Persia, Alexander took the Van region, and after his death it became part of the Seleucid empire. When the Romans overthrew the Seleucids, the region passed for a time into Roman hands.

Romans and
Armenians

In the 1st C BC, claiming he was heir to the Romans, the Armenian King Tigranes the Great, of the family of Artaksias of the Huns, captured Van from the Romans and founded the first Armenian kingdom here, called Vaspurakan. Later, in 66 BC, the Romans under Pompey recaptured Van once more, but in the 3rd C AD the Sassanians

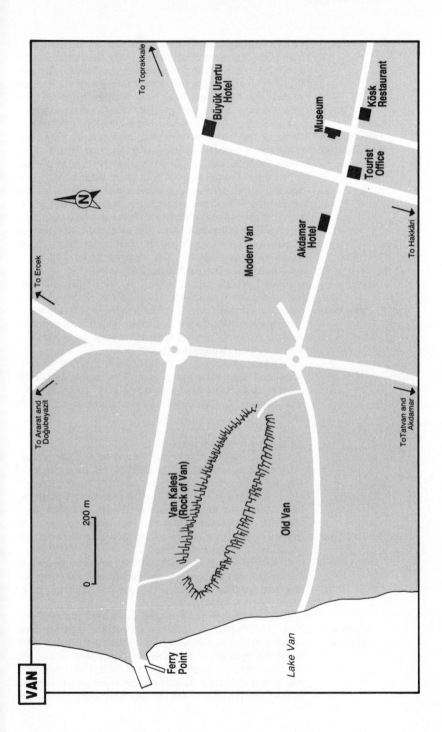

VAN

To Toprakkale

Büyük Urartu Hotel

Museum

Kösk Restaurant

Tourist Office

To Hakkâri

Akdamar Hotel

Modern Van

N

To Ercek

To Ararat and Doğubeyazit

ToTatvan and Akdamar

Van Kalesi (Rock of Van)

0   200 m

Old Van

Ferry Point

Lake Van

251

of Iran scattered the Romans from Van, killing the Armenian King Khosrow Parhis and forcing the Armenians to adopt their religion. So unhappy were the Armenians under this state of affairs that they joined forces with the Romans to oust the Sassanians, and from then on for some time Van was ruled by Armenians under Roman domination.

Arabs, Seljuks and Mongols

The Roman Empire's control here ended with the outsurge of the Arabs in the 640s, who captured Van and converted it to Islam. Then in 1054 the first Turkish raids on the Vaspurakan kingdom began at the time of the Seljuks under Tugrul Bey. A few years later in 1071, the famous Seljuk warrior Alp Arslan won his great victory against the Byzantines at Manzikert which opened the way for the Turks to move westwards into the whole of Anatolia. But then followed in the 13th, 14th and 15th C a series of attacks, first by the Mongols, then by the Black Sheep Turcomans, and again by the Mongols under Tamerlane who, needless to say, destroyed Van Kalesi.

Ottomans

From 1503 the region ws held by the Iranian Safavids for a time, until in 1514 at Çaldıran the Ottoman Sultan Selim the Grim defeated the Iranian Shah and incorporated the region into the Ottoman Empire with a local governor at Van. All of these successive rulers used the rebuilt Van Kalesi as their stronghold.

German scholars of the 19th C were the first to write about and begin excavations in the Van region, and in this century Americans have conducted excavations at Tilkitepe (near Van airport) and at Van Kalesi from 1937 to 1939.

Exploring Van and Environs

In the Van region today you can enjoy several particularly worthwhile excursions: to the freakish Urartian citadel of Van Kalesi on the lake edge; to the annihilated town of old Van below it; to the Urartian palace at Çavuştepe; to the fairy-tale Kurdish castle at Hoşap; and then on to the wild remoteness of the Hakkâri gorge and the Zab river. To visit these places a bare minimum of two nights is needed in Van, ideally three.

A visit to Van Kalesi is best done towards the end of the day so that you can get the benefit of sunset over the lake and mountains. It takes three to four hours to make a thorough exploration.

A choice of approach

There are two ways of visiting Van Kalesi and Old Van. Your first option is to follow the yellow sign for 3 km straight to Van Kalesi along the potholed road that leads along the right (northern) and less precipitous side of the citadel. Leaving the car at the end by a little tea house, you will notice next to it the large stone block remains of the **Urartian jetty** which the lake once came up to. This

Approaching the highest point of Van Kalesi

road links up to that which runs down to the current landing stage for the train ferries and other boats, now some 500 metres away. From the tea house you can climb up a steepish but short path to explore the hilltop fortress, then returning to the car in order to drive round to the other side of the outcrop where the ruins of Old Van lie.

The second option is to drive straight to Old Van first, then walk across the flattened city and climb up the sheer side of the citadel to explore and then return. The first way involves less energy and is shorter and quicker, but the second is more satisfying because you discover the magnificence of the setting gradually and see all the sections of the long thin citadel which you might otherwise miss.

Old Van

Also called the Rock of Van, the citadel is a narrow outcrop nearly 2 km long, rising 100 metres, with sheer sides to the south. The flatness of the surrounding land makes it look particularly striking, a strange aberration. One Turkish traveller of the last century described it as a kneeling camel in profile. As you approach the citadel, look out for an earth road leading off left at right angles about 300 metres before the citadel outcrop. It is not possible to turn left at the foot of the outcrop itself because the municipality has fenced the whole area off and is apparently planning to build a recreation area here. You follow the earth road for some 300 metres, then turn right where it meets a more major but still unsurfaced road. Follow this in the direction of the lake, still not really visible at this point, past some small mud-built hovels, till you arrive after 500 metres directly opposite the citadel near the first of the large Ottoman mosques close to the road on the right.

From here you now walk across the rubble-like mounds of **Old Van** towards the citadel. This town, once surrounded by 16th C Ottoman walls, had one of the largest populations in Anatolia, and its bustling streets were so attractive that the Turks said everyone should see Van at least once in his lifetime. Today it must be one of the most vivid examples anywhere in the world of a town which has been quite literally razed to the ground, and nothing you will have read can prepare you for the total devastation here.

Beyond the southern walls to the left of the earth mound, two conical **türbes** with columned supports for the domes stand like a memorial to the dead city. Within the walls, mud mounds are all that remain where the walls of houses once stood, and grass grows inside. Apart from the two mosques near the road, the only other buildings left standing are a ruined hammam near the foot of the citadel and another two older mosques with minarets. The first of the mosques near the road is 16th C, the **Kaya Celebi Camii,** now just a shell, totally ruined and covered in grafitti inside, but still with surprisingly lovely lace-like lattice work mihrab in white stone. The second Ottoman mosque, closer to the lake, is now being restored. It is called the **Husrev Paşa Camii** (1567) and has the tomb of Husrev Paşa attached to its eastern side. The two colours of stone used give it the distinctive striped look seen so often in Diyarbakır's mosques. The mosque directly under the cliff to the left (lakeside) was the 13th C **Ulu Cami** and the steps of its broken brick minaret can still be climbed. On its walls was once rich decoration of geometric forms and flowers, looking Persian in influence. Set halfway up the cliff face above this minaret is a huge flattened piece of rock like a colossal plaque with a cuneiform inscription in Babylonian, Persian and Median, of the 5th C BC. The man who carved this must have hung over the rock edge on ropes for many weeks.

Massacre of the Armenians and the Destruction of Old Van

Throughout the vicissitudes of Van's history, the Armenians remained in the majority until the early 20th C. An English visitor to the town in the 1890s found two-thirds of the population to be Armenian. The town beneath the citadel was at that time totally walled with four gates built by the Ottomans, with narrow streets, wooden balconied houses and crowded bazaars, and was inhabited by Moslems and Christians. On the site of today's modern Van was the so-called 'garden suburb' where many of the wealthier Armenian Christians lived separately, going into the walled medieval city to conduct their business. They also had six churches in the old town, all made of wood, so they burnt easily. A bad earthquake in the 1950s destroyed what was left of the fine Armenian houses in the garden suburb.

The Van version of events told today is that the town was burnt down by the Armenians when the Turks were away fighting the Russians in 1914, and it was in revenge

for this that the Turks later drove the Armenians from Van. The Russians had provoked the Armenians in Van to side with them and the Allies against the Turks in the war. Then in 1915 the Russians occupied Van for nearly three years, during which time the Armenians tried to oust the Turks, killing many who refused to leave. When the Russians withdrew, unable to sustain the war effort because of the revolution at home, the Turks recaptured the city and punished the Armenians for their treachery by burning it and killing many of its inhabitants. The Turks say that the Armenians realised their hopes of setting up their own independent state were ruined, so they left Van and the surrounding towns of their own accord. They do, however, admit that the city was destroyed so utterly that it was uninhabitable, so they had to rebuild a new city from scratch.

Up to the late 19th C the official Turkish attitude to the Armenians was one of careless tolerance. Under the Ottomans, the Armenians, led by the patriarch of the Armenian Church, had their own General Assembly and their own councils to control education, law and property.

Much of the blame for why this tolerant relationship went wrong is laid at the door of Russia, who, disguised as the protector of the Christian communities in Turkey, set Armenians and Turks against one another with a view to ultimately controlling the Bosphorus. The Crimean War (1856), too, was a struggle for influence in Turkey and for the control of the military and trade routes. The victory of the British and the French inclined some Armenians to turn to the West for support in a bid for independence. The governor of Sivas told Frederick Burnaby, travelling here in 1876: '25 years ago the Turks and the Christians got on very well together, but ever since the Crimean War the Russian government has been actively engaged in tampering with the Armenian subjects of the Porte and has been doing its best to sow the seeds of dissension amongst the younger Armenians, by promising to make them counts and dukes in the event of their rising in arms against the Porte'.

The Pasha of Erzinczan, whom Burnaby spoke to in 1877, ominously predicted: 'If there be a war in Asia Minor, the Russians will do their best to excite our Kurds to massacre the Armenians in the neighbourhood of Van, and will then throw all the blame upon our shoulders'.

The Kurds have long been enemies of the Armenians, a conflict born not only of religion, but also of lifestyle, with the contempt of a nomadic and marauding people for settled townsfolk dealing in commerce. The Armenians also had the gift of irritating the Moslems by their often arrogant manner. When the Young Turk dictatorship ordered the removal of the two million or so Armenians, many were only too happy to oblige. The feeling was, however, mutual, and the Armenian volunteers on the Russian side, when Turkey collapsed, also took their revenge. More than 600,000 Kurds are said to have been killed in eastern Anatolia between 1915 and 1918. The Turkish view on the matter is that the Armenians were a disloyal minority who connived with the Russians to partition Turkey and set up an Armenian state. As traitors to their country at a time of national crisis, they deserved their fate, however extreme.

Armenian disloyalty

The Armenians see things differently, and cite the words of British Prime Minister David Lloyd George spoken in 1922: 'Since 1914 the Turks, according to testimony — official testimony — we have received, have slaughtered in cold blood one million and a half Armenians, men, women and children, and five hundred thousand Greeks without any provocation at all'.

The Armenian argument

During the period from 1908 to 1918, Turkey was dominated by the Young Turks. They came to power by a revolution proclaiming liberty, equality and fraternity. But far from establishing a democracy, by 1914 the Young Turks had established, under a triumvirate, an absolute dictatorship, silencing all opposition, including liberal and westernised Turks.

Already in 1911 at a Congress of Young Turks the following secret resolution had been carried: 'Sooner or later the complete Ottomisation of all Turkish subjects must be realised. It must, however, be clear that this objective can never be attained by persuasion. On the contrary, it must be achieved by force of arms'.

A history of massacres

Even before the rise of the Young Turks, the Armenians had suffered: in 1895 and 1896, tens of thousands of Armenians perished in officially instigated massacres; at Urfa over 2000 people including women and children were burnt

An 18th C European vision of Van

alive in their cathedral. Another massacre, in 1909, said to have claimed 30,000 Armenian lives in the province of Adana, was deliberately prepared by the government, as a local Young Turk member later admitted.

Nevertheless, far from being disloyal, at the outbreak of the First World War over 250,000 Armenians were serving in the Turkish army, and they only established an independent state in 1918 with the collapse of the Ottoman empire and in response to the gross violence they had suffered.

The holocaust reached its peak from 1915 to 1918. In 1915 the Minister of the Interior, Talaat Bey, a member of the Young Turks triumvirate, ordered: 'All rights of the Armenians to live and work on Turkish soil have been completely cancelled, and with regard to this the Government takes all responsibility on itself, and has commanded that even babies in the cradle are not to be spared'. A German journalist and eyewitness of the events which followed wrote: 'This diabolical crime was committed solely **Turkish** because of the Turkish feeling of economic and intellectual **inferiority** inferiority to that non-Turkish element, for the set purpose of obtaining handsome compensation for themselves'. That compensation, apart from laying waste to Armenian civilisation in Turkey, amounted to seizing material wealth valued at 14 billion dollars in gold. Henry Morgenthau, the American Ambassador to Turkey at the time, wrote: 'If this plan of murdering a race is to succeed it would be necessary to render all Armenian soldiers powerless and to deprive of their arms the Armenians in every city and town. Before Armenia could be slaughtered, Armenia must be made defenceless'. In 1918 the Minister of War, Enver Pasha, another of the triumvirate, announced 'an order for the whole Armenian race': Armenian civilians from the age of five 'to be taken out of the towns and slaughtered', and Armenian soldiers 'to be taken into solitary places away from the public eye and shot'.

Viscount James Bryce said in 1920: 'About the middle of 1915, as soon as the fear that Constantinople might be captured by the British Fleet had vanished, Talaat and Enver issued orders for the slaughter of all the adult males among the Armenian Christians in the Asiatic parts of the Empire, and for the expulsion from their homes and enslavement or transportation into the desert of Northern Arabia and Mesopotamia, of the women and children. These orders were carried out. Nearly a million persons were killed, many of them with horrible tortures, some, including bishops and other ecclesiastics, roasted to death'. The English historian Arnold Toynbee wrote of the deportations and slaughters: 'They fell behind and were bayonetted and thrown into the river, and their bodies floated down to the sea, or lodged in the shallow river on rocks where they remained for ten or twelve days and putrified. All this horror, both the concerted crime and its local embellishments, was inflicted upon the Armenians without a shadow of provocation'.

Of the Turkish and Armenian arguments you can take your pick.

Anyone involved personally in the massacres would have to be very old today, and the Turks do not feel guilt for the deeds of their fathers. But the fathers felt no guilt either, and this character trait seems to be reflected in two Turkish proverbs: 'The cat which eats her kittens swears they look like mice', and 'Even if guilt were made of sable, no one would choose to wear it'.

Not guilty

Before the First World War the population of Van was 80,000 (315,000 in the whole province). When the first census of the new Turkish Republic was taken in 1927, Van's population was 6,931 (75,437 in the province). By 1986, however, the Van population was 92,000 (570,000 in the province).

Ascent of Van Kalesi

Looking at the sheer face of the citadel, it does not look as if it can easily be climbed. Legend says that there are 1000 steps cut into the rock, and though as you approach, short runs of steps can be seen, none of them link up so it is not, alas, possible just to climb an enormous flight of steps to the top. If, however, you head for the lowest end of the outcrop, to your right, you will notice one short flight of steps quite close to the ground. It is a very easy five-minute scramble from here up to the lowest walls. At the walls you follow the path to the right, where you can clamber through a breach, and a path then leads over the crest of the **citadel.**

Had you approached the citadel as described in the first option (straight from Van rather than via Old Van), you could climb up from the tea house to a small cemetery where there is an oratory and a tomb. Above this shrine (but below you if you are already atop the citadel) is a platform of limestone rock, **site of an Urartian temple,** with a curved-back bench cut out of the rock wall. Two huge arched niches are carved here which the locals say once held two gold statues of ancient goddesses. The Americans, they say, took them away after their excavations in 1935–37. The western or lakeside niche has a black basalt statue base with a cuneiform inscription recording the work of the great warrior and builder King Menua.

If heights do not bother you, an alternative route along the citadel follows the narrow path along the **top of the battlements.** At one point a path forks down left and leads round to an impressive flight of wide **rock-cut steps** down to a wide terrace on the cliff edge which appears man-made.

Vast royal tomb From the platform a further five steps lead up to a huge tomb entrance hollowed out of the sheer rock face, a cave-like opening readily visible from Old Van below. Inside is a large square cut chamber with smaller rooms leading off from each of the three side walls. It must have taken years to hollow out this vast area, for the ceilings are very high. This is the **tomb of Sardur II** (c765–733 BC), a warrior Urartian king, and the chambers were probably used for various rituals and sacrifices. In the last century they were also used as quarters for troops or dungeons for prisoners.

A castle sits within the citadel walls and from here the path to it is quite tricky to find. If you continue along the battlement walkway, you come soon to a huge cleft in the rock which divides the lower citadel from the upper citadel. Only experienced rock climbers would be advised to attempt bridging this gap. Retracing your steps a short way, you discover a path forking down towards the oratory below and then running along the side of the citadel for 200 metres or so until it leads up to a slope of slippery mud which you have to clamber up to get to the castle on the higher level of the citadel. A telegraph pole marks this point and is a useful landmark to remember for your return route.

To the top of the castle You can now climb up to the highest point of the castle, a large open grassy area on which stands the inevitable representation of the great Atatürk. (Lower down, near the cleft between the two halves of the citadel, another path leads down to the Old Van side of the outcrop and round to another flattened terrace, this time with two large rock-cut tombs in the cliff face. Each one has the same three chambers leading off the main one as before. These are the **tombs of King Ispuini,** 815–807 BC, **and Menua,** 804–790 BC.) But following the path off along the citadel crest you pass several crumbling **Ottoman buildings,** including barracks, a madrasa and a mosque which still has its minaret and steps inside, until you come to the **castle.** In Ottoman times Van castle was an important military base, and the 17th C Turkish traveller Evliya Celebi said that up to 3000 Janissaries and artillery men lived in it. The castle construction shows clearly the large blocks of the original Urartian fortress at the bottom, then the smaller blocks of the Armenian castle, then topped with the mortar and clays of later Turkish periods. An **inscription** in one corner of the cyclo-pean walls boasts: 'I, Sardur, the illustrious king, the **King of the castle** mighty king, the king of the universe, the king of all lands, a king without equal, I erected these walls'.

Following the wide ramp-like path slightly downhill and through an arch, you now reach the open flattened-out part of the mountain top with white limestone sides and floor. (It is this flattened area you reach first if you have climbed up from the tea house from the Van side.) Over on the far side of this, overlooking Old Van, iron railings and a gate now block off access to the rock-cut steps which lead down the cliff face to the **tomb of King Argistis** (790–765 BC), son of Menua. The vertical rock face around this tomb is covered in **Urartian cuneiform inscriptions,** heavily defaced, dating from 765 BC. The local tourist office says it was tourists who came and hacked off pieces of the inscription to take away as souvenirs, so it had to be sealed off for protection. If you do not mind heights, you can in fact climb down a second outer staircase just below the railings, which, though more damaged, is still manageable. If you want to go into the tomb a flashlight is necessary as there is a large hole inside which you cannot see by natural light. One tourist recently fell down this hole and hit his head badly, so care is called for. In front of the cave a large footprint in the rock is claimed by some locals as the devil's, while others say it is that of Ali, the Prophet Mohammed's son-in-law.

Devil's footprint

Wandering round Van Kalesi up and down the little paths and gullies is a very enjoyable experience, rather like exploring an adventure playground, and is especially lovely at sunset. As you make your way back towards the lower citadel for the climb down to Old Van, the view over towards the mountains growing pink in the light is an unforgettable sight.

Toprakkale
The large outcrop of mountain rising above the town of modern Van with a radio mast on top and white slogans carved into it alongside the star and crescent is **Toprakkale** (Earth Castle), site of another 8th C BC Urartian palace citadel, the next largest after Van. Some talk of an underground palace here, a huge room 25 by 50 metres cut into the rock reached by a flight of rock-cut spiral steps. It is in fact no more than a cistern. The site lies within a military area and is only visitable by obtaining a permit from the local wali (governor). The remains on the hilltop are no longer considered worth visiting anymore anyway, and certainly a perhaps premature state of ruination often seems to accompany historic sites which find themselves in military zones.

Other Excursions from Van
In the immediate Van area a few other sites are now closed to tourists. The Armenian **Yedi Kilise Monastery** (Warak Vank), on a bad dirt road 20 km east-southeast of Van, on a slope of the Warak mountain under Susan Dağı (2750 metres) is heavily damaged and no visits are permit-

ted until restoration is completed. The once famous monastery, founded in the 8th C, housed 300 monks in its heyday. King Gagik's daughter and her husband are buried here. The locals claim that earthquakes over the centuries have taken their toll on it which is why the remains are so fragmentary. In the last century, rich Armenians used to come here on summer outings, but now Kurdish peasants live in the ruins. The largest of the seven churches that remains, dedicated to Mary, has been whitewashed and is used as a grain store.

Other monasteries exist, extremely remote, in the region but are not visitable without a guide and long journeys. For the totally undauntable there is the excursion to the **convents of Aparank,** southwest of Van, a three-day excursion involving 216 km in a jeep and 20 hours on horseback. The riding begins from the village of Bahçesaray (Garden Palace) up a track to the right from the tarmac road to Çatak. Near the Kurdish village of Vatas (Aparank) are five Armenian churches ranging from the 10th to the 17th C. The best preserved ones are, as ever, used by the locals as stables and stores.

Armenian churches become Kurdish stables

Çatak is an attractive mountain town 86 km from Van, reached by forking off south a few kilometres before Gevas. In its streams excellent trout can be caught, and in its forests there is hunting for partridges, ducks, hares, mountain goats and foxes. Some 60 km along this road a lovely **waterfall** where the Ganiyisippi (Persian for White Spring) gushes over a cliff. The trout is never available in restaurants in Van, nor is it sold commercially. Bears, wild boars, wolves, beavers and stone martens can be hunted at the right season in the **Zilvan valley** near Erciş.

TOWARDS HAKKÂRI

Leaving Van on the road past the tourist office, the main road runs to the south towards Hakkâri, 204 km away. The dauntless Freya Stark recalls this remote mountainous corner of Turkey in the 1950s as 'one of those dwindling regions where a four-footed animal is still the only help to locomotion'. Today there is a good road and the drive without stopping takes just over three hours.

On the way there are two highly interesting and unusual sites: the Urartian palace at Çavuştepe and the Kurdish castle at Hoşap. It is in fact possible to visit Çavuştepe, have a picnic at Hoşap, drive on to Hakkâri town, and then drive back again to reach Van before dark if you wish. Though this involves a faster pace of travel than is usually thought desirable, it does at least have the advantage of another night at the comfortable hotels of Van rather than those of Hakkâri.

Urartian Palace

As soon as you are clear of the outskirts of Van, the road begins to climb and soon reaches a low pass at 2225 metres before dropping quickly down to a major fork in the road, right to Elazığ and Gürpinar, left to Hakkâri. The hills are more barren along this initial stretch than on the southern shore of Lake Van. The road arrives at Çavuştepe after some 10 km of flat road from the junction, and only 22 km from Van. As you drive through the village you will notice to your right a characteristic long thin hill, the shape favoured by the Urartians for their palaces, and on this is the **royal citadel of Çavuştepe.** The buildings on the summit were for the king and his family only, while the Urartian laypeople lived down on the flat, roughly where the present village now lies. The fact that ordinary people never appear at all in Urartian art — the players are all kings, priests and gods — has led some scholars to speculate that the Urartians might have been a slave society.

Upstairs, downstairs

A yellow sign points off to the right on a straightforward earth road up to the citadel shortly after passing through the modern village, and you can drive up to the lowest collar on the citadel crest. From here a courteous guardian is usually waiting for you and will show you photos of the Turkish excavations which took place here in the 1970s, before accompanying you round the palace. There is no entrance fee and no refreshments are on offer here, only a few postcards. On a hot day the bare hilltop can be punishing with no shade at all, so make sure you have your own supply of drinks.

The guardian leads you first along the so-called lower temple area, following a path, then up steps and along a broad corridor, almost like a sacred way, which runs along the crest and links the temple area to the palace. A stone basin near the path was used for holy water. The **temple** has a superb series of highly polished black basalt stone blocks, so smooth that it feels like the highest quality marble to the touch, beautifully carved in Urartian cuneiform. Nearby is a **sacrificial altar** where the Urartians honoured or appeased their gods. An extraordinarily advanced **water system** with a series of large cisterns hollowed out of the rock to collect the rain or snow is evident. Below the citadel there are still traces of a huge water channel system that brought water from the mountains.

The **palace,** at the far end of the hill crest, would originally have been a three-storeyed building; archaeologists have drawn impressive reconstructions of what it would have looked like. It has a recognisable *harem* area, and in the corner, just on the edge of the hill, is a neat little *water closet* with a drainage tunnel leading hygienically off down the hill.

Returning now to the car park and climbing up to the upper section of the citadel, you come to a flattened area of limestone with an **upper temple.** The standard of preservation and the masonry is not, however, of the same quality as that of the lower temple.

Kurdish Fortress

Onwards from Çavuştepe the road remains largely flat and fairly straight till it reaches a quarry where a dam is being built, and major road works force a small diversion. The road then climbs slightly, still keeping straight, through bare and somewhat gaunt hills, and suddenly, on crossing the brow of a hill, the unmistakable **castle of Hoşap** appears before you, standing on a hill above a small village. As you descend gradually into the valley, the magnificent castle seems unreal, like a hallucination from a fairy tale, with its crenellated battlements and turrets, the whole perched precariously on its hill. Built by Sarı Sulayman, a local Kurdish despot of the Mahmudi tribe, in 1643 when Ottoman power was slipping, it is the best example of a Kurdish castle to be seen in Turkey today. Its appearance is such that you might be inclined to believe the local tradition that the Kurdish bey had the hands of the architect cut off after it was finished, to ensure no similar castle could be built elsewhere.

Fairy-tale castle

The Kurdish fortress at Hoşap

In the village just below the castle, a fine **bridge** of light and dark stone, built at the same time as the castle, crosses the little stream which gives the village its name Güzelsu, Beautiful Water (Hoşap means the same in Kurdish). Passing by the bridge and continuing a little beyond the foot of the castle, a yellow sign announces it and a dirt road forks off left, over a modern bridge, and then winds on round the back of the hill to the castle's main entrance. If locked, the guardian or his son will soon materialise with the key. The **entrance gate** is very impressive indeed, set in a powerful and colossal round tower. Carved above it are inscriptions in Farsi script and a medallion in the shape of a tear drop with a stylised lion on either side. The initial entrance way appears to lead into the hillside itself with a fine vaulted ceiling carved from the rock. A dark tunnel-like passage leads up into the interior of the castle, which suddenly becomes very open and grassy. Parts of it are like a meadow, and you almost expect to see cows and sheep grazing inside. There is in fact considerably less left inside than you would expect from the outside walls.

You come first to a large circular area of wall which you look down into from above. This is said to have been the **conference hall,** a sort of Knights of the Round Table room, and beam holes in the wall show that it originally had two storeys. The path then leads on up to an edge of the castle with a heavily ruined bath, mosque and madrasa, so heavily ruined in fact that you simply have to take the guardian's word for it. Tiny traces of blue decoration are left round the inside of some of the windows. The castle is known to have had 360 rooms, two mosques, three baths, dungeons, fountains, store-rooms and a well.

Looking over to the east, away from the road, you can follow the line of mud **defence walls** running over the nearby hills, once encircling the town below. Freya Stark graphically describes their crumbling aspect: 'The flesh of their battlements [had been] sucked by weather to look like the skeletons of caterpillars creeping about the lower hillocks'. A higher path climbs higher still up to the **keep** which is the best preserved part of the fortress.

Caterpillar walls

Lured on by Mountains

After Hoşap the road follows the river valley for a few kilometres, then begins a steep climb over a pass of 2790 metres where snow lies even in late May. The landscapes up to this point, though mountainous, are not particularly striking, mainly due to the absence of any greenery, even in springtime. In the distance, the mountain massif of the Çilo Dağ and Sat Dağ, the main mountains of the Hakkâri region, rise before you, luring you on ever deeper into the remote valleys. Freya Stark commented that in her opinion international congresses should be held in quiet places like this instead of in busy capital cities, 'places where the grassy skyline is a lifting of earth untroubled with houses, and cattle grazing along the coolness of buried waters bring the smoothness of their own lives into the mind of the gazer — if an international congress ever has time to gaze'.

From here on there are no particular monuments to visit, and the journey to Hakkâri is really for the magnificent scenery which begins at the Zab valley. In the past the main reason for foreigners to come here was for the mountaineering in the peaks east of Hakkâri and south of Yuksekova, and pack animals and guides could always be found at both these towns. But with the problem of Kurdish insurgents, climbing in the Hakkâri region has been totally forbidden since 1985. Until the political situation is more settled, you would be advised to stick to the main routes and not head up small tracks into the villages. The main road, however, remains perfectly safe. 12 km from Başkale, and exactly 100 km from Van, there is an army checkpoint, the only one until near Hakkâri, which stops all traffic, checks papers and passports and searches all vehicles. Since Hakkâri is a province still under martial law and with guerilla activity nearby, it is perhaps surprising that this is the only checkpoint along this main road. The soldiers are very good-natured and inspect your baggage quite gently, doing their best to restrain their curiosity. They have obviously been instructed not to hassle people who are evidently tourists. It continues to function after dark, and there is no question of the road being closed at night.

Guerillas and checkpoints

In more quiet times an excursion could be made from near this check point left, up a narrow stabilised road 12 km to the town of **Albayrak.** This town consists largely of the buildings of the former Armenian **Bartholomew Monastery.** The monks did not live in one large central building, but in separate houses like a small village. A military station is housed here today. The church looks like a Greek temple. Its roof collapsed in a recent earthquake. To visit it you need permission from the military post, but it should only be attempted if you are a competent Turkish speaker or have a good local guide with you. The church has many features reminiscent of Persian Sassanid style with many fine relief carvings. This road continues along the valley of the Greater Zab, and after 20 km in superb landscapes you reach the village of **Soradır** (2400 metres), only 15 km from the Iranian border. It has a yellow Armenian church of c600 standing alone on a hillock, seen as the forerunner in style to Akdamar and resembling the style of church still found in the Soviet Republic of Armenia. It is used today as a grain store.

From the check point the main road now climbs gradually up to **Başkale,** at 2500 metres the highest town in Turkey. Huddled up against a slope of the mountain, it looks like a God forsaken place on a bleak treeless plateau and must be truly grim in winter. Today's inhabitants are totally Kurdish, and the houses are either old mud hovels or new ugly concrete blocks — there is nothing in between. The road continues along the plateau, then begins a slow descent into the Zab valley, leading eventually to Hakkâri town. The Zab river flows through Hakkâri to join the Tigris below Mosul in Iraq. From this point on the scenery becomes more grand as the road winds round the valley with very lush fields and brilliant green grass, so bright it is almost dazzling higher up the mountain slopes. There are no villages here at all, and all you pass are flocks of sheep and goats and small herds of cows.

On the lush grassy river banks the occasional black nomad tent can be seen in idyllic settings. The colourfully dressed children happily playing on the river banks, their clothes glinting in the sun, look as if they could not have a more perfect place to grow up. As Freya Stark writes:

'The life of insecurity is the nomad's achievement. He does not try, like our building world, to believe in a stability which is non-existent; and in his constant movement with the seasons, in the lightness of his hold, puts something right, about which we are constantly wrong. His is in fact the reality, to which the most solid of our structures are illusion; and the ramshackle tents in their crooked gaiety, with cooking-pots propped up before them and animals about, show what a current flows round all the stone erections of the ages. The finest ruin need only be lamented with moderation, since its living essence long ago entered the common stream. No thought of this kind is likely to come into the head of the Turkish Yürük (though it could be familiar to the imagination of the Arab); they are happy to shelter their goats in the warmth or the shade that they find, whether the ruins be of Nineveh or Rome. Their women were cheerful and fierce, unlike the peasant, and dressed in brighter colours — equals of their men or of anyone, as one may be if one lives under the hardness of necessity and makes insecurity one's refuge'.

The road now reaches a fork, left to Yüksekova across the river, with an intriguing yellow sign marking Iran as if it were a tourist attraction. The crossing into Iran here is quicker than via Doğubeyazit to the north. **Yüksekova** used to be the commonest base for mountaineers to make their departures to the Çilo and Sat peaks, though its appearance, set on a high open plateau, is not remotely mountainous.

The road to Hakkâri stays on the right-hand side of the

Nomad encampment in the Zab valley

Precarious bridges

river, and the ever beckoning snow-covered mountains in the distance get closer and closer as you wind on through the valley. Spanning the river along the way are several extraordinarily precarious looking bridges used by the nomads and their livestock. There is also one chair-lift style bridge, worked on a wynch. The Greater Zab countrymen, and women too for that matter, must suspend themselves by a pulley, and then heave their way across the turbulent river. Landslides and flash floods after summer thunderstorms cut the roads off quite frequently here.

The Nestorians

A deserted village on the left bank could, with its mud brick houses and grassy roofs, be mistaken for any field and can be easily missed altogether. This might be the abandoned Nestorian village which early accounts have seen in this valley. Isolated and rugged, the history of the region is one of villages, not of empires. The armies of conquerors by-passed it, preferring to stay on the flatter ground, and though the Urartians and Akkadians came from here, they moved north when the time was ripe to found their empires elsewhere.

Until the First World War there were many Nestorian Christians living in the villages here. The doctrine of Nestorius, Bishop of Constantinople from 428 to 431, was rejected as a heresy in 431 at the Council of Ephesus, but welcomed in Syria and Persia. Nestorius' works were burnt by papal order, and he was carried off and mutilated by Nubians, dying finally in the Egyptian desert in 451. Their centre grew up first in Edessa (Urfa), but when in 489 the Edessa school was closed, the students and teachers moved to Nisibis (Nusaybin) and then on to Persia, where their school flourished under the protection of the Sassanids. The Mongols and Tamerlane later destroyed their centres in Persia and in Baghdad, and in the 15th C many Nestorians fled north to these mountain valleys where they lived alongside the Kurds. They were good and industrious farmers, carefully building terraced fields and irrigation systems which are still in use today. Their houses and churches were simply and neatly built of stone, and they were wholly opposed to the use of images in their churches.

Their patriarchal church, **Mar Shalita,** lies on a high platform some 20 km to the northeast of Hakkâri, reachable today only on foot and with a guide. It is used by shepherds as a dung cake store. Scattered in the mountains are said to be around 20 more Nestorian churches: the simplicity of their architecture is disappointing, but the beauty of the landscape compensates.

Centuries of isolation in Hakkâri surrounded by Moslems made the Nestorians a distinct people, but originally they were Syrians from northern Mesopotamia, and they still spoke a form of Syriac. They believed in the predominantly human nature of Christ, and that Mary was Mother

A human Christ of Christ, not Mother of God. The Syrian Orthodox Church holds the opposite doctrine, that Christ's human nature was absorbed in the divine, while the Greek Orthodox and Roman churches hold the more subtle view of two natures, unmixed, unchangeable, indistinguishable and inseparable.

The relations of the Nestorians with the Kurds deteriorated in the 19th C, and in 1852 the British Embassy in Constantinople heard reports of massacres of Nestorians by Kurds and the selling of women and children as slaves into the Arab parts of the Ottoman Empire. The ambassador of the time, Sir Stratford Canning, actually rescued some of the slaves, buying them back with money raised by public subscription. In 1915 the Nestorian patriarch lent his support to the Allies against the Turks, but the Russians failed them and they were forced to leave their little farms to escape east to Iran and Iraq, where a few still live today. The Kurds moved into their abandoned houses, still called nesturi, and all that remains in Turkey to remember them by is the coloured cross knitted on the toe of the woollen socks by the local Kurdish women.

A Nestorian church was also described in early accounts as being in this stretch of the Zab valley, but it must now be so heavily disguised as a cow shed that it is invisible to all but the well-trained eye.

Wild Hakkâri

In the final 10 km before Hakkâri the road makes a spectacularly steep climb out of the Zab valley to higher mountain slopes of poplar trees and green grass. Here stands **Hakkâri,** directly facing the 4135-metre massif of Çilo Dağ. From a distance it has almost the look of an Alpine ski resort in summer; it is certainly unlike any other town you have visited in Turkey. Although you feel it must be higher, at 1700 metres it is in fact marginally lower than Van. With a population of 18,000, almost entirely Kurdish, it is a small place but very spread out. The road winds up and through it for at least 3km, passing first the petrol station and then on past other newish buildings until it reaches the centre of town, recognisable by the bust of Atatürk. The Turistik Hotel is just on this square, while the supposedly better Callı Hotel is off a turn to the left.

In Hakkâri itself the atmosphere is most curious. All women are veiled with scarcely even their eyes showing and wear black from head to toe. The passport photographs **Veiled women** of these women would present customs officials with real difficulties. The town is highly traditional and Ramadan is very strictly observed with no alcohol being served at all throughout the month. The men, in drab black or grey trousers and jackets, wander aimlessly round the streets. The atmosphere is tense and you feel a wildness bubbling just below the surface. Hakkâri is the name of the Kurdish nomadic tribe which settled here in the 13th C.

In winter the main road through from Van to the Iranian border is kept open by snow ploughs and is only shut for a day or so if there have been large avalanches. The remoter side valleys, however, are cut off for nearly half the year by heavy snow, though by way of compensation it is not as cold as it is on the bitter and windswept hills further north. The Kurdish tribes who live here are semi-nomadic, living in the villages in the winter and moving up to the high pastures for the summer, often no more than half a day's walk away.

PRACTICAL INFORMATION

TATVAN
Denizcelik Bankası Otel, sometimes also called the Van Gölü Hotel (1-star). This is by far the best in the western area of the lake, as it was built originally for rail-way passengers waiting for the ferry across to Van. It does not expect much casual custom from independent travellers, so unless you know where to look you will never find it. As you drive along the main

street of Tatvan from Bitlis, you should be looking out for a white H on a blue background, the standard hospital sign on the left-hand side of the road, about two-thirds of the way through the town and some 300 metres after the PTT office. This H sign points left towards the lake, and you turn into this unlikely and pothole-ridden road, following it round as it curves to the right, then veers off left straight towards the lake, and then runs along the edge of the lake past a defunct-looking landing stage. From here the road leads back inland to a blue 2-storey building, clearly a converted barracks, set 100 metres back from the lake with trees and a garden in front. The rooms on the first floor are the best, comfortable, carpeted, with private bathrooms and a pleasant view over the lake. In cold weather the efficient central heating keeps the whole place nice and warm, something of a rarity in these parts. The restaurant, however, is somewhat limited and service can be surly. Because it is the best in the area it does get full.

Karaman Hotel. Very basic rooms where you have to stay if the Van Gölü is full, but mercifully with no smell from the drains. High on the cockroach rating.

For breakfast there are several **pasta-hanes** near the Karaman where you can eat hot börek with cheese and hot sweet tea in large beakers. The **lokanta** opposite the Karaman is surprisingly good, and above the nearby Yapı Kredi Bank is a **beer hall** on the first floor, which unusually continues serving throughout Ramadan, and where the locals come to get very drunk.

Passenger **ferries,** also taking cars, run from here to Van 3 or 4 times a week.

Nemrut Dağ Crater is closed by snow for all but July and August. An ordinary car will get you to the top in the summer.

GEVAS (AKDAMAR ISLAND)

Details of how the **boats** run across to the island are given in the text. A **restaurant and picnic area** are laid out at the roadside opposite the ferry point. There are no refreshments available on the island.

VAN

Akdamar Hotel (2-star), Tel: 1894. One of the best hotels in Eastern Turkey, with 75 good rooms and a very spacious and pleasant bar on the first floor. Breakfast can be taken in your room and freshly squeezed orange juice ordered. Good attentive service, though the range in the restaurant is disappointingly limited.

Büyük Urartu (2-star), Tel: 12173. Van's newest hotel and very comfortable and stylishly decorated.

Büyük Asur (1-star), Tel: 3753. 48 rooms with lift and central heating. American bar. 5-storeyed modern block in main street.

Beş Kardeş (1-star), Tel: 1116. 50 rooms, a bit old now, built in 1970.

The standard of **food** in the good hotels like the Akdamar and the Büyük Urartu falls far short of the level you would expect from this class. When challenged about why they do not serve the Van fish (supposedly available in abundance from April until June) they just look at you and grin uncomprehendingly and explain with a baffling logic that the fish is eaten in people's homes, not in restaurants. One restaurant, the Kösk (see plan), a rather unsavoury looking place with no sign, claims to offer the fish. The other speciality, sometimes available if you ask, is otlupeynir, herbal cheese, a Kurdish delicacy, a full creamy cheese with 2 types of herb. These herbs, grown in the mountains, are said to have certain curative properties for the kidneys and urinal channels.

There are **flights** to Ankara daily except Thursdays and Saturdays ($1\frac{1}{2}$ hours), with connections to İstanbul ($3\frac{3}{4}$ hours including transfer). Arrival by plane in Van is an experience to be relished, giving you a superb view in clear weather down into the crater lake of Nemrut Dağ and the northern volcano cone of Suphan Dağı, then crossing the lake and landing close by Van Kalesi, whose curious appearance is enhanced from the air.

Trains run direct from Van to İstanbul or İzmir, via Ankara, 3 times a week, and on to Tabriz and Teheran 4 times a week.

The large **ferry steamers** run direct across the lake from Tatvan to Van to connect the railways 4 times a day. In addition, **smaller ferry boats** link the other points of the shore with Van and Tatvan, and there are landing stages at Ahlat, Adilcevaz, and Erciş on the north side, and Edremit, Gevas, and Reşadiye on the south side. The trip along the northern shore takes 1½ days, and along the southern shore 8 hours. The latter is the more impressive route. The express service from Van to Tatvan takes 3¾ hours.

In Ottoman times Van was famous for its finely worked silver, in the form of belts, necklaces, bracelets, cigarette cases and holders, pipe mouthpieces and the like. As the local tourist leaflet euphemistically puts it: 'Today this craftsmanship has almost disappeared'. The silversmiths were all Armenians, so the reasons for its disappearance are evident. **Handicrafts** which are still going strong, however, are the weaving of Van kilims or rugs. The predominant colours in these are red, white and dark blue. The designs are usually geometric, with occasional stylised motifs of animals or plants. They are all handmade and natural dyes from local plants and roots are still used.

A **festival** is held on 2 April, when the end of Russia's First World War occupation is celebrated.

The **winter** is very long, from September to May, and the **summer** season is really only the three months of June, July and August when it gets very hot during the day, but cools off very quickly at night. The air and water here are both very revitalising and healthy. Swimming begins from mid to late May at the earliest, unless you are a masochist. The water then heats very quickly throughout June, July and August, cooling down again very quickly at the end of September.

Average temperature (Celsius):

J	F	M	A	M	J
−5.6	−5.5	−1.7	5.1	11.6	16.4
J	A	S	O	N	D
20.0	18.7	13.8	7.2	1.8	−3.0

Maximum temperature:

J	F	M	A	M	J
12.6	14.3	20.4	24.0	26.7	33.5
J	A	S	O	N	D
37.5	36.7	32.6	28.8	20.1	14.5

Minimum temperature:

J	F	M	A	M	J
−28.7	−28.2	−19.6	−17.5	−6.6	−2.6
J	A	S	O	N	D
3.6	5.0	2.2	−14.0	−20.5	−21.3

HAKKÂRI

Callı Hotel A modernish red and yellow block, it looks totally unprepossessing from the outside, but is not too bad inside apart from the surliness of the service. It has a fine terrace at the back facing over the mountain. The rooms have their own basin and shower, but no integral WCs. These are shared and some are of the sitting, some of the squatting variety. By Eastern Turkey standards, the place is quite clean though somewhat spartan.

May is really too early to enjoy Hakkâri, as the temperature is too cold to sit outside. June, July and August are the **best times to visit.**

NORTH EASTERN TURKEY

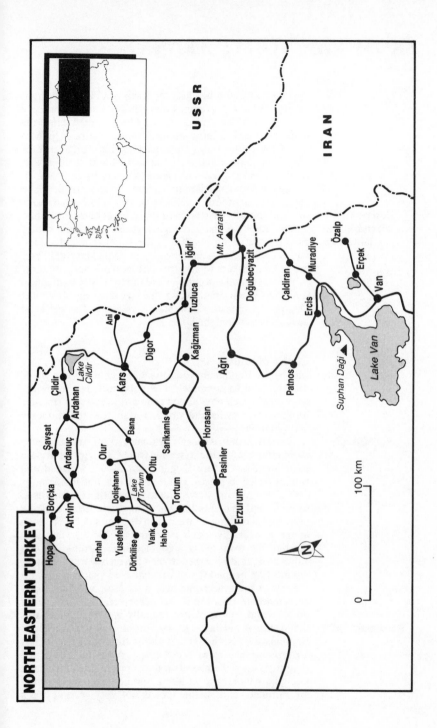

NORTH EASTERN TURKEY

USSR

IRAN

Hopa
Borçka
Artvin
Şavşat
Ardanuç
Ardahan
Çıldır
Lake Çıldır
Parhal
Yusefeli
Dörtkilise
Vank
Haho
Dolişhane
Lake Tortum
Oltu
Olur
Bana
Kars
Ani
Digor
Sarıkamış
Tortum
Pasinler
Horasan
Erzurum
Kağızman
Tuzluca
Iğdır
Mt. Ararat
Doğubeyazıt
Ağrı
Patnos
Çaldıran
Muradiye
Erciş
Suphan Dağı
Lake Van
Özalp
Erçek
Van

N

0   100 km

275

FROM VAN TO MT ARARAT

As you leave Van heading off north towards Mt Ararat, the turn-off to Özalp comes very quickly, almost while you are still on the outskirts. 10 km up this turn-off stands the **castle of Anzaf**, a more minor Urartian fortress, built to guard the trade routes from Iran to the capital at Van. Like Çavuştepe, it has an upper and a lower section, with colossal blocks of stone surviving to two or three layers.

Most beautiful stretch of the lakeshore

The main road north remains dead flat and straight, passing, 20 km out of Van, a yellow sign off 10 km down towards the lake shore. This stretch of shoreline is known as **Amik**, famous for its orchards and natural beaches, and widely used by picnicking families in the summer months. Dolmuşes and minibuses running between Van and Amik ferry the holidaymakers to and fro. The beaches here are long, a mixture of sand and pebbles and the spot, with its plentiful trees and green grass facing the volcanic one of Suphan Dağ on the opposite shoreline, is thought of as the most beautiful stretch of the lake.

Choice of Routes

Just before Bendimahi you can make a choice about which road to take to continue to Doğubeyazıt: left along the main road which does a loop round to the west, a straightforward if somewhat dull drive, or right towards Muradiye and Çaldıran.

Via Muradiye

This latter route is shorter by some 150 km, and scenically more interesting, but the section from Çaldıran to the main road just 3 km before Doğubeyazıt, is not surfaced and is a bit rough in places. Before May it is not passable for cars as the melting snows create a river which is too deep to be forded at one point, but at any time from mid-May onwards till mid-September it can be done safely. The road as far as **Muradiye** itself is good and straight. You pass through the town along a cobbled road turning left at a T-junction, rejoining the tarmac 1 km on towards Çaldıran. About 7 km beyond the town a battered yellow plaque on the left of the road announces a 'köprü', a **Seljuk single-arched bridge**, over the Bendamahi river. Just 1 km further on a second yellow plaque, equally battered, announces

Bendimahi Falls

the **Muradiye Şelalesi**. These waterfalls, also known as the Bendimahi Falls, though not visible from the road, lie just a short distance along a dirt track. A bridge crosses the river just below them, and on the opposite side of the bank a few huts looking a bit like a building site emplacement are grouped, and so the spot is not very suitable for a picnic. The falls themselves, however, are pretty, but not particularly impressive as they are quite low, only about 10 metres, and their setting is nothing special. Where this river runs into the lake, Van fish are found in the greatest abundance.

Driving along virtually empty roads you arrive at **Çaldıran**, a bustling place with a large military base. North along the stretch of unsurfaced road closest to the Iranian border there are police patrols which stop you to ask to see your passport and then wave you on. Their manner towards foreigners is very friendly. The road closes after 5pm, so make sure you allow yourself plenty of time — three hours should do. Iranian border posts are visible at many points, and in one village you pass through you should be careful to take a left fork as the right one leads into Iran. The worst section of road surface is the final 15 km before Doğubeyazıt where it skirts the edge of an old lava field.

Turn right for Iran

If you choose to stick to the main road however, the route continues very straight to **Erciş**, passing a recently restored conical türbe just on the left of the road as you fork right on the town by-pass. Built in 1458, it contains the body of the mother of a Black Sheep emir, for Erciş was once the capital of the Black Sheep Turcomans.

Via Agrı

From Erciş onwards the huge cone of Suphan Dağ rises to the left, dominating the landscape for the next 50 km as far as Patnos. The Patnos road continues very straight and driving is therefore quite fast. The total trip to Doğubeyazıt from Van takes around four hours on this route. **Patnos** is now one huge military camp. In all parts of the town are various military zones with their accompanying playgrounds full of ropes and climbing apparatus, painted in the military red and white stripes. Two Urartian sites which once existed on small hillocks to the left of the road as you leave are now clearly within military areas. The road on to Tutak leads through very dull and featureless steppeland. It continues to be dead straight but the surface is riddled with potholes which you vainly hoped to have left behind. After Tutak the scenery becomes more interesting as the road follows the course of a river along a shallow gorge.

Arriving at **Ağrı**, a faceless modern town, you turn right before entering the town proper, towards Doğubeyazıt. This road continues in a straight line eastwards toward distant hills and mountains, and then unmistakably, **Mt Ararat** itself looms up as you cross a small ridge in the road. To its right stands Little Ararat, like a child beside its parent. Ararat at 5165 metres is Turkey's highest mountain. In summer the snow line retreats up the mountain to cover the top third only, while in winter it comes right down

The roof of the world

to the base. As the surrounding plateau, itself at 1800 metres, is so flat, the colossal cone of Ararat dominates the landscape for over 50 km in every direction. From afar its sides look smooth and deceptively easy to climb, but in practice the jagged lava fields are very tricky to negotiate. It was first climbed in 1829 by a Professor Parrot, and then by a succession of German, Russian, British and most recent Turkish mountaineers. Sudden changes in weather are the mountain's speciality and people have been killed in the ascent. Leopards and huge snakes and bears are also said to number among its surprises.

Armenian tradition has Ararat as the centre of their universe, with a belief that the Armenians themselves came down from the slopes of Ararat. Ararat is also cited in *Genesis* as the final resting place of Noah's Ark after the Flood. 'And after the end of the hundred and fifty days the waters were abated. And the Ark rested on the seventh month, on the seventeenth day of the month, upon the mountains of Ararat.' In recent years the search for the **The search for** Ark has gained momentum, with the convinced and ever- **Noah's Ark** hopeful making the ascent from base at Doğubeyazıt, some claiming to have returned with pieces of it. Written official permission from the authorities in Ankara is needed nowa- days for an ascent because of its proximity to the Russian border. The American astronaut and born-again Christian James Irwin has been the most zealous of the climbers, making several attempts since 1982. Given that the volcano has erupted many times since the Flood (the most recent being in 1840) a sceptic is inclined to view the Ark's chances of escape from total burial under tons of lava as decidedly slim.

Ararat was long considered by the Arabs to be the roof of the world. Here, it was believed, the two great rivers, the Tigris and Euphrates, had their source, bringing life and civilisation to the open plains of Mesopotamia. The British climber-scholar Viscount James Bryce, who scaled Ararat in 1876, wrote these moving words from the summit: **Cradle of the** 'Below and around, included in this single view, seemed **human race** to lie the whole cradle of the human race, from Mesopota- mia in the south to the great wall of the Caucasus that covered the northern horizon, the boundary for some many ages of the civilised world. If it was indeed here that man first set foot on the unpeopled earth, one could imagine how the great dispersal went as the races spread themselves down from these sacred heights along the course of the great rivers down to the Black and Caspian Seas, and over the Assyrian plain to the shores of the Southern Ocean, whence they were wafted away to the other continents and isles. No more imposing centre of the world could be imagined.'

This stretch of road from Ağrı to Doğubeyazıt has very light traffic now with only a few trucks. The transit traffic along this road into Iran, only 35 km away, used to be two to three thousand trucks a day, mainly oil tankers, but since the Iran–Iraq war it has dwindled to almost nothing.

ISHAK PASHA SARAY: THE TAJ OF TURKEY

Doğubeyazıt is a small dirty drab frontier town huddled miserably at the foot of a mountain range opposite Ararat. It has nothing to recommend it apart from its one quite good hotel, the Isfehan. Here you can overnight comfortably and, if you are searching for the Ark, use it as your base to make the five-day ascent of Ararat, or more usually to visit the famous **Ishak Pasha Saray**, 6 km away.

This much photographed palace, the ultimate 'Turkish chateau', is even for many people who have never visited Turkey one of its most familiar scenes, as the Taj Mahal is to India. It has often served on the front covers of books and evidently conjures up in the mind of many romantics an image of what Turkey is all about — palaces in bleak landscapes, exotic harems with seductive houris in pointed slippers and diaphanous veils, eunuchs with scimitars and pashas with healthy sexual appetites, rich on the trade of silk and spice caravans.

The Approach to the Saray

The road from Doğubeyazıt to the palace is up a dead end road to the south. You continue along the main street until you reach a small roundabout and the yellow signs point you straight over it for 5 km. The road, a dirt track, is quite steep in parts, but not too difficult as even coaches manage it. Driving up towards the mountains behind Doğubeyazıt you now see the palace for the first time in the distance, raised up dramatically on a terrace like a stage set straight ahead of you. As the road winds on up you pass through whole slopes of ruined houses crumbling away on the hillside. This was **Eski Doğubeyazıt**, originally a Seljuk town, which had at its peak 120,000 houses and a population of 250,000. Doğubeyazıt's population today is less than 20,000. The town was totally abandoned in 1930, when, according to the locals, the people left to go to the cities and find more lucrative work than farming. This defensive explanation neatly sidesteps the fact that the Turks destroyed the town and dispersed its population after its involvement in a Kurdish revolt against the authorities. A photograph taken in 1897 shows it as a thriving town of stone-built flat-roofed houses, but from its appearance today you could be forgiven for mistaking it for a medieval ruin. This is largely because all the woodwork and timbers and some of the stone blocks have been removed to build

Razed Kurdish town

the modern hovel town of Doğubeyazıt below. The population today is still predominantly Kurdish, though in the past there were also many Armenians living here. At the bottom of the ruined town there is an attractive area of grassy land enclosed by a stone wall in the middle of which is a ruined house on a rock outcrop — this is apparently still owned by an Armenian who lives away in İstanbul.

Glimpse of the harem garden

As you approach the Saray you can see the dark wooden arched door set low down in the walls which led out onto the grassy terrace at the foot of the palace. This was the harem garden, a secluded spot not visible from any part of the castle except the harem. The palace is usually open daily from 8am to 4pm, but on fine days it can sometimes stay open as late as 6pm. Coach tours always visit the palace in the late afternoon or early morning, so if you get here late morning or early afternoon you are virtually guaranteed to have the place to yourself. You enter through a huge wide gateway into the vast courtyard where the guardian has his little ticket office tucked to the left.

Nineteenth Century Folly

This remarkable building was only built c1800 on the orders of Ishak Pasha, the feudal overlord of this area nominally under Ottoman control. He is thought variously to have been a Kurd, a Georgian, an Armenian or a Jew, and made his money by dominating the lucrative silk caravan routes from his palace vantage point. In its architecture the palace is equally mixed, with elements of Seljuk, Persian, Georgian, Armenian and baroque Ottoman style.

Sybarite's delight

Frederick Burnaby, travelling here only 80 years after it was built, says it belonged to a Kurdish chieftain 'who expressed the wish to have the most beautiful residence in the world, and, after conversing with numerous architects upon this subject, had accepted the service of an Armenian'. The Armenian proceeded to design a magnificent palace with large stained glass windows and every possible comfort. The pasha was pleased and to ensure that the Armenian could not construct a similar one for a rival chieftain, ordered his hands to be cut off. The poor man died shortly afterwards as a beggar. The pasha met with his just desserts, dying of a snake bite 'after committing all sorts of excesses'. At the time of Burnaby's visit, the palace was being used as a barracks in the run-up to the preparations for war against Russia in 1877. The large stained glass windows which had been bought at great expense had all disappeared and their place was filled with sheets of Turkish newspaper. The marble pillars and alabaster carving over the portico was chipped and hacked at, and in the harem 400 soldiers slept in the rooms the pasha had intended for his 14 concubines.

The Ishak Paşa Saray

The palace has a sybaritic feel to it and was definitely conceived more as a pleasure dome than as a defensive castle. Yet the Russians, too, occupied it on other occasions and they are blamed by the Turks for the blackened cooking residues that coat the walls of rooms designed for more elegant purposes. They also ran off with the gold-plated doors of the entrance during the 1917 invasion, and these are in a museum in Moscow. A fair degree of restoration was carried out in 1956; for all its hotchpotch elements, it is hard to dislike anything in it.

Touring the Saray

From the outer courtyard you pass through an elaborately carved portal into the slightly smaller inner courtyard. Directly ahead lies the entrance to the harem or women's quarters, and to the right is the entrance to the mosque and the selamlik or men's quarters, with a reception area and audience hall. Over on the left are the remains of store houses. In the right hand corner of the courtyard are the little free-standing tombs of the pasha and his favourite wife, with steps leading down to the grave chambers.

The women's quarters

The entrance to the **harem** is the most richly ornate of the three portals. It leads into a maze-like series of rooms, with a large blackened kitchen and dining area, still with its roof intact. Next to it are two charming circular bathrooms, one the hot the other the cold. On the cliff edge all around the palace are the long thin *harem bedrooms*, 14 in all, each with its fireplace at the end and its window overlooking the valley. Near the bathrooms, on the outer edge of the palace, is an equally charming water closet with a large window. In the centre of the harem is the superbly colonnaded *feast room*, with mirrors in the blind arches so that the harem women could partake of the feast but not be seen by the guests of the pasha. To get an overview of the harem it is fun to climb up some steps to the roof level and walk along the tops of the walls looking down into all the rooms.

The men's quarters

Entering the **selamlik** and mosque area you pass through an open-roofed courtroom where the pasha also gave audience. On the outer edge are a few more long thin bedrooms, used by male guests, one of them still with the remains of its carved wooden balcony overlooking the side valley below. The **mosque** is especially fine, divided into two parts with marble pillars in one half. It still has much of its original decoration and stone carving on the ceiling and columns, with the original lamp chains. A gallery runs along beneath the dome, but access to this and the minaret is now locked. The little stone carved minbar is also charming and you can still climb the steps and deliver orations to the imagined masses. If you coincide with a coach tour, they will not be imagined. The mosque is no longer in use so there is no need for you to feel particularly reverent. In its time as a barracks the mosque has doubtless witnessed much irreverence.

Over on the far side of a little cleft in the valley the earth road leads on from the palace to a large mosque with a new concrete dome and an **Urartian castle** lowering over it. The best approach is from behind, where a breach in the walls can be climbed through after scrambling over a rocky path from the road. On the walls facing out over

Urartian sacrifice

the valley is a *relief* showing a man with his arms outstretched to sacrifice a goat to a woman, thought to be a goddess, holding out her arms to receive the sacrifice. The style of the figures and their dress is Assyrian, and they are thought to date from as early as the 9th C BC.

TO KARS AND ANI

From Doğubeyazıt the drive on to Kars non-stop via Kağız-man takes three hours on a road in generally good condition. The stretch along as far as Iğdir, skirting past the foot of Mt Ararat, is very picturesque. Ararat is usually cloaked in cloud and mist, looking totally unreal. The occasions when it stands unobscured in all its glory are few and far between, but the most likely time is early morning.

Nomads around Ararat

All round the foothills of Ararat are the nomad tents stretched over circular stone walls with wooden struts for support like Mongolian yurts. These are the central Asian tents on which the Seljuk türbe is thought to be modelled, with its circular drum and conical dome. The nomads' flocks of sheep are enormous.

Along the Soviet Border

Iğdir looks like an oasis of sudden greenery, lined with tall poplar trees bending in the strong wind. From Iğdir on to Tuzluca the scenery is very pretty, remaining much greener than it has been to the south. The road here passes quite close to the border with the Soviet Socialist Republic of Armenia, and the hills you see to the north are all in the Soviet Union.

Tuzluca has salt mines (tuz means salt), and as you drive out of the town you can see the entrance to the mines cut in the cliff to the right of the road. A few kilometres out of Tuzluca a road leads off north 48 km to **Digor**, the former Armenian village of Tekor. This route to Kars is more direct, though it is not often chosen because it used to require a permit due to its proximity to the Russian border. Now however it can be driven without qualms and it passes through interesting scenery with several nomad encampments. One hour's walk from Digor is an 11th C Armenian church, **Beşkilise**, with its domed roof built by a Bagratid king. The road then passes through **Duzgeçit** near the ancient Armenian church of **Mren** where there are the imposing remains of a 7th C cathedral with fine reliefs on its façade. The dome is also very well-preserved.

No photography

As it is so close to the border, no photography should be attempted here.

The usual route to Kars is via Kötek, ie turning right off the main road to Erzurum just after Kağızman. This road begins a long and winding ascent up to a pass at 2625 metres, then winds down to bleak open plains with many sheep flocks wandering over the road. Sections towards the northern end are being widened and repaired and you are apt to find you have to drive through great mud sections. Trucks travelling uphill from the opposite direction often get bogged here and can cause a total blockage of the road.

Arrival at Kars

On reaching the T-junction with the main road from Erzurum, the final 12 km towards Kars is through a bleak dirty landscape along a heavily potholed road. It can often be the case that the supposedly more major roads are in worse condition than the minor ones because they have to carry a greater volume of traffic.

Armpit of Eastern Turkey Kars in wet weather is the armpit of Eastern Turkey. This is not a totally subjective view, for even in 1877 when Frederick Burnaby arrived here, he was horrified: 'The streets of Kars were in a filthy state. The whole sewerage of the population had been thrown in front of the buildings.' Today the situation is marginally better, but the culprit is still the mud. The main street, awash with mud and potholes, makes Tatvan's main thoroughfare appear like the Champs Elysées. Nearly every building in this ex-Russian town is decaying, neglected and filthy. Even in the summer months the mud remains, unable to dry up and turn to dust because of the numerous leaks in the drainage system.

The more interesting sections of town, off up the side streets are not apparent from the main street and have to be searched for. In the old part through which you enter as you cross the first bridge, many of the houses are virtually caves. This traditional form of housing, burrowing into the earth, is evidently still the best way to protect yourself against a winter spent in Kars. The word itself means snow in Turkish, and Kars can get up to 13 metres of it.

The main reason to come to Kars, however, and which does make it all worthwhile, is to visit the haunting Ani, a true Armenian ghost town, unlike Ahlat, on the Soviet **Security procedures** border 42 km east. Because of its location in the 700 metres of no man's land between Russia and Turkey, a special permit is required to make the visit, obtainable in under half an hour from the tourist office. As you enter Kars on the main road, you should look out for the grey building on the left with a red flag, the Emniyet Müdürlügü (The Security Headquarters). Just opposite is a turning to the right which you follow for about 250 metres, passing the Jandarma building on your right, until you reach on the left of the road the new Kültür ve Turizm building. The tourist office is in this building on the first floor, and its hours are 8.30am to 12.30pm and 1.30pm to 5.30pm. Here you must bring your passport (and car registration number if you are driving yourself) and fill in the application form for the visit. With the completed form you must then return to the Emniyet Müdürlügü on the main street and get the

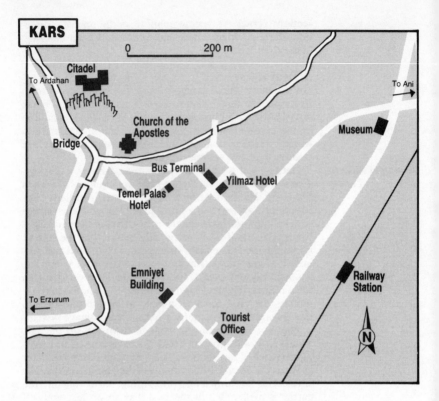

papers signed and stamped. The process is perfectly routine.

To visit Ani on the same day as your arrival you must be at the tourist office no later than 2.30pm. Trips are not usually arranged on Sundays. The tour of the ruins takes one to one and a half hours, so the entire trip from Kars takes a good half day.

The Excursion to Ani

From the east of Kars a narrow potholed tarmac road crosses the railway line and heads towards the Soviet border. The drive takes about 40 minutes, passing through a bleak landscape suitable for the approach to Russia, with a handful of blighted villages with stone-built houses enroute. In the second village a large red notice announces the turn-off right to the Jandarma camp where you must show your permit and hand in your camera at the guard hut. No photos are permitted at all in the whole of this border region and you will find yourself in deep trouble if you disobey this. A large arch leads into the main part of the camp with the slogan over it *Her şay watan için*, Everything for the homeland, and flanked by two almost cartoon-character soldiers giving a two-fingered salute.

The road now continues for the final 10 km to the last village just before the ruins, which you drive through and on to the Jandarma post to the left of the road. Here you show your permit again and a soldier used to be delegated to accompany you round the ruins to make sure you stuck to the approved route. This rule has recently been relaxed, but even if it is reintroduced, the soldiers are generally very friendly and will wait for you while you linger and poke in the churches.

As you approach from a distance, your first sight of **Ani** is not very impressive. You draw up in a parking area in front of the walls where there is a little kiosk selling drinks, beer, biscuits and postcards. From here you walk with or without your military escort through the main double gate, **Alp Arslan Kapısı**, and it is from here that the site of Ani

first hits you. In front of you is an eerie scene of a destroyed city stretching ahead and to the sides over green grassy land towards the Russian hills. Of Ani, city of a hundred gates and a thousand churches, all that remains today is the rubble and the shells of a few of its most robust churches. The colossal sand-coloured walls are a triumph of Armenian architecture, and no where else this side of the Iron Curtain will you see an entirely walled city of this type. Looking back up at the gate tower from the inside, you will see the age-old swastika motif inset in black in the sandy walls.

The origins of the swastika are unknown. It has been used for thousands of years as a symbol of the sun, of infinity and continuing recreation and fertility in Sumeria, China, India, Egypt, Greece, Scandinavia, the Americas and elsewhere. It has been found in the catacombs of Rome, on the textiles of the Incas and on relics unearthed at Troy. It is also one of the sacred signs of Buddhism.

The word comes from the Sanskrit *svastika* for prosperity, and it was thought to bring good luck. As a decorative motif, it exists in many distorted forms on the doors of nearly all Seljuk and Ottoman buildings, notably on the gateways of Diyarbakır, and in the gateway of the Karatay Mosque in Konya. Some extremist Teutonic nationalists in Austria began to use it in the mistaken belief that the swastika was of Indian origin and therefore an Aryan motif symbolising their self-designated racial superiority. Hitler himself saw it as symbolising, in his own words, 'the fight for victory of Aryan man and of the idea of creative work, which in itself eternally has been anti-Semitic and eternally will be anti-Semitic'.

Walls form the third side of a triangle, the other two sides of which are the deep ravines of two rivers, the Arpa Çayı and the Alaca Çayı.

History of Ani

The name Ani comes from Anahid, an ancient Persian goddess identified with Aphrodite. Before Gregory the Illuminator, the founder of the Armenian Church, she was one of the chief deities of the Armenians. The city grew up here on a major east–west caravan route, amassing great wealth which its Armenian rulers later used to endow the city with sumptuous churches. The Bagratid kings who transferred their capital here from Kars, claiming descent from the kings David and Solomon of Israel, were one of the leading princely families to survive after AD 428 when Armenia was divided between the Byzantines and the Persians. It was such semi-autonomous families who preserved the Armenian and also the Georgian nationhood, for the Bagratid family and its various offshoots provided the rulers in both Armenia and Georgia for many hundreds of years.

Rival to the great cities of the East

In its size and magnificence in the mid-10th C, nothing in Europe could touch Ani, and in the East only Constantinople, Cairo and Baghdad were its rivals. In the superb architecture of Ani you have the inspiration for much that we now call Seljuk: the powerfully built walls and the graceful türbe shapes that became the standard mausoleum shape for the next few centuries. The Armenians were renowned stonemasons and the quality of workmanship of what remains at Ani bears witness to their technical virtuosity, the best in the world at that time.

The Mongol raids, combined with a severe earthquake in 1319, and the *coup de grâce* of Tamerlane, destroyed forever this town whose population at its height was said to number 200,000, nearly four times the current population of Kars.

Wandering About the Ruined City

Inside, the area has been laid out in neat paths with signposts labelling the major landmarks. From the main gate the soldier leads you off first along the path to the semicircular shell of a half-collapsed circular church, the **Chapel of the Redeemer**. Built in the early 11th C, the fact that one half stands intact while the other half has vanished adds to the curiously unreal scene.

The loveliest church

From here you walk on towards the edge of the ravine and down some rough steps to **St Gregory's Church**, labelled Resimli Kilise, the church with pictures, the most lovely of Ani's remaining churches, built in 1215 with beautiful coloured *murals* inside and out. All are painted on the deep royal blue background of the Sassanid tradition. Most of the frescoes depict scenes from the life of Gregory the Illuminator, apostle to the Armenians. On its south (river) wall is a sun dial, a common Armenian feature. The dome and walls are delicately carved with animals like peacocks, stags and dragons amid garlands of foliage. Set on a lower terrace of the ravine, this is the closest you will come to the Soviet border which is formed by the Arpa Çayı itself. Over to the left, set in a slight hollow some **Silent atmosphere** 500 metres from the ravine, is a large Russian camp. The border posts of the Russian side, in green, are visible across the ravine but you would need binoculars to see a guard and binoculars are not allowed. The Turkish posts are grey. The atmosphere is totally silent and almost haunting, though not in any way frightening — on the contrary, it is a pleasure to find somewhere at last that is unpopulated, quiet and empty. No young children can pester you here for money or pens. No cars or buses can interrupt your enjoyment of the site; a unique experience to be savoured.

From the Church of St Gregory you are next walked across towards the **Cathedral of Ani** itself. This late 10th C building, superbly proportioned, still has its roof for the most part, but there are sections where you look through gaping holes in the dome to the sky. Its architect was the famous Trdat who rebuilt the Haghia Sophia dome when it collapsed in the earthquake of 989. Like most Armenian architecture, it is unusual in having a very high ceiling for its length and width, and its height is equal to its width (c22 metres) with its length c40 metres. It is in fact by far the largest Armenian church left standing in Turkey. With no murals, its beauty lies totally in its bare style and proportions. From the outside it has the characteristic graceful blind arches. There is superb use of two-coloured stone on the columns inside, black and red.

From here the path now leads on to an 11th C mosque, the **Menüçer Camii**, with a minaret standing on the edge of the ravine. This most unusual building feels inside more like a palace than a mosque, and though built in 1072, eight years after the Seljuk conquest, it seems to have been built by Armenians, evidently converted into a mosque later. Inside, its ceiling is beautifully decorated with the two red and black stones with geometric designs and a stars in heaven motif. Sitting on the windowsill of the mosque you have a magnificent view over the gorge and towards the Soviet border. In the total silence you can hear the lovely rushing sound of the river in the gorge below. Clearly not all have found it so peaceful here, for a German tourist is said to have committed suicide by jumping off the

The Armenian cathedral at Ani

minaret. Since then access to it has been kept locked.

Down in the gorge to the right is what appears to be an island in the river, but which is in fact a peninsula jutting out from the Turkish side. On the summit of this hillock-shaped peninsula is a building with three vaulted arches. The Turkish sign labels this as **Young Girls' Church** or convent. Above it, at the top of the ravine, is the **citadel** with its defence walls rising up the hillside. This whole section is, however, out of bounds and your military escort will not let you approach any further than the mosque.

From the mosque you now walk off away from the ravine towards a little kümbet-style church, the **Church of the Holy Apostles** (1031). Its dome is still intact but it has no murals. Its floor space is particularly tiny for its height. Just beyond this church you can look down into the other side of the gorge, this being the Alaca Çayı, where the ravine has widened considerably. Right on the banks of the river potatoes and tomatoes are being cultivated.

Your escort now leads you to the collapsed circular **Church of Gagik I** (989–1019), not the same king as the earlier Gagik of Akdamar. This building, impressive

Round experiment

Interior of Ani cathedral, looking east

because of its huge scale, has survived less well because its roundness made it an inherently weaker structure. Built in 1001, its circular style with an interior circle of columns is unique in Armenian architecture. Earthquakes got the better of the experiment. In its centre is a deep well, maybe some kind of sacred spring, an idea the Armenians were keen on.

From this point you walk back towards the main gate, passing a heavily ruined **caravanserai** in the centre of the flattened area. Of all Ani's other buildings nothing remains except foundations and rubble. As an Armenian poet mourned: 'Where are the thrones of our kings? They are seen nowhere. Where are the legions of soldiers that massed before them like dense cloud formations, colourful as the flowers of spring, and resplendent in their uniforms? They are nowhere to be seen. Where is our great and marvellous pontifical throne? Today it is vacant, deprived of its occupant, denuded of its ornaments, filled with dust and spiders' webs, and the heir to the throne removed to a foreign land as a captive and a prisoner. The voices and the sermons of the priests are silent now. The chandeliers are extinguished now and the lamps dimmed, the sweet fragrance of incense is gone, the altar of Our Lord is covered with dust and ashes. Now if all that we have related has befallen us because of our wickedness, then tell heaven and all that abide in it, tell the mountains and the hills, the trees of the dense woodlands, that they too may weep over our destruction.'

Poet's lament

In the vicinity of Ani there are several fine Armenian monasteries and a particularly fine Armenian castle, called **Magazbert**, of the 10th C, in almost perfect preservation, two hours walk away to the southwest. All of these, alas, are out of bounds today because of their closeness to the Russian border. The same would ordinarily be true of Ani, but the authorities have made an exception here because of the touristic importance of the site.

Back to Kars Again

Returning from Ani to Kars, you might like to go shopping (fairly sophisticated here); the local honey is to be recommended. Depending on your timings, you may wish to drive on to Sarıkamiş to avoid a night in the execrable Kars hotels.

Originally an Armenian town founded in the 8th C, Kars was always to be overshadowed by Ani. Taken in the 11th C by Alp Arslan for the Seljuks, it then spent three centuries under Georgian control before bowing to the Ottoman Empire in 1514. Because of its position so close to the Russian border, it was a frontier garrison town of the Sultans against the Russians in the 19th C. It was besieged in 1807 and 1828, put under a five month siege in 1855 during the Crimean War, then taken properly in 1878 and held in Russian hands until the end of the First World War. It was then given back to Turkey with the rest of the province in 1925.

What to see in Kars

The town today has little to offer and the most interesting things are the **Russian buildings**, erected during their 40-year occupation, now neglected and slowly disintegrating.

These once fine neo-classical style buildings are used by the Turks as endless administrative offices, various müdür-lügü of one sort or another. They are largely to be found on the higher streets in the town, up to the left of the main road as you enter, so they are mercifully spared the worst of the mud. One Russian Orthodox Church has been converted to an electricity distribution centre.

Russian power

Besides the Russian architecture, Kars has its Armenian **Church of the Apostles**, its Ottoman **bridge** and its Ottoman **citadel**, all built in crude black basalt and none of them easy on the eye. The church, built in 932–38 by the Armenian Bagratids, is set in a scruffy clearing near the river and the bridge and was once the museum, but this has now been moved to a new site on the other side of the town and much extended. The church has none of the grace and charm of the Ani churches or of Akdamar. The carvings of the Twelve Apostles on the outside of the dome which give the church its name, are so crude they look like comic strip characters, gargoyle-like, faintly grotesque. The church will be opened or locked depending on the mood of the guardian, but inside there is nothing special to see, so you are not missing anything either way. It served as a mosque under the Turks and again as a church under the Russians.

Just by the old black bridge is a **Turkish bath**, men only, the sort of place you enter in fear of your life. Again near the bridge is another decaying Armenian church, now heavily ruined and serving as a tramps' home. Above on the hill overlooking the town is the squat black lowering citadel, still used as a military camp and not visitable without special permission. It was destroyed in the siege of 1855 and had to be rebuilt.

The new **museum** is worth a visit. The kilim collection is especially good. Most of the exhibits are ethnographical rather than archaeological.

Still the age of steam

Kars' only other claim to fame is its steam engines, for it is one of the few places left where steam locomotives are still in use. The train journey from Erzurum to Kars takes seven hours.

Routes North and West

Towards the Black Sea

From Kars it is possible to drive direct to the Black Sea coast at Hopa, avoiding Erzurum altogether, but passing through the highly scenic mountain region which was once the heartland of Georgia. Remote Georgian churches can still be visited here, but the problem is the absence of places to stay between Kars and Artvin. By making a very early start it is however possible to leave Kars and head north towards Lake Çıldır, then across through Ardahan and Savşat to Artvin, stopping off briefly enroute to see churches at Çıldır, Tbeti and Dolişhane.

Passing through Arpaçay, you reach after 73 km the village of **Doğruyol** on the eastern shore of **Lake Çıldır**. A domed Armenian church lies near here, not visible from the road. On the island of Ağçakale in the lake are the picturesque remains of a castle and a church. Along the lakeshore are several monastery and church ruins, often difficult to reach. The road winds round the northern shore, and near the northwestern tip of the lake is **Urta** with a domed Georgian basilica used today as the village mosque. A road forks off south along the west shore of the lake but is very difficult for a car. A jeep or minibus can do this, however, and can thus visit **Pekresin** with the ruins of a double church and a Kurdish cemetery. On this high and remote mountain lakeshore, at 1900 metres, 200 metres higher than Lake Van, large colonies of waterbirds can be watched. The land is under snow for eight months of the year, and the lake itself is frozen over from November to April. 14 km north of Çıldır stands a medieval fortress often called the **Devil's Castle** close to the Soviet border. Military passes are necessary before undertaking a visit.

From Çıldır the road continues via Çamlıçatak to **Ardahan**, set in an austere high steppeland on a riverbank opposite a mighty citadel rebuilt by Selim the Grim in the 16th C. The town was occupied by Russia from 1873 until 1921 and in the heavy fighting many buildings were destroyed and rebuilt, giving the town quite a modern aspect with broad streets and pretty gardens. The road on to Artvin continues via **Şavşat**, an attractive mountain town dominated by a fine Georgian ruined fortress.

The challenge of mountain driving

From Ardahan an alternative route to Artvin can be taken, via Ardanuç, 12 km longer than the Şavşat route, ie 142 km instead of 130 km. This route takes you over the Yalnız Cam Pass (2650 metres) the highest road pass in Turkey, and as driving is slower at least an extra hour should be allowed. If you enjoy the challenge of difficult mountain driving and you are in a hired car, you will relish this route. Allow three and a half hours from Ardahan to reach Artvin.

The continuation of both these routes to Artvin, giving details of the churches at Tbeti and Dolişhane, is described later.

West to Sarıkamış

The drive on from Kars southwest to Sarıkamış, is along good flat road. A few kilometres beyond Kars you pass through the hamlet of **Kümbetli**, which gets its name from the little Armenian kümbet standing off to the left in the plough fields looking as if it is on the verge of collapse. It certainly does not appear to warrant the muddy walk across the fields to reach it. Just 3 km before Sarıkamış you enter a sudden pocket of beautifully conifered hillsides. All the hills around Sarıkamış are still tree-covered for some reason, transforming the landscape into an almost Scandinavian scene. The trees are being cut down all the time and no doubt in another 20 years or so even this last pocket will have disappeared, not to be replaced. Atatürk, as ever the forward thinker, made it a capital offence to cut down a tree, but even this drastic measure came too late to save Anatolia's once beautiful and lush forests.

Blood-stained slopes

It was in these hillsides that a fierce three day battle was fought in heavy snow in December 1914 between the Russians and the Turks under Enver Pasha. The Turkish Third Army, usually stationed at Erzurum, was virtually annihilated, and the blood of 75,000 men stained the white slopes of Sarıkamış. At the entrance to **Sarıkamış** you pass two petrol stations in quick succession, and the road then leads round to the left into the small main square with the man himself in black on his horse. From here the road leading to the left is the one to Erzurum, though in the dearth of signposts your instinct is to go right. If you wish to spend the night here in the comfortable Sartur Motel you take the road leading straight up the cobbled hill opposite to a T-junction at the brow where you turn left, then first right and right again to the gate in the walls of the motel. It chooses not to announce itself as it is obviously not expecting any passing custom.

Sarıkamış' average annual temperature is the coldest in Turkey. Once a resort of the Russian Czar, it is now a minor ski resort.

ERZURUM

The finest bridge

From Sarıkamış the road on to Horasan is very pretty, passing through heavily wooded hillsides along the course of a river valley. Near Horasan a graceful six-arched bridge, the **Çoban Köprü**, Shepherd's Bridge, spans the river. It was constructed in the 16th C by the famous Sinan, architect of İstanbul's greatest mosques, and is the finest old bridge still in use in Turkey. From Horasan onwards the scenery becomes bleaker and flatter. A fair number of trucks travel along this route between Erzurum and Doğubeyazıt, transitting into Iran, but despite this the road is still in fair condition for Eastern Turkey. Some 25 km beyond Horasan you pass Pasinler and the village of **Hasankale** with its ruined Armenian castle, later used by the White Sheep Turcomans.

Bright Lights

Arriving in **Erzurum** from the east is like hitting a pocket of civilisation, for it is the finest proper city you have visited since Diyarbakır. Essentially a god-forsaken place, mercilessly cold in winter, high on its plateau, Erzurum, with its life and streets of shops and lights at night can nevertheless seem like a haven of modernity. It does, too, have the definite bonus of a good hotel, the Oral.

Set in a great bowl at nearly 2000 metres, Turkey's highest provincial capital, and ringed by broad eroded mountains rather than by dramatic peaks, Erzurum has always been a bleak place. The landscape is harsh and the dull grey stone of the buildings is in perfect harmony with it. Always called a 'garrison town' on the route of armies marching to and fro across central Asia, this is less true today than it has been in the past. Eastern Turkey's main university is located here, chosen in 1958 in preference to Van. Wolves have been seen roaming the campus in the winter months. It is said to be difficult to get teachers from Ankara and İstanbul as they are unwilling to come to the harsh climate and limited entertainment of Erzurum unless they are dedicated archaeologists or agricultural experimentists, the two strongest faculties at the university.

Campus wolves

The destruction left by the Russians in the 19th C and by the earthquake of the late 1930s is being gradually replaced by wide new boulevards and tall white concrete buildings.

The town was passed to and fro between Byzantines, Persian Sassanids, Arabs and Armenians until in 1071 after the Battle of Manzikert the Seljuk Turks took it. The Mongols overwhelmed it in 1241, and it then passed to the

Ottomans as their northern outpost in 1514. It was captured by the Russians in 1882 and in 1916, but not for long. In July 1919 Atatürk called the Congress of Erzurum where the outlines of post-Ottoman Turkish foreign policy and **Land of the** Turkey's modern boundaries were drawn up. It was the **Romans** Arabs who first called it 'Arz Er-Rum', land of the Romans, (ie Byzantines), and the Seljuk Turks kept the name.

Apart from the **walls of the citadel**, there is nothing left in Erzurum which predates the Seljuk conquest in the 11th C. Severe earthquakes and years of wars have taken their toll but there are still some fine buildings to see near the centre of town.

On the left of the main road as you approach from the Oral Hotel, you will notice in an open park area the **Yaku-tiye Madrasa**, and just beyond, the Ottoman Lala Pasha Mosque. The madrasa, built in 1310 by the Ilhan Mongol rulers of Persia, with its pretty turquoise tiling on the minaret and traces of green and yellow in the portal, is the most attractive building in Erzurum. On the sides of its portals two lions and an eagle stand astride a palm tree. The whole conception of this façade shows marked Persian **Feminine touch** influence. It is noticeable how there is often, in Persian-style buildings, a more feminine quality than is usually to be found in Arab or Turkish architecture. The Turks are themselves aware of this femininity, referring contemptuously to the Persians as 'a nation of women'. Burnaby discovered this in conversation with his Turkish companion when he made a brief trip to Persia.

'These Persians are ridiculous creatures,' said the Turk. 'Only think of the men dying their beards red! One would have thought that black would have been a more appropriate colour.'

'Some of our English women dye their hair a light colour', Burnaby remarked.

'With women I can understand it', said the Turk. 'Every part of a woman is false, from her tongue to her smile; dyeing her hair red enables her to carry on the deception; but for men to dye their hair red — they might as well form part of a harem at once!'

The madrasa is kept locked and appears to be used as a military depot of some sort, which is a pity since the carving on the inside is said to be very beautiful.

The **Lala Pasha Mosque** next door is very much open and in use, but has no particular virtue, being typically 16th C Ottoman in style with no great architectural merit.

Erzurum's most Continuing on to the main square you can now see to **famous monument** the right, set back some 20 metres from the main road, the **Çifte Minare Madrasa** (Twin Minaretted Madrasa), Erzurum's most famous building. In photographs it looks larger than it is in reality. Founded in 1253 by the Seljuk

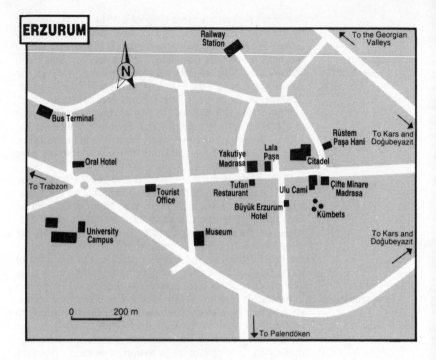

Sultan Alaeddin Keykubad II, grandson of the great builder of the fortress of Alanya, it was built in honour of his daughter Huant Hatun, whose mausoleum is part of the madrasa at the back. For years used as a military store, it has been undergoing a lengthy restoration since 1977 from which it now seems finally to be emerging. Inside it has been restored but is already going into a decline of neglect again. Like the church in Kars it is usually shut but occasionally decides to open for no discernable reason. Seen head on with its squat towers it is involuntarily reminiscent of Battersea power station, and lacks the grace of its half sister of the same name in Sivas. The museum was moved from here in 1968 to a new building nearer the outskirts of town, leaving this madrasa functionless and unsure of its role. Its two fluted brick minarets have far fewer turquoise tiles than the Yakutiye Madrasa.

Walking on behind the Çifte Minare Madrasa you will pass some squalid houses, still inhabited, but looking as if they should have been derelict for years, and come after some 100 metres to a scruffy playground area containing **Circumcised** three Seljuk conical **kümbets** (Üç Kümbet), similar to those **kümbet** seen in the Van area. The one on the left is in two-tone stone and differs from the others in that its cone appears circumcised. Entry into all three is not possible. A fourth midget kümbet has been constructed behind the circumcised one, and in the scruffy park an empty ornamental pool and chickens pecking about in the dirt complete the air of neglect.

Returning to the main street, the building immediately on your left is the **Ulu Cami** (1179), an austere squat building with little decoration inside or out. Six arched vaults supported by a forest of columns run its length, and in the centre is a stalactite dome carved with a central window. Some 20 years ago the roof fell in but has now been repaired.

Directly opposite, a road leads off towards the old **citadel** 300 metres from the main road. The high walls enclose a large area now used as a football pitch by the local youths,

A street corner in Erzurum

The madrasa of twin minarets at Erzurum

with a couple of incongruous rusting cannons lying around. Originally of 5th C Byzantine construction, it was rebuilt several times. Its curious clock tower began life as an 11th C Seljuk minaret. The Russians are said to have run off with the clock in 1830, but this is a handy explanation for anything missing in Erzurum. In Ottoman times it was the eastern stronghold for many years of the dreaded Janissaries, the Ottoman SS. From its edge you can look down the hill over the houses below, with their filthy-looking corrugated iron roofs sprawling over the hillsides. Just 25 years ago this view was of picturesque flat grass-roofed houses. Now you are hard pressed to spot one such roof among the modern sprawl. Each of these roofs had its stone roller for use after rain, and with this care they provided good insulation against heat and cold. In summer the grass was used to fatten sheep and chickens. Sometimes, however, the livestock got too fat and fell through, and the villagers used to have to repair their roofs quite frequently.

Sheep falling through the roofs

In all the shops of Erzurum near the Ulu Cami you will notice windows full of rather flashy gold used for the setting of the local black jet, called Oltutaş, stone from Oltu, a small town to the north in the Georgian valleys. It is moulded into necklaces, worry-beads, ornaments and just about anything. Slightly down the hill from the Ulu Cami, 75 metres on, you will come to a severe dark stone caravanserai on your right, called **Rüstem Pasha Hanı**, still used today as a covered bazaar, but exclusively for the sale of black jet objects. Each stall sells identical worry-beads, yet each seems to do a thriving trade.

South of Erzurum 4 km out of town on a new straight road past modern tenement buildings, you can see the winter ski resort of **Palendöken**. The resort is meagre to say the least, consisting of one chair left going off up the mountain and one restaurant next to it.

Well worth a visit is the new Erzurum **museum**, now in the modern outskirts of town, with its own car park. Downstairs among the well laid-out exhibits are mammoth bones, fine Urartian drinking vessels in the shape of horses' or rams' heads, and a huge bronze bell, unlabelled, cast **The bric-a-brac** in Croydon, which once adorned the clock tower in the **of eons** citadel. Many items of Ottoman jewellery and clothing are displayed with some fine Ottoman silver breastplates, quaintly translated as 'pinafores', Turkish 'gogüşlükler'. There is one exquisite set of Ottoman bed linen, beautifully embroidered with colourful flowers. To lie in a bed with these must have felt like sleeping in a spring meadow. Upstairs are weapons and coins, and also several highly decorated Korans. One is so tiny that the script and illuminations are almost microscopic. Out in the garden around the front of the museum are all sorts of unexplained objects. Stone rams, possibly representing the Black Sheep or the White Sheep, stand near the entrance and several elaborately carved Seljuk tombstones are scattered all around.

THE GEORGIAN VALLEYS

From Erzurum there are two major routes northwards to the Black Sea coast. The route via Aşkale, Bayburt and Gümüşhane to Trabzon is the most commonly used and is the way most coach tours take. The road is good and leads through the spectacular scenery of the Pontic mountains over the Zigana Pass at 2025 metres, the highest major road pass in Turkey. This route is described in detail later from Trabzon.

An alternative route, however, far less used and equally if not more spectacular is north via Lake Tortum and Artvin to the Black Sea at Hopa, a charming little resort and Turkey's easternmost port on the Black Sea, just 22 km from the Soviet border. This route can be driven in one long day from Erzurum to Hopa, stopping off to see several Georgian churches on the way. You can also stay at Artvin where you can base yourself at the comfortable Hotel Karahan for a couple of nights if you want to explore all the churches reachable by car in these remote but beautiful valleys. The churches are visited only rarely and while a few of the more enterprising German coach tours do come on this route, they only stop at one church, Dolişhane.

The Georgians

A race apart

The villagers in this region, descendants of the Georgians, are like a different race from the inhabitants of Erzurum or Doğubeyazıt. Many still have ginger hair and freckles, and they are more dignified in manner and the children less urchin-like. You will not be made to feel here like a tourist curiosity to be peered and poked at, but like a guest who has taken the trouble to come and visit the remoter parts of the country.

Religion and architecture

The Georgians have had little influence on the history of Turkey. They speak a non Indo-European language which belongs, like Laz (the language spoken on the Black Sea), to the Caucasian group. At the controversial Council of Chalcedon in the 5th C when the Armenian and Nestorian churches broke away from the Greek Orthodox Church, the Georgians sided with the Greeks, and there were always close links between Byzantium and Georgia. Byzantine emperors endowed churches here, sending craftsmen, architects and masons to build and decorate them. The Georgians themselves drew almost entirely on Armenian and Byzantine models, and though they provided little architectural inspiration of their own, they may well have been the channel through which Byzantine influence passed into Russia. The churches all have the

Armenian drum and conical dome, later incorporating the basilical plan. The carving on the outer stonework of the walls, with animals and rich garlands are also highly reminiscent of Armenian styles. There are still some 50,000 Georgians in Turkey and the language is still spoken in the remoter valleys and mountains of the extreme northeast.

Though ethnically distinct, the Armenians and the Georgians shared a similar history of invasions and counter invasions, and through frequent intermarriage they became to some extent mixed. The Bagratid family for example featured large in both Armenian history, as rulers of Ani and Kars, and in Georgian history, as rulers of the upper Çoruh valley at Bayburt, Ispir and Ardanuç. There were many branches of the Bagratid family and rivalries were constant, with various barons controlling small sections independently of each other. The Seljuk conquest in the 11th C put an end to these little fiefdoms for a time, but by the early 12th C a new young king, David the Restorer, attempted to re-establish authority over the semi-independent barons, then drove the Seljuks out of the Georgian heartlands and recaptured Ispir and even Tiflis, the ancient Armenian capital in the east, now in Soviet Armenia.

Queen Tamara   After David's death in 1125, Georgia entered a period of relative peace, reaching a high point under the leadership of Tamara, a gentle and humane leader, also a shrewd administrator and diplomat. She maintained close ties with Constantinople and gave refuge to Alexius and David Comnenos when they fled after the Fourth Crusade. She provided them with the troops necessary to establish their dynasty in Trebizond which was to last 250 years. She pursued an aggressive foreign policy, and during her reign Kars was recaptured and successful raids were made into northern Persia. On her death in 1212 in her capital Tiflis, her kingdom extended to include Armenians, Kipchaks, Kurds and Azerbaijanis; Moslems and Christians alike.

In the 13th and 14th C Georgia suffered heavily under Mongol attacks, especially that of Tamerlane. He had singled out Georgia as the bulwark of Christianity in Asia, and inflicted an especially vicious series of invasions, leaving its cities, towns and villages in ruins. Georgia never really recovered from the onslaught. The land was depopulated, the remaining inhabitants exhausted and without central authority. A few semi-independent barons again set up small domains, but in this weakened condition Georgia could not withstand Ottoman power. When the Trebizond Comnene empire fell to the Ottomans in 1461, it was the beginning of the end for Georgia. By 1552 a detachment of Janissaries was stationed in the ancient Bagratid fortress of Ardanuç.

In the 18th and 19th C the Georgians, like the Armenians, saw in the Russians a fellow Christian ally, and like the Armenians they were punished by their Turkish masters. The Ottomans held only loose control over Georgia, content to let the princes and barons squabble among themselves in their endless family feuding. Russian advances, however, were seen by the Porte as attempts to extend her borders southwards using Georgia as a stepping stone, and this inevitably was to lead to war between Russia and Turkey, a series of wars in fact, each more horrible than the last, culminating in the bloody battle of Sarıkamış during the First World War.

In Search of Georgian Churches

Leaving Erzurum on the Artvin road, the first stretch of 50-odd km to Tortum is on a good straight and relatively flat road, with only the occasional pothole. **Tortum** chooses not to announce itself so you must deduce you have arrived when you pass through the only town on the route. It is a small place, with a petrol station, and seems to be mainly engaged in the timber trade with many felled trees at the roadside.

From here the road now enters the beginning of a gorge, the muddy Tortum river running through it. The scenery as the gorge begins to narrow becomes very pretty with bright green trees and lush vegetation on the hillsides. The population throughout this valley is very sparse with only the tiniest of villages appearing occasionally on the river banks. Most of the villages in fact lie up in the side valleys, approached by narrow dirt tracks from the main road and it is in these that most of the Georgian churches lie, either derelict shells or renovated by the villagers and converted into the village mosque.

A few kilometres after Tortum, an unsignposted road leads off to the left to the village of **Tortum Kale** named after its derelict Georgian castle, a stronghold of one of the Bagratid princes. Some 10 km beyond this turn-off, another fine castle can be seen rising on the right on an inaccessible clifftop with no apparent road to it. An approach would have to be made on foot and would take at least two hours. 25 km from Tortum you reach a recently built pointed-arch bridge crossing the river.

At this point stands a square yellow plaque, somewhat battered, with Bağbası as the first word on it, and this is the new Turkish name of the village, 8 km from the main road, in which the 10th C Georgian church of Haho lies. Accounts written some ten years or so ago tell you that to reach it involves a two and a half hour walk. Now however, the dirt road is motorable even after wet weather when much of the track is muddy. Crossing the bridge you follow the track to the right as it winds round a little hillside and then up a river valley. The road leads through various small villages. At a junction in the road in one village, you take the left fork, then a couple of kilometres further on at a junction with a timber works, you take the right fork which is marked with a blue sign to Bağbası. After a total of 8 km of careful driving along this very pretty lush valley with a rushing river flanked by poplar trees and flowery meadows you arrive at **Bağbası** village. Continuing on through the village and bearing left whenever there is a choice, you reach the church some 300 metres beyond the centre, identifiable by the little breeze block ablution huts built just on the right of the road.

The interesting **church** with its typical but distinctive conical dome in the lovely soft yellowy colour of the local sandstone was originally part of a monastic complex with a 9th C chapel built by King David the Restorer and a 10th C church of the Mother of God. It has been carefully retored by the locals and converted to their village mosque. Most of the Georgians in this area converted to Islam in the 17th C.

If you can contrive to get here shortly before noon you will be present to witness the arrival of the various male elders of the village staggering up here from the village to the noon-day prayer. The mosque is usually kept locked but will be opened at this time and you will be gladly invited in to join the congregation. One toothless 90-year old still proudly wears his medals from previous wars under his coat, while another, cupping his hands over his ears, eyes closed and swaying trancelike begins to wail into a loud-speaker the most tuneless of calls to prayer you are ever likely to hear.

The galleried entrance where he stands to wail is a later Moslem addition and is now used as a school for the children. You can still clearly see the join where this abuts the original nave. On either side of the entrance to the original church, stone reliefs can be seen. To the right of the entrance is a very comic *relief of Jonah and the Whale*, reminiscent of the monster in the Akdamar reliefs, looking like a pig with teeth. The Georgians had no more idea of what a whale looked like than the Armenians and simply copied the Armenian version: it was the blind leading the blind. Underneath this is a *cockerel*, and a little further to the right is a heavily blackened niche where a carving of the Virgin Mary once stood. To the left of the entrance a *lion and a griffin-like beast* are busy devouring some prey. Inside, a mihrab has been added, yet traces of blue paint and murals remain in the apse and *five apostles* are visible. The feel is still very much of a church, though whitewashed like a mosque. A wood-burning stove has been added

Armenian-style reliefs

Georgian church at Haho

where the altar would once have stood to make the winter prayers more bearable. Walking around the church gardens you pass, at the back of the building, a semi-collapsed and now unused aisle. The part in use has had its roof replaced with corrugated iron in places. The tomb of some saint lies within railings and overgrown grass.

Returning to the main road you now continue on through the valley for a further 15 km until you reach an unmarked turn-off to the left again on an earth road. This is the turn-off to the colossal **Vank monastery church**, 7 km up the track. To help pinpoint the turn-off, it is 4 km after the Petrol Ofisi station which stands by itself at the left of the road. The valley at this point is much wider than before. The earth road leads across the open flat valley, passing after less than a kilometre through a curious ghost village, then on along the right hand side of a valley. The track, easily motorable and somewhat easier in fact than the track to Haho, used to be described as a two-hour walk, but is now a straightforward drive with no confusing turn-offs, just climbing a little in the final kilometre.

Vast shell   The church is instantly visible as you approach, rising up with its conical dome from the houses and trees clustered around it. A derelict shell in the heart of the village, it is used now merely as covered parking for a local Renault and its nave has been turned into a sheltered volleyball playground for the children. You cannot pay a visit without attracting the interest of the entire village. The children will follow you round but will not pester or beg, and the villagers are genuinely friendly and almost honoured that you should have made this detour to visit their church.

In its porch a carefully shaped tree trunk has been ingeniously slotted in to replace one of the broken stone columns. To the left of the tree trunk notice the very fine and elaborately *carved pillar* and *paintings* of angels, Mary, Jesus and one other unknown figure. The faces of these are still very well-preserved, and have been dated to the 11th C. Shrubs and greenery grow from the roof and there are *reliefs of lions and bulls* adorning the facade, with the archangels Michael and Gabriel high in the gable. Inside, it is no more than a huge shell, its roof having long ago collapsed. The scale and height of its *dome* are, however, still very impressive. Within the front entrance are traces of murals.

Like Haho, Vank too was originally part of a 10th C monastery with only its church, dedicated to the Deisis (Christ, the Virgin and John the Baptist), now remaining.

Dramatic Drive

Returning to the main road, you now come after just a few hundred metres to the southern tip of **Lake Tortum**, a fine blue sliver 10 km long and 1 km wide. It has a strangely man-made look, with sheer sides and no real shoreline, but was in fact formed by a landslide damming the Tortum river three centuries ago. For many years a spectacular new road has been in the process of construction

Most dramatic landscape in Eastern Turkey   in the left cliff side of the lake, now nearing completion. Spiralling round above the lake, often very steep indeed, this road is one of the most spectacular in Turkey, with sheer drops and dizzy views. The scenery here, with the lushly treed hillsides, the lake and the gorge, is in many ways the most dramatic stretch of landscape in Eastern Turkey, certainly more attractive and impressive than the drive through the Zab valley to Hakkâri.

Dropping down to the shore level about half way along the length of the lake, a spit of land sticks out into the water with a track leading out onto it. This is one of the very few places where you can approach the lake shore, and is a superb picnic spot where you can feast on strawberries and Turkish champagne bought in Erzurum. The lake has a stillness that is almost eerie and its colour ranges from a clear blue to an opaque green, depending on the angle of your gaze.

At the northern end of the lake you come on a small settlement which has grown up as a result of the industrial development of the lake. The Tortum **waterfalls** which once fell from this end of the lake were the biggest waterfalls in Turkey, 48 metres high, but have now been regulated by the construction of a dam completed in 1960. From May onwards for the summer months there are no waterfalls to be seen at all, but in the winter months you can follow the pebbled road which leads off to the right down into the new dam settlement with its whitewashed mosque, and then turn right to follow the road round to the falls, less than a kilometre away. Their setting is especially lovely, in wild and unspoilt scenery. Though you can hear the water thundering from a distance, the falls are not visible from the road, and you come upon them very suddenly.

As the main road north now drops down through a village flanked with leafy trees, some of them walnut, and lush greenery, you reach a section of road that has often caused problems. Landslips prompted by the extensive road construction here can often create delays and the road may be closed for periods of several hours while the blockage is cleared. From 1987 this construction should be largely **Fording a river** complete, so you should be spared the appalling road surface from here to the Yusefeli turn-off, entailing rough boulders, wet clay and the fording of two foaming rivers which simply gush across the road. Should you still encounter these rivers, where there is a choice of an upper or lower crossing point, take the upper one as it is fractionally shallower. Rest assured that buses, trucks and cars have all driven through and survived.

The road winds on through the gorge which becomes narrower and much more dramatic, flanked with high cliffs.

Some 35 km on from the Vank turn-off, you reach a fork off to the right to Olur, crossing a bridge at the confluence of two rivers. The main road to Artvin continues straight on. This is the fork you must take to visit **İşhan**, the third of the Georgian churches, once a bishop's church, which has the most lovely setting of the three. Though in the centre of the village, it is beside some small ponds on a terrace overlooking the mountains. From the tarmac road to Olur, an earth track, often difficult, with hairpin bends and vertiginous drops, leads left 9 km up to the church. The original church here, the **Church of the Mother of God**, was 7th C, extended in the 11th C. The windows, as is usual in the Georgian tradition, are richly decorated with stone carving. The east facade has two fine blind niches. The roofs have fallen in, so the *dome* in the centre appears to float on the corner pillars. Inside in the dome and near the windows several *murals* of flying angels are still preserved. A famous solid gold processional cross found here last century is now in the state museum of Tbilisi, ancient Tiflis, capital of the Soviet Republic of Georgia.

Remote Churches for Enthusiasts

From Olur, those with a lot of time on their hands and keen to explore the remoter churches, can make a difficult 13 km excursion, much of it on foot, to the interesting round **church of Bana**, by the village of Penek, which was not destroyed till 1877 in the Russian–Turkish war. 2 km further on up the valley is the heavily ruined **Harap Kilise**, and two further hours hard climb leads up to **Salomonkale**, Solomon's Castle, with an 11th C chapel and murals and frescoes in a cliff chapel.

The main road continues north and 8 km after the Olur turnoff a road leads off left 10 km to **Yusefeli**, a picturesque mountain town. Simple accommodation is available here which can be used as a base to visit another two remote churches, Dörtkilise and Parhal. Leaving Yusefeli to the south in the direction of İspir, after following the Çoruh river for 15 km you will see a castle with a chapel, after which you reach a village. Turning off right in the village you follow a small stream for 8 km until you reach the 10th C church ruins. Though **Dörtkilise** means Four Churches, only one remains, with its stone-tiled roof still partly preserved. Traces of murals can be seen inside.

To reach the 10th C **Parhal Church** you set off northwards from Yusefeli towards Sarıgöl. This church is still in use as the local mosque and is therefore quite well-preserved. In style it resembles Dörtkilise, and still has traces of painting.

These churches are really only for enthusiasts, and most people will prefer to drive on towards Artvin or even Hopa for the night.

Back on the Road to Artvin

The road follows the dramatic gorge, quite narrow now at times, with the river often muddy and brown in the spring months after the melting snows have swelled its waters. Attractive dark timbered houses can be seen clustered in small villages on the steep slopes of the valley above the river, almost Swiss chalet style, with gabled roofs and wooden overhanging balconies. At several points **Rickety bridges** extraordinarily rickety wooden bridges are strung over the

Along the Artvin valley

gorge: some are evidently disused and are slowly falling piece by piece into the rushing river below; others are intriguing as they appear to lead into a sheer rock face with no visible path or village on the far side.

Shortly before Artvin, the gorge widens out and then you see for the first time, high on the left, the houses of **Artvin** lying in a magnificent setting on the upper slopes of the valley, looking just like an Alpine ski resort in summer. An impressive 15th C **castle** at its foot looms up on a piece of jagged cliff with an enormous sheer drop to the river below. Sometimes described as 'where Turkey and the Caucasus meet', Artvin makes an excellent base for exploring these Georgian heartlands, and the name itself is Georgian. Both Russian- and Greek-style buildings can be seen. On its Alpine meadow, the spring flowers in the region are very plentiful, especially in June and July.

In the eastern valley opposite Artvin there was once such a wealth of monasteries that the area was called the Georgian Mt Athos. Some of these are still relatively well-preserved and can be visited on driveable dirt tracks. The first and most commonly visited of all the Georgian churches is at **Dolişhane**, which even some German coach tours now incorporate in their itinerary. Returning south to the Şavşat turn-off you follow this eastwards for some 10 km, then taking a left turn up a dirt track for about

The Mt Athos of Georgia

4 km. The track is steep in parts, but quite driveable with care. The village in which the church stands is called **Hamamlıköy** and the 10th C church now serves as the village mosque, with the lower level in use as a stable.

Returning to the main Şavşat road, the next churches, **Barta**, **Opiza** and **Porta**, all lie in the hills to the left of the road and are heavily ruined: a visit is really only for enthusiasts. Shortly before Şavşat a turn-off left to Veliköy brings you after 6 km to another left turn leading to the **church of Tbeti**. In wet weather the track is difficult for cars. The church stands in a fertile valley among the trees and is not visible from afar as a result. Although heavily ruined, the quality of construction was evidently very high. Inside remains of fine frescoes are visible, eg Christ on a throne with outstretched arms surrounded by angels and saints, still with strong colours.

Bagratid fortress

In the southern slopes of the Imerhevi valley, a further excursion can be made to the town of **Ardanuç**, once a Bagratid stronghold, by taking a right turn off the Şavşat road opposite the Dolişhane turn-off. Slightly apart from the new town stands a mighty cliff on top of which are the remains of a large fortification in a dramatic setting overlooking a gorge. At the foot of the cliff a smaller old village is huddled, but the inhabitants are increasingly moving to the new town as the rock above has been pronounced unstable. The cliff can be climbed by a steep twisting path and a flight of rickety steps, but apart from a few outer walls and towers, little remains on top, though its setting remains impressive. About 5 km east (an hour's walk) of Ardanuç, is the 9th C **Monastery of Yeni Rabat**. The ruined church lies in a wooded hollow and is therefore not visible from afar. With richly decorated window frames and well-preserved dome, this monastery was once a school of book illustration for the monks.

To the Black Sea

Continuing from Artvin northwards to the Black Sea you come after 26 km of driving along the valley to **Borçka**, a very Russian looking town, not to be confused with the soup. Clinging to both sides of the river with a bridge linking it, it is heavily militarised as two roads lead off east from here to the Soviet border.

From this point on the road begins to climb over the final range of the Pontic mountains 37 km to the coast at Hopa, leaving the Çoruh river valley behind. After dark or early in the morning this route is prone to extremely dense fog and visibility is so poor that it can take over an hour to drive this last stretch from Borçka. The road winds and snakes through heavily wooded hills, passing several pretty mountain villages with beautifully built stone hump-backed bridges over small rushing streams. You reach a small pass summit at 690 metres and as you descend towards Hopa through these rain-soaked northern facing slopes, you pass through the first of the lush green tea plantations which characterise this coast. You also have your first view of the sea, and after weeks spent in the harsh interior you too can share the relief felt by Xenophon's Ten Thousand Greeks when after their long retreat from Babylon they saw the sea and shouted 'Thálassa, thálassa!'

The sea, the sea!

Reaching the coast at a T-junction on the **Hopa** esplanade you turn right to reach the town proper, a charming little resort with only 10,000 inhabitants, strung out along one main street. The hotels are to be found about 1 km along this road, facing out over the sea. You have now returned to the fringes of civilisation.

PRACTICAL INFORMATION

DOĞUBEYAZIT
Hotel Isfehan (2-star), Tel: 139. Formerly called the Ararat Hotel, the best by far in the town. To reach it you turn into the town of Doğubeyazıt, leaving the main road and following the yellow signs to the Ishak Pasha Saray, then turn up right into the main street, lined with shops. Continue up this for c200 metres until the Müdürüğlü office building on the left, then take the fork right just opposite this. Along this side street are several hotels and the Isfehan is the very last on the right with a car park to its side, sealed off by an ex-railway crossing barrier. All the coaches stop here, and the cream of the local businessmen gather here in the evening to drink at the bar and pick up female tourists. It has its own Turkish bath, for men only, as ever. The restaurant is unusually good for Eastern Turkey, and the place is well-run, with waiters dressed up in national costume and colourfully embroidered jackets. The effect is somewhat marred by the tracksuit-bottom trousers which they wear with embroidery sewn along the leg. 56 rooms.

Sim-Er-Turistik Tesisleri (2-star), Tel: 601. 38 rooms on the eastern edge of town on the road to Iran. A modern hotel, formerly catering for transit traffic to Iran. Similar price to the Isfehan.

Is-Mer Motel offers good accommodation.

KARS
The notorious two, the Yılmaz and the Temel Palas, have now been abandoned by the tours because of their squalor and their bad food. A new hotel is being built opposite the Yilmaz so the Kars accommodation problem may be resolved fairly soon.

Average Temperature (Celsius):

J	F	M	A	M	J
−11.8	−10.0	−3.9	4.7	10.2	13.4
J	A	S	O	N	D
17.2	17.3	13.2	7.0	0.4	−7.3

Maximum Temperature:

J	F	M	A	M	J
5.2	11.0	18.8	24.2	26.5	31.0
J	A	S	O	N	D
34.8	34.6	32.4	26.1	21.2	11.2

Minimum Temperature:

J	F	M	A	M	J
−39.6	−37.0	−33.3	−22.6	−7.0	−4.0
J	A	S	O	N	D
1.8	−1.9	−6.0	−17.5	−30.0	−35.0

ANI

Full details of how to arrange a journey are given in the text. If you do not have your own car, a taxi is the only way to see the ruins. The tourist office can arrange this for you, hiring it for the half day.

SARIKAMIŞ

Sartur Motel (1-star). This motel, beautifully set in pine trees in walled grounds, is a real bonus to come upon here, as an escape from the awful hotels of Kars. It does not announce itself in the town, so follow the directions given in the text to find it. Catering very much for groups, it clearly does not expect any casual passing custom, and so if it does not have a tour booked in it is inclined to close altogether, with the hot water turned off and all the restaurant staff sent home. The food is good and all the rooms have showers. The plumbing is somewhat temperamental and the techniques for use of the various water systems is usually explained. The hotel has a pool which is open from mid-June until September.

In the winter Sarıkamış is a **ski resort** for the locals. Cross country skiing here, with wolves and all, must be quite exciting.

ERZURUM

Oral Hotel (2-star), Tel: 19740. Erzurum's best by far, built quite recently. You have to do battle here with the tours, but the hotel is large (90 rooms), so even with several groups passing through you can usually keep yourself at a certain distance. Service in the ground floor restaurant can be a bit trying. Avoid the temptation of ordering Nescafé at breakfast here after your weeks of abstinence, as you will find your breakfast bill exceeds your dinner bill. The rooms have good bathrooms, but you must ask for the hotel plug if your room does not have one. Hot water is available only after 8pm. No breakfast is served in the rooms.

Büyük Erzurum Hotel (1-star), Tel: 16201. The second best choice, in the centre of town, with a top floor restaurant, good to get an aerial view of the greyness of Erzurum.

The local bastırma, beef dried in the sun in spices and then served thinly sliced, is a speciality. A kind of variation on a theme of Parma ham, it is also found in Trabzon and Hopa.

Daily **flights** at noon to Ankara ($1\frac{1}{4}$ hours), all connecting to İstanbul ($4\frac{1}{2}$ hours including transfer).

In winter on this high plateau temperatures can get as low as $-43°$C, while in summer it can climb to $+37°$C. In Erzurum the first snow begins in October and lies on the ground until April.

Average Temperature (Celsius)

J	F	M	A	M	J
−8.6	−7.0	−2.7	−5.2	10.8	14.9
J	A	S	O	N	D
19.2	19.6	15.0	8.5	18	−5.2

Maximum Temperature:

J	F	M	A	M	J
8.0	10.6	17.8	23.5	29.6	32.2
J	A	S	O	N	D
34.0	34.0	31.4	27.0	20.7	12.3

Minimum Temperature:

J	F	M	A	M	J
−30.1	−27.5	−24.8	−18.5	−6.4	−3.2
J	A	S	O	N	D
1.0	1.2	−3.8	−12.0	−25.6	−28.0

ARTVIN

Hotel Karahan (1-star), Tel. 1800. A surprisingly good and clean hotel to come upon in this remote and beautiful town. The central heating and hot water is efficient, and there is a good restaurant with a fine terrace.

THE BLACK SEA COAST

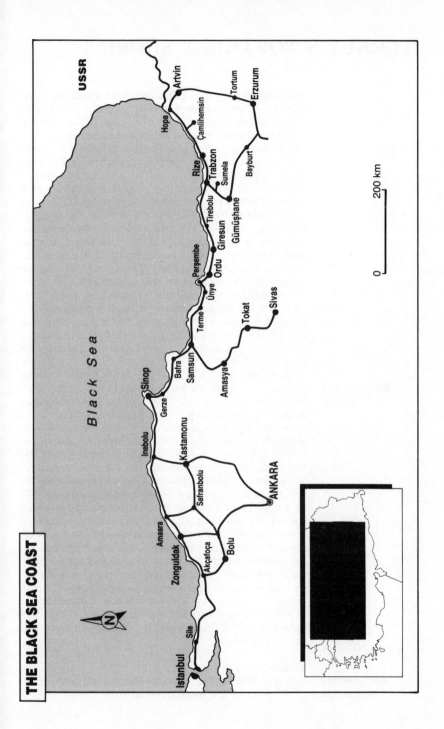

THE BLACK SEA COAST

0   200 km

Black Sea

USSR

Istanbul
Şile
Zonguldak
Amasra
Akçafoça
Bolu
Safranbolu
ANKARA
Kastamonu
İnebolu
Sinop
Gerze
Batra
Samsun
Terme
Ünye
Perşembe
Ordu
Giresun
Tirebolu
Rize
Trabzon
Sümela
Gümüşhane
Bayburt
Erzurum
Tortum
Artvin
Hopa
Çamlihemşin
Amasya
Tokat
Sivas

315

TURKEY'S NORTHERN SHORE

There are two main surprises about the Black Sea coast. The first is how green and lavishly vegetated it is, and the second is how built-up it is. The name 'Black Sea' has somehow always managed to conjure up for most people a drab bleak coastline and certainly not a heavily populated one. Yet in practice the coastline has a near unbroken string of development along it, much of it recent and brought about to a large extent by the prosperity of the tea plantations. These deck the extensive slopes of the Pontic range all the way to the crest of the north, seaward-facing slopes, dropping right down in terraces like a gently descending staircase, to touch the edge of the road along the coast itself. This road, which runs the length of the coast from Hopa to Sinop, is good pothole-free asphalt, following the water's edge for much of the way, winding through ribbon development round endless headlands and inlets. Traffic on it is quite heavy, far heavier than anything you will have been used to after the deserted roads of the east, and travel is consequently quite slow and rather strenuous, consisting of an endless series of trucks, buses and vans to be overtaken.

Black Sea and White Sea

Quite why the Turks (and the Arabs for that matter) call this the *Black* Sea and the Mediterranean the *White* Sea, is not known for sure. The most plausible explanation is that the sun glinting on the Mediterranean gives it a white sheen whereas the rain of the north makes the water seem blacker here. This difference in climate between Turkey's north and south coasts is also the explanation of why the north has been less favoured as a tourist destination. Even in the height of summer it can rain heavily any day and the temperature can fluctuate from a pleasant 30°C to a cool 18°C. There is often a breeze, and feasibility studies are currently being conducted on wind-driven power stations. While the coast is used by the Turks and resident expatriates for holidays, this lack of reliability in the weather means that the Black Sea will never receive the attentions of developers and tour operators in the way that the Aegean and Mediterranean coasts have. The main resorts are within easy striking distance of İstanbul, west at Kilios, east at Şile, Akçafoça and Amasra, but the most attractive part of the coastline in fact does not begin until east of Samsun.

Fringe History

Jason and the Argonauts

In historical terms the region has also lacked the dynamism of the Aegean and Mediterranean coasts, and the major events of history seem largely to have passed it by. For most people it is associated with Jason and the Argonauts who sailed along it in their search for the Golden Fleece.

The earliest known foundations here were in the 7th and 8th C BC by the enterprising colonists from Miletos, the greatest of the ancient Greek Ionian cities. These Milesians established the leading sea trade city of the Greek world, founding nearly 100 colonies on the shores of the Hellespont, the Sea of Marmara and the Black Sea coast. Sinop, Samsun, Ordu, Giresun and Trabzon were all Greek Milesian colonies. None of them ever attained much status or produced a famous citizen apart from Diogenes the Cynic, and the only really significant kingdom to rule here was that of the Pontic kings which sprang up after the confusion following Alexander's death in the 4th C BC. These kings, called Mithradates, were troublesome to the Romans for centuries, and the Roman legions finally managed to put an end to them.

When Xenophon and the Ten Thousand reached Trabzon after their tough retreat from Babylon, they took their time returning back along the coast before returning to Greece. As Sir William Ramsey has put it: 'Hardly any of these great armies has failed to leave behind some part of its numbers', and it all added to the already varied racial mix of Anatolia.

HOPA TO TRABZON

From Hopa it is only 22 km east to the Russian border and the town of Batum at the mouth of the Çoruh, the river which you drove along in the Georgian valleys. There is talk of this border crossing being opened to tourists with visas soon, at which stage it would be possible to continue your travels east into the Caucasus and the Russian Republics of Georgia and Armenia. For the moment however, it is only possible to go west and the initial stretch of coastline from Hopa for a few kilometres until you enter a 100 metre road tunnel, is the least developed stretch of coastline you will see, with nothing but the lush green vegetation on the steep hillsides tumbling down to the road.

Village Sprawl

After this, the coastline begins to get more built-up with a fairly continuous stream of larger or smaller towns and villages sprawling along the roadside. A few of these only are in the old style with gables and wooden balconies. Most are rather ugly new blocks of flats, often looking half-finished, and those that are finished look as if they are starting to fall down. Washing adorns the windows and balconies on every day of the week. To judge from this sheer quantity of washing the inhabitants must be obsessed with cleanliness, but if this is the case, it is not evident in the streets and houses.

Perhaps it is just a reflection on the size of the families, where seven to eight children is the norm. Turkey's most recent census in fact gave the country something of a shock. In the five years to October 1985 the population increased from 44.7 million to 51.4 million. At that rate of increase it will double in 28 years. Almost 40 percent of these Turks are under 15, and the government is hurriedly introducing **Women ...** birth control campaigns dispensing free contraceptives. These campaigns have had a warmer reception from women than from men. For many Turkish women, giving birth is just a day off from the fields. Many of them want smaller families, and one survey showed that 80 percent of women did not want more than three children. Abortion has been legal in Turkey since 1983 and there are no religious objections to birth control.

The women, dressed in quite colourful clothes and white headscarves, can be seen in the terraced tea plantations on the steep slopes working non-stop at all times of the day, clipping the tea and collecting it into bags. These are then emptied into colossal baskets which they carry off to the store. Some of the older ones are bent double under the weight and from the back as you pass them on the road, all you can see is the bouncing basket and a pair of feet sticking out from the bottom.

Meanwhile the men can be seen at all times of the day, strolling round the streets in small groups, chatting, twiddling with their worry beads and watching the passing traffic **... and men** with the curiosity of people who have nothing better to do. Michael Periera, when walking in this part of Turkey in the 1970s, noticed how the seats of the men's trousers were 'often highly polished from long contact with coffee-house chairs'. Life expectancy for the men is far higher than for the women. The latter are probably so crippled by heavy work that in their old age they can hardly move from the house, and it is certainly noticeable that far more old men than old women are to be seen out in the streets. These practices are by no means general throughout Turkey, and in many Central Anatolian regions the men are much more in evidence working with the women in the fields.

The people in this part of Turkey are often Laz, a sea-faring race of obscure Caucasian origins. They are like remote cousins of the Georgians, but with the important difference that they converted to Islam early and remained **Unlazy Laz** staunch Moslems. As such they were loyal to the Turks in the wars against Russia, while the Christian Georgians and Armenians were suspect. Their language too is related to Georgian and is still spoken in the villages, though not written. They are the indigenous inhabitants of the Rize area and the women do much of the work in the tea plantations. The women are self-contained and hard-working and the men are fond of dancing and playing bagpipes. their houses are unlike any others in Turkey, well-made of timber and stone and always set in gardens. They are never clustered together in rows or terraces but are spread out along ridges so that villages are often strung along the tops of ridges to ensure breathing space. The ancient Greeks wrote of them as being savage tribesmen and they have a reputation for being fiercely aggressive as enemies but generous as friends. Rather like most Turks, they are patient and good-natured until pushed beyond a certain point. 'The Laz talks with a pistol', runs a local saying.

Sights Along the Way

Shortly before Pazar, some 40 km from Hopa, a yellow sign points off to **Aydar Kaplıcaları**, thermal springs in the hills near Çemlihemsin. These are probably much in demand by the local women to ease their crippled limbs. At **Çemlihemsin** itself you can still see a typical Laz village with all its neat wooden houses laid out in a row, each in its own garden. 12 km south of Çemlihemsin the romantic castle of **Zil Kale** perches on a heavily forested hill with trees growing out of its turrets.

Tea power

Rize, the tea capital, some 60 km further on, is the largest town on the coast east of Trabzon. It is a modern town, its prosperity built totally on tea, and there is nothing of particular interest to the passer through. It has no deep water harbour and larger ships have to anchor off the coast using smaller boats to ferry cargo to a long pier. Tea has only relatively recently become a popular drink in Turkey, largely because of the high cost of imported coffee. The Russians began planting tea in Georgia at the end of the last century, and it was first planted in Turkey in 1935. Since 1945 production has rocketed bringing prosperity to these parts. Unfortunately the 1986 harvest had to be destroyed since it was irradiated to unacceptably high levels after the Chernobyl disaster. The tea farmers were compensated and the crop was buried at various sites in eastern Turkey. The 1987 harvest was pronounced safe.

At 25 km beyond Rize a sign points off inland to Çaykara. The road is not good, but if you are interested in bridges you might like to make the detour 26 km to see the remarkable old wooden **roofed bridge** at Çaykara, unlike any other in Turkey, though rather heavily and obviously restored. Some 13 km beyond the Çaykara turn-off you come to the town of Sürmene. 4 km before Surmene, hidden from the road by a high hedge, is the so-called **Kestel Kale** or Kastelli Mansion or even Memisağa Konagı, now derelict. This is a quite magnificent and unusual building, built in c1800 by local 'lords of the valley'. Its lower story is in reddish brickwork and its two upper storeys are in white with timbered frames and elaborate wooden lattice windows. The whole is then capped by a spectacular wide overhanging roof on timbered supports which makes the building look like a gigantic mushroom. It also has interesting dungeons.

At 5 km beyond Sürmene a yellow sign announces the 13th C Byzantine **castle of Araklı**, on a lump by the side of the sea. There is absolutely nothing to see beyond a few fragmentary walls, but the local province is so short of important places to signpost along this stretch that anything gets a yellow sign.

TRABZON

'Fabled Trebizond lies like a green Eden at the foot of the Pontic mountains, a little Constantinople on the Black Sea coast.' If you have read anything like this about Trabzon you have read a fable indeed. Rose Macaulay's towers are equally illusory and you have to hunt long and hard to find a view of the walls that is even remotely impressive. The approach from the sea gives the best overall impression. That said, as long as you arrive with expectations suitably deflated, Trabzon does have some interesting things to offer and can even begin to grow on you after a couple of days.

Historical Background

The Cathedral of Haghia Sophia, 3 km west of the main square, is rightly the most famous site, outshining all Trabzon's other architectural monuments. These include ten churches, a number of them converted to mosques by the Ottomans, a convent and an Armenian monastery, all relics of the Comnene dynasty which fled Constantinople just before its fall to the Fourth Crusade in 1204. Alexius Comnenus, 22-year old son of the Byzantine Emperor Manuel I, established himself as king here with the help of the Georgian Queen Tamara, to whom he was related. The dynasty and the city flourished through its position, the skill of its traders and a string of beautiful and marriagable princesses: these helped to cement useful alliances with potentially troublesome neighbours like the Black and White Sheep Turcomans. Though the size of a province, it posed as an empire, Byzantium in exile. It sustained its pretensions with a court of pomp and ceremony, and acquired a reputation beyond its achievements through diplomatic manoeuvring, palace revolutions and civil wars — certainly Byzantine in the popular sense of the word. From Constantinople its art and architecture drew inspiration, though it was influenced also by Cappadocian, Georgian, Armenian, Syrian and Seljuk styles, introduced by imported craftsmen. It never developed from these a style of its own.

Trebizond's Greek roots went back to the 7th C BC when it was founded by the great Ionian sea-trading city of Miletos. It was a typical site for a Greek colony, with a good harbour and an acropolis (which gave it its name Trapezus, table); its climate could support olives and, across difficult mountains, it managed a trade route to Persia. To Trebizond came camel caravans from Erzurum and Tabriz carrying silk and spices, and it even benefited during Byzantine

Byzantium in exile

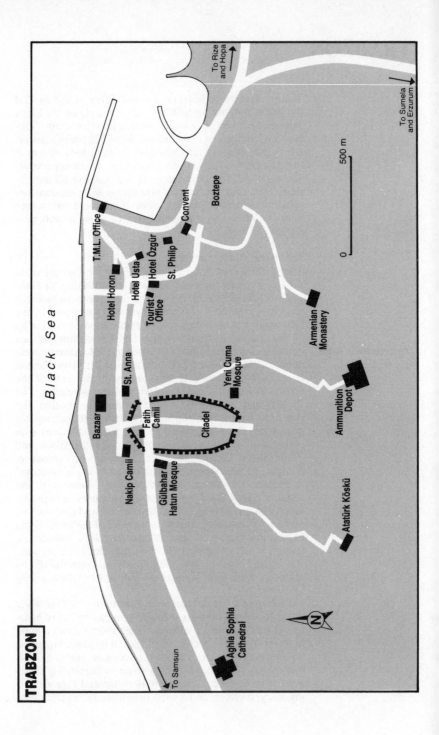

TRABZON

Black Sea

To Samsun

Aghia Sophia
Cathedral

N

Nakip Camii

Gülbahar
Hatun Mosque

Fatih
Camii

Citadel

Bazaar

St. Anna

Hotel Horon

Hotel Usta

Tourist
Office

Hotel Özgür

St. Philip

T.M.L. Office

Convent

Boztepe

Yeni Cuma
Mosque

Armenian
Monastery

Ammunition
Depot

Atatürk Köskü

To Rize
and Hopa

To Sumela
and Erzurum

500 m

0

times from Arab incursions into Anatolia which redirected the overland trade between Constantinople and the East through the Black Sea.

When Constantinople fell a second and final time, to the Ottomans in 1453, Trebizond and the Comnenes held out for a further eight years. As the last flicker of Byzantium it acquired a certain romantic mystique in Europe as the distant Christian outpost in Asia still defiant against Islam.

Decline ... and new life

Though the birthplace of Süleyman the Magnificent in 1494, under the Ottomans it fell into decline. The overland trade routes were made secure and commerce passed Trebizond by. The city suffered in the First World War when it was bombarded and occupied by the Russians. But the Turkish republic's policy of reorienting the country towards Anatolia has brought some life back to Trabzon, to use the Turkish name, turning it into a major port.

Seeing the Town

Setting off from the main square, Park Meydanı, you can begin by walking along Uzun Yol, Long Street, which heads off towards the citadel. Distances however, are not long, and it is fun to do this on foot as you can peer in all the shops along the way, this being the main shopping street of Trabzon. The leather shops here are particularly good for such things as bags, belts and wallets, and the food shops are also interesting, many of them selling the thinly sliced pastırma, a local speciality excellent for picnics.

The first little church you come to is up a small side street to the left just as the road begins to go downhill. A neat little stone building, this is **St Anna**, Trabzon's oldest church, dating from the 7th C and restored in the 9th C. This is its only claim to fame however, for it is now kept locked, is devoid of decoration or frescoes, and is only of interest to experts in Byzantine architecture. (The Church of St Basil was on the other side of the street, used as a storehouse in the metalworking section of the bazaar. It recently collapsed and was razed to the ground.) The Nakip Camii, north of the citadel nearer the sea, is thought to have been the **Church of St Andrew**, who, according to tradition, introduced Christianity to Trebizond. Today almost in ruins, it was built in the 10th or 11th C.

Byzantine churches and Ottoman mosques

Shortly after the St Anna Church, the Uzun Yol takes you across a road bridge with white railings over a gully to the **citadel**. Climbing uphill slightly on the other side of the bridge, you reach an open square with an elegant neo-classical government hall on the left, and in the centre, the unmistakable **Fatih** or **Ortahisar Camii** with ochre walls. Until the Ottoman conquest this was the Byzantine **Church of Panaghia Chrysocephalus**, the Golden-Topped

Virgin, because of its copper dome. The principal church of Trebizond, it was built in the 10th C and much enlarged after 1204. For all its historical significance, its Islamic embellishments are a living testimony to tastelessness.

The 16th C **Gülbahar Hatun Mosque** beyond the narrow citadel on the far side is almost as ugly as the Fatih, with crass new colours and garish capets. It was built in 1514 by Selim the Grim in honour of his mother who was known in her later years as Gülbahar, the Rose of Spring.

The **Yeni Cuma Mosque**, difficult to find up a maze of streets was also originally a church (**St Eugenios**), and does at least still look like one. It is kept shut except at prayer times when you could slip in to see its fine carved mihrab.

Returning to the Fatih Cami at the centre of the citadel, you can now walk up the long steep hill to the summit where there are fragments of the keep. Little children will appear as you approach, to take you to the 'Kale'. This is no bad thing as you need to cross a few people's back gardens to reach the edge, and it would be difficult to find unaided. Here, you can walk along the battlements that look down 100 metres or so into the gulley below. Windows with some decoration are still visible in the taller fragments of walls, liberally covered now with ivy and creepers. It was in this high corner that the Palace of the Comnene experors and their lovely princesses is thought to have been located, and it is from here that you get the best feel for what Trebizond must once have been like.

Royal view

Haghia Sophia as it was in the 19th C

As you walk back towards the main square you can still notice in the backstreets behind the Uzun Yol the occasional grand Greek dwelling, often four storeys high with attractive carving on the doors and windows. Trabzon had until 1923 and the exchange of populations one of the largest Greek populations in Turkey. Many are now derelict, some with boarded or smashed windows. No attempt is being made to restore them, and in some parts of town, the only attention being paid to them is that of the bulldozer, while cheap ugly breeze block buildings are hurriedly put up in their place.

A visit to the **Haghia Sophia Cathedral** on the outskirts of town is best done by car or taxi as it is a good hour's walk from the centre. In pictures taken 20 years ago the church stands by itself, raised on a terrace overlooking the sea where once Hadrian built a Temple to Apollo. Now the jerry-building of Trabzon has caught up with it and its setting has been lost.

The Haghia Sophia was built in the mid-13th C as a monastery church in the heyday of the Comnene Empire and converted to a mosque after the Ottoman conquest of 1461. As is usual in this process, the walls were whitewashed and covered with hard plaster, and the rescue of the murals from under these layers has been lengthy and involved. The Turks have also used it as a military storehouse and at the turn of the century, as a fever hospital. Now it is classified as a museum and therefore has the standard museum opening hours, closing on Mondays.

The tall grey stone building is the old *bell tower* built in 1427. Marble columns are used within the church and in the arcaded porches; in the south porch a *frieze* above the arches depicts the *Garden of Eden, Adam and Eve* and the *Temptation*. The style shows Armenian and Eastern influences, while much of the decorative carving of the church, especially the stalactite work in the porches, geometric medallions, the lotus flower and star motifs are Seljuk, added when the church was converted to a mosque.

The famous frescoes The magnificent *frescoes* for which the cathedral is famous adorn the walls and ceiling of the *narthex*. Among the most beautiful is the *Marriage at Cana*, the colours vivid as Christ turns water into wine. Among the other miracles depicted are the *Feeding of the Five Thousand, Christ walking on the water*, and the *Miracle of the boy possessed of a demon*. One of the labels on the frescoes has a delightful mistranslation in its English version: 'Angel adoring the Holy Towel' (instead of Shroud). These paintings were all done in the late 13th C and are in the tradition of Constantinople with some Cappadocian influence: they are thought to have all been the work of one individual.

Inside the church are more frescoes and fragments of

the original marble mosaic flooring with elaborate geo-metric designs. In the dome a huge half-effaced *Christ Pan-tokrator* looks down. Restoration work began in 1957 and went on for six consecutive summers under the supervision of David Talbot Rice.

Walking round the outside to the sea terrace on the northern side, the porch shows a heart-rending *fresco* labelled 'Job plagued by boils'.

The most pleasantly situated building in Trabzon is the Kızlar Manastiri, originally the **Theokephastos Convent**, set up on one of the hills overlooking the town and the sea. To reach it you follow the yellow sign to Boztepe, a picnic and recreational area on a hill above the city. The road leads inland from the Hotel Usta end of the main square, and winds on uphill for about 1.5 km. Then, as you approach a right bend with a large pink hospital building on your right, you will notice a smaller tarmac road leading straight on from the bend, and an even smaller tarmac road leading steeply downhill. The first road is the one that leads to Boztepe, soon passing a football ground on the right, and the second is the road that leads steeply down for 20 metres and then forks off uphill for 10 metres to the convent entrance.

The guardian will soon materialise. He is the local prim-ary school teacher and has been entrusted with the care of the convent in return for being allowed to grow his vege-tables in its grounds. He says the convent is shortly to be restored and put firmly on the tourist map. For the moment, however, it is rarely visited and the atmosphere, Peace once within the high walls, is beautifully peaceful, a wel-come escape from the bustle of the town. Much remains, including a rock cave church, a second church, a bell tower, a bathroom, the refectory and hall. Faint traces of 15th C murals are still visible in the blackened walls of the rock church. A spring in the cave is associated with eternal youth. Walking up through the vegetable garden you come to a little folly, like an ornamental well. It is in fact a tomb. From here the views out across Trabzon with the convent in the foreground are memorable.

A Couple of Excursions near Trabzon
From here with a few spare hours you can make an excur-sion further inland to the even more rarely visited Arme-nian monastery, **Kaymaklı Manastiri**, occupied by monks until 1923 and now used as a farm. The reward of this somewhat bizarre visit is the pleasure of discovering a truly remote site, with no village nearby, and of seeing the highly Poking about in an unusual frescoes in the church, now used as a barn. As Armenian long as you behave respectfully and politely, the family

Armenian monastery near Trabzon

monastery cum farmyard will let you poke about, as the part they live in is a modern breeze block construction which has no interest for you.

Continue uphill on the main road that you turned off to see the Kızlar Manastiri, and after about 1 km when you reach a T-junction turn right and following the pot-holed road for 2 km as it runs between hazelnut groves and vineyards. 10 metres or so after a newly built mosque, an earth road runs obliquely left off down the hill. In wet weather this earth road is tricky for cars because the gradient is steep, so you are best advised to walk the remaining 500 metres down the hillside. Like the convent, the monastery has high walls punctuated with windows on two storeys facing out over the valley.

The church stands in a grassy courtyard. Beyond it is

Atatürk's kösk near Trabzon

a little chapel, now a chicken coop. The farmyard animals, chickens, dogs and cows, will all set up a rumpus as you approach, and the mother yells things at you which sound like rather fierce abuse as she carries on with her heavy labour in the yard, but be reassured that this is just her normal manner. By opening the doors wide you have enough light to see the astonishing *frescoes* on three walls. **Hell in a barn** The most memorable is a fantastic *depiction of hell*, with the red river of hellfire running the length of the wall. The devil crouches in various gleeful and beckoning postures along it as he lures people further and further down into the pit, and Cerebus, the black dog of Hades, and other typically Armenian fantastical creatures like griffins, lurk behind bushes along the way. This painting is unlike anything to be seen in Cappadocian or Byzantine churches, which depict standard scenes from the Bible. The colours are still quite strong, protected from the light.

Another short excursion, definitely worthwhile, is to Atatürk's Summer House, **Atatürk Köskü**, 4 km behind Trabzon high up in heavily pine-wooded hills. The house is an attractive white stucco villa which could have been lifted straight out of any European riviera, set in its own extensive and beautifully tended gardens. It serves today as a museum of Atatürk memorabilia.

To reach the Kösk you must drive from the main square off towards the citadel, as for Haghia Sophia; on the far side of the citadel you will see yellow signs pointing to the Atatürk Köskü. It is from this stretch of road that you get the best view of the citadel walls and that the fable of Trabizond's towers comes closest to reality.

Revered Villa The road winds higher than the Kızlar Manastiri, high enough in spring often to be shrouded in mist. You then come quite suddenly on the elegant white house. There is a small entrance fee. Two gardeners are instructed by ten supervisors where to weed. Rubbish (cöp) containers are laid out every 5 metres, not that anyone would dare drop litter here, such is the atmosphere of reverence. It is, for the tourist, delightfully obsessive, and all for a house that Atatürk graced for only three days, in 1921. Inside are photos of Atatürk in every conceivable pose and the desk drawers are stuffed full of further memorabilia that there is no room to display. A guard follows you everywhere, not so much to check you do not steal anything, as to make sure you do not defile with your touch.

SUMELA: VIRGIN OF THE BLACK ROCK

The excursion from Trabzon 48 km inland to the superb mountain **Monastery of Sumela** takes a full half day but is well worth the effort. It is its setting, clinging Tibetan-style to a sheer rock face above steep and heavily wooded slopes, that makes the trip memorable, together with the stiff 30 minute walk required to reach it. Far from any village or habitation and often shrouded in mists, the monastery has a haunting quality despite the huge numbers of visitors who flock here in the summer months. East of Ankara, it is probably Turkey's most visited site after Nemrut Dağ.

Joining the Throng
The road follows the course of the river Değirmendere in a wide valley with wooded slopes rising either side. This is the main road to Erzurum, up over the Zigana pass at the end of the Pontic mountains and descending onto the plateau of the Anatolian hinterland. A busy road, carrying much truck traffic, this is also the main coach route for tours leaving Trabzon and having to reach Erzurum that

Vandalising graffiti at Sumela

night. Because of this, the tours depart very early from Trabzon, and so between 8.30am and 12.30pm the monastery is at its most crowded with continuous streams of people plodding up and down the mountain path. If you time your arrival for 1pm or later, however, you have a very good chance of having it to yourself, and as it stays open until 5pm you can have lunch afterwards rather than before if you would rather not make the ascent on a full stomach.

Reaching Maçka on the main south road after 25 km from Erzurum, the turn-off left to Sumela is clearly marked with the usual yellow sign: the signposting is in fact almost excessive for the 17 km hereafter. The path up to the monastery can get muddy after wet weather so it is as well to have suitable shoes. Many a tourist has decided against the ascent as a result of his open-toed sandals. A fee is charged at the top.

From below, the monastery is often not visible because of mist, so as you climb zigzagging your way up the mountain side, your first glimpse of it levitating above the trees is thrilling. The ascent from the restaurant below takes 25 to 30 minutes or longer depending on your fitness. The monastery is 1250 metres above sea level, but though the ascent only climbs through 250 of these, the distance of the path is 1100 metres with 25 zigzags.

Levitation

Once inside, you can see how heavily ruined the monastery is behind its imposing facade. A few crumbling rooms remain which were, to judge from their smallness, the monks' cells. Founded in the 6th C to house the icon of the Virgin painted by St Luke (Panaghia tou Melas, Virgin of the Black Rock, corrupted in the Pontic dialect to Soumelas, then to Sumela) the monastery was inhabited till 1923 when the Greeks were expelled from the country in the exchange of populations. Alexius Comnenus III was crowned Emperor of Trebizond here in 1349. Most of the facade dates only from the 18th C, and the monastery's sorry state today is the result of a fire just after its monks were forced out in 1923, together with subsequent neglect and vandalism.

Outstanding of what remains are the *frescoes* on the facade and, inside, on the ceiling of the cave church. On the facade, the top row of paintings are a fascinating *Adam and Eve* series to be read like a cartoon from left to right. In the top left Adam is lying down naked having a chat with God; next Adam and Eve stand together naked (Adam with his penis defaced) and a snake in the background; the middle picture is too defaced to make out; next Adam and Eve are standing with their fig leaves, looking guilty and ashamed next to God; finally, on the far right side, Adam and Eve are out in the world without God. On the right hand side of the facade you can just make out a painting of *St George* killing the dragon. Inside the cave church the frescoes are heavily defaced but the strong colours and the sheer number of paintings still makes them impressive. Where the later plaster has fallen off, it has revealed older frescoes underneath. Look for the particularly fine *Virgin and Child* seated on a magnificent gold throne.

Vandalism Nowhere in Turkey except perhaps in the Göreme churches of Cappadocia, is there anything to equal the degree of defacement found here. Great chunks of fresco have been gouged out over the years and the surfaces covered in graffiti. As in Cappadocia, the names carved are mainly Turkish and Greek, with just the odd German or French addition.

For the More Adventurous

In dry weather you can visit a second far more remote and unknown monastery nearby, called **Vazelon**. You follow the main road towards Erzurum for another 10 km from Maçka. As the road climbs along the left-hand slope of the valley, at a sharp hairpin bend to the left a dirt road leads right, or rather straight on, quite steeply downhill. There is no signpost here, but you can look out for the red and white striped chevron road sign indicating a sharp bend. The dirt track can be very muddy after rain and is not then suitable for a car. It leads down to the bottom of the valley, crosses the river, and then climbs back up the other side, winding round the hill to the monastery set above the road in the cliff face, a total of 6 km from the main road. It was founded in the 5th C.

A third and even remoter monastery, built in the time of Justinian, can be visited by keen walkers on the return to Trabzon from Sumela, or preferably as a day trip from Trabzon. This is to the convent of **St George in Peristera**, also called Hızır Ilyas Manastir, near Küştül village. From Eşiroğlu, 19 km from Trabzon on the main Sumela-Erzurum road, you fork left 4 km to Liboda and then on to Küştül village. In dry weather the tracks are drivable with a car, but more usually it is a three-hour walk and you are advised to take a guide from Eşiroğlu with you, as the maze of tracks is very confusing. Built on a rock, a 93-step stairway leads up to the monastery. It was once very wealthy, but in 1906 a severe fire badly destroyed the building and then the monks had to leave for good in 1923. It was later converted to a mosque.

The Greek Orthodox Monastery of Sumela hangs on the rock face

TRABZON TO ERZURUM: THE ZIGANA PASS

From the Black Sea the commonest route inland is over the **Zigana pass** to Erzurum, following the first great caravan route overland to Persia that brought Trabzon its wealth. The climb through the valley beyond Maçka is impressive, winding up through heavily wooded conifer hillsides, though the scenery and mountains are in many ways less dramatic than the less used route inland described earlier, from Hopa through the Tortum Gorge. The most striking moment comes when you reach the abrupt transition from the lush green vegetation of the coastal zone to the bleakness of the central Anatolian plateau.

Xenophon's route
This was the route which Xenophon and his Ten Thousand followed from Babylon in 400 BC and from where, as they reached the summit, they caught their first glimpse of the sea: 'So Xenophon mounted on his horse and, taking Lycus and the cavalry with him, rode forward to give support, and, quite soon, they heard the soldiers shouting out "The sea! The sea!" and began passing the word down the column. Then suddenly they all began to run, the rear guard and all, and drove on the baggage animals and the horses at full speed, and when they had all got to the top, the soldiers, with tears in their eyes, embraced each other and their generals and captives'.

Some 40 km after the summit of the pass you reach **Gümüşhane**, a new town built after the First World War. It takes its name (Silver Caravan) from the silver mines in the neighbourhood, now closed down. The old town, in ruins 4 km away, was once a summer resort for wealthy merchants of Trabzon and had a large Greek population. It was occupied by the Russians in 1916 and subsequently so thoroughly destroyed that it necessitated the construction of the new town. A further 80 km brings you to **Bayburt**, a larger and more appealing town than Gümüşhane, dominated by impressive fortifications running along a high ridge to the north. Originally Armenian, it was rebuilt by the Romans, Seljuks and Ottomans. Marco Polo stayed there on his way to China. Despite the excellent state of the outer walls, little remains inside the castle. A river runs around the foot of the castle hill, and along its banks attractive houses have continuous wooden balconies on props overhanging the water.

Marco Polo slept here

Beyond Bayburt you climb over a second pass at **Kopdağı**, 2390 metres, higher than the Zigana but nowhere near as spectacular. In winter it is notorious for its sudden blizzards when whole caravans used to be snowed in and frozen to death. Xenophon describes it: 'The snow was six feet deep and many of the animals and slaves perished in it, as did about 30 of the soldiers. . . . Soldiers who had lost the use of their eyes through snow blindness or whose toes had dropped off from frost bite were left behind'.

A drive through uneventful scenery for the final 70 km brings you then to Erzurum.

TRABZON TO SAMSUN

Black Sea ferries

Trabzon is now the easternmost port of call for the TML ferries from İstanbul. A few years ago these ferries used to go as far east as Hopa and stop off at many more ports like Giresun and Sinop on the way. Now however the service has, in their own words, been 'streamlined' and the ferry does the return voyage just once a week, calling only at Samsun. Whereas the old ferries used to take cars with difficulty, using a crane to lift them off the quayside onto the open deck, the new ones in use since winter 1986 are fully fledged roll-on roll-off car ferries. Fares for cars are very reasonable.

If you still have the energy after Eastern Turkey, however, it is enjoyable to drive the stretch between Trabzon and Samsun, spend the night in luxury at Samsun, and then get on the boat the following morning to arrive at İstanbul the next day. To drive along this coast is the only way to see it now, for whereas the old ferries used to hug the coast, the new ones keep so far out that you can scarcely see the coast at all.

Driving Along the Coast

The 365 km drive from Trabzon to Samsun, though passing through quite built-up areas of the coast, is nevertheless an interesting one and in good weather you can stop for a seaside picnic or eat in one of the good restaurants along the way. The drive takes four and a half hours without allowing for stops. Because this is the only road west, traffic tends to be quite heavy in relation to what you have grown used to in the eastern areas, and with the ferry only linking these towns once a week and with no railways, the road inevitably takes the brunt of all the commercial traffic.

The road west from Trabzon leads off alongside the sea with the by now familiar deep green tea plantations covering the hillsides to the left. Some 15 km from Trabzon, a yellow sign marks the 13th C Byzantine **castle of Akçakale** on the sea, but nothing of it remains to hold your attention for long, just walls with vegetable gardens growing right up to them.

Beaches

Beyond Akçaabat the beaches are black sand with black rocks along the shore, the green hills still coming right down to the edge. The road passes a series of pretty beaches. The anchovy caught in quantity all along the coast is very cheap and forms the staple diet of the fishing villages. Otherwise the commonest varieties are red mullet, tuna, bluefish and turbot.

A String of Castles

Shortly before Tirebolu, 97 km east of Trabzon, a yellow sign points inland up a valley just before crossing a river to **Bedrama Kalesi**, a castle built by the Genoese, who were active traders all along the Black Sea from Seljuk times onwards. At Tirebolu, an imposing fortification on a promontory is anounced by another yellow sign as **St Jean Castle**, with steps leading up to it. Below is an attractive tea house and restaurant on the pretty curve of Tirebolu harbour. A little outside the town is a good sandy beach. From Espiye, 110 km from Trabzon, another yellow sign points off inland to **Andoz Kalesi**, again built by the Genoese.

You now reach **Giresun**, a bustling town of 56,000 inhabitants, about one and three quarter hours' drive from Trabzon. At a roundabout a yellow sign points inland to **Giresun Kalesesi**, the castle which stands on the top of the wooded headland you passed, and was once the acropolis of the Milesian colony of Cerasus. It was from here that the Roman General Lucullus, who captured the town in the Pontic wars in 69 BC, brought back the first cherry trees to Europe. The name Cerasus is the origin of our European words ceirios, cerise and cherry. Just offshore is a small island with a second castle. Jason and the Argonauts are said to have put in here on their quest for the Golden Fleece and were attacked by birds dropping feathered darts. Now called **Büyük Ada** (Big Island), it was once the ancient island of Aretias where an Amazon queen founded a temple to Ares, god of war. Inhabited today by fishermen, the island can be visited by boat.

Cherries

A Change in Climate

Perşembe, on a headland 16 km beyond Urdu, is one of the most attractive towns and harbours along this coast. West from Perşembe the coastline becomes much prettier. The towns are more resort-like, cleaner and less sprawling. The trees on the slopes are spectacular and cover the hillside right down to the edge of the road. Were it indeed not for the road they would only end at the sea. The tea plantation region has been left behind; these trees are all either hazelnut (findik), an important Turkish export, or cherry. In early May the hills blossom.

The weather from here westwards is less prone to rain showers and gets more sunshine. When the sun is out along this coast is transforms the colours of the scenery. The sea immediately becomes intensely blue and the greens of the coast become even greener. The occasional picnic area with wooden tables and benches is laid out on the shore by the roadside. If you do not stop at one of these, it can be difficult to find a beach where it is not already built up. One possible place to stop is near the spectacular **bird island** just before a road tunnel, an island that almost seems to move, it is so covered in gulls and other sea birds. The road here is quite high above the sea so you cannot get down to the beach, but the view is very fine.

The road continues on to Boloman, and between here and Fatsa, where large sulphur reserves have been found, there are a number of good comfortable hotels on the sea. Just before Ünye, a road leads inland to Niksar. There is no yellow sign here, but 6 km up this road stands the striking **castle of Çaleoğlu** on a volcanic hill. At a high **Seal caves** point within its walls is the entrance to a tunnel of 400 steps down to the water, built by Mithradates, King of Pontus. Along the rocky shore near the town of Ünye there are caves inhabited by seals.

From Ünye onwards the road straightens out as it leaves the coast. From Terme on to Samsun it is dead straight and passes through fertile landscape of a very different kind to the hilly coastline. The land here is in fact the large delta formed by the Yeşilırmak and the main cash crop is the famous Turkish tobacco. Primitive peasants' farmhouses line the road on either side, but set down some 5 metres below it. The road has been built on an artificially raised section to avoid flooding. Down in the gullies, except in summer a lot of water still collects. Livestock is plentiful with many chickens and cows strolling about feeding on the lush grass. The women are, as ever, humping heavy burdens around while the children play and the men stroll and chat.

This final stretch of some 80 km to Samsun is very fast on a good straight road where overtaking is no problem. You now approach the outskirts of **Samsun**, the biggest town and port on the Black Sea with 280,000 inhabitants, a population that has more than doubled in the last ten years.

SAMSUN AND WEST

As you come in along the main coast road, Samsun's luxury hotel, the Büyük Samsun Oteli, is on the coast to the right of the road, impossible to overlook. The turn-off to the TML office and port for the ferry is 600 metres beyond the Büyük Samsun.

Samsun, as ancient Amisos, was founded by Greeks from Miletos in the 7th C BC and was later ruled by the Pontic kings, the Romans, the Byzantines and the Seljuks, who gave it its present name. When it fell to the Ottomans in the 15th C, the Genoese, who were given trading privileges here by the Seljuks, burned the city down, which is why nothing of historical interest remains to be seen today.

Atatürk Rallies His Forces

In more recent history, Samsun is the point where Atatürk landed on 19 May 1919 and began organising the defence against the Greek army which had landed at İzmir at about the same time. The date is therefore taken as the beginning of the Turkish War of Independence, and 19 Mayıs is a national holiday in Turkey as well as a frequent street name. Samsun welcomed Atatürk with bands and cheering crowds and has been staunchly republican ever since. The town commemorates the event with a colossal equestrian statue of Atatürk, surpassed in size only by that in Ankara. In July the town has a regional Black Sea Fair which can make accommodation difficult to find.

To Sinop

The coast west of Samsun is generally not as attractive as the stretch to the east, with the exception of the stretch from Bafra to Sinop. The total drive to Sinop takes two hours, following the coast for most of the way except where you cross the broad delta of the Kızılırmak.

Caviar

The road west first passes through **Bafra**, a tobacco growing centre on the Kızılırmak. It is also famous for its caviar.

The road rejoins the coast some 25 km on and then reaches the fishing town of Cerze. Leaving the coast again you soon come to **Sinop**, the only natural harbour along the Black Sea. Situated on a peninsula easily defended from attack and protected from the west and north winds, Sinop is known to have served as a port as early as Hittite times for the capital of Hattuşaş due south of here. Because of its setting, it was chosen for the largest Milesian colony in the 8th C BC, and it was from here that the Greek colonists made subcolonies to the east in Giresun and Trabzon. It remained prosperous under the Pontic kings, for whom it served as a capital city for a time, and later under the Romans. It passed from the Byzantines to the Seljuks in the 13th C, and then fell to the local emirs of Kastamonu in the hills inland, who allowed the Genoese to use it as the centre for their Black Sea trade. After being taken by the Ottomans in 1458, it became secondary to Samsun as a port.

The town still makes its living from the sea and a good meal can be had in the fish restaurants on the quayside. Little remains of its illustrious past beyond the ruined **Genoese castle**, the 13th C **Alaeddin Cami** and the **Alaiye Madrasa**, now a museum with a fine Seljuk portal. The only citizen of any note produced by the Milesian colonies along the Black Sea, Diogenes the Cynic, was born in Sinop in 413 BC. But it was not here, rather at Corinth in Greece, that Alexander the Great encountered Diogenes who, shunning worldly pleasures, chose to live inside a barrel.

The philosopher and the virgin

Taking pity on this abject figure, Alexander asked if there was anything he wanted. 'Yes', replied Diogenes, 'stand aside a little, for you are blocking the sun'. 'If I had not been Alexander', came the reply, 'I would have wanted to be Diogenes'.

The town's name is said to come from an Amazon queen called Sinope. Zeus, attracted by her charms, came to court her and offered her any gift she desired. She chose everlasting virginity and lived happily ever after.

Amazon Country

The land around the Black Sea was anciently associated with the Amazons. These remarkably independent women were described by Strabo: 'The Amazons spend ten months of the year off to themselves performing their individual tasks, such as ploughing, planting, pasturing cattle, or particularly in training horses, though the bravest engage in hunting on horseback and practice warlike exercises. The right breasts of all are seared when they are infants, so that they can easily use their right hands for any purpose, and especially that of throwing the javelin. They also use bows and arrows and light shields, and make the skins of wild animals serve as helmets, clothing and girdles. They have two months in spring when they go up into the neighbouring mountain which separates them from the Gagarians. The Gagarians, also in accordance with an ancient custom, go thither to offer sacrifice with the Amazons and also to have intercourse with them for the sake of begetting children, doing this in secrecy and darkness, any Gagarian

at random with any Amazon; and after making them preg-
nant they send them away; and the females that are born
are retained by the Amazons, but the males are taken to
the Gagarians to be brought up; and each Gagarian to
whom a child is brought adopts the child as his own, regarding the child as his son because of the uncertainty'.

Popular Resorts

There are good swimming beaches outside Sinop, and at
Aklıman, 15 km from the town, the forest comes down to
the beach and the bay is dotted with attractive little islands
ideal for camping.

**Good swimming
and camping**

Between Sinop and Ayancık the road is still unsurfaced
though there are plans to remedy this soon. The scenery
is attractive as far as Abana and Inebolu, where there are
more good swimming beaches. From Inebolu a good road
leads inland to Kastamonu and then via Çankiri to Ankara.
Kastamonu is an extremely picturesque town with square
half-timbered houses, one of them housing the **museum**
with a good collection of Roman sculpture. The 13th C
Atabey Mosque is also worth a visit. But following the coast
from Inebolu the road winds on to **Amasra**, a pretty resort.
Founded by the Milesians, beautifully situated on its own
well-treed peninsula, it has a Genoese castle on its citadel.

The road then dips inland 23 km to **Bartin** along splendid
scenery. Here, and especially further inland at **Safranbolu**,
the attractive black-timbered white-washed houses with
their overhanging balconies can be seen in profusion, similar in style to the houses around Bursa.

From Amasra westwards the coast becomes quite industrial until Akçafoça, with Zonguldak a coal mining centre
and busy industrial port, and Ereğli with its colossal steel
mill. After Samsun, Zonguldak is the largest city in the
Black Sea Region.

Akçafoça is a pretty resort with another Genoese castle
and is often crowded with families from the large industrial
towns. Inland, **Bolu** (Roman Polis) lies in the mountains
that separate Ankara from the sea, and is the centre of
the region's most popular mountain recreation area. The
hills here are not as steep as further east along the Black
Sea, but are heavily forested with many deciduous trees
like oak, rarely seen in Turkey today, and making a welcome change from the heavy and somewhat monotonous
dark green of the coniferous trees of the Pontic Alps. **Lake
Abant** to the south is especially beautiful and is full of
trout for the fisherman. Skiing is at **Kartalkaya** to the south
west of Bolu.

West from Akçafoça there is no real beach until you
come to **Şile** with another Genoese castle. Only 71 km from

İstanbul, this resort is crowded with the poorer İstanbul families during holiday times.

PRACTICAL INFORMATION

The best time to visit the Black Sea is early June. Summer temperatures rarely exceed 28°C. East of Ünye the rainfall is higher because of the mountains, but it can rain any time winter or summer.

Accommodation along the Black Sea is not as developed as on the Aegean and Mediterranean coasts, and still tends to consist of small family-run establishments with friendly service.

HOPA

Hotel Papila (1-star), Tel: 1440. Charming and well-run little hotel with balconies overlooking the sea and a good restaurant with a terrace onto the shore. The beaches here are pebbly.

Hotel Cıhan, next door to the Papila, is the next best.

TRABZON

Hotel Usta (2-star), Tel: 12195. Up a side street shortly before the main square, this is considered the best hotel, especially if you get a room on the top floors. It has no restaurant, however, though it does serve breakfast either on a rooftop terrace or downstairs in the reception. 72 rooms. The Avis office has its desk here, a convenient point for collecting or handing in a hired car.
Hotel Özgür (1-star), Tel: 11319. 45 rooms on the main square; reckoned to have the best restaurant, though its rooms are not as good as those of the Usta. Prices are the same.
Hotel Horon (1-star), Tel: 11199. 42 rooms, the third best, slightly cheaper than the other two.

For **orientation** it is worth noting that the main street, the Uzun Yol, is one-way eastwards.

The Trabzon **restaurant** on the main square opposite the Özgür is the best with an unusually pleasant ambiance. Fresh fish is usually on offer here, and it serves alcohol: not all restaurants by any means will serve alcohol, and in Trabzon about 60 percent of them would normally serve it, but at Ramadan it drops to only 2 or 3. The decision to close down during the day, or not to serve alcohol during Ramadan, is a personal one, up to each owner. Many close because they feel if they remain open they may lose at lot of custom from their more traditional clientele.

Food along the Black Sea is generally good, far better than in Eastern Turkey, but also more expensive. The fish available vary with the season. In April there is turbot (kalkan), and from May onwards there is red mullet (barbunya), tuna (palamut) and anchovies (hamsi). Anchovies are the most abundant and the cheapest and are the staple diet of the fishing villages.

Without your own **transport in Trabzon**, you can take a taxi or dolmuş out to Haghia Sophia or the Atatürk Kösk. For **Sumela** you can get a bus to Maçka and then take taxis to the monastery. Dolmuşes only run on weekends to Sumela.

Regular **buses** link Samsun with Trabzon, Rize and Hopa.

There is no **railway** linking Samsun and Trabzon, as Samsun is the terminus of the route from Sivas via Amasya.

There are daily **flights** to Ankara (1 hour 20 minutes), with connections to İstanbul (3½ hours including transfer time) and in summer a direct flight straight to İstanbul (1½ hours).

Turkish Maritime Lines **ferries** now run just once a week from İstanbul to Trabzon and back again, calling only at Samsun. Because the roads are bad and there is no railway, it acts more like a public transport service than a cruise, and local custom accounts for up to 90 percent of the passengers. Prices are reasonable, especially for cars. It leaves İstanbul on Mondays at 5.30pm, arriving Samsun 7.30pm on Tuesdays, leaving 1½ hours later at 9pm and arriving at Trabzon at 8am on Wednesdays. It stays docked all day at Trabzon until 10pm, then sets sail for Samsun arriving at 8am on Thursdays. Its stop here is again just for 1½ hours before it sets off for İstanbul arriving at 11am on Fridays and docking just under the Topkapı Palace right in the centre of İstanbul. In practice it often arrives home early which means that to make sure of your view of the Bosphorus and its superb houses and palaces lining the shore, you should have breakfasted, packed and be up on deck by 9pm. The new boats were built in Poland, are similar in size to a British cross-channel ferry, and have a side car-loading hatch because they have side docking. It is worth booking in advance as with only one sailing a week you can have your plans totally wrecked if it is full. The A class cabins are all the same, small but well-designed, with comfortable twin beds and an integral WC and shower. The B class are the same but with no windows, and the C class have no bathroom and no windows. These new boats travel a long way out from the shore, so that you can hardly see the coast most of the time. The days when people said a steamer was the best way to see the coast are now gone. The boat has good sun decks, a small swimming pool, a restaurant and a cafeteria. The restaurant serves one set meal only, there is no element of choice: the food is pretty average but after Eastern Turkey it seems rather good. Meals are only available between fixed hours and payment for them is by vouchers, bought in books from the information desk. Buy less rather than more than you need, as any surplus is not transferable back to cash.

Average temperature (Celsius):

J	F	M	A	M	J
7.2	7.4	8.2	11.6	15.8	20.0
J	A	S	O	N	D
22.6	23.0	20.0	16.4	13.1	9.6

Maximum temperature:

J	F	M	A	M	J
25.9	28.2	35.2	37.6	38.2	36.6
J	A	S	O	N	D
32.6	38.2	32.2	33.8	32.8	26.4

Minimum temperature:

J	F	M	A	M	J
−7.0	−7.4	−5.8	−0.8	4.7	9.2
J	A	S	O	N	D
13.5	13.5	7.3	3.4	−1.6	−3.3

GIRESUN
Hotel Giresun (1-star), Tel: 3017. 29 rooms.

FATSA
Dolyman Motel, between Fatsa and Bolaman, with a fine cliff setting overlooking the sea.

ÜNYE
Cemlik Hotel, 13 rooms, in pine forests by the sea.

SAMSUN
Büyük Turban Samsun Otel (3-star), Tel: 10750. 117 rooms on the beach, semi-luxury class, air conditioning, swimming pool.
Vindili Oteli (1-star), Tel: 16050. 65 rooms, the best bet if you do not want the expense of the Büyük.

Average temperature:

J	F	M	A	M	J
6.9	6.9	7.7	11.0	15.6	20.0
J	A	S	O	N	D
23.0	23.2	19.8	16.2	12.9	9.5

Maximum temperature:

J	F	M	A	M	J
23.4	26.5	33.4	37.0	37.4	36.2
J	A	S	O	N	D
36.1	39.0	38.3	35.4	32.4	26.9

Minimum temperature:

J	F	M	A	M	J
−8.1	−9.8	−6.4	−2.4	2.8	7.8
J	A	S	O	N	D
13.4	12.4	6.8	3.3	−2.8	−5.0

BAFRA
Bafra Belediye (1-star), Tel: 1524. 12 rooms.

SINOP
Melia Kasım Hotel (1-star), Tel: 163. 60 rooms.

AMASRA
Nur Aile Pension (1-star), Tel; 1015. Simple pension with 19 rooms on the

beach. Now rather rundown, with dubious plumbing.

BOLU
Koru Motel (2-star), Tel: 601. 16 km outside Bolu on the İstanbul road. 26 rooms set in a pleasant forest.

ABANT
Turban Abant Hotel (2-star), Tel: 04. 94

rooms in detached bungalow style. Sauna and pool.

ANÇAKOCA
Yeni Çinar Oteli (1-star), Tel: 1566 or 1567. Good simple hotel on the main road. Beach.

ŞILE
Değirmen Oteli (1-star), Tel: 48. 73 rooms on the beach.

INDEX

(P indicates an entry in the Practical Information section)

Maps and Plans

NOTES

NOTES